A GREAT EXPECTATION

STUDIES IN THE HISTORY
OF
CHRISTIAN THOUGHT

EDITED BY

HEIKO A. OBERMAN, Tübingen

IN COOPERATION WITH

HENRY CHADWICK, Oxford
EDWARD A. DOWEY, Princeton, N.J.
JAROSLAV PELIKAN, New Haven, Conn.
BRIAN TIERNEY, Ithaca, N.Y.
E. DAVID WILLIS, San Anselmo, California

VOLUME XII
BRYAN W. BALL
A GREAT EXPECTATION

LEIDEN
E. J. BRILL
1975

A GREAT
EXPECTATION

ESCHATOLOGICAL THOUGHT
IN ENGLISH PROTESTANTISM TO 1660

BY

BRYAN W. BALL

LEIDEN
E. J. BRILL
1975

ISBN 90 04 04315 2

PRINTED IN THE NETHERLANDS

To
DAWN

CONTENTS

PREFACE

In the last few years what is loosely called millenarianism has received considerable and increasing attention in seventeenth-century studies. The belief that the return of Christ is imminent, and that the end of the world is in sight, must always have far-reaching implications when held deeply and by more than a few people. Historians have been fascinated by its impact on social and political programmes during the Commonwealth and Protectorate. More than one monograph has been devoted to the Fifth Monarchists. In itself, however, belief in Christ's return is a religious and theological phenomenon. It is curious that at this level any sustained presentation, with attention to the cardinal Scriptural passages, has been lacking. Without such exposition, understanding can be uncomfortably superficial.

In *A Great Expectation* Dr. Ball provides what is needed. He demonstrates 'the breadth of eschatological involvement' within the century. Faith in Christ's return was then in the main stream of Christian thought, not in a backwater of sects and splinter groups. Fifth Monarchism he shows to have been only one, and a very minor, expression of the contemporary eschatological urge and surge. Millenarianism fostered it, but by no means all eschatological hope was millenarian, and not all millenarians were radical or violent.

In Chapter I Dr. Ball puts the subject in context. He looks back to Luther and Osiander and to Joye and Latimer as well as at such seventeenth-century divines as Sibbes, Bolton, Ussher and Baxter. In Chapter II we come to grips with the interpretation of prophecy, especially in the books of Daniel and Revelation, by the four men whose writings were seminal: Napier, Brightman, Dent and Mede. In Chapter III we observe a variety of what were taken to be 'signs of the end', and the several numerical calculations are explained which pointed to 1655/6/7 or to 1666 as the year of the end. Chapter IV provides the evidence for the belief that Antichrist, whether Rome or the Turk, was being defeated and the conversion of Israel begun. In Chapter V we come to 'the millennial rule of Jesus'. While Fifth Monarchist interpretation of this was literal and outward, an inward and spiritual interpretation was adopted by the Quakers, and the Quakers appropriately introduce a final chapter on the relation of the eschatological hope to devotion and the pursuit of holiness.

Dr. Ball regards his book as 'more in the context of historical theology than theological history'. Whichever it is, he is insatiably inquisitive and asks many questions of both history and theology. He has read widely in seventeenth-century writers and has taken the trouble to study how these men thought. He also possesses a qualification essential but all too rare in that he is at home in the biblical material and understands the premisses from which argument proceeded. With patience in unwinding tangled skeins he combines sensitiveness to variety in shades of colouring and the ability to distinguish weighty from light-weight. While preserving a historian's detachment he writes as one engaged and sympathetic; but he is not above an absurd quotation or two and on occasion can be sardonic. At times the vitality and 'warmth of anticipation, almost a *joie de vivre*' which he finds in his sources flow over into his own writing. In this way he conveys feeling as well as logic and theology, and we sense something of the subject's power over men's hearts.

New College, London   GEOFFREY F. NUTTALL

ACKNOWLEDGEMENTS

This book owes its origin to the scholarly guidance and encouragement of the Rev. Dr. G.F. Nuttall, of New College, London, under whose supervision my study of eschatology in English Puritanism culminated in a doctoral thesis presented to the Faculty of Theology in the University of London in 1970. I am additionally grateful to Dr. Nuttall for consenting to write the preface to this revised study.

I am indebted to Professor V.N. Olsen, now of Loma Linda University, for imparting an initial interest in the history of the Christian church, an interest which later was to converge on the Reformation and its theology, and to Professor H.A. Oberman of Tübingen for including this work in the series under his direction, "Studies in the History of Christian Thought".

The task of revising the study for publication was aided by Dr. A.J. Woodfield and Mr. H.I. Dunton, and by Mr. D.S. Porter of the Bodleian Library, who read the manuscript in final draft, and I am grateful for their helpful comments and suggestions. For any errors or blemishes which may remain I am solely responsible.

Many friends have shown their interest and offered help in various ways, and I wish to express my thanks to them all, particularly to Miss Helen Savage, my secretary, for long hours spent in helping with compiling the indices.

I am deeply grateful to my wife for her help throughout, particularly for typing the manuscript, and to my family for often forgoing the companionship of their father. Any reward is theirs as much as mine.

Nottingham, 1975.   B.W.B.

TABLE OF ABBREVIATIONS USED WITH
PRIMARY SOURCES

A short title as used in the footnotes is entered only when it differs
from the first words of the original title.

Bolton, Robert:
   Last Things — *Mr. Boltons Last and Learned Worke of the Foure last Things.*

Burrough, Edward:
   Severall Queries — *Answers to Severall Queries.*

Cotton, John:
   Revelation — *An Exposition Upon The thirteenth Chapter of the Revelation.*
   Church Members — *Of the Holinesse of Church-Members.*
   Seven Vials — *The Powring out of the Seven Vials.*

Coverdale, Miles:
   Letters — *Certain most godly, fruitful, and comfortable letters.*

Finch, Henry:
   Great Restavration — *The Worlds Great Restavration.*

Fox, George:
   The Kingdom — *To all that would know the Way to the Kingdome.*

Goodwin, Thomas:
   States & Kingdomes — *The Great Interest of States & Kingdomes.*

Hall, Thomas:
   Commentary — *A Practical and Polemical Commentary or Exposition.*

Haughton, Edward:
   Antichrist — *The Rise, Growth, and Fall of Antichrist.*

Homes, Nathaniel:
   Ten Exercitations — *The Resurrection-Revealed Raised Above Doubts and Difficulties in Ten Exercitations.*

Huit, Ephraim:
   Daniel — *The whole Prophecie of Daniel Explained.*

Owen, John:
   Hebrews — *A Continuation of the Exposition of the Epistle ... to the Hebrews.*

Parker, Thomas:
   Daniel — *The Visions and Prophecies of Daniel Expounded.*

Seagar, John:
   World to Come — *A Discoverie of the World to Come.*

Shepheard, William:
   Foure Last Things — *Of The Foure Last and Greatest Things.*

Sibbes, Richard:
   Philippians — *An Exposition of the Third Chapter of the Epistle ... to the Philippians.*
   Emanuell — *A Miracle of Miracles or Christ in our nature.*

Stephens, Nathaniel:
   Number of the Beast — *A Plaine and Easie Calculation of the ... Number ... of the Beast.*

Strong, William:
   Sermons — *XXXI Select Sermons.*

Taylor, Thomas:
   Titvs — *A Commentarie upon the epistle ... to Titvs.*

INTRODUCTION

When addressing the Star Chamber in 1616, it is recorded that James I spoke of "the latter dayes drawing on".[1] Such convictions were neither wholly new nor yet fully developed in the religious thought of the age. A tide of opinion concerning the second coming of Christ and the end of the world had begun to flow early in Elizabeth's reign and would not ebb until its high-watermark had been reached in the middle decades of the seventeenth century. That this period marked the apogee of eschatological expectation has been recognised for some time. Of the 1630's Professor H. R. Trevor-Roper writes, "In many an English manor-house, in many a vicarage or college-cell, old computations were revised and new elaborated."[2] The computations were those arising from the study of apocalyptic prophecy, and converged upon the years between 1640 and 1660.[3] Dr. G. F. Nuttall's statement that "many Puritans believed themselves to be living in a remarkable age, a new age, perhaps the last age",[4] and Alexander Gordon's earlier remark that by the time of the Commonwealth, "the idea of a speedy approach of our Lord's millennial reign was very widely diffused among all classes of religionists",[5] are complemented by Dr. Christopher Hill's observation that "many in the seventeenth century believed the end of the world was imminent."[6]

Much of the attention that hitherto has been given to this subject has centred on millenarianism, its more radical extension in the Fifth Monarchy movement, and the convictions of sectarian eccentrics. Robert Barclay and Dr. E. A. Payne represent a long-established tradition in drawing attention to the extent of

---

[1] James I, 'A Speach in the Starre-Chamber, 1616', in *The Workes of the most High and mightie Prince Iames* (1616), p. 554.

[2] H. R. Trevor-Roper, *Religion, the Reformation and Social Change, and Other Essays* (1967), p. 247.

[3] *Ibid.*, p. 47. The suggestion that eschatological expectation decreased as the 1640's progressed may have been true of radical millenarianism, P. Toon, *Puritans and Calvinism* (Swengel, Pennsylvania, 1973), p. 40; a wider eschatology continued, however, see J. A. De Jong, *As the Waters Cover the Sea: Millennial Expectations in the Rise of Anglo-American Missions, 1640—1810* (Kampen, 1970), p. 36.

[4] G. F. Nuttall, *The Holy Spirit in Puritan Faith and Experience* (Oxford, 1946), pp. 102, 109.

[5] A. Gordon, in *The Dictionary of National Biography*, s.v. C. Feake.

[6] C. Hill, *Puritanism and Revolution* (1958), p. 325.

Fifth Monarchy views,[7] and P. G. Rogers sees Fifth Monarchism as a "creed of the seventeenth century."[8] More recently B. S. Capp has noted the disdain with which the Fifth Monarchy Men have been regarded by modern historians—"an irrational movement, beyond the pale of analysis."[9] In tracing the history of the quest for a Utopian socialism, W. H. G. Armytage draws attention to the millenarian assumptions of Familists, Behmenists, Diggers, Levellers, Muggletonians, and "other persecuted minorities".[10] L. F. Solt takes the millenarian hope from the lips of the radical William Erbury, whose theology was suspect on a number of counts.[11] The effect is inevitably to associate eschatological expectation with the fanatical fringe. But "excessive immersion in the Bible" did not turn all heads, if it turned some,[12] and the presence of this extreme element is itself an argument for the existence of a more restrained and representative corpus of eschatological thought.

Before the millenarianism and Fifth Monarchism of the mid-seventeenth century, contemporary with them, and long after them, there existed such a moderate doctrine of the last things which focussed primarily on belief in Christ's second coming. The moderate, and eloquent, Richard Sibbes enquired of his congregation:

> If Abraham rejoyced to foresee, by the eye of Faith, the first comming of Christ in the flesh, how should we joy by Faith to see the second comming of Christ? If Iohn Baptist leaped in the wombe for joy, at the presence of Mary, the Mother of our Lord, how will our hearts dance when we shall see the Lord himselfe in the great glory

---

[7] See R. Barclay, *The Inner Life of the Religious Societies of the Commonwealth* (1876), p. 182, and E. A. Payne, *The Baptists of Berkshire Through Three Centuries* (1951), p. 17. See also L. F. Brown, *The Political Activities of the Baptists and Fifth Monarchy Men in England During the Interregnum* (Washington, 1912), *passim*, and P. Zagorin, *A History of Political Thought in the English Revolution* (1954), ch. VIII, 'The Fifth-Monarchy Men'.

[8] P. G. Rogers, *The Fifth Monarchy Men* (1966), p. 132.

[9] B. S. Capp, *The Fifth Monarchy Men* (1972), pp. 15, 16. Capp's study of the movement is the most thorough to date. The chapter on developing millenarianism in England is a useful survey, although perhaps lacking the sensitivity of a theological approach. See also Tai Liu, *Discord in Zion: The Puritan Divines and the Puritan Revolution 1640—1660* (The Hague, 1973), *passim*.

[10] W. H. G. Armytage, *Heavens Below: Utopian Experiments in England 1560—1960* (1961), pp. 11—25.

[11] L. F. Solt, *Saints in Arms: Puritanism and Democracy in Cromwell's Army* (Stanford, 1959), p. 73. On Erbury see *Dictionary of National Biography* s.v., where it is stated that his doctrinal deviations included universal redemption, a denial of the divinity of Christ, and a curious belief that the Holy Spirit had departed after the apostolic age.

[12] Armytage, *op. cit.*, p. 16.

and Majesty of Heaven? If Peter was so ravished with a little droppe and glimpse of Heaven, when hee saw the transfiguration of Christ in the mount, so that hee even lost and forgat himselfe, and wist not what he said, how shall we be affected, think you, when wee shall see Christ, not in his transfiguration, but in his glorification for ever? [13]

There is a lot of truth in the distinctions that not all who believed in the second coming were millenarians, and that not all millenarians were Fifth Monarchy Men. It is this wider belief in the more general doctrine of Christ's return which is a key, not only to the chiliasm which became so rife after 1640, but also to the more basic issues of understanding both the religious nature of the age itself, and beyond that, the eschatological emphases which recur in English-speaking Protestantism.

There has been some indication of a tendency to recognize this wider eschatological involvement and its importance to the interpretation of the seventeenth century. E. L. Tuveson's *Millennium and Utopia* (1949) remarks that apocalyptic study was a "serious business which concerned Lutheran, Calvinist, and Anglican of every variety", [14] and describes Fifth Monarchism as "the poor man's millennial doctrine ... opposed by the more responsible interpreters". [15] Perez Zagorin, in *A History of Political Thought in the English Revolution* (1954), rightly distinguishes between Fifth Monarchism and the universal Christian belief in Christ's second coming, [16] and even suggests that the Fifth Monarchy movement as a whole remained more spiritual than secular. [17] More recent studies by William Lamont, John Wilson and Tai Liu have again pointed to the broad interest generated in the seventeenth century in a theology of the last things. [18] The titles given

---

[13] Richard Sibbes, *The Brides Longing for her Bridegroomes second comming* (1638), pp. 59, 60.

[14] E. L. Tuveson, *Millennium and Utopia: A Study in the Background of the Idea of Progress* (New York, 1964), p. 29.

[15] *Ibid.*, p. 89.

[16] Zagorin, *op. cit.*, p. 96; cf. Capp, *op. cit.*, p. 14.

[17] *Ibid.*, p. 97.

[18] W. M. Lamont, *Godly Rule: Politics and Religion 1603—1660* (1969), p. 31; J. F. Wilson, *Pulpit in Parliament: Puritanism during the English Civil Wars, 1640—1648* (Princeton, 1969), pp. 189—196. Tai Liu rightly notes that "the millenarian strain in Puritanism has usually been considered in the past as an aberration rather than an essential part of the Puritan mind." The attitudes of historians to the eschatological conceptions of Puritanism are changing, however, and "The Puritan vision of a glorious millennium of Christ's kingdom here on earth is no longer regarded merely as the ideology of the reckless Fifth Monarchy Men; on the contrary, it is now considered a central theme in Puritanism during the whole course of the Puritan Revolution," Tai Liu, *Discord in Zion*, pp. 2, 3. It will be argued that even this conclusion falls short of the facts, and that eschatology in its broader sense, as opposed only to millenarianism, was restricted neither to Puritanism nor to the period of the English revolution.

to most of the studies referred to thus far, however, indicate the primary concern of modern scholarship, and it seems appropriate to suggest that an adequate appreciation of the eschatological impulse is severely limited if restricted to its involvement with social and political movements. [19] It remains demonstrably true that millenarians were not necessarily Fifth Monarchy Men, [20] that John Rogers was not "one of ... the most moderate of the millenarian preachers", [21] that all Bible readers were not proletarian, [22] and that John Foxe did not make "the pursuit of the Millennium respectable and orthodox."[23] The attraction of apocalyptic prophecy must be explained on other grounds than as a factor in the development of the theory of war, [24] or as a key to the politics of the seventeenth century, secular or ecclesiastical, [25] or even as an aid to a satisfactory philosophy of history, [26] relevant though any of these may have been. The causative, and therefore central, factor in eschatology is necessarily theology, and the essentially religious nature of the seventeenth century makes it desirable to approach its eschatology first from a theological standpoint. [27]

The intrinsic theological nature of the eschatological surge can

---

[19]   Even Mr. Peter Toon recommends his edited collection of essays on Puritan eschatology on the strength of its usefulness to the interpretation of the Puritan revolution. Though sketchy and poorly documented and suffering from a predisposition to stress millenarianism, it is, nevertheless, *per se*, a helpful introduction to the eschatological thought of the period; P. Toon (Ed.), *Puritans, The Millennium and the Future of Israel: Puritan Eschatology 1600—1660* (Cambridge, 1970).

[20]   E.g. Zagorin, *op cit.*, pp. 97—105.

[21]   *Ibid.*, p. 103.

[22]   Armytage, *op cit.*, p. 16.

[23]   Lamont, *op. cit.*, p. 33. Foxe held to the view that the millennium had already been fulfilled in the history of the church; see his *Actes and Monuments* (1576 Edit.), p. 743.

[24]   M. Walzer, *The Revolution of the Saints: A Study in the Origins of Radical Politics* (1966), p. 290—299.

[25]   Lamont, *op. cit., passim.*

[26]   Tuveson, *op. cit.*, p. 75.

[27]   The study of historical and contemporary millenarian movements, however helpful to the social historian and the student of behavioural science, will suffer limitations if divorced from the basic discipline of theology; cf. Sylvia L. Thrupp (ed.) 'Millennial Dreams in Action', *Comparative Studies in Society and History*, Supplement II, the Hague, 1962. The exclusion of the theological roots of English millenarianism and of the wider eschatology from which it emerged is a serious omission militating against historical objectivity. F. S. Plotkin has correctly noted the essentially theological nature of millenarianism and the advisability of seeing it primarily in this context. "To speak of it in any other terms is to distort its essential nature and significance", F. S. Plotkin, 'Sighs from Sion: A Study of Radical Puritan Eschatology in England 1640—1660', unpublished Ph.D. thesis, Colombia University (1966), p. 207. The dangers awaiting those who approach what is, after all, principally a religious question without due regard for its theological implications are illustrated by

hardly be overstated. The seventeenth century in England is the age, *par excellence*, of intensity in religious belief, when religion touches life at every level and leaves its mark in some way on every individual, [28] and a discernment of this predominant bias is prerequisite to any sensitive understanding of the age. But this religiousness, which is so vital a key to the understanding of the times, cannot itself be fully comprehended without a thorough appreciation of the breadth and depth of the eschatological convictions which rose to their zenith in the middle decades of the century. Generally speaking the men of the seventeenth century, and this must be granted to include members of Parliament and others of influence as well as the lower classes, gave as much attention to religion as to politics. Preaching on the end of the world, the Congregational spokesman at the Westminster Assembly, Jeremiah Burroughes, exclaimed in 1645:

> ... we find there are mighty stirrings abroad in the world, the hearts of men are more raised to expect it then ever they were before ... truly there is the greatest expectation of the Saints of God, and those that are the most strict and holy, the greatest expectation of these times, as ever yet was ... [29]

Professor Wilson's *Pulpit in Parliament* tends much to the same conclusion by arguing the importance of the eschatological element in the Parliamentary sermons of the time. [30] It may be inferred that what the preachers judged as necessary for the spiritual diet of the Commons and Lords, they would also have thought necessary for the people. The stirrings and expectations which moved Jeremiah Burroughes and thousands beside him sprang almost wholly from a fulfilling eschatology.

Various reasons have been advanced for the engrossment of seventeenth-century England with the latter-day events. Not the least of these suggested causes is the lingering influence of mediaeval thought. Professor Cohn has observed that the happenings of the last days for mediaeval people were "not a phantasy about some remote and indefinite future, but a prophecy which was

---

the definition of postmillennialism and premillennialism, in a recent study, as the view which puts the millennium in the past and in the future, respectively; P. K. Christianson, 'English Protestant Apocalyptic Visions, c. 1536—1642', unpublished Ph.D. thesis, University of Minnesota (1971), introd., p. ix.

[28]   Men did not go to church only for news, see C. Hill, *Society and Puritanism in Pre-Revolutionary England* (1969), p. 33; the preacher was, above all, to use Haller's phrase, a 'physician of the soul'.

[29]   Jeremiah Burroughes, *Jerusalem's Glory Breaking forth into the World* (1675), p. 111.

[30]   Wilson, *op. cit.*, pp. 150, 151, 195.

infallible, and which at almost any given moment was felt to be
on the point of fulfilment." [31] This view takes on added significance in the light of Perry Miller's argument that the men of the
seventeenth century were fundamentally mediaeval in their
thinking. [32] Closely related to this position is that which sees
"the revolutionary nature of the age" [33] as a predisposing factor
to millenarianism and its kindred doctrines. Cohn, again, has
argued this idea in his fascinating work *The Pursuit of the Millennium.* A society which is at the same time politically disrupted,
economically expanding, and intellectually enquiring, is a seed-
bed peculiarly suited to the generation of chiliastic hopes, [34] and
in England this was the prevailing milieu in the early part of the
seventeenth century. Trevor-Roper places the rise of apocalyptic
hope during the 1630's against the dark background of economic
depression, political inexpertise, and the threatened extinction of
Protestantism. "The 1620's had been a terrible decade ... It was
the end of an era ...". [35] A further motivation is seen in that
general Utopianism which is a part of the human spirit, and
which from time to time breaks out, more often than not in
times of national and social hardship. This "still-living tradition
of Renaissance utopianism", [36] this "ancient myth of a Golden
Age", [37] is seen to underlie a developing millenarianism. Indeed,
the arrival of this dream world is something which "only chiliastic radicalism dared hope for." [38]

Such are some of the root causes which are said to have predisposed men to eschatological convictions. Nor are they without
their significance, for in the turbulent waters of the contemporary religious thought the effect of these undercurrents is not

---

[31]   N. Cohn, *The Pursuit of the Millennium* (1957), p. 115.
[32]   P. Miller, *Errand into the Wilderness* (Cambridge, Massachusetts, 1956), p. 218.
[33]   G. F. Nuttall, *The Welsh Saints, 1640–1660* (Cardiff, 1957), p. 44; cf. Tai Liu,
Discord in Zion, p. 64.
[34]   Cohn, *op. cit.*, p. 311. It is further maintained that such a situation creates a
"sense of helpless exposure, disorientation, and guilt" resulting in mass paranoia, and
in this is seen a further cause for millenarian excitement. While this may have been true
to some extent of the early Continental extreme millenarianism of Thomas Müntzer
and John Mathijs, it can have little bearing on the overall development of eschatological teachings in England.
[35]   Trevor-Roper, *op. cit.*, pp. 246–247.
[36]   A. S. P. Woodhouse, *Puritanism and Liberty: Being the Army Debates
(1647–9) from the Clarke Manuscripts with Supplementary Documents* (1938), Introduction, p. 47.
[37]   C. H. & K. George, *The Protestant Mind of the English Reformation 1570–1640*
(Princeton, 1961), p. 118.
[38]   *Loc. cit.*

wholly to be discounted. But to regard such factors as basic causes of the eschatology which developed in seventeenth-century England would be to overlook that which is of the utmost significance—the inherent religious feeling of the age, built on the twin foundation of the great historical tradition of Reformation theology and the complete contemporary reliance upon the Bible as the source of revealed truth. It is impossible to arrive at a satisfactory interpretation of the eschatological thinking of the seventeenth century while disregarding the far-reaching influence of these two factors, and when King James divulged his convictions to the members of the Star Chamber, it is fairly safe to assume that these were the influences which had largely shaped his thinking.

This study, then, is primarily concerned with the theological concepts which formed the basis of the fervent eschatological expectations of seventeenth-century England. In the view of Professor Wilson "insufficient attention has been devoted to the speculation regarding the *eschaton* which developed in conjunction with late Elizabethan and early Stuart Puritanism."[39] Dr. G. F. Nuttall's comment may also be noted:

> For an understanding of Puritan piety which is more than superficial few aids are, in fact, more needed than a fresh presentation of the developing millenarian argument, with its manifold sources and ramifications and its equally manifold attractions and effects. [40]

If any further justification is necessary for such a study it may be found in the preceding paragraphs. Considerably more attention will be paid to moderate opinion than to the views of millenarians or Fifth Monarchy Men. Enough has already been written concerning their beliefs and activities and they will be examined here only for a theological relationship to the overall eschato-

---

[39] Wilson, *op. cit.*, p. 214. Commenting on the historico-apocalyptic Reformation view of church history as background to the eschatology which appeared in sixteenth and seventeenth-century England, Professor V. Norskov Olsen, in his penetrating study of John Foxe, remarks, "It is difficult for the twentieth-century theologian and historian to realise that chiliasm and apocalyptic eschatology were more than a phenomenon seen in Radical enthusiasts at the time of Luther or by [sic, in?] the Fifth Monarchy men in England during the Civil War ... we must acknowledge that there were a "normal" millennialism and a "normal" apocalyptic eschatology which were not alien to, but played a prominent role in, the Reformers' total involvement in the life of church and society", V.N. Olsen, *John Foxe and the Elizabethan Church* (Berkeley, Los Angeles and London, 1973), p. 22.
[40] G. F. Nuttall, *Visible Saints: The Congregational Way 1640—1660* (Oxford, 1957), p. 157.

logical pattern, and in order to set their extremer views in what is
believed to be true perspective.

Two things deserve to be said briefly about J. F. Wilson's view
as quoted above. In the first place it correctly recognises that
caution will be required in any attempt to isolate the years between 1640 and 1660 from the preceding decades. The lines may
have been clearly drawn politically and ecclesiastically; theologically there is no such sharp distinction. Religious convictions
rarely mature sufficiently in one generation to contribute to an
upheaval as profound as that which shook England between 1642
and 1660. The eschatological excitement of the Civil War and
Interregnum years was not a phenomenon isolated from the previous developments in English theology. By the middle of the
seventeenth century men had believed for almost a hundred years
that the end of the world was at hand. In the second place,
however, it may be emphasised that caution is again called for in
attempting to isolate the views which arose within Puritanism
from those which belonged to the English church as a whole.
From an eschatological viewpoint there is ground to conclude
that the thesis argued by C. H. and K. George of a basic affinity
in doctrinal matters between Anglican and Puritan is essentially
correct. [41] Indeed, the earliest interest in the Apocalypse and the
Antichrist preceded the rise of Puritanism by a good many years.
Even Foxe could not lay claim to pioneering the field of apocalyptic interpretation. [42] It may also be noted that while this enquiry closes for convenience with 1662 and the Act of Unifor-
mity, it would not be judicious to assume that all interest in
eschatology ceased with the re-establishment of Episcopacy. The
last forty years of the seventeenth century alone offer a fruitful
field for the further investigation of latter-day thought in English
theology. If, after 1660, Hartlib, Durie, and Comenius would not
concern themselves again with "the Millennium, the Messiah or
the number of the Beast," [43] there were many for whom the
attractions of eschatology would remain potent.

For these reasons this study attempts to set the eschatological

---

[41] C. H. and K. George, *op. cit.*, pp. 71, 72; cf. O. Chadwick, *The Reformation*
(1968), p. 226.
    [42] Lamont, *op. cit.*, p. 50. Foxe was preceded by John Bale and John Sleidan, see
Olsen, *op. cit.*, pp. 22, 41. Heinrich Bullinger's *In Apocalypsim Iesu Christi* (1557)
must also be included in this context. Professor Olsen's study *passim* is crucial to an
evaluation of Foxe's eschatology and its significance to the development of eschatological thought in England over the next hundred years.
    [43] Trevor-Roper, *op. cit.*, p. 293.

beliefs so rife after 1640 in the context of a gradual development over three or four generations and, what is fundamentally important, to ascertain the extent of those beliefs in terms of the whole theological spectrum. Who believed in Christ's second coming and the imminent end of the world? What form, or forms, did those beliefs take, and how widespread and lasting were they? On what were they based, and could they reasonably be defended? Were the causative factors of that eschatology peculiar to the age? What kind of men were its chief protagonists? What was millenarianism and how far can it be identified with the total eschatology of the time? What effect did the expectant spirit have on the life of the church and on the spiritual well-being of the individual believer? These are some of the questions to which answers are necessary if the eschatological upsurge of the seventeenth century is to be seen in its rightful context in secular and religious history.

A further question may be raised. How germinal was this early English eschatology to the eschatological thought of later generations? For three hundred years or so, the course of Protestantism was determined very largely by developments within the English church in the seventeenth century. Of course, changes came with the passing of years, and particularly in the twentieth century the modifications in theology have been profound.[44] It is nonetheless true that traditional Anglo-Saxon Protestantism remains rooted in the Reformation and Puritan cras. Theological and doctrinal patterns constitute a significant part of the tradition derived by Protestantism from its formative years. Bibles and prayer-books, confessions and creeds, as well as Episcopacy, Presbyterianism, and the broader lines of dissenting denominational demarcation emerged from the age of the later Tudors and early Stuarts. Their influence has been incalculable. If it is conceded that the church as custodian of truth is of greater import than the church as an institution, then the onflow of thought and doctrine is of immense significance. Even allowing for subsequent modifications, this continuity from the past with any relevance it may have for the present cannot be dismissed lightly.

From an eschatological standpoint, the suggestion of any such continuity poses further significant questions. Did the fanatical millenarianism which undoubtedly existed in mid-seventeenth century England lead, *ipso facto*, to a rejection of the more

---

[44] Developments in eschatology over the past fifty years or so are discussed briefly by A. L. Moore, *The Parousia in the New Testament* (Leiden 1966), pp. 1—6.

restrained eschatology from which it emerged, or did the moderate views persist as both church and state moved away from the concepts of immediate eschatological fulfilment? Were the more moderate opinions, held by many of the most respected preachers and theologians, so inherently naïve and ill-considered, or so peculiarly related to the times, that they were to merit no further serious consideration in the outworking of the church's eschatological hope? Conversely, did the extremer elements disappear from the seventeenth-century scene as the kingdom they had thought to herald evaporated before their eyes, or was their disappearance merely transitory and were they to reappear later clad in new and more attractive garb? Has subsequent eschatological thought been reluctant to return to what might be considered a more biblically-oriented position as a result of the persistent image of fanaticism attached to the views which have become associated with the seventeenth century? [45] In short, can the eschatological present be divorced entirely from the eschatological past?

Certainly many aspects of contemporary eschatology indicate an affinity with the divergent emphases which appeared in seventeenth-century England. The militant and exclusive self-confidence of the Fifth Monarchy Men, for instance, bears some resemblance to the eschatological convictions of the present-day Jehovah's Witness movement. The highly personalised and experiential aspects of early Quakerism are similar to corresponding stresses in modern Pentecostalism, neo-Pentecostal groups and even the more radical exponents of 'realised eschatology'. Pronouncements of self-styled prophets in the mould of John Rogers and Mary Cary, called to rally the faithful and usher in the kingdom, resemble, to some extent, the claims of Joseph Smith and the Latter-Day Saints. The post-millennialism of John Cotton and Edmund Hall was taken up by Daniel Whitby in the eighteenth century and re-appeared again in Methodism, Anglicanism, and The Brethren with, for example, Adam Clarke, Thomas Scott, and Alexander Campbell respectively. [46] The insistence of the Puritan preachers on a scriptural basis for eschatological hope would have found ready acceptance with Baptists, Seventh-day Adventists, and others more within the mainstream

---

[45] Individuals and minority groups have perpetuated the more traditional New Testament emphasis, with differing variations. A wider movement of prophetic interpretation recurred early in the nineteenth century, see L. E. Froom, *The Prophetic Faith of our Fathers* (Washington, DC. 1946—1954), III, pt. II, *passim.*

[46] Froom, *op. cit.*, IV, pp. 121—122, 412.

of Christian thought and having respect for a fundamentally biblical eschatology. A. L. Moore sees "a serious impoverishment of
the church's witness" devolving from a neglect of the Parousia
hope. [47] Clearly no such impoverishment existed in the English
church of the seventeenth century, and Moore's commendable
study tends towards the conclusion that there exists within the
established church today a spirit approaching that which prompted Richard Baxter, Joseph Hall, and James Ussher to cherish the
hope of a completely fulfilled eschatology. Much in contemporary eschatological thought, both at the centre and on the wings,
can be more readily comprehended and more accurately ap-
praised against the background of the eschatology that developed
in England as the seventeenth century progressed. [48]

The primary sources examined in pursuit of these related
eschatological themes are those available to the student of any
aspect of seventeenth-century theology. Commentaries on the
Bible, in whole or part, form a significant portion of the total. To
the numerous expositions of Daniel and The Revelation must be
added interpretative works on other books: Thomas Taylor's
Commentarie ... upon Titvs, Jeremiah Burroughes' *Exposition of
the Prophesie of Hosea*; Thomas Adams on II Peter, Thomas Hall
on II Timothy 3 and 4, or William Jenkyn on Jude. Specific
doctrinal treatises like Henry Denne's *The Man of Sin Discovered*
or John Durant's *The Salvation of the Saints by the Appearances*

---

[47] Moore, *op. cit.,* p. 4.

[48] The tendency to isolate various contemporary eschatological viewpoints from a
historical point of origin beyond the nineteenth century and hence from a historico-
theological perspective perpetuates misunderstanding and the fragmentation of the
church's eschatological witness. The confusion of Seventh-day Adventist eschatology
with that of the Jehovah's Witness movement may be cited as a case in point. It is
incorrect to represent the Adventist position as declaring that only 144,000 will be
saved at Christ's second coming, D. L. Edwards, *Religion and Change* (1970), p. 262,
or as exhibiting a tendency to calculate the time of the second advent, Moore, *op cit.,*
pp. 216, 217. Moore's dependence here on secondary source material of dubious reliability is unfortunate. The essentially Christological character of Seventh-day Adventist
eschatology places it in a different category from that of Jehovah's Witness, and would
agree very largely with Moore's own conclusion, "that where the person and work of
Jesus Christ is evaluated in terms of eschatology *and* grace, there too the present time
will be recognised both as eschatological and the provision of grace. The End will be
regarded indeed as near, as ready to break in at any moment, as held back only by the
merciful patience of God who wills that men should repent whilst there is time ...',
Moore, *op. cit.,* p. 218. In Adventism, as in Puritan eschatology, the end is the soteriological climax to the outworking of the divine purpose in history, and will thus break
in when that purpose is accomplished. The historical background is therefore an important key to a sensitive understanding of these and other contemporary eschatological
emphases.

of Christ, or Joseph Mede's *The Apostasy of the Latter Times*,
provide much vital eschatological material. In an age given to controversy and debate, polemical works assume particular relevance: Alexander Petrie's *Chiliasto-mastix* and Thomas Hall's
Chiliasto-mastix redivivus are typical in this respect. Devotional
writings in the great tradition of Baxter's *Saints Everlasting Rest*
and Brooks' *Heaven on Earth* illustrate the accepted relationship
of eschatological hope to the basic tenets of Christian belief. The
custom of printing sermons, both singly and in collections, has
preserved a considerable number of discourses, invaluable as a
guide to the exegetical thought of preachers and expositors. Sermons in the mode of *A Sermon of Commemoration of the Lady
Davers*, by John Donne, *Noah's flood Returning*, by Robert Gell,
A Sermon of Iudgement, by Richard Baxter exemplify the eschatological element in contemporary preaching, as do also collections such as William Strong's *XXXI Select Sermons*, or Jeremiah
Burroughes' *Jerusalem's Glory Breaking forth into the World*.
Further information, often of considerable significance, is to be
found in the poetry, correspondence, and miscellaneous writings
of clergy and laity alike. The vast amount of source material
available demands that an investigation of this nature be representative rather than exhaustive.

The original study has been carefully revised in view of subsequent cognate works, and the appendix on conditional immortality and resurrection is new. It will already have been recognised
that what follows is more in the context of historical theology
than theological history, a distinction which, in view of the continuing interest in the history of the period, both religious and
secular, merits note. In chapter one we survey the basic doctrine
of Christ's second advent as inherited from early Protestantism
and understood by representative moderate writers of the period.
Chapter two examines the concept of the end of the age, with
reference to the exegesis of the apocalyptic books of Daniel and
The Revelation. Attention is then centred on the two major arguments advanced in support of an imminent advent, the interpretation of latter-day signs, and the computation of specific chronological prophecies. In the following chapter the concept of the
kingdom of God and its ultimate succession over all earthly
powers is set forth, with special attention to the Papacy, the
Turks, and the Jews. This leads to an examination of millenarianism and Fifth Monarchism as they emerged from an already
accepted eschatological pattern, and of their place in that wider
scheme. Finally, the relationship of eschatological belief to the

life of faith and the quest for godliness is examined, first as it appears in early Quakerism and then in the experience of the individual and the church at large. Original spelling and punctuation have been retained and, unless otherwise indicated, all books cited were published in London. Biographical information on sixteenth and seventeenth-century English theological writers may be found in *The Dictionary of National Biography* (DNB) if no other reference is given in the footnotes.

A word remains to be said of terminological usage. Certain terms recurring with some frequency are basic to the nature of the argument. Thus 'prophecy' and 'prophetic' are used in the more narrow sense of predictive rather than in the more etymologically correct sense of proclamatory. 'Apocalyptic', in this context, is restricted to that type of prophetic utterance which is couched in cryptic symbolism, rather than in the wider sense of revelational. 'Chiliasm' and 'chiliastic' are derived from the Greek χιλιας, thousand, and refer to belief in a coming millennium, usually with a connotation of extremism. Millenarianism, unless otherwise qualified, is the belief in a coming thousand-year reign of the church on earth prior to the last judgement. Finally, eschatology is the doctrine of the last things in a universal sense, Christ's second coming, the resurrection of the dead, the end of the world, as opposed to an individual relationship to death, judgement, heaven and hell.

Protestant eschatological optimism deriving from the Reformation achieved its most lucid expression with English theologians in the Puritan era. That optimism included the certainty that time would see the fulfilment of biblical prophecy, belief in the triumph of good over evil, and hope in the ultimate realisation of the will of God on earth. That such optimism was unfounded in the immediate historical context, and that it was sometimes expressed in forms unacceptable to a more mature theological orientation should not be allowed to preclude the more fundamental aspects of Christian hope it sought to express. At a time when the significance of seventeenth-century religious thought is widely recognised, and when there also appears to be a renewed attentiveness to a biblically-related eschatology it is hoped that this study may contribute to a more informed understanding of both. [49]

---

[49] The "growing consensus in New Testament scholarship that the Kingdom of God is in some sense both present and future", G. E. Ladd, *Jesus and the Kingdom* (1966), p. 3, would have been well understood by seventeenth-century interpreters.

Other recent works reflecting a movement towards an eschatology of biblical realism include: O. Cullmann, *Christ and Time*, 1951, and *Immortality of the Soul or Resurrection of the Dead?*, 1958; J. Jeremias, *The Parables of Jesus*, 1954; G. R. Beasley-Murray, *A Commentary on Mark Thirteen*, 1957; G. Lundström, *The Kingdom of God in the Teaching of Jesus*, 1963; J. P. Martin, *The Last Judgment in Protestant Theology from Orthodoxy to Ritschl*, 1963; N. Perrin, *The Kingdom of God in the Teaching of Jesus*, 1963; A. L. Moore, *The Parousia in the New Testament*, 1966,; see also: G. E. Ladd, *The Presence of the Future*, 1974. The 'eschatology of biblical realism' describes the attempt to evaluate New Testament eschatology from the viewpoint of its writers as distinct from interpretations latterly imposed by modern scholarship. In contemporary eschatological *schemata* it may be placed between the Continental 'consistent eschatology' of Schweitzer and Werner, *inter alios*, which interprets the New Testament eschatological emphasis in terms of a mistaken apocalypticism on the part of Jesus, and the Anglo-Saxon 'realised eschatology' of Dodd, Glasson, and Robinson, *inter alios*, which postulates that eternity and the kingdom are already here in the person of Christ, leaving little or no room for a future consummation; cf. Moore, *op. cit.*, pp. 35—66.

CHAPTER ONE

THE WORD OF GOD
AND THE SECOND COMING OF CHRIST

The view that "Luther performed all his deeds in the conviction that the Last Days were at hand"[1] deserves further serious consideration. An eschatological interest, at times approaching an emphasis, appears consistently in his writings, as it does with other sixteenth-century Continental theologians, and the expectant spirit of the Reformers in general may be regarded as germinal to the more mature eschatology which appeared in the seventeenth century. In recognising this element in Continental antecedents, the English theologians felt an affinity with the impetus to restore to the body of faith the New Testament ingredient of hope.

Luther himself had early expressed faith in the approaching end. In 1519 he wrote to the Elector Frederick of Saxony of "these evil latter times."[2] "The end of the world is not far away",[3] he declared four years later. When considering the claims of the Papacy and the priesthood he remarked, "If the Last Day were not close at hand, it would be no wonder if heaven and earth were to crumble because of such blasphemy. However, since God is able to endure this, this day cannot be far off".[4] Luther's subject for an Advent sermon was "The Signs of Christ's Coming", and was taken from the words of Christ in Luke 21:

> I would compell no man to believe me, and yet in this matter I will not yield up my Judgement to any other, namely, that the Last Day is not far off ... Let us not therefore be wanting to ourselves, disregarding the most diligent premonition and prophesie of Christ our Saviour; but seeing in our Age the Signs foretold by him, do often come to pass, let us not think that the coming of Christ is far off.[5]

---

[1] Cohn, *Pursuit of the Millennium*, p. 261.
[2] Martin Luther, 'Luther an Kurfürst Friedrich 13th/19th January 1519', in *D. Martin Luthers Werke* (Weimar), Briefwechsel, I, p. 307, quoted from *Luther's Works* (American Edition), 48, p. 104.
[3] Luther, 'Epistel S. Petri, gepredigt und ausgelegt', *Werke*, 12, p. 293, quoted from *Works*, 30, p. 38.
[4] Luther, 'Von den Konziliis und Kirchen', *Werke*, 50, p. 513, quoted from *Works*, 41, p. 13; cf. *Works*, p. 65, where the last day is said to be "imminent".
[5] [Luther], *The Signs of Christs coming, and Of the last Day* (1661), pp. 4, 28.

Luther is followed closely by Melanchthon who speaks of "these laste perellous dayes",[6] of "Cryste with his laste coming now at hād",[7] and, "he shall come agene shortely".[8] Even Calvin, who is generally less explicitly concerned with future events,[9] epitomises earlier Reformation thought on the question of the second advent:

> ... wee must alwayes remember the comming of our lord Iesus Christ. For were it not for this, we should faint euerie minute of an houre ... there is no other meanes to confirme vs to stande stedfastly, and to follow the right way, but onely to know, that our Lorde Iesus Christ will come and restore all things that are now out of square ... True it is, that according to our fleshly senses, it cannot sinke into our heades that the comming of our Lord Iesus Christ is at hand ... And though our flesh be not able to reach vnto it, yet we must beholde it with the eyes of faith ... let vs loue this comming of the Sonne of God ... [10]

This relationship between belief in Christ's coming and the present experience of the believer was to prove one of Calvin's great contributions to spiritual life within the English church.

The seeds thus sown in the early spring of the Reformation were borne across the English Channel to take root in a climate favourable to their further development. It is not surprising, therefore, to find the English Reformers expanding the eschatological theme introduced by their brethren on the Continent. Bishop Latimer, for instance, has left abundant testimony to his

---

Probably a translation of the *Ainchristliche und vast wolgegründe beweysung von dem Jüngsten Tag* (Augsburg, 1522).

[6] In George Joye, *The exposicioun of Daniel the Prophete gathered oute of Philip Melancthon, Johan Ecolampadius, Chonrade Pellicane & out of Johan Draconite* (Geneva, 1545), fol. 5 v.

[7] *Ibid.*, fol. 7r.

[8] *Ibid.*, fol. 244 v. Although the title suggests that Joye has drawn from several Reformers, the work appears primarily to reflect the views of Melanchthon. His dedicatory epistle is translated verbatim, and the summary of the book's argument is also attributed to him. There is no further indication as to which of the original authors, if any, Joye is following.

[9] But cf. "It is of the essence of Calvin's whole theology that it is impossible to treat his eschatology as a separate part ... If we call Luther the theologian of faith we may, even if with exaggeration, characterize Calvin as the theologian of hope. All his declarations are, so to speak, concerned with the future," H. Quistorp, *Calvin's Doctrine of the Last Things* (1955), p. 15. It is in seventeenth-century England that this Calvinistic eschatology finds its most lucid expression.

[10] John Calvin, *Sermons de Iean Calvin sur les deux Epistres Sainct Paul à Timothee, & sur l'Epistre a Tite* (Geneva, 1563), pp. 502, 503, quoted from *Sermons ... on the Epistles of S. Paule to Timothie and Titus* (1579), pp. 994—996.

belief in the second advent. Preaching in the presence of Edward
VI, in 1549, he maintained: "the end of the world is neare at
hand. For there is lacke of fayeth now. Also the defection is
come and swarving frō the faith. Antichrist the man of synne the
sonne of iniquity is reveled, y latter dai is at hand." [11] Latimer
subsequently developed this theme in a sermon before the Duch-
ess of Suffolk. The passage is quoted at some length in view of
the basic eschatological concepts to which it gave an early expression:

> Saincte Paule sayeth, Non veniat dum nisi veniat defectio. The Lorde
> wyll not come tyll the swarvyng from faythe commeth, whyche thyng
> is already done and past: Antichrist is knowē thorought al the world.
> Wherfore the daye is not farre of. Lette us beware, for it wyll one
> daye fall uppon oure heades. Saincte Peter Sayeth. Finis omnium
> appropinquat, The ende of all thinges draweth very nere. Yff Peter
> sayd so at his tyme, how muche more shall we saye so: For it is a
> longe tyme sence Saincte Peter spake these woordes. The worlde was
> ordeyned to endure (as all learned men affirme and prove it with
> scripture) syxe thousande yeare. Nowe of that number there bee paste
> fyve thousande [five hundred] [12] fyftie two, so that there is no more
> left but foure hundred and forty eighte. And furthermore those dayes
> shal bee shortened, it shall not bee full syxe thousande yeare, Nam
> abbreuiabuntur dies propter electos, the dayes shall bee shortened for
> the electes sake. Therefore all those excellent learned men, which
> withoute doute God hath sente into this world in these latter dayes to
> give the world warnyng: all those men doe gather oute of Scripture
> that the laste daye can not be farre of. [13]

This, it may be observed, was the mature confession of one of
England's prominent Reformers, and a belief which remained
with him to the very end. Writing from his last prison in Oxford,
in 1555, to the "unfeigned lovers of God's truth", Latimer pointed them to the day "when our Christ shall come in his glory,
which I trust will be shortly". [14]

John Bradford, chaplain to bishop Ridley and prebendary of
St. Paul's repeatedly refers to the last events in his writings: "I
trust our redemers comming is at hande"; [15] "the commyng of

---

[11]   Hugh Latimer, *Certayne Godly Sermons* (1562), pt. II, fol. 59r.
[12]   The phrase in parenthesis is omitted in the original, also in the 1571 and 1578
editions. The omission is obviously unintentional.
[13]   Latimer, *op. cit.*, pt. I, fol. 21r.
[14]   Latimer, *The Works of Hugh Latimer,* II (Cambridge, 1845), p. 441.
[15]   John Bradford, 'To my deare Brother in the Lorde Mayster Rychard Hopkyns',
in *Certain most godly, fruitful, and comfortable letters of such true Saintes and holy
Martyrs of God,* ed. M. Coverdale (1564), p. 348.

the Lorde, whyche is at hande"; [16] "for suerlye the coming of our Sauiour wyl shortlye appeire in glorie." [17] A vivid description of Bradford's concept of the day of judgement, with its contrasting effects of joy and despair on saints and sinners, appears in his "Meditation on the Coming of Christ to Judgement", published in 1562. John Jewel, the Anglican apologist and bishop of Salisbury, added to the eschatological literature in 1583 with *An Exposition vpon the two Epistles of Sainct Paule to the Thessalonians*. The learned Edwin Sandys, successively bishop of London and archbishop of York, believed that he lived in "the last houre" [18] and that the judge was "euen at the doore". [19] In a letter to the bishop of Chester, in 1583, Sandys wrote:

> When I look, venerable brother, at the course and condition of this world lost in impiety; what triumphs Satan obtains, how far and wide vice bears rule, how numerous and crowded are the assemblies of ungodly men, how weak, how withered, or rather how entirely gone from the earth is faith, is piety; it seems to me that we are now arrived at the last and ungodly times of this world, drawing near to destruction. [20]

If this tended towards pessimism, it is balanced by the more optimistic "joyful day for God's children", Sandys' description of the second advent in a sermon preached at Paul's cross. [21]

The developing eschatological consciousness is further demonstrated in two little works which appeared in the mid-sixteenth century, George Joye's translation of Andreas Osiander's *Vermutung von den letzten Zeiten und dem Ende der Welt aus der heiligen Schrift gezogen* (Nürnberg, 1545), [22] and the translation by Thomas Rogers from the Dutch of Sheltoo à Geveren entitled *Of the ende of this worlde, and the second comming of Christ* (1577). The four conjectures, or methods of calculating when the end of the world would occur, which Osiander had propounded to the people of Germany were faithfully imparted

---

[16]   Bradford, 'To my good Syster Mystres Elizabeth Browne', in *Letters*, p. 413.

[17]   Bradford, *The Hvrte of Hering Masse* [1561?], sig. Eir.

[18]   Edwin Sandys, *Sermons made by the most reuerende Father in God, Edwin, Archbishop of Yorke* (1585), p. 345.

[19]   *Ibid.*, p. 186.

[20]   Sandys, *The Sermons of Edwin Sandys, D.D.* (1841), p. 439. The original Latin MS. of this letter is in the library of Emmanuel College, Cambridge, and is quoted by Strype in *Annals of the Reformation* (1824), III, pt. II, p. 257.

[21]   *Ibid.* p. 390.

[22]   Andreas Osiander, Lutheran theologian and professor of theology at Königsberg. The title of Joye's translation was *The coniectures of the ende of the worlde* (Antwerp, 1548).

to the English readers of Joye's book. The first argument was based on an oft-quoted prophecy of Jewish origin, reputed to have been recorded in various places in Talmudic writings. [23] This prophecy had foretold that the world would last for approximately six thousand years, two thousand before the law, [24] two thousand under the law, and two thousand under the Messiah. The six millennia were compared to the six days of creation, it being reasoned that as the sixth day of creation had been shortened and the time thus gained added to the seventh day of rest, so the sixth millennium would similarly be curtailed in order to usher in the final era of world history, the era of eternal rest:

> For as in the lawe, the sixt daye was not hole graunted to worke therein to the full end as to the midnyght, but a good part therof was anticipated and cut off, added to the Sabboth daye, even so shall not the sixt millenarie be all full hole geven to the labourouse last mortal lyfe, but y most gloryouse beutyfull parte therof about the euenying shal be anteuorted and preuented of that blessed and euerlastynge reste ... [25]

In view of the parallel, and also in view of the fact that nearly five thousand five hundred years had elapsed since the creation, it seemed certain that the end drew on apace.

All this, however, was still somewhat vague and to make a more specific reckoning, Joye drew the attention of his readers to the second and third conjectures from Osiander. Christ's own comparison of the last days to the Noachian age, especially the phrase "As the days of Noe were ..." [26], was interpreted to refer particularly to the time element involved. Thus the period from Adam to the Flood was representative of the time from the "second Adam" to the final visitation of judgement. Since the antediluvian period had lasted 1656 years, it was "very like that in y yeare of our Lorde. Mccccclvi. the end of the world shall becomen ..." [27] This calculation was strengthened by the third postulate, based on a comparison to the duration of our Lord's life on earth, thirty-three years and a few days. The inference

---

[23]   According to Dr. Max Seligsohn, the view had originated with Rabbi Kattina, or Ketina a Babylonian amora of the third century; see *The Jewish Encyclopedia* (1925), 7, p. 452. For examples of its appearance in the Talmud, see 'Rosh Hashanah', *The Talmud* (1938), Mo 'Ed. VII, p. 146, and Sanhedrin II, *The Talmud* (1935), Nezikin VI, p. 657.

[24]   Not the Sinaitic law, but the law of circumcision, given to Abraham.

[25]   Joye, *The coniectures of the ende of the worlde* (Antwerp, 1548), sig. Aviiiv.

[26]   Matt. xxiv: 27.

[27]   Joye, *op. cit.*, sig. Biir.

drawn from this particular period was that He would likewise spend thirty-three years spiritually with His church on earth, before returning literally in glory at the end of the age. Those years were to be reckoned as "great yeares", corresponding to the Jubilees of the Israelites and so each of fifty literal years' duration. Thus, thirty-three of these 'Jubilee' years, plus the few additional years required by the days in excess of Christ's thirty-three actual years on earth, also pointed to the year 1656 or thereabouts. "Wherefor it is very lyke that aftir the xxxiii Jubeley year of y church which shal be shortly after the year from Christes birth or resurreccioun. Mcccccl. the ende of the worlde shall be at hande ..." [28]

These calculations considerably limited the possible extent of the sixth millennium. But there was still a difficulty. Should the computations be taken from the time of Christ's birth, or from the time of His resurrection? This question was largely answered by the fourth, and most significant, of Osiander's propositions. The Bible had foretold that Rome was to enjoy a two-fold era of power, both aspects of which had been designated in Scripture. When the second era came to its appointed end "then doubtless is the end of the worlde at hand". The first era, that of Pagan Rome, had extended until a little after the time of Constantine. The second era, foretold by Paul in II Thessalonians and by John in the Apocalypse, was still in existence but would "not long dure". This era was destined to last for 1260 years, calculated from 412 A.D. and thus reaching down to 1672. "It can not be doubted but that, these yeares once fulfilled, the ende of the worlde is anone at hande". [29] On the basis of this final conjecture, Osiander stated that the two previous propositions were to be calculated from the time of the resurrection rather than the nativity. This would bring all the dates into a closer harmony and Osiander finally concluded, "it shall come to passe that the ende of bothe the Pope and of Rome, and of the worlde shall fall into the yeare of our Lorde, about m.ccccc.lxxxviii. Whiles the fall of the Pope is lyke to come in the yeare of Christ, about m.ccccc.lxxii." [30]

Joye, however, was not entirely satisfied with Osiander's computations and added one of his own, stemming from the 1290

---

[28] *Ibid.*, sig. C*ir*. Joye thought himself that 1672 or 1677 were possibilities, *loc. cit.*

[29] *Ibid.*, sig. G*viir*.

[30] *Ibid.*, sig. G*viiiv*; i.e. in 1688 and 1672 respectively.

days of Daniel chapter xii. Signifying years, this period had commenced with Diocletian's abdication, which had precipitated the revelation of the beast of the Apocalypse who, according to Joye's interpretation, was to reign during these 1290 years. His conclusion is almost predictable. "Wherefor", he said, "me thinketh it shuld be at an ende within these xxxvii yeres or in lxxvii, if we rekē frō the resurreccion of Christ." [31] It seems that Joye thus anticipated the end between 1582 and 1622. [32] He also allowed for the possibility that the 1260 year period could have commenced in 307 A.D., thus bringing the time of the end appreciably nearer. Which of the two sets of dates Joye regarded as the more probable he does not indicate. What is beyond doubt is that he expected Christ's second appearance well within the limits suggested by Osiander, and most probably before the turn of the century.

The first edition of Thomas Rogers' *Of the ende of this worlde and second comming of Christ* appeared in 1577. [33] While the influence of the earlier work is evident, the particular concern of this author is to underline the conclusion that Joye had reached, that the second coming of Christ was to be expected before the sixteenth century expired. Three arguments pointed in that direction. In the first place, there appeared to be an obvious parallel between the time of the Mosaic jurisdiction in Israel and the time of the church's rule on earth under the Gospel. The former dispensation had ended with the destruction of Jerusalem by Titus, a period of 1583 years, and it was not "to be doubted of any, but that that destruction ... is a manifest figure of the last ruine of this world". [34] Secondly, a current astrological prediction forecast that in 1584 there would occur "eyther a greeuous alteration of Empyres ... or els an vtter destruction of this world". [35] Finally, a deduction was drawn from the time between the birth of Christ and the destruction of Jerusalem. If

---

[31] *Ibid.*, sig. Hiiv. Joye's computations here are somewhat abstruse. Just how the issue of dating from Christ's birth or resurrection affects this particular calculation of the 1290 years, is not easy to see.

[32] Sidney Lee gives 1585—1625 as the period within which Joye expected Christ to come. He has apparently overlooked the fact that Joye was calculating from the time of writing in 1545, and not from publication in 1548; see *DNB*, 30, p. 221.

[33] Further editions were issued in 1578, 1582, 1589. Rogers was later to become chaplain and literary aide to Archbishop Bancroft.

[34] Thomas Rogers, *Of the ende of this worlde, and second comming of Christ* (1577), fol. 18r.

[35] *Ibid.*, fol. 18v.

taken from the rebirth of the gospel in 1517, a similar period would expire in 1588.[36] It was difficult to avoid the conclusion, in view of the "wonderfull agreeing togeather of yeares",[37] that the end would come between 1583 and 1588.

As time passed this latter year, 1588, became particularly popular as a projected date at which the last day would occur, and it cannot be doubted that the publication of the foregoing views did much to bring it constantly before the minds of the people. The widespread expectations which came to focus on that year are noted by no less a figure than the renowned theologian of early Puritanism, William Perkins. In his first written work,[38] *A Fruitfull Dialogue Concerning the end of the World*, an imaginary conversation between a 'Christian' and a 'Worldling' and published only a year before the anticipated event, Perkins observed that "they say everywhere, that the next yeare eighty-eight, Doomes day will be."[39] 'Worldling', quite convinced that time will prove the truth of this prognostication, reminds 'Christian' who appears more sceptical and who is obviously Perkins' spokesman, of a rhyme currently in circulation portraying this common view:

> When after Christs birth there be expired,
> of hundreds fifteene, yeares eighty eight,
> Then comes the time of dangers to be feared,
> and all mankind with dolors it shall freight,
> For if the world in that yeare doe not fall,
> if sea and land then perish ne decay.
> Yet Empires all, and Kingdomes alter shall,
> and man to ease himselfe shall have no way.[40]

Perkins himself, as might be expected, is not moved by fancies which set the time of the second coming for next year or, for that matter, in any year. It is not possible, nor is it the will of God, that man should have prior knowledge of the exact time.[41]

That no attempt should be made to date the end of the world, however, does not preclude belief in an imminent second coming.

---

[36]   *Ibid.,* fol. 20r.

[37]   *Ibid.,* fol. 21r.

[38]   See William Crashaw, To The Right Honourable Thomas Lord Scroope, in 'A Fruitfull Dialogue Concerning the end of the World', *The Workes of M. W. Perkins*, III, (1631).

[39]   William Perkins, 'A Fruitfull Dialogue Concerning the end of the World' (1587), in *Workes*, III, p. 467.

[40]   *Loc. cit.* This piece of doggerel had also appeared in Rogers' *Of the ende of this worlde*, fol. 19v.

[41]   Perkins, *op. cit.,* p. 473.

On the contrary, Perkins is clearly committed to the doctrine of an early advent. Although, as has been noted, he dismisses the specifying of 1588 as the probable time, nevertheless these are the "last days" and the end is "most certaine". [42] Only the conversion of the Jews remains to be accomplished before the final act in the drama. [43] Both in this work and elsewhere, Perkins discusses at some length the signs which are to precede Christ's coming, "all which are almost past, and therefore the end cannot be far off." [44]

It is, then, perhaps not without significance that in this very year 1588, King James first published his exposition of part of the twentieth chapter of Revelation. [45] This royal interest in prophecy may be seen as a reflection of the growing attention now being given to the prophetic portions of the sacred canon, particularly to the books of Daniel and Revelation. Already several notable expositions of these fascinating prophetic books had appeared both on the Continent and in England, [46] and the coming years were to witness the publication of many more. "Of all the Scriptures", the King wrote, "the buik of the Reuelatioun is maist meit for this our last age ..." [47] And when could its final fulfilment be expected? "Iudge yif this be not ye tyme quhairof this place that I have maid chois of doeth meane, and sa ye dew tyme for the reueiling of this prophecie." [48] By the time the crown had passed from Tudors to Stuarts there had developed within English Protestantism a marked awareness of those doctrines which concerned the end of time and the final consummation of history. The last age had come. These days were the last days. The second coming of Christ could be expected in the foreseeable future. As the sixteenth century passed and as the seventeenth century commenced, the tide was already well on its way in. [49]

---

[42] *Ibid.*, p. 474.

[43] *Ibid.*, p. 470.

[44] Perkins, 'An Exposition of the Symbole, or Creed of the Apostles' (1595), in *Workes,* I (1626), p. 261.

[45] James I, *Ane frvitfvll Meditatioun contening ane plane and facill expositioun of ye 7.8.9. and 10 versis of the 20 Chap. of the Reuelatioun* (Edinburgh, 1588).

[46] E.g. John Bale, *The Image of bothe churches after the moste wonderfull and heauenly Reuelacion of Sainct John the Euangelist* (1548?); Henry Bullinger, *A Hvndred Sermons vpo the Apocalips of Jesu Christe* (1561); John Foxe, *Eicasmi seu Meditationes in Sacram Apocalypsin* (1587).

[47] James I, *frvitfvll Meditatioun,* sig. Aiiir.

[48] *Ibid.,* sig. Biiv.

[49] Other sixteenth-century works of eschatological importance include: George

The other fundamental element which underlay the eschatology of the seventeenth century was the complete contemporary acceptance of the Bible as the sole source of faith and doctrine. This utter reliance upon Scripture was itself the continued out-working of a principle flowing directly from the main stream of Reformation thought. Such explicit phraseology as "the sole source of authority",[50] "a revelation complete and unalterable",[51] and "the all-sufficient book",[52] has been employed by modern scholarship in defining this almost universal attitude to the written Word.[53] If Puritanism was "a child of the Reformation",[54] then this insistence upon biblical authority was one of the more salient family characteristics.

This stand upon the unquestioned and unquestionable supremacy of the Bible was the platform of all theological debate, the *sine qua non* of reasonable discussion, and was frequently defended by contemporary apologists. Thus James Ussher, the archbishop of Armagh, propounds the basic tenets of the Christian faith having first established the trustworthiness of their foundation: "the bookes of Holy Scripture are so sufficient for the

---

Gascoigne (tr.), *The Droomme of Doomesday* (1576), a clear statement of the doctrines of the imminent advent and judgement, sig. Eii-Ev; Francis Shakelton, *A blazyng Starre or burnyng Beacon* (1580), occasioned by the appearance of a comet on October 10th, 1579, and written to warn the world of the "seconde commyng of Christ in the cloudes", ep. ded; and Philip Stubbes, *The Anatomie of Abuses* (1583), in which the decay of society is argued as evidence that "the daie of the Lorde can not bee farre of", fol. 123r. Evidence of a continuing interest in the last things is a later MS. dedicated to the Chancellor of Cambridge University in the Sloane collection in the British Museum: 'A most sure and certaine prophecie of That which is past, present, and to come, Rev. 15:1. Historically comprised in the seven last plagues, probably interpreted of yt which is past from ye times of ye Waldenses, and yet to come in and before ye second comming of Christ to iudgment', British Museum, Sloane MS. 1004.

[50] A. Simpson, *Puritanism in Old and New England* (Chicago, 1955), p. 6.

[51] Woodhouse, *Puritanism and Liberty*, Introduction, p. 45.

[52] W. Haller, *Liberty and Reformation in the Puritan Revolution* (New York, 1955), p. 139.

[53] Horton Davies and C. H. and K. George have shown that this intrinsic Biblicism extended far beyond the bounds of conventional Puritanism. Cf. the statement that both the Established and Puritan clergy "subscribed to the Sixth of the Thirty-Nine Articles", H. Davies, *The Worship of the English Puritans* (1948), p. 3, with "The view that scripture is the primary and final source of authority and truth in Christianity ... is by no means limited to a group of extremists in English Protestantism ... Protestantism as a whole is indeed characterized by this emphasis ... (a) universal acceptance of Scripture as the Word of God over any and all merely human authority or tradition", C. H. and K. George, *The Protestant Mind*, pp. 341—342.

[54] G. F. Nuttall, *The Puritan Spirit* (1967), p. 81.

knowledge of Christian Religion, that they doe most plentifully contain all Doctrine necessary to salvation ..." [55] The judicious Richard Baxter, in setting forth his celebrated *Saints Everlasting Rest*, devotes most of the second part to a vindication of his authority maintaining "that the Scripture promising that Rest to us, is The perfect infallible Word and Law of God". [56] Likewise Christopher Love, the injudicious Presbyterian, [57] in the clearest possible terms exhorts his hearers to "Be sure you make the Word of God to bee the Standard by which you try and prove all Doctrines that you heare, and if there bee anything preached (although it should be by an Angell from Heaven) that is not according to the Word of God, beleive it not". [58] When a preacher or a writer wished to prove a point he turned instinctively to the Bible for support and could readily provide relevant references to substantiate an argument. This was the ultimate court of appeal, "more sure ... then if wee should heare a voyce from Heaven." [59]

The crux of the matter was that this divine revelation extended to the delineation of coming events. The Bible was authoritative not only in its record of the past and in its guidance for the present life and doctrine of church and believer, but equally in its pronouncements of future consummation. This intrinsic relationship between past, present, and future was ably argued by John White, rector of Lambeth, and another member of the Westminster Assembly:

> Whatsoever things were written aforehand, were written for our learning, saith the Apostle, Rom. 15.4. The Lawes for our Direction: The Prophecies for Observation of their Accomplishment in answerable Events: The Promises for our Comfort and Consolation. The Examples of Evill for Caution, of Good for Imitation: And lastly the Events, ordered by the Wisdome, and Providence of God, for Precedents and Patternes, representing our State and Condition, either

---

[55] James Ussher, *A Body of Divinitie* (1645), p. 18.

[56] Richard Baxter, *The Saints Everlasting Rest* (1650), pt. II, Title Page.

[57] Love was accused of being implicated in a plot to overthrow the Commonwealth, and was subsequently executed in 1651. The impression given by W. A. Shaw in the *DNB* is of a man often at variance with authority. The temptation to prejudge his theology and religious motivations in the light of this picture must be avoided. The restraint and scholarship which generally characterize his writings reveal him as a principled man of honest conviction, a victim, perhaps, of his age rather than of any censurable crime; see *DNB*, s.v.

[58] Christopher Love, *A Christians Duty and Safety in Evill Times* (1653), p. 82.

[59] *Ibid.*, p. 83.

> What it is at Present, and why so, or what wee are to Expect it may be hereafter. [60]

The validity of past and present is in their ultimate fulfilment in the future. The entire Bible, in all its manifold revelations, is thus "a word more firme then the foundation of the earth, setled forever in heaven". [61]

Two indispensable factors in seeking to understand the promptings which led men like Ussher, Baxter, Love and a multitude of their contemporaries to study the Bible with such reverent attention are, on the one hand, an inexorable compulsion to return to the theology and practice of the early New Testament church and, on the other hand, a similarly impelling desire to move forward to the discovery of new truth. Protestantism in general "saw itself to be not a new faith based on a new revelation, but rather a protest against novelties conceived by others, and therefore a re-formation of the original church of Christ." [62] The Protestantism of the seventeenth century was undoubtedly typical of this orientation, and the resultant bibliocentric preaching and writing of its exponents is the clearest evidence of this concern to return, as far as possible, to the principles of primitive Christianity. John Robinson's frequently quoted admonition to the Pilgrims at the time of their departure to the New World illustrates the other tendency. Edward Winslow's account of this "wholsome counsell" [63] given by Robinson records that:

> He was very confident the Lord had more truth and light yet to breake forth out of his holy Word ... For, saith he, It is not possible the Christian world should come so lately out of such thick Antichristian darknesse, and that full perfection of knowledge should breake forth at once. [64]

Together, these two principles made a serious study of the Bible a continual necessity.

---

[60] John White, *The Troubles of Jerusalems Restauration, or The Churches Reformation* (1646), p. 1.

[61] *Ibid.*, p. 18.

[62] C. H. and K. George, *op. cit.*, p. 382.

[63] Edward Winslow, *Hypocrisie Unmasked* (1646), p. 97.

[64] *Ibid.*, pp. 97–98. There is no original copy of this address, Winslow's account being the first known record. Cotton Mather, in 1702, was the first to turn Robinson's advice into the first person, *Magnalia Christi Americana* (1702), I, p. 14; see *DNB*, s.v. John Robinson. The general feeling that new truth awaited discovery may be seen in the belief in a progressive understanding of the Bible, particularly prophecy; see Burroughes, *Jerusalem's Glory*, pp. 41–42, and infra, pp. 64, 65.

Nowhere did the application of these apparently opposing principles seem to meet in common focus more than in the exposition of those numerous Scriptural prophecies which concerned the future of man and of the world, the fulfilment of which came to be expected in the years close at hand. When devout men studied the Bible, particularly the New Testament, they became increasingly aware of a recurring eschatological emphasis. They found that Christ Himself had spoken, at some length, of the latter days [65] and that, on more than one occasion, He had given what seemed to be an unequivocal promise to return to the earth at the end of time in a dramatic consummation of human destiny. [66] They discovered that the early Christians had gone forth on their world mission sustained in the hope of an early fulfilment of these promises. [67] When they read Paul they read of a day of resurrection, a day of judgment, a day of ultimate reward, [68] and when they turned to the Catholic epistles they found further amplification of the theme of Christ's coming and its attendant course of events. [69] In the light of these more unassailable pronouncements they considered also the more difficult passages of apocalyptic imagery, the mysterious prophecies of Daniel and the book of Revelation, and saw in them confirmation of hopes already engendered by the words of Christ and His apostles. It was inevitable, therefore, that religious thought in Puritan England, stemming as it did from the Bible, should develop an eschatology rooted in the "infallible Word of God." [70]

Nothing was more positive in the whole gamut of resulting latter-day thought than that the Lord Jesus Himself would assuredly come again. This simple, undeveloped statement of second advent belief was the keynote of the entire theme which eventually became so complicated, and although there were many who were to strain the doctrine beyond even the limits of seventeenth-century credibility, there were many others who sought to defend it as biblical and tenable. Indeed, that a belief in the certainty of Christ's second coming was widely dissemi-

---

[65] Cf. Matt xxiv, Mark xiii and Luke xxi.

[66] E.g. Matt. xvi, 27: Luke xviii, 8 and John xiv, 3, 18, 28.

[67] Cf. the promise of the angels at the time of the ascension, Acts i, 9–11, with Paul's assertion "the day is at hand", Rom. xiii, 12 and John's "it is the last time", I John ii, 18. See also Heb. i, 2 and James v. 8, and cf. bishop Joseph Hall's reference to this apostolic belief, "They did then believe that Christ was at the doore", Joseph Hall, *The Revelation Unrevealed* (1650), p. 224.

[68] E.g. I Thess. iv, 15–17, II Tim. iv, 1 and 8.

[69] E.g. James v, I Peter iii, Jude.

[70] Baxter, *Saints Rest,* p. 250.

nated among people and preachers alike is one of the inescapable
conclusions deriving from a thorough appraisal of the religious
literature of the period.

Among the more orthodox exponents of the doctrine were
preachers and writers widely known in their day, as well as men
of lesser repute. Richard Baxter, whose works reveal an unexcel-
led rapport with the times, and who has come to be recognised as
representative of the more conservative element in Puritanism, [71]
left ample evidence in *The Saints Everlasting Rest* of his understanding of the second advent hope. [72] Referring to Christ's coming as the first of "four great Preparatives to our Rest" [73] , Baxter
continues:

> And well may the Coming of Christ be reckoned in to his peoples
> Glory, and annumerated [sic] with those ingredients that compound
> this precious Antidote of Rest: For to this end is it intended; and to
> this end is it of apparent Necessity. For his peoples sakes he sanctified
> himself to his office: For their sakes he came into the world, suffered,
> dyed, rose, ascended: And for their sakes it is that he will Return ... [74]
> This is most clear, that to this end will Christ come again, to receive
> his people to himself, that where he is, there they may be also, John
> 14:3. The Bridegrooms departure was not upon divorce: He did not
> leave us with a purpose to return no more: He hath left pledges
> enough to assure us; We have his Word in pawn, his many Promises,
> his Sacraments, which shew forth his death till he Come; and his
> Spirit, to direct, sanctifie, and comfort, till he Return. [75]

A careful appraisal of The *Saints Rest,* written at a time when its
author lived almost daily in the expectation of death, makes it
evident that this was not merely a theological concept for Baxter,
but a vital element in his own personal faith. "Hasten, O my
Saviour, the time of thy return, send forth thine Angels, and let
that dreadful, joyful Trumpet sound," he entreated. "O blessed

---

[71]   See Nuttall, *Holy Spirit,* p. 10. Although Baxter himself preferred to avoid the
division which formal classification of denomination inevitably implied, he nevertheless
leans fairly clearly towards a moderate episcopacy; cf. his *Reliquiae Baxterianae*
(1696), pt. I, p. 62; pt. II, p. 149.

[72]   The bulk of Baxter's enormous output was published after 1662, and is thus
beyond the scope of this study. It may be noted, however, that in 1691 he entered the
millenarian controversy with *The Glorious Kingdom of Christ,* in which he opposed the
views of Thomas Beverley's *The Catechism of the Kingdom of our Lord Jesus Christ, in
the Thousand Years* (1690). There is no evidence in this later work by Baxter to
suggest that he abandoned, or even altered, the position he had taken in 1650.

[73]   Baxter, *Saints Rest,* p. 44.

[74]   On the intrinsic relationship between the two comings of Christ which is here
implied, see *infra,* pp. 47 ff.

[75]   Baxter, *op. cit.,* pp. 45, 46.

day ... how neer is that most blessed joyful day? it comes apace, even he that comes will come, and will not tarry." [76]

A decade or more previously Richard Sibbes had expressed similar sentiments. "We must take it for granted", he had said, "That there will be a second glorious comming of Christ." [77] Sibbes returned to this subject repeatedly in the later years of his life. In addition to the work already noted, there were *The Chvrches Eccho* (1638) [78], *A Miracle of Miracles* (1638), *An Exposition of the Third Chapter of ... Philippians* (1647), and *The Gloriovs Feast of the Gospel* (1650), all published posthumously and all containing further exposition of the advent doctrine. In the latter, Sibbes, like Baxter, emphasised the biblical foundation of the belief:

> Now since the comming of Christ, the character of the New Testament, is, to wait for Christs appearance. 'There is a Crowne of glory for me, and not onely for me, but for all them that love his appearance.' That is an ingredient in waiting, when we love the thing we wait for. And so Titus 2. last 'The grace of God that teacheth to deny ungodlinesse and worldly lusts, and to live holily, and justly, and soberly in this present evill world, looking for, and waiting for this glorious appearing of Jesus Christ' ... You have scarce any Epistle, but you have time described for looking for the comming of Christ; as Jude, 'Preserve your selves in the love of God and wait for the comming of Christ.' [79]

In the same year in which Baxter's *Saints Rest* and this latter work of Sibbes had been published, there also appeared another important contribution to the growing body of more sober second advent literature. John Seagar's [80] *A Discoverie of the World to Come* (1650) deserves particular attention since its author was openly opposed to "The Doctrine of Millenaries". [81] Despite this confessed disinclination to millenarianism, there are few works which give a clearer exposition of the various aspects of the second advent doctrine. In section five, "Touching the Second

---

[76] *Ibid.*, pp. 837, 791. Extracts from *The Saints Rest*, with a preface by C. H. Spurgeon, appeared in 1858 under the title *The Second Coming of Christ*, one of many nineteenth-century editions of Baxter's enduring work.

[77] Sibbes, *The Brides Longing*, p. 34.

[78] In *Beames of Divine Light* (1639).

[79] Sibbes, *The Gloriovs Feast of the Gospel*, p. 120.

[80] John Seagar, or Seager, (d. 1656) received the living of Broadclyst, Devon, in 1631. In 1648 he subscribed his name to the *Joint Testimonie* of the Ministers of Devon; see *DNB*, s.v. Francis Segar, and *Calamy Revised*, p. 554.

[81] The inscription on the Title page reads, "The Doctrine of Millenaries touching a new Reformed Church in the latter times, which they call a new World, is confuted".

Coming of Christ in the Flesh", Seagar sets forth the certainty of the second advent as an integral part of the total biblical witness:

> ... the Word of God ... informeth us, That the second Coming of Christ in the Flesh shall be most sure and certain: And we may not doubt hereof, because it is confirmed unto us by many plain testimonies of Scripture; (Jude 14, Psa. 50. 3, Matt. 24.30, Matt. 25. 31 and 26. 34, Luke 21. 27, John 14. 3, Acts 1. 11, I Thess. 4. 15, 16, James 5. 7. 8.) And if the second Coming of Christ in the Flesh be confirmed unto us by so many plain testimonies of Scripture, we should not doubt hereof, but should look upon it as upon that which shall be most sure and certain. [82]

If the sheer weight of the biblical evidence was any criterion, Seagar's work was above criticism.

An even fuller treatment of the subject was afforded by another decided anti-millenarian, the Presbyterian Christopher Love. In *The Penitent Pardoned* (1657) in which he, too, considered "the opinion of the Chiliasts" and "solidly confuted" [83] it, Love argued that the certainty of Christ's coming rested on the three biblical foundations of "The immutability of God's decree ... the infallibility of Christs promise ... the Impartiality of his Justice", [84] and represented it as "the great Pillar of our hopes." [85] Commenting on the nature of the assurance given by Christ Himself to return, Love noted that it was "a promise made by Christ", [86] and although it perhaps seemed a long time in reaching its fulfilment "yet the time appointed will bee true, it is certaine, though it be long". [87]

Love here takes up a line of thought previously argued by Sibbes, that the sureness of Christ's return rests on the immuta-

---

[82]   John Seagar, *A Discoverie of the World to Come* (1650), pp. 77, 78.

[83]   Christopher Love, *The Penitent Pardoned*, Title page, see also pp. 158—173. Other noteworthy advocates of the second advent who also opposed millenarianism include Alexander Petrie, *Chiliasto-mastix* (1644); Joseph Hall, *The Revelation Unrevealed* (1650); William Sclater, *The Grand Assizes* (1653), and *The Crowne of Righteousnes* (1654), and Thomas Hall, *Chiliasto-mastix redivivus* (1657), and *A Practical and Polemical Commentary or Exposition upon the Third and Fourth Chapters of the latter Epistle of Saint Paul to Timothy*, (1658). See also Thomas Brooks, *The Glorious day of the Saints Appearance* (1648) and Samuel Smith, *The Great Assize or Day of Ivbilee* (1618). This latter work had gone through twenty-three editions by 1670 and, continuing in popularity long after its author's death in 1665, eventually reached thirty-nine editions by the turn of the century. Petrie, first minister of the Presbyterian church in Rotterdam 1643—62, and Sclater (the Younger) both died shortly after the Restoration. Hall, Brooks and Smith were all ejected in 1662.

[84]   Love, *Penitent Pardoned*, p. 173.

[85]   *Ibid.*, p. 174.

[86]   *Ibid.*, p. 137.

[87]   *Loc. cit.*

bility of the divine purpose and the expression of that purpose in the promises of Scripture. The promises themselves were not only evident for all to see throughout the New Testament, but went right back to the statements of divine intent in the Old Testament where they were "delivered and repeated againe and againe". [88] Therefore, since "the hearts of the Children of God are plyable to Divine Truths, to yeeld to the whole Word of God, especially to the good Word of God, viz. the Promises", they inevitably yield "of all Promises, to the Promise of Promises, the second comming of Christ". [89] Later Sibbes added, "Now as God giveth grace to wait, so he will performe what wee waite for ... God will at length make good what hee hath promised; and what his truth hath promised, his power will performe". [90] There is little distinction in all this between the immutable purpose of God and the irreducible promises which gave it expression. To Sibbes, in this instance at least, the difference was marginal. Both sustained the same argument. Christ's coming was certain.

A further important deduction, seen in the writing of Baxter and others, supported this conclusion. Prophecy had not only depicted the consummation of world history, it had also focussed on important events all through the long ages of the church's existence, paramount among which had been the circumstances surrounding the earthly life of our Lord, particularly those concerned with His birth. These prophetic utterances, it was argued, had been completely fulfilled and it was only logical to assume that predictions dealing with His second coming to earth would be as certainly realised as had those foretelling the Incarnation. "As Christ failed not to come in the fulness of time, even then when Daniel and others had foretold his coming; so in the fulness and fitness of time will his second coming be", [91] wrote Baxter. The point was underlined by William Jenkyn, Presbyterian vicar of Christ Church, Newgate, and an associate of Christopher Love, who asked:

> The Scripture is in no one point more full and plentifull, then in assuring us that this day shall certainly come; and if the other predictions in Scripture, particularly those concerning the first coming of Christ, have truly come to passe, why should we doubt of the truth of Christs second appearance? [92]

---

[88]   Sibbes, *The Brides Longing*, pp. 6, 7.
[89]   *Ibid.*, p. 12.
[90]   Sibbes, *Gloriovs Feast*, pp. 120, 121.
[91]   Baxter, *op. cit.*, p. 92.
[92]   William Jenkyn, *An Exposition of the Epistle of Jude*, pt. I (1652), p. 537.

George Hammon, in replying to Hezekiah Holland's survey of the
"most choice" commentaries on Revelation [93], had also noted
the logic of accepting fulfilled prophecy as a ground for believing
that which was, as yet, unfulfilled:

> Hence it came to passe that that all which was spoken of Christ to be
> fulfilled in the daies of his flesh, was accomplished in the very letter
> of the Scriptures ... and so shall all those Scriptures that speak of his
> glory ... be fulfilled in their time. [94]

For all good churchmen of the day these were reasons [95] more
than adequate to establish the certainty of Christ's coming at the
end of days, and to demonstrate the credibility with which the
doctrine could be accepted.

To enquiring minds, however, and this would include perhaps
the majority in the seventeenth century, the mere statement of
the unelaborated fact that Christ would come again was not sufficient. There were a number of consequential questions which
soon became evident to any who gave the matter much thought,
and each of these contingent matters demanded clarification. If,
for instance, it was to be regarded as established fact that Christ
would return to earth as certainly as He had come the first time,
then in what manner would this second advent occur? Would it
again be a literal, personal coming, or perhaps would He come
this time in some spiritual sense, as a manifestation of the Holy
Spirit working gloriously in the church? If His coming was to be
literal, how would it compare with the Incarnation at Bethle-
hem? That had been a notably inauspicious event. Did the Bible

---

[93] Hezekiah Holland, *An Exposition or ... Epitome of the most choice Commentaries upon the Revelation* (1650). Despite the title, Holland in the main follows the
exposition of David Pareus (or Paré) 1548—1622, Professor of Sacred Literature at
Heidelberg University. On Pareus see J. Le Long, *Bibliotheca Sacra,* II (1723), p. 893.
Pareus's work *In Divinam Apocalypsin ... Commentarius* (Heidelbergae, 1618) had
been translated into English by Elias Arnold, and published in Amsterdam as *A Commentary Upon the Divine Revelation* (1644). On Holland, vicar of Sutton Valence,
Kent (1653), see *Walker Revised,* p. 225, s.v. Rob. Smith. On Arnold, vicar of Ring-
mer, Sussex, 1654—60, see *Calamy Revised,* s.v.

[94] George Hammon, *Syons Redemption* (1658) pp. 189, 190. On Hammon, (to be
distinguished from Geo. Hamond (*Calamy Revised,* s.v.)), pastor of the General Baptist
Church at Biddenden, Kent, see Whitley, *A Baptist Bibliography,* s.v., and Adam Taylor, *The History of the English General Baptists* (1818), pt. I, pp. 166, 167.

[95] There were other lines of reasoning, besides those purely biblical, which sought
to establish the certainty of the advent. Cf. William Durham's interesting argument
from conscience — "only unrivet the secret Cabine of thy brest, and thou shalt find
this doctrine legible; Whence else arise those secret twinges & girds of thy conscience,
which like an under-officer, bind thee over to the great Assize?", William Durham,
Maran-atha: The Second Advent, or, Christ's Coming to Judgement (1652), p. 10.

portray the second advent in a similar light? Such questions, as others which inevitably followed, gave rise to larger issues running into virtually every aspect of eschatological thought, and will be examined in more detail later. It is necessary now to note the position taken on these related aspects of doctrine by what has been referred to as the more moderate, middle-of-the-road opinion of the time. What answers did men such as Baxter, Sibbes, Seagar, and Love, and those of similar calibre give to questions like these and others which were asked with no less insistence? The vast amount of source material which appeared in the first part of the century, particularly in the years after 1640, [96] makes it abundantly evident that much thought was given to these emergent issues of second advent theology.

In the first place, it was not to be doubted that Christ's coming would be literal and personal, "in the Flesh", to note again the phrase of John Seagar. Seagar's emphasis that the bodily return of Christ was to be carefully distinguished from any spiritual 'comings' to the individual soul through the immediacy of the Holy Spirit [97] was argued at greater length by Christopher Love, who maintained that "Christ shal not only come certainly, but he shal come personally ... in his Body ..." [98] Love took the trouble to point out that the idea of a spiritualised second advent could be traced back to Origen, and that it should in no way be regarded as biblical:

> It was the great mistake of Origen, though hee holds for the coming of Christ againe, that he pleades for the coming of Christ in spirit, therefore the Text where it is said, you shall see the Sonne of Man coming in the Clouds of Heaven, Origen understands by the Cloudes, to bee the Saints, because it is mentioned in Scripture, that the Beleevers are a cloud of witnesses. Now this is to pervert the whole letter of the Bible, and turne all the Scripture into an Allegory and Metaphoricall sense ... I onely mention this to confute those that follow the conceit of Origen, meerly to make Christs coming to be but a spiritual coming, a coming in the hearts of Saints. [99]

---

[96] Dr. Nuttall refers to the fact that the Dutch theologian Grotius reported that about eighty different works on the subject had appeared in England by 1649, Nuttall, *Visible Saints,* p. 157. If commentaries, expositions, and polemical writings, which frequently dealt with various aspects of the subject, are included the figure mentioned by Grotius must be regarded as a conservative estimate. Certainly by 1660 the number is far in excess of eighty.

[97] Seagar, *op. cit.,* pp. 76, 94, 95.

[98] Love, *Penitent Pardoned,* p. 175.

[99] *Ibid.,* pp. 175, 176.

Love's exhortations did not fall on deaf ears, and revived concepts of a spiritualised second coming belong largely to later generations. [100]

Like many careful students of Scripture, Love came to see that the Bible mentioned several comings, or revelations, of Christ. In an important work issued in 1653, *Heavens Glory, Hells Terror*, [101] a series of sermons preached ten years previously on Coloss. iii, 4, he drew attention to three appearances of Christ, one in the flesh at the Incarnation, another spiritual through the gospel, and the third, his final appearance to judgement, at the last day. [102] Love pointed out that it was this last coming which was depicted in both Coloss. iii, 4 and John xiv, 3, the texts on which his *Heavens Glory* and *The Penitent Pardoned* were respectively based, and hence "By Christs appearing here, is meant that glorious manifestation of Jesus Christ upon earth at the time, when he shall come at the last day", [103] and "The same Jesus that you saw Ascend, shall descend, so that it cannot bee Christ in his spirit, but in his person." [104]

There is possibly no point of wider agreement concerning the whole subject, apart from the basic certainty of the advent, than on what Love here describes as a "glorious manifestation". Robert Bolton's "comming in the clouds of heaven with power and great glory", James Ussher's "environed with a flame of fire, attended with all the host of the elect Angels", John Owen's "Illustrious Appearance" filling "the whole World with the beams of it", and Thomas Taylor's "in such glorie as neither the tongue can vtter, nor the mind of man can conceiue", [105] are

---

[100]   Although, of course, Quaker literature was beginning to appear by this time, and Love may have had this in mind.
[101]   The work was re-issued in 1671, and again in 1805 and 1810, and also in Dutch, as late as 1857.
[102]   Love, *Heavens Glory, Hells Terror* (1653), pp. 4, 5. He also recognised a fourth interpretation, a coming to inaugurate the thousand year kingdom, without allowing its validity; see *Penitent Pardoned*, p. 136. It was, in fact, the millenarians who usually stressed the necessity of differentiating between the various comings referred to in the Bible; e.g. Edmund Hall, Ἡ Αποστασια ὁ ἀντιχριστος: *or, a Scriptural discourse of the Apostasie and the Antichrist* (1653), p. 15, and William Hicks, ἈΠΟΚΑΛΤΨΙΣ ἈΠΟΚΑΛΤΨΕΩΣ, *or, The Revelation Revealed* (1659), p. 25. But see also Thomas Adams, *A Commentary or Exposition upon the Divine Second Epistle Generall, written by the Blessed Apostle St. Peter* (1633), p. 1166.
[103]   Love, *Heavens Glory*, p. 32.
[104]   Love, *Penitent Pardoned*, p. 176.
[105]   Robert Bolton, *Mr. Boltons Last and Learned Worke of the Foure last Things* (1632), p. 87; Ussher, *Body of Divinitie*, p. 477; John Owen, *A Continuation of the Exposition of the Epistle ... to the Hebrews* (1680), p. 470; Thomas Taylor, *A Commentarie upon the Epistle of Saint Paul written to Titvs* (Cambridge, 1619), p. 480.

descriptions of the nature of the advent all of which are thoroughly representative. The picture thus evoked is further illuminated by Baxter's vivid depiction:

> Methinks I see him coming in the clouds , with the attendants of his Angels in Majesty, and in Glory! ... If there be such cutting down of boughs and spreading of Garments, and crying Hosanna, to one that comes into Jerusalem riding on an Asse; what will there be when he comes with his Angels in his Glory? If they that heard him preach the Gospel of the Kingdom, have their hearts turned within them, that they returne and say, Never man spake like this Man: Then sure they that behold his Majesty in his Kingdom, will say, There was never glory like this Glory ... O then what a day will it be, when he will once more shake, not the Earth only, but the Heavens also, and remove the things that are shaken? When this Sun shall be taken out of the firmament, and be everlastingly darkened with the brightness of his Glory? [106]

Notwithstanding the numerous specific biblical allusions to the glorious manner of the second advent, it was deemed beneficial to elucidate these concepts by comparison with the first advent. Here was an event, which although unseen was neither unknown nor irrelevant, and which could provide a good basis for attempting to apprehend that supernal glory which it was expected would characterize the last day. Reasoning thus from the known to the unknown, these writers succeeded in imparting an indelible impression of what they believed the Bible taught regarding the manner of the second advent. Baxter, again, makes this comparison, although he was preceded by others:

> It will not be such a Coming as his first was, in meanness, and poverty, and contempt ... And yet that coming, which was necessarily in Infirmity and Reproach, for our sakes, wanted not its Glory. If the Angels of heaven must be the messengers of that Coming, as being tydings of Joy to all people; And the Heavenly Hoast must go before, or accompany for the Celebration of his Nativity ... Oh then with what shoutings will Angels and Saints at that day proclaim, 'Glory to God and Peace and Good will toward men?' If the stars of heaven must lead men from Remote parts of the world to come to worship a child in a manger, how will the Glory of his next appearing constrain all the world to acknowledg [sic] his Soveraignty? [107]

Samuel Smith had previously noted the biblical emphasis on a visibly glorious advent:

[106]   Baxter, *op. cit.*, pp. 791, 776, 777.
[107]   *Ibid.*, p. 47.

> When our Sauiour Iesus Christ liued on earth, hee came in misery, very base and lowly; euery child durst looke him in the face ... But now, Hee shall come as a King, full of maiesty and glory, guarded and attended vpon with many thousands of heauenly Souldiours, euen all his holy Angells; ... [108]

Christopher Love had been even more explicit:

> When Christ first appeared, he appeared in the form of a servant; at his second appearing he shall appear in Majesty as a King. In his first appearing he appeared in contempt in a manger, in his second he shall shine in glory in the clouds: In his first appearing, he had onely beasts to be his companions, in his second appearing he shall have Saints and Angels to be his attendants. [109]

It seems fairly certain that these views concerning the manner of the second advent were also part of the tradition handed down from an earlier generation. William Perkins had emphasised the nature of the advent, contrasting it with the Incarnation, "His first comming was in humilitie, borne of a poore virgin ... but his second comming is with glorie, majestie, and dominion in the clouds". [110] Also early in the century, in 1614, Sir William Alexander, Earl of Stirling, statesman and poet, and tutor to Prince Henry, son of James VI of Scotland, had first published *Doomsday, or, The Great Day of the Lords Iudgement*, an epic of almost fourteen hundred stanzas, in which he described in great detail the 'twelve hours' of the Day of Judgement. [111] In the context of the poem, Sir William expected Christ's coming to take place in the third hour, and asked:

> Who can abide the Glory of That sight,
> Which kills the living, and the dead doth rayse,
> With squadrons compass'de, Angels flaming bright,
> Whom thousands serve, Ten thousand thousands praise?
> My soule entranc'd is ravish'd with that light,
> Which in a moment shall the world amaze;
>   That of our sprite which doth the powers condense,
>   Of muddy mortalls farre transcends the sense. [112]

The New Testament record depicted Christ coming at the end of days "in his glory" and "in the glory of his Father" with "all the

---

[108]   Samuel Smith, *The Great Assize, or Day of Ivbilee* (1628 Ed.), p. 21.
[109]   Love, *Heavens Glory*, pp. 38, 39.
[110]   Perkins, 'Commentarie vpon the first three Chapters of the Reuelation' (1595), in *Workes,* III, p. 230.
[111]   With some poetic licence, also.
[112]   William Alexander, 'Dooms-day, or The Great Day of the Lords Iudgement' (1614), in *Recreations with the Mvses* (1637), p. 48 (separate pagination).

holy angels with him", [113] and no respectable theologian in the seventeenth century sought any other interpretation.

Further questions to which answers were required concerned the purposes of Christ's coming. Why, in the secret conclaves of heaven, had it been predetermined that the Son should twice become personally involved in the affairs of men on earth? The purpose of His first coming was clear enough, but what necessity could be argued for a second advent? What would happen to the present order of things when He did come? A final solution to these problems, if that were possible even in the terms of seventeenth-century eschatology, would require a thorough investigation of the many facets and ramifications of millenarianism, and this again must be reserved for attention later. [114] It may be said here, however, that basically two reasons were understood to make the second advent imperative. His coming would, in the first place, usher in the day of judgement and, secondly, establish His long-awaited kingdom.

It is certainly difficult for twentieth-century minds to regard the seventeenth-century emphasis on judgement, finality, and dissolution, without a suspicion of eccentricity. It is equally certain that seventeenth-century minds would have been dismayed at what they would have considered a failure to assess their opinions objectively and as a logical extension of a sincere approach to the interpretation of Scripture. Few things were more certain to them than that God had revealed quite definitely that every man, living or dead, must ultimately be brought to judgement to receive his due reward. Human experience, the justice of God, and prevalent conditions in the world showed that a divine visitation of judgement was an urgent necessity. That this final day of reckoning was a corollary to the second coming and, indeed, often, synonymous with it appears in the titles frequently given to works dealing with the subject. [115]

The Puritan divine, Robert Bolton, had shown a marked awareness of this association between advent and judgement in his *Foure last Things* (1632). [116] There were also two Assize

---

[113]   Matt. xvi, 27 and xxv, 31.
[114]   See *infra,* Chap. V, 'Last Events and The Millennial Rule of Jesus'.
[115]   E.g. William Alexander, 'Dooms-day: The Great Day of the Lords Iudgement'; William Durham, *Maran-atha: The Second Advent, or Christ's Coming to Judgement;* William Sclater, *The Grand Assizes: or, the Doctrine of the Last Generall Judgement* (1653).
[116]   See Robert Bolton, *Last Things,* pp. 87–95.

sermons preached at Northampton, in which he had said that when the number of the elect was complete,

> ... the world shall stand no longer, but the heavens shall shrivell together like a scrole and passe away with a noise, the whole frame of this inferiour world, shall be turned into a ball of fire ... the Trumpet will sound, and we shall all come to the Iudgement of that great, and last day. [117]

Christopher Love maintained that "at the last day" Christ would "judge both quick and dead, those that are living at the day of judgement, and those that are already dead before that day." [118] Thomas Hall of Kings Norton, later to be ejected from his living, was strongly opposed to any form of millenarianism, and wrote in his virulent *Chiliasto-mastix redivivus*, "And we shall oft find in Scripture that the appearing of Christ in glory, and his coming to judgment are joyned together, as being one and the self same thing at the same time. Matt. 24. 30. 2 Tim. 4. 8. Colos. 3. 4." [119] William Durham thought that it was only just that Christ, who once had been "Judged by his Creatures", should "in his second coming ... judge his Judges", [120] and Thomas Adams felt that the great contrast between the two advents would be largely due to the fact that the second advent would reveal "the Iudge thundring out his finall Sentence". [121] Although this day would be "Terrible" to the sinner, yet it would be "Joyful" to the saint. [122]

---

[117]   Robert Bolton, *Two Sermons Preached at Northampton at Two Severall Assizes There* (1635), p. 67.

[118]   Love, *Heavens Glory*, p. 32.

[119]   Thomas Hall, *Chiliasto-mastix redivivus* (1657), p. 55.

[120]   Durham, *Maran-atha*, p. 4.

[121]   Adams, *Commentary*, p. 1308.

[122]   Baxter, *op. cit.*, p. 57. J. F. H. New has concluded that a fundamental difference existed between the Anglican and Puritan concepts of judgement; "we may ... characterize the two eschatologies as mercy versus impartial justice, joy versus condemnation, and subjective optimism versus objective pessimism", J. F. H. New, *Anglican and Puritan* (1964), p. 81. This view must be reconsidered in the light of Puritan attitudes as reflected by Baxter and Durham. Noting the fact that Christ is to be man's judge at the last day, Baxter says, 'Oh what inexpressible joy may this afford to a Beleever? That our dear Lord, who loveth our Souls, and whom our Souls love shall be our Judg? Will a man fear to be judged by his deerest friend? ... fellow Christians, let the terror of that day be never so great, surely our Lord can mean no ill to us in all", Baxter, *op. cit.*, p. 62. Durham concludes his sermon at Warwick Assizes on an optimistic note, "Here's the balme of Gilead for the fainting soule, and abundant consolation for him that is opprest; 'tis doubtless a great asswagement to a Christian's misery, to think that Christ is ready to come to judgement", Durham, *op. cit.*, p. 32. That there were two eschatologies, or rather perhaps, two emphases in one eschatology, may be valid. That they were synonymous with Anglicanism and Puritanism is a conclusion

The other reason which required that Christ should come again arose from the traditional Christian hope of the kingdom. For an accurate assessment of the total eschatological thinking of the age, it is necessary to realise that the second advent doctrine in general gravitated towards the existence of an ultimate future state of which Christ would be head, and in which righteousness and truth would prevail. Although even here among those who did not espouse the millenarian view there were indications of the wide differences of opinion regarding this kingdom which were to arise within the chiliastic groups, the main line of argument illustrates the universality of the hope that the second coming would, in some way, terminate the present world order in favour of something nobler and better. To Baxter, this kingdom would follow immediately after the judgement and would be the just reward of the Saints, purposed for them by God from all eternity,[123] while to Love it was the due inheritance of Christ, whose ultimate right to rule an everlasting kingdom had been made incontrovertible through His first coming.[124] To Alexander Petrie, the Scottish Presbyterian, the kingdom was to be "an heavenly kingdome" for "the reward of the godly is in heaven",[125] but to James Durham, professor of Divinity at Glasgow, it was to be an earthly kingdom, in a re-created earth, "after the general Judgement", the old earth having been destroyed by fire.[126] That which united these men was a common conviction that the present evil world must be superseded by something infinitely superior, as well as a common opposition to the millenarian belief that it would be in the form of an earthly kingdom of a thousand years' duration, prior to the last judgement. The kingdom would logically succeed the judgement, and both would thus follow the second advent.

---

argued on too slender a basis. New's distinction rests on a comparision of the comments of one Puritan and one Anglican on the eschatological proposition in the Creed "from thence He shall come to judge the quick and the dead". The delimitations here restrict the scope of comment, even if William Perkins' Of the Creed (1600), and John Pearson's Exposition of the Creed (1659) can be considered representative. The developments in eschatology in the intervening sixty years must also be taken into account.

[123] Baxter, op. cit., pp. 65, 66.

[124] Love, op. cit., pp. 50, 68.

[125] Alexander Petrie, Chiliasto-mastix (Roterdame, 1644), pp. 62, 63.

[126] James Durham, A Commentarie Upon the Book of the Revelation (1658), pp. 749, 750. Judged by Robert Baillie's attack on millenarianism in his Dissuasive from the Errours of the Time (1645), the fact that he agreed to write the preface to Durham's book is some indication of Durham's own anti-millenarian convictions.

The view advocated by Durham, of a renewed and renovated earth as the ultimate home of the saints, had been the main thesis of John Seagar's *A Discoverie of the World to Come*. Seagar, although ostensibly not in favour of millenarian views was, perhaps, much nearer to them than he would have cared to admit. The kingdom of Christ was to be on earth, he declared, but for ever and not merely for a thousand years. The Bible, Seagar continued, repeatedly mentioned a world to come, and this was not to be understood as simply another term for Heaven. [127] It was a seperate, distinct place, created by God, but would not exist until the dissolution of the present, evil world. [128] This catastrophic change would take place at the second coming, [129] at which time the earth would be reformed and become the inheritance of the Saints for ever. [130] Thus the kingdom of Christ is a new earth, universal, righteous, and eternal.[131] These hopes also, it may be added, were not new but had been propounded several years previously by Arthur Dent, who had placed the thousand years of the millennium in the past, proclaiming the nearness of the last judgement, to be followed immediately by a literal new earth. [132]

There was, of course, a pre-requisite to the effective execution of judgement, as there was also to the establishment of the kingdom. We are speaking now of the resurrection of the dead, without which neither of the two foregoing eventualities could possibly occur. The resurrection can thus be seen as a third cause necessitating Christ's return to earth. At His appearance Christ would "in a moment both raise the dead with their own bodies and every part thereof though never so dispersed"; [133] he would "roll away the stone, and unseal our Graves, and reach us his hand and deliver us alive to our Father." [134] Baxter associates the second advent with these its three major consequences by describing them together as the "four great preparatives" to the eternal rest of the Saints, [135] and under the "heads of divinity"

---

[127]   Seagar, *op. cit.*, p. 7.
[128]   *Ibid.*, p. 25.
[129]   *Ibid.*, p. 42.
[130]   *Ibid.*, pp. 37, 38.
[131]   *Ibid.*, pp. 143—145.
[132]   Arthur Dent, *The Rvine of Rome* (1603), pp. 271—297. This work had left a lasting impression on the first half of the century, going through ten reprints before 1662.
[133]   Ussher, *op. cit.*, p. 447.
[134]   Baxter, *op. cit.*, pp. 56, 57.
[135]   *Ibid.*, pp. 44, 45.

to be taught to children he sets forth clearly the chronological
sequence of events:

> ... when the full number of these elect are called home, Christ will
> come down from heaven again, and raise all the dead, and set them
> before him to be judged; And all that have loved God above all, and
> believed in Christ, and been willing that he should reign over them,
> and have improved their mercies in the day of grace, them he will
> Justifie, and sentence them to inherit the Everlasting Kingdom of
> Glory, and those that were not such, he will condemn to Everlasting
> fire. [136]

Second advent, resurrection of the dead, judgement, eternal rewards, in this order the events of the last days were to occur.

Important as these matters were in arriving at a satisfactory
understanding of the second advent doctrine as a whole, no question was more pressing or provocative than that which concerned
the time when all those tremendous events would take place. Was
it possible that all would be accomplished within a limited future, maybe within the century, or even before? In attempting to
provide an answer to this tantalising question the religious think-
ers of the day were aware that they were wrestling with a problem
that went back to the earliest days of Christianity. They were
also aware that the problem had recurred, with added implications, since the Reformation and that the relentless passing of
time had only added to the urgency of providing an acceptable
answer. Within the context of Reformation theology, which itself
was contained within the framework of the New Testament,
there was but one answer which could be given. Christ would
come soon. The end of the world was imminent. This had been
the answer given by their forefathers in the faith, and there was
every reason for thinking that it was now even more timely. As
Thomas Hall wrote: "... the dayes we live in, are the last dayes.
Our times are the last times ... This is the last hour ... and upon
us the ends of the world are come ..." [137] Hall's logic was hard to
escape, "If the Apostle thought the day of the Lord was at hand
1600. yeares agoe, we may well conclude that it is neer
now". [138] Henry Symons added, with measurable conviction:

> ... it will not be long before this Judge comes, though I dare not say
> with Alsted in his Chronol. that 1657 should be the yeare, because the
> numeral letters are found in mundi conflagratio; nor yet with Napier

[136]   *Ibid.*, p. 550.
[137]   Thomas Hall, *Commentary*, p. 7.
[138]   *Loc. cit.*

that 1688 shal be the year, for those are Arcana coeli; yet I may say
with Bucanon, if 1660 yeares agoe were ultimum tempus, that then
this is ultimum temporis. I may say with Tertullian, this is clausulum
seculi: with Austin, Christ is in proximo: with Cyprian, he is supra
caput; yea, I may say of some here as was said of Simeon, they shall
not depart this life before they shall see the Lord's Christ ... he is on
the wing, he comes post, he will be here before most are aware. [139]

Neither the appeal to the Fathers nor the nuances of the Latin
were wholly lost on Symons' readers.

Beyond associating belief in an imminent advent with the New
Testament and immediate post New-Testament periods, these
views are worthy of consideration on two grounds. In the first
place they demonstrate the absolute certainty with which it was
held that Christ's coming was very near. They also illustrate,
lucidly, that it was altogether possible to maintain this position
without becoming involved in capricious date-setting or the unre-
strained interpretation of prophecy. There is no lack of evidence
to establish the truth of these contentions with regard to the
middle decades of the seventeenth century. To Richard Baxter,
the eventful day is "approaching", "not far off", and "comes
apace". [140] The signs of Christ's coming "foretold by himself,
dayly come to pass". [141] "The day is appearing, and the Spring is
come." [142] John Seagar, who discreetly reminded his readers that
the exact time of the advent was known only to God, [143] pointed out that it was nonetheless near:

> ... we should not think the time of this his second Coming to be far
> off, because the Scripture speaks of it as of that which is near at hand.
> Luke 21.71. Rom. 13.12. Phil. 4.5. I Peter 4.7. Rev. 22.10. James 5.8.
> wherefore, if we will judg according to Scripture, we should judg it to
> be near at hand ... [144]

It is needless to add further statements merely to demonstrate
widespread anticipation of an imminent day of judgement, [145] a

---

[139]   Henry Symons, Ανδριδικαστης Αρχιδικατης *The Lord Jesus His Commission*
(1657) pp. 35, 36. On Symons, Rector of Southfleet, Kent, 1646–60, see *Calamy
Revised* s.v. On Alsted and Napier see *infra* pp. 119, 59 respectively. On Bucanon see
DNB, s.v. Buchanan.

[140]   Baxter, *op. cit.*, pp. 105, 49, 791.

[141]   *Ibid.*, p. 46.

[142]   *Ibid.*, 804.

[143]   Seagar, *op. cit.*, p. 87; cf. Matt. xxiv, 36.

[144]   *Ibid.*, p. 87.

[145]   Similar expressions of the nearness of the second coming include "neer at
hand", Hall, *Revelation Unrevealed*, p. 10; "These are the last dayes", Durham, *Maran-
atha:*, p. 1; "at hand", Brooks, *Heaven on Earth*, p. 596; and "nearer ... then thou
thinkest for", Taylor, *Titvs*, p. 490.

fact which, in any case, has been recognised for some time. [146]

In the second place many concurred with Henry Symons in accepting the doctrine, while at the same time rejecting the necessity to stipulate a definite date. Thomas Adams had cautioned against becoming too pre-occupied with future events lest the exigencies of the present in the Christian life should be forgotten:

> ... his first comming was long looked for; yet the day not precisely knowne. He promised to send the holy Ghost; yet his Apostles knew not the day when; but were commanded to abide at Ierusalem, till they were endued with power from on High: they must tarry the good houre. Much lesse is the terme of his last comming notified to any sonne of man. Let all our care be to finde Christ in our hearts, before wee see him in the clouds. [147]

Despite what he saw as an obvious need in some quarters for this advice, Adams went on, "... so deepe are we fallen into the latter end of these last dayes, that (for ought we know) before we depart this place, we may looke for the last fire to flash in our faces. We are they, upon whom the ends of the world are come." [148] Christopher Love went even nearer to the thought of Henry Symons in dissociating himself from time-setting:

> Some held that the world should last as long after Christs birth, as 'twas from the creation to the flood, viz. 1656. years; by this account it should be 10. years hence. Others say that it shall be as long from Christs birth to the end of the world, as it was from Moses to Christ, viz. 1582. years. Beloved, I only name these for this end, lest when you should read fancies about this time, you should be insnared and taken in a trap, to think to know that determinately, which Christ as man did not know. [149]

Again, however, "the Scripture laies down some Prognosticks, whereby you may know that the day and hour is not farr off", [150] and hence "most Interpreters say 'tis near." [151]

It is thus a matter of fact that the right to believe in "Christ's expected advent and triumph" [152] was not the prerogative of

---

[146]   Cf. Hill, *Puritanism and Revolution*, pp. 325, 326, and Nuttall, *Visible Saints*, pp. 146, 147.

[147]   Adams, *op. cit.*, p. 1134.

[148]   *Ibid.*, pp. 1136, 1137.

[149]   Love, *op. cit.*, pp. 59, 60. There is an apparent awareness here of the ideas set forth a century beforehand by George Joye and Thomas Rogers; cf. *supra*, pp. 19 ff.

[150]   Love, *op. cit.*, p. 61.

[151]   *Ibid.*, p. 62.

[152]   Haller, *Liberty and Reformation*, p. 101. Toon lists eschatological hope, "A strong sense that the last days had dawned ... that Christ was soon to return to earth in glory", as one of six criteria basic to the definition of a Puritan, Toon, *Puritans and Calvinism*, p. 10.

visionaries and fanatics, nor even of millenarians, however moderate. It appears as an accepted article of faith in the body of Christian dogma, and its inclusion in the Westminster Confession of Faith and the Catechisms indicates the measure of its respectability. These documents reflect the doctrine as it existed in English theology as a whole at the beginning of the Interregnum. In the words of the Confession, "God hath appointed a day wherein he will judge the World in righteousness by Jesus Christ", [153] who "... shall return to judge men, and Angels, at the end of the World." [154]   The Catechism is more explicit. Christ

> ... is to be exalted in his coming again to judge the World, in that he who was unjustly judged and condemned by wicked men, shall come again at the last day in great power, and in the full manifestation of his own glory, and of his Fathers, with all his holy Angels, with a shout, with the voice of the Archangel, and with the trumpet of God, to judge the world in righteousness. [155]

If this was the ultimate official pronouncement of Puritan dogma, Professor Owen Chadwick's comment should not be overlooked: "the momentous difference between Puritan and episcopalian was rather devotional than doctrinal." [156]

To come to a thorough understanding of the doctrine and its various involvements, however, was only one concern of seventeenth-century theologians. They were also anxious that the second advent should be seen in perspective, both in a theological and historical sense, and that its place in the divine will for human redemption should be clearly recognised. It is not surprising, then, that as much effort was given to defending the orthodoxy of belief in the second advent, and to setting it in its context in the overall scheme of Christian theology, as to the mere promulgation of the belief and the interpretation of its various facets. It is this desire to see the intrinsic rightness and historicity of belief in latter-day events which, perhaps more than anything else, takes seventeenth-century eschatological expectation as a whole out of the ranks of extremism, and necessitates an objective analysis of the entire subject.

Christopher Love's *The Penitent Pardoned*, in which a lengthy section devoted to the second advent was based on Christ's own

---

[153]   *The Humble Advice of The Assembly of Divines ... Concerning A Confession of Faith ...* (1658), Ch. XXXIII, p. 106.
[154]   *Ibid.*, Ch. VIII, p. 33.
[155]   *The Humble Advice of The Assembly of Divines ... Concerning A Larger Catechisme ...* [1658], p. 29.
[156]   O. Chadwick, *The Reformation* (1968), p. 226.

promise to return, indicates that Love regarded the doctrine as an integral part of the historic faith. On John xiv, 3 Love commented, "This Text contains in it, the most materiall and fundamentall points of all the Doctrine of Christianity", notably "the great Doctrine of Christ's second comming ..." [157] Another biblical reference which was felt to carry a lot of weight was that found in Heb. ix, 28, which accordingly received considerable attention, particularly in commentaries, as in that of John Owen. [158] "Christ's Appearance the Second time", said Owen, "his Return from Heaven to compleat the Salvation of the Church, is the great Fundamental Principle of our Faith and Hope." [159]

Richard Sibbes had already carried this point a step further when he had argued that since the doctrine was a fundamental article of the Christian tradition, it was therefore something which should be desired by the church. This attitude had marked the faithful prior to Christ's first coming, and Sibbes says:

> Such is the disposition of the Church, that before Christ was come, good people were knowne by the desire of his comming. And therefore it was the description of holy men that they waited for the consolation of Israel. Oh Lord come quickly, come in the flesh. But now the first comming is past, they desire as much his second comming and therefore they are described in the Epistle of Saint Paul, to be such as love and long for the appearing of Christ ... [160]

Writing further about the Messianic expectation of the Jews prior to the first advent Sibbes urged, "... let us haue thoughts of the second coming of Emanuell as they had thoughts of the first ..." [161] A desire for Christ's appearance was a characteristic of the true church, the espoused bride of the heavenly Bridegroom,[162] and Sibbes continues "As in civill Marriage, there is a contract; so here, in the Spirituall: and seeing there is a contract, there is also

[157] Love, *Penitent Pardoned,* p. 115.
[158] The first volume of Owen's *Exposition of the Epistle ... to the Hebrews* was published in 1668. Owen was by this time fully aware of the eschatological debate, having already made important contributions himself, e.g. *The Shaking and Translating of Heaven and Earth* (1649), *The Advantage of the Kingdome of Christ* (Oxford, 1651), and *A Sermon Preached to The Parliament, Octob. 13. 1652 ... Concerning the Kingdome of Christ,* (Oxford, 1652).
[159] Owen, *Hebrews,* p. 471.
[160] Sibbes, *The Brides Longing,* pp. 55, 56.
[161] Sibbes, *A Miracle of Miracles, or Christ in our nature* (1638), p. 21 (the second so numbered. The running head reads 'Emanuell, God with us').
[162] Cf. Rev. xix, 7 and xxii, 20, the latter being the text from which Sibbes had preached *The Brides Longing,* originally a funeral sermon for Sir Thomas Crew.

an assent to the second comming of Christ; the contracted
Spouse must needs say Amen, to the Marriage-day." [163] Indeed,
belief in Christ's coming was widely assumed to be part of the
historic witness of Christianity, a fact which in itself is strong
evidence for the doctrine's popularity. It is extremely difficult to
find any extended comment in the relevant literature in which, if
no clear assertion of the doctrine's historicity is made, this assumption is not self-evident.

While at this juncture it is not proposed to examine millenarianism, it will not be out of place to call attention to the views of
John Durant, [164] as set forth in *The Salvation of the Saints*
(1653), a comprehensive and restrained treatise on the soteriological relationship between Christ's priesthood and His second coming. Touching every aspect of second advent doctrine Durant,
like Owen, notes the significance of Heb. ix, 28, saying:

> In the whole verse ... wee have two fundamental points of our Chris-
> tian religion held forth and confirmed. The first concerns the Passion
> of Christ; the second his coming againe. The not right and full beleev-
> ing of these, indangers the very foundation of our faith. [165]

The fact that current belief in an imminent, glorious second advent
was widespread across the theological spectrum—Durant mentions
that men of all parties, "many both Prelatical and Presbyterian" as well as Independent, subscribed even to millenarian
views [166] —seems added proof that the doctrine was felt to belong
to the main stream of Christian thought, rather than to the back-
waters of sects and splinter groups. Viewed as an intrinsic element in the Christian message, the second advent doctrine thus
came to assume considerable theological significance. It was not
an appendage to the main body of belief, merely a convenient

---

[163]   Sibbes, *op. cit.*, p. 15.

[164]   John Durant, or Durance, an Independent, and pastor of the Congregational
Church in Canterbury from 1646—89, held moderate millenarian views, but in *The
Salvation of the Saints* was concerned almost entirely with the doctrine of the second
advent, mentioning the millennium only as a secondary issue. The close similarity of
Durant's views to those of Sibbes, Love, Seagar, Baxter and others on all aspects of the
second coming is a notable argument in favour of the contention that millenarianism,
in its moderate form, was only a step removed from accepted orthodoxy. An outline of
Durant's interesting career may be deduced from various statements in *DNB*, s.v., and
Calamy Revised; see also G. F. Nuttall, 'Dissenting Churches in Kent before 1700', *The
Journal of Ecclesiastical History*, XIV, No. 2, pp. 180, 181. Durant appears from the
latter as a leader among the Congregational Churches in Kent.

[165]   John Durant, *The Salvation of the Saints By the Appearances of Christ* (1653),
pp. 201, 202.

[166]   *Ibid.*, pp. 217, 218; see also pp. 197, 198.

way of bringing to a conclusion the logical sequence of Christian theology. It was, *per se*, of cardinal importance on a number grounds and no survey of the doctrine would be adequate that did not examine these arguments.

Certain links between the first and second advents have already been noted. There was, however, it was believed, a much stronger association between the two events than a mere comparison of the manner of their fulfilment or any similarity in pre-advent expectancy. William Gouge stated the case succinctly when he implied that a second advent was a necessary and inevitable theological sequel to the first advent. [167] "The first and second comming of Christ, are of so neere connexion," Richard Sibbes had argued, "that oftentimes they are comprised together, as the regeneration of our soules, & the regeneration of our bodies, the Adoption of our soules and the Adoption of our bodies, the redemption of our soules, and the Redemption of our bodies." [168] "And he will come to make an end of what he hath begun," he wrote on another occasion, explaining:

> He came to redeeme our soules, hee must, and he will come to redeeme our bodies from corruption. Hee came to be judged, and to die for us, he must come to be judge of the quick, and dead; he came to contract us, he will come againe to marry us, and to take us where he is. He loved us so, that he came from heaven to earth where we are, to take our nature, that he might be a fit Husband, but hee will come to take us to himselfe ... Hee will come; there is no question of that. [169]

This latter statement of Sibbes underlines two major antecedents for maintaining that a theological relationship existed between the two advents, namely the soteriological necessity to complete the salvation of the elect and the moral necessity laid upon Christ to finish the work He had begun. [170] The first of these arguments, particularly, is of great significance in evaluating the importance attached to the doctrine as a whole, and finds expression in a number of pertinent forms.

---

[167]   William Gouge, *A Learned ... Commentary on ... Hebrews* (1655), II, pp. 412, 413.

[168]   Sibbes, *The Brides Longing*, p. 72.

[169]   Richard Sibbes, 'The Chvrches Eccho', p. 107, in *Beames of Divine Light* (1639).

[170]   The line of demarcation between these two principles appears to be very fine. The distinction was clear enough in contemporary argument, however, to warrant separate consideration here. They may be understood better, perhaps, as the human and divine aspects of one soteriology.

The basic idea was nowhere put more forcibly than in John Durant's introduction to *The Salvation of the Saints*. The unqualified statement that "salvation is onely yours: at the last day" [171] might well have laid his theology open to suspicion on the part of orthodox Calvinists—and even Arminians—of the day, and so, possibly to avoid the imputation of heresy, Durant proceeded to explain his position. It was, he said, his experience that the majority of Christians were content to go no further in appreciating the work of Christ than in obtaining an understanding of the work wrought on the cross. In Durant's view this was singularly unfortunate, since the total salvation of man depended also on the work Christ accomplished after His passion. While it was not to be disputed that the death of Christ lay at the very heart of human redemption, yet it was not the whole of His redemptive work. Although it was the "medium impetrationis" it was not the "medium applicationis". Salvation had been "purchased" but not "compleated". Beyond the cross "there remained a great deal more to bee done ... to apply it unto us." This remaining work of Christ had been greatly furthered through His priestly ministry, and would culminate at His second coming. [172] Feeling that even this did not state his understanding of the matter as clearly as might be wished Durant returns to the argument again, now with the emphasis that at the second advent salvation would become an actual reality. A believer's salvation was now in hope, at a distance, as the rightful, though suspended inheritance of an heir under age. While accomplished and assured it was not yet a positive reality, although he did hasten to add that it was "as safe as if you had it". [173] The Robe had been provided, as had the Crown, and at His coming the Lord would deliver both. "Christ keeps the Crowne till the day of his appearance, and Kingdome, and in that day hee will give it you". [174]

While all this might possibly have been interpreted as sufficient cause to question Durant's orthodoxy on the Atonement, there is no reason to suspect that it was so regarded, or that Durant had any fears that it would be. He was, after all, only supporting a view that had been argued by men more eminent than himself. Sibbes had said that at the second coming "he shall perfect our

---

[171]   Durant, *op. cit.,* ep. ded., sig. A4*v*.
[172]   *Ibid.,* To the Reader, sig. A7*r*.
[173]   *Ibid.,* p. 221.
[174]   *Loc. cit.*

salvation",[175] Love that "you shall then be saved to the uttermost",[176] and John Owen, with a little more finesse, added:

> The End of his appearance is εἰς σωτηριαν, the Salvation of them that look for him. If this word relate immediately unto his Appearance; the meaning is, to bestow, to collate Salvation upon them, Eternal Salvation. If it respect them that look for him, it expresseth the qualification of their persons, by the Object of their Faith and Hope; they look for him to be perfectly and compleatly saved by him. [177]

It could hardly be disputed that a perfect salvation should be perfectly effected, and if this was the purpose of the second advent few would be disposed to disagree.

The expression of this conviction that a second coming was necessary for the completion of the salvation of the elect was given another turn by John Milton.[178] Milton based his argument for the necessity of a second advent on his doctrine of "Perfect Glorification". In chapter twenty-five of his *Treatise on Christian Doctrine* Milton describes the "in perfect glorification to which believers attain in this life". Subsequently, in chapter thirty-three, he turns to a consideration of the "perfect glorification which is effected in eternity" and writes: "Its fulfillment and consummation will commence from the period of Christ's second coming to judgment, and the resurrection of the dead. Luke xxi. 28."[179] Milton thus sees the glorification of a Christian as the ultimate purpose of the gospel. It is a process which begins in this life, but which is not fully achieved until the sec-

---

[175]   Richard Sibbes, *An Exposition of the Third Chapter of the Epistle of St. Paul to the Philippians* (1639), p. 225.

[176]   Love, *Heavens Glory*, p. 51.

[177]   Owen, *op. cit.,* p. 470.

[178]   The significance of Milton's theology is indicated by A. H. Strong's view that "as Dante was the poet of the Roman Catholic Church, so John Milton was the poet of the Protestant Reformation", and that "Milton, of all the great poets, was the one and only systematic theologian"; A. H. Strong, *The Great Poets and Their Theology* (Philadelphia, 1899), pp. 231, 257. This latter reference is to Milton's *De Doctrina Christiana,* or *A Treatise on Christian Doctrine,* in which he set forth, in the form of a dogmatic theology, the fundamental tenets of Christian faith. This work was not published until 1825, after it had lain unrecognised in the State Paper office for a hundred and fifty years, discarded as "dangerous rubbish", *Encyclopaedia Britannica* (1955), 15, p. 513. The *Treatise on Christian Doctrine* affords a clear picture of Milton's well-defined views on eschatology, which although not published in his lifetime should, perhaps, be assessed in the light of the judgement which sees Milton as "a first-rate student of Scripture and a competent Biblical critic", G. N. Conklin, *Biblical Criticism and Heresy in Milton* (New York, 1949), p. 85; see also W. Haller, *The Rise of Puritanism* (New York, 1938), p. 356.

[179]   John Milton, 'A Treatise on Christian Doctrine', *The Works of John Milton* (New York, 1931), XVI, p. 337.

ond advent. Christopher Love was only a shade removed from this concept of glorification. To him it was essentially the future, eternal state of the believer "that we shall enjoy with Christ, when the world is ended", [180] and which would materialize when Christ "shall appear to judge the world". [181] Thomas Brooks also wrote "when he shall appear the second time ... he shall appear glorious, and so shall all his Saints". [182] To Milton, Love and Brooks alike the glorification of a believer was an essential purpose of the gospel and was contingent upon the second advent.

The soteriological necessity of the second advent was further argued by Christopher Love in his conclusion to *The Penitent Pardoned*, and by Richard Baxter. Salvation meant the restoration of the whole man, body and soul, to fellowship with God, which Love described as the receiving of believers to Himself. [183] A partial receiving of a believer into Christ's presence occurred before the last day, at death, when the soul ascended to heaven. But the "totall and compleat reception" of believers would not take place until the second advent at which time the body also would be received. [184] This, indeed, was "the maine end of Christs coming againe". [185] There is an unmistakable similarity here to what may be regarded as the main proposition of Baxter's *Saints Everlasting Rest*. The transparent hope which illuminates this great work sprang from the biblical assurance that "there remaineth therefore a rest to the people of God". [186] On the strength of this promise Baxter reiterated the basic Christian premise of a life to come, depicting it as the eternal rest of the saints. But when does the saint inherit this promised rest? At death, or at the last day? Baxter replied that the believer's reward began at death, but was not full or perfect until the body and soul were eventually re-united at the coming of Christ and the Resurrection:

> This Rest containeth, the Highest Degree of the Saints personal perfection; both of Soul and Body ... Now thy Salvation is not perfected ... Now thy Sanctification is imperfect and thy pardon, and Justification not so compleat as then it shall be ... The Lord indeed is risen,

---

[180] Love, *op. cit.*, p. 4.
[181] *Ibid.*, p. 6.
[182] Thomas Brooks, *The Glorious day of the Saints Appearance* (1648), p. 6.
[183] Love, *Penitent Pardoned*, pp. 185–188.
[184] *Ibid.*, pp. 187, 188. Love argued strongly against the doctrine of the soul's non-immortality.
[185] *Ibid.*, p. 197.
[186] Heb. iv, 9.

and hath here appeared to thee; and behold he is gone before us into Rest, and ... is now preparing a place for them, and will come again and take them to himself. [187]

Whether, then, it was to make salvation a reality, or to perfect and complete it, or to effect the believer's glorification, or to receive the saint to himself, it was clear that the final chapter in the saga of human redemption could not be written until Christ had descended once more into the realm of creaturely existence.

The other side to this argument which saw a distinct doctrinal relationship between Christ's two advents, the first necessitating the second, placed the emphasis on what was seen as a divine obligation, imposed by the very nature of deity. Not only was it essential that Christ should finish His redemptive work for the sake of man, but it was equally essential as far as He was concerned Himself. He had begun a work, and it was unthinkable that He should leave it unfinished. Having undertaken the restoration of man to the fulness of fellowship with God and having, at His first coming, through the propitiatory act on the cross, achieved atonement between man and God, it was incumbent on Him now to bring everything to a just and satisfactory conclusion. This He would do, and could only do, at His second appearing.

Richard Sibbes had seen the force of this argument, and had declared that Christ must come "to make an end of what he hath begun". [188] Sibbes also suggested that the second advent would perfect, not only the church, and the individual believer, but even Christ Himself. "Christ is in some sort imperfect till the latter day, till his second comming" he continued, adding:

> ... the mysticall body of Christ is his fulnesse; Christ is our fulnesse, and wee are his fulnesse; now Christs fulnesse is made up, when all the members of his mystical body are gathered and united together; the head and the members make but one naturall body ... Christ in this sense is not fully glorious therefore till that time. [189]

It was needful, then, for Christ Himself, as well as for His people that He should come again and "bee glorious in himselfe." [190]

The most forcible defence of this argument, however, came from the logic of what may be termed the continuity of Christ's work for man. This called for a realisation of the truth that

---

[187] Baxter, *op. cit.*, pp. 22, 35, 42.
[188] Sibbes, 'Chvrches Eccho', p. 107, in *Beames of Divine Light*.
[189] Sibbes, *The Brides Longing*, pp. 50, 51.
[190] *Ibid.*, p. 51.

Christ's involvement with humanity was not to be seen merely as one act at one period in history, but rather as a continuous and contemporaneous fact. In this way Christopher Love saw the second advent, not as an isolated event at the end of time, but as part of this unceasing process which moved towards the ultimate complete and harmonious restoration of unity between man and God. This process had been manifest since the cross and included, in succession, Christ's ascension to heaven, His priestly ministry in heaven, His second advent, the resurrection of the dead and "the great Doctrine of that everlasting Communion that the Saints shal have with Christ in Heaven ..." [191]

Both Love and Durant felt that if Christ's ascension to heaven and subsequent priesthood could be shown as necessary to this continuous work, then it would naturally follow that the second advent, with its outcomes of resurrection and restored fellowship, would be seen in the same way. Accordingly Love, before he discusses the second advent, stresses the importance of the mediatorial ministry of Christ who "is entred into the very heavens, that he might appear before God for us ..." [192] The intercession of Christ was to be regarded as even more necessary than His personal presence, for

> Jesus Christ could never have fulfilled the office of the Priest-hood to make intercession for all the Elect, if Christ had not gone bodily into heaven ... Christ must goe to heaven and there hee is a Priest; now if hee were upon the earth hee could not be a Priest for us, therefore we have great advantage by CHRISTS going into heaven. [193]

John Durant drew his analogy from the tabernacle ritual of the Israelites:

> ... it was not enough for the sacrifice to be kild without the campe, but the blood must be carried into the holy of holies. All was not done, till that was done. Indeed, when Christ dyed, the Sacrifice was slaine, the blood was shed, there was no more sacrifice to succeed, all was finished in that respect; but yet all was not done untill the blood of Christ was carried into the holy places, which was not till Christ went to Heaven, to appeare, as our High-priest. [194]

Having thus established the essential nature of the priestly ministry of Christ in heaven, both Love and Durant could now proceed to an examination of the second advent in its logical se-

---

[191]   Love, *op. cit.*, p. 115.
[192]   *Ibid.*, p. 122.
[193]   *Loc. cit.*
[194]   Durant, *op. cit.*, pp. 48, 49.

quence in the total work of Christ for man. If it was remembered that He had voluntarily undertaken the salvation of humanity, with all that that involved, and that the entire work had been initiated by God in response to human need, then the moral obligation to finish this work was manifestly indisputable.

Thus a two-fold constraint was effectually laid upon Christ. Both on account of the very nature of God's redemptive purpose, rooted as it was in the divine character and on account of the beneficiaries of that purpose, the church, His people, "there must be a second comming of Christ". [195] Not until that occurred would Christ's work, or the saint's salvation, be complete. In the final outworking of grace the second advent was indispensable.

One further concern was shared by these exponents of the imminent second advent regarding their belief. They had sought clearly to understand the biblical doctrine and faithfully to impart that understanding to their people. Similarly, they had endeavoured to see it in the overall context of Christian faith and to lead the saints to a recognition of its proven significance. But it would be a great mistake to conclude that these men were satisfied, either for themselves or for their flocks, with a mere intellectual understanding of so great truth. This belief, as with every other teaching of Scripture, must be translated from theory to reality. It must be living not dead, relevant not meaningless. The final test of truth in the milieu of seventeenth-century religion came at the individual level. Not unmindful of this fact Baxter asked, "how should it then be the character of a Christian, to wait for the Son of God from Heaven?" [196] An answer to this question had already been supplied by Sibbes, "it is the disposition of a gracious heart, to desire the glorious comming of Christ Iesus";[197] "wee may know wee have benefit by the first comming of Emanuell, if wee have a serious desire of the second comming"; [198] "we patiently waite for the second comming of Christ. This is the disposition of every sound Christian". [199] This conviction was re-echoed by Love:

---

[195]   Sibbes, 'Chvrches Eccho', p. 107, in *Beames of Divine Light.*
[196]   Baxter, *op. cit.,* p. 50.
[197]   Sibbes, *The Brides Longing,* p. 48.
[198]   Sibbes, *Emanuell,* p. 22 (the second so numbered).
[199]   Sibbes, *Philippians,* p. 226.

> Beloved, you should learn from this Doctrine of Christs appearing in glory, to have your desires quickened, that this day might be. Cry, as the Spouse, Come Lord Jesus, come quickly. Luther in his exposition upon Matth. 6. on that petition of the Lords prayer, Thy Kingdome come, hath this expression, He cannot be a true Christian, nor can he ever truly pray the Lord's prayer, unless he hath these wishes in his soul ... [200]

The preachers and writers who shaped the religious thought of the age were not satisfied until the truths they handled became alive in the hearts and minds of their hearers. [201]

Belief, then, in the imminent, glorious return of Christ as Judge and King was to be seen not only as an integral element in the historic tradition of Christianity, or as an arguable theological necessity, or as a characteristic of the true church, vital as these concepts unquestionably were. It was to be cherished as something more personal and more tangible than any mere academic argument could make it appear. It was, in essence, the sign of a true believer in Jesus Christ:

> And now, Christians, should we not put up that Petition heartily, Let thy Kingdom come? for the Spirit and the Bride say, Come; and let every Christian, that heareth and readeth, say, Come; And our Lord himself saith, Surely I come quickly. Amen, Even so, Come Lord Jesus, Revel. 22. 17, 20. [202]

This stress, perhaps more than anything else, helps to explain the wide measure of appeal which the doctrine of the second advent enjoyed in the English church of the seventeenth century. In the final analysis it was more than a tenet of faith, more than an article of doctrine. It was a guide to personal godliness, an impetus to piety. It was, to use John Trapp's simile, as the badge pinned "to the sleeve of every true believer". [203]

---

[200]   Love, *Heavens Glory,* p. 50.
[201]   Cf. Haller, *Rise of Puritanism,* ch. III, "The Calling of the Saints".
[202]   Baxter, *op. cit.,* p. 50.
[203]   John Trapp, *A Commentary or Exposition upon All the Epistles and the Revelation of John the Divine* (1647), p. 269 (the second so numbered). Trapp, noted for his "profound scholarship", was head-master of Stratford-upon-Avon school, and later rector of Welford-on-Avon.

CHAPTER TWO

APOCALYPTIC INTERPRETATION
AND THE END OF THE AGE

Ben Jonson's allusions to "the two legs, and the fourth Beast", and "the stone" which "falls on the other foure straight",[1] would undoubtedly appear obscure to many in a modern audience. That a contemporary playwright could refer so patently to apocalyptic imagery is some indication of a widespread familiarity with those passages of Scripture which today rarely receive much attention. There was certainly nothing strange about this in the seventeenth century. If the message of the Bible was heard at all, it was heard in its entirety and by a considerable proportion of the rank and file of ordinary people[2] and Ben Jonson, who was astute enough to realise that most of his hearers had been subjected to these biblical influences, had no fear that his references to the book of Daniel would be incomprehensible. Even the most cursory examination of the contemporary literature reveals that it was deemed as proper to think about the future as it was to be concerned with the present, and as necessary to give attention to the messages contained in the books of Daniel and The Revelation as it was to read the Psalms or the Gospels. In an age when the entire Bible was universally held to be an inspired revelation, it was inevitable that this interest in future events should manifest itself in the writings of prominent men, and that it should focus upon those portions of Scripture which were regarded as essentially prophetic.

At the beginning of the century, as previously noted,[3] there had already been a marked interest in prophecy. King James's *Ane frvitfvll Meditatioun*, first published in Scotland in 1588, had been reprinted in England in 1603, in addition to being issued in French in 1589 and in Latin in 1596, 1603 and 1608. Ussher's biographer records that in a sermon soon after his ordination in 1601, he referred to Ezek. iv. 6 "... thou shalt bear the

---

[1] Ben Jonson, *The Alchemist* (1612), Act 4, Sc. 5; cf. Dan. ii, 31—35 and vii, 7.

[2] Cf. Haller's "holy endeavour to popularize the sacred book", Haller, *Rise of Puritanism*, p. 128, and Hugh Barbour's statement that the Authorised Version "carried its own authority into every home", Hugh Barbour, *The Quakers in Puritan England* (New Haven and London, 1964), p. 6.

[3] See *supra*, p. 23.

iniquity of the house of Judah forty days: I have appointed thee each day for a year", and applied it to the future of Ireland. "From this year will I reckon the sin of Ireland, that those whom you now imbrace shall be your ruine, and you shall beare this iniquity".[4] When the Irish rebellion occurred in 1641 some who recalled his earlier words wondered if he, too, had received the gift of prophecy.[5] Later in the century Joseph Hall's *The Revelation Unrevealed* argued against a too literal interpretation of the millennium, warning against extremism such as of those who "have gone so far, as already to date their Letters from New Jerusalem",[6] but defending a more restrained study of the books of Daniel and The Revelation in the belief that "the world is near to its last period ... our Lord Jesus is at hand for his finall judgement."[7]

If a king, an archbishop, and a bishop could regard the future and the study of prophecy as a serious and necessary matter, it cannot be surprising that other men should come to think likewise. Thomas Hall maintained, "it is our duty to take notice of the Prophecies delivered to us in the Word of God. As they are not sealed by him, but left open for our use; so they must not by our negligence be as a sealed Book to us."[8] His brother, Edmund, took the argument further:

> It is a sin to be wilfully negligent in the searching into those Prophesies, which give light to the times we live in: in the Revelations there are shallows as well as depths; there both the Lamb may wade, and the Elephant may swim ... . The not understanding, or neglect of searching to understand the prophetick texts of the Old Testament, was the cause of the greatest sin and scandal in the Church that ever was committed, and that was the murthering of Christ: and I am confident the self-same ignorance and neglect hath been the cause of the greatest sin & scandal that ever was committed in the Gospel-Church, and that is the slaying of the witnesses.[9]

---

[4] Nicholas Bernard, *The Life & Death of ... Dr. James Usher* (1656), p. 39.

[5] *Ibid.*, p. 40. Bernard, chaplain to both James Ussher and Oliver Cromwell, states that one of the works Ussher submitted for his D.D. degree in 1612 was an exposition of Revelation xx and the prophecy of the thousand years. It is one of Ussher's few works which have not survived; *ibid.*, p. 48.

[6] Joseph Hall, *Revelation Unrevealed*, p. 15.

[7] *Ibid.*, pp. 226, 227. The significance of Hall's views can be judged from his successive tenure of the bishoprics of Exeter and Norwich, and from his authorship of *Episcopacie by Divine Right* (1640).

[8] Thomas Hall, *Commentary*, p. 5.

[9] Edmund Hall, *Manus Testium movens* (1651), Epistle to the Reader, sig. A2r. The "slaying of the witnesses" Hall interpreted as the removal of Magistracy and Ministry by "the Beast", Cromwell's government, which had been accomplished "when he set up ... his Sword-power ... in Anno 1647", *ibid.*, p. 44. Hall, an ardent Presbyte-

Hall's argument that a failure to interpret prophecy had contributed to Israel's rejection of the Messiah would not have passed unnoticed in the seventeenth century, with its concern for the ultimate salvation of the Jews. Thomas Parker, commenting on the visions of Daniel, had said:

> ... it was not for Daniel to search and understand the time, two times and a half, at the end whereof the Kingdom must begin to be set up; howbeit these times are to be unsealed to the last age ... And therefore as in the time of Christ, the Saints were to be stirred up to watchfulnesse, because the time of the end was unknown: so now they are to be stirred up to watchfulnesse, because the time of the end is known. [10]

With convictions such as these disseminated among churchmen of all shades of opinion, it is not surprising that many believed that those Scriptural passages which concerned the future should be understood and expounded with the diligence becoming good shepherds of the Lord's people. This basic attitude to prophecy and divine revelation explains, to a large extent, the very considerable amount of literature relating to future events that was published and re-published by theologians and preachers of all groups.

Besides emphasising the need to study prophecy, the foregoing statements identify the specific portions of the Bible where this divine illumination was to be found. While the books of Daniel and The Revelation were not the only prophetic passages in the Bible to receive careful scrutiny, [11] it is very evident that together they occupied a place of prime importance in the thinking of all who were concerned with prophetic enquiry. The tendency

---

rian and Royalist, was imprisoned for the blatant attack on Cromwell which followed, *loc. cit.* He had anticipated "the downfall of Cromwell and his Army" sometime in 1651, to be followed by the millennial kingdom of Christ, pp. 87, 50. Although thus clearly a millenarian himself, his antagonism to others holding similar views, notably Nathaniel Homes, as well as to Cromwell and Independency in general, illustrates that those holding millenarian views were not confined to Independents and the smaller sects, and also the need for avoiding too sweeping a classification of millenarians at this period.

[10] Thomas Parker, *The Visions and Prophecies of Daniel Expounded* (1646), pp. 128, 129. On Parker, first pastor at Newbury, Mass., and formerly minister at Newbury, Berkshire, see *Dictionary of American Biography*, s.v.

[11] Many saw the Song of Solomon as an apocalyptic prophecy, e.g. Thomas Brightman, *A Commentary on the Canticles* (1644), John Cotton, *A Brief Exposition of ... Canticles* (1642), and Nathaniel Homes, *A Commentary ... on Canticles* (1652); see Appendix I. Various parts of the New Testament were also recognised as significant, e.g., II Timothy, iii and iv, see Thomas Hall, *Commentary;* and II Peter iii, see Thomas Adams, *Commentary.*

to dismiss the serious study of these writings as the fad of a minority in the seventeenth century is no longer defensible, and a judicious insight into the backgrounds of these men and their times, with a sensitive appreciation of the attitudes in which they attempted to interpret the visions of the apocalyptic prophets, is increasingly necessary if anything more than a superficial understanding of their conclusions is to be reached.

The intense interest shown in these symbolic predictions in the mid-seventeenth century was neither a new phenomenon, nor a sudden development of thought. In much the same way as belief in the imminent second advent, this absorption with prophecy can be traced back to the earliest years of the Reformation. Luther had written a commentary on Daniel, and Bullinger's *In Apocalypsim Iesu Christi*, published originally in 1557, had appeared in English in 1561 as *A Hvndred Sermons vpō the Apocalips of Jesu Christe*. William Perkins' exposition of the first three chapters of The Revelation defended its canonicity as "of equall authority with the rest of Gods Booke", [12] an opinion which undoubtedly exerted a powerful influence on later attitudes, both by virtue of his own standing as a scholar [13] and also since the work often re-appeared in the early years of the following century. William Lamont has noted the influence of John Foxe on later apocalyptic study, particularly on Thomas Brightman who, to use Lamont's phrase, "acknowledged his debt to 'our John Foxe' for his pioneer labours in the field of apocalyptic interpretation". [14] In the ultimate, however, Foxe's contribution did not prove as influential as that of his disciple, for it is not until the sixteenth century has passed that the interpretation of apocalyptic prophecy reaches its most significant period in English Reformation thought. [15]

---

[12]   Perkins, 'A Godly and learned Exposition', in *Workes,* III, p. 207. Among the reasons he advanced for this view, were the apostolic character of its doctrine, the book's general reception in the church as part of the canon, and the fulfilment of many of its prophecies. The same reasons were given more than sixty years later by William Hicks in his *The Revelation Revealed*, pp. 4, 5.

[13]   Cf. Miller's judgement of Perkins, "a towering figure in Puritan eyes", Perry Miller, *Errand into the Wilderness,* p. 57, with that of Ziff, "England's most influential religious thinker", Larzer Ziff, *The Career of John Cotton* (Princeton, 1962), p. 16.

[14]   William Lamont, *Marginal Prynne 1600—1669* (1963), p. 59. The "great gulf between Foxe and Brightman" would not have been so noticeable to contemporaries as it is to later historians, who can see the significance of Brightman's views in relation to the developing millenarianism, see V. N. Olsen, *John Foxe,* pp. 83, 84.

[15]   John Foxe, *Eicasmi sev Meditationes in Sacram Apocalypsin* (1587); Foxe's work, published posthumously by his son, was never reprinted or translated. The same is true of other sixteenth-century works on prophecy, see e.g., *supra*, p. 23, n. 46, which were seldom, if at all, reprinted. Cf. Olsen, *op. cit.,* p. 87.

With Brightman, we come to one of four men in the early years of the seventeenth century whose efforts to popularise the prophecies of Daniel and The Revelation met with notable success, and whose work was destined to have a more far-reaching influence than any of them could possibly have imagined. Together with John Napier, Arthur Dent, and Joseph Mede, [16] Brightman gave to prophetic study a sense of urgency which it had never previously enjoyed in the history of English religious thought, and a respectability which it never wholly regained after the century had passed. While others were also attracted to the fascinating imagery and chronology described by Daniel and John, [17] even making significant contributions in their own time, it remains true that the foundation upon which all succeeding generations raised their prophetic hopes was laid in the early years by these four learned men.

The arguments substantiating this contention are the repeated reprinting of the works of these earlier writers and continual references to them, particularly to Brightman and Mede, in the writings of later expositors. Napier's book, *A Plaine Discouery of the whole Reuelation of Saint Iohn*, had been issued first in 1593 and was reprinted in 1594, 1611, 1641 and 1645, in addition to being published twice in Dutch and four times in French, all between 1600 and 1607. Arthur Dent's *The Rvine of Rome*, also an exposition of The Revelation, enjoyed an even greater popularity among English readers, going through at least eleven printings between 1603 and 1662. [18] Brightman's interest in prophecy

---

[16] Joseph Mede (or Mead), an Anglican loyal to Episcopal principles, stands out in this early group, if not among all expositors in the seventeenth century, for his colossal contributions to prophetic interpretation and for his learning in many other fields. As "a man of encyclopaedic information" and exceptional memory (*DNB*), he was, among other things, noted as a philologist, mathematician, historian, physicist, botanist, and anatomist. With due regard for this impressive list of accomplishments, J. Bass Mullinger in the *DNB* states that his chief work remained his *Clavis Apocalyptica,* of which Doddridge commented that it contained "a good many thoughts not to be found anywhere else". This work enjoyed the almost universal praise of contemporaries, both at home and abroad, and left an enduring impression on the development of eschatological thought in English Protestantism. On Mede, see *DNB*, s.v. Mead, and John Worthington, 'The Author's Life', in Joseph Mede, *The Works of ... Joseph Mede,* (3rd ed., 1672). The earlier influence of Napier, 1550—1617, Laird of Merchiston, mathematician and inventor of logarithms, can only be marginally less than that of Mede.

[17] E.g. Hugh Broughton, *Daniel his Chaldy Visions and his Ebrew* (1596) and *A Revelation of the Holy Apocalyps* (1610); Patrick Forbes, *An Exqvisite Commentarie vpon the Revelation of Saint Iohn* (1613); Richard Bernard, *A Key of Knowledge for the Opening of the Secret Mysteries of St. Iohns Mysticall Reuelation* (1617).

[18] The eleven known editions may be calculated from dates variously given in *DNB* (s.v. Arthur Dent) and in both the *Short-Title Catalogues* of Pollard and Redgrave, and of Wing.

extended to both the book of Daniel and the Song of Solomon, as well as to the Apocalypse. His *Exposition ... of the Prophecie of Daniel* appeared first in 1614, and then in 1635 and 1644, while the *Revelation of the Revelation*, which was issued first in Latin in 1609 and again three years later, was published in English in 1611, 1615, 1616, and 1644. His *Commentary on the Canticles* was first included in a 1644 edition of his complete works. The erudite Joseph Mede was undoubtedly the most prolific and influential writer of this early group. His most significant works included *Clavis Apocalyptica* (1627), issued three times in Latin and three times in English between 1627 and 1650, and again in 1833;[19] *The Apostasy of the Latter Times* (1641, 1642, 1650, 1652); and *Daniel's Weeks* (1643).[20] Together with the *Diatribae* (1642), the foregoing constituted the bulk of his *Works*, which were published in 1648, 1663-4, 1672 and 1677.[21]

Thus, when in the 1650's Edmund and Thomas Hall stressed the duty of searching into the prophecies, they did not consider this to be an attempt to defend the discredited views of an insignificant, or extreme, minority. They saw themselves rather, if indeed they thought at all of their position as different from that of an overwhelming majority of contemporaries, as custodians of a tradition established early in the century by scholars such as Mede and his predecessors. John Napier had already asked, with a forceful degree of logic, "to what effect were the Prophecies of Daniel, and of the Reuelation giuen to the Church ... if God had appointed the same to be neuer knowne or vnderstood ... ? "[22] Arthur Dent, with characteristic candour, had gone further, laying the responsibility for imparting the meaning of the Revelation squarely on the shoulders of the ministry: "I holde that every Minister of the Gospell standeth bounde as much as in him lyeth, to Preach the doctrine of the Apocalyps to his particular charge and congregation".[23]

---

[19]   The seventeenth-century English translations were by Richard More and the nineteenth-century version, a fresh translation, by R. Bransby Cooper.

[20]   Mede's 'Epistles', in *Works* (1672) contain further material on prophecy and the extensive correspondence with prominent men of his day, including James Ussher, William Twisse, Samuel Hartlib and Sir William Boswell, *inter alios*, again largely on questions of prophetic interpretation and chronology.

[21]   Wing gives a further edition of 1667. Of the 1672 edition, Tillotson wrote, "a monument likely to stand as long as learning and religion shall continue in the world."

[22]   John Napier, *A Plaine Discouery of the whole Reuelation of Saint Iohn* (1593), p. 18.

[23]   Arthur Dent, *The Rvine of Rome*, Epistle to the Reader, sig. aalv.

It is as unnecessary to multiply statements of this nature as it is to stress that the throng of interpreters who travelled this same road in the middle decades of the century set off from the same starting-point. The premise that the books of Daniel and Revelation were an integral part of inspired scripture and therefore to be accepted and understood, was as fundamental to the Baptist pastor, George Hammon, as it was to the Anglican scholar, Joseph Mede. When men of the stature of Thomas Goodwin, Jonn Cotton, Joseph Mede, Nathaniel Homes or James Durham wrote at length on the prophecies, expanding and enlarging and sometimes correcting the views of an earlier generation, and always seeing fulfilment in their own time, it is not to be thought surprising that a host of lesser men arose, of equal sincerity and, in many cases, of equal scholarship to shine forth as lights dispelling the darkness of the "Antichristian world". [24] William Hicks, in *The Revelation Revealed* (1659), a commentary on the Apocalypse expressly intended "for the keeping the Saints feet streight, in not stumbling by a false Interpreting and Applying of this Book of Prophesies", [25] and as a corrective to "wilde Applications" [26] of its symbolism, nevertheless maintained that "the things represented in this Book are no more mysteries and hidden things, but as clear and accomplished Acts unto us." [27] Such convictions, fostered in the years when the schemes of militant Fifth Monarchists were fast coming to a head, indicate again that those other than extremists had a serious concern to understand and proclaim the message of prophecy. *The Revelation Revealed* was one of the last in a long line of works between Napier's *Plaine Discouery* of 1593 and 1660, which endeavoured to set the study of apocalyptic prophecy fairly within the context of orthodox Christian thought.

Beneath all this, however, lay a deep conviction which gave to these arguments an immediate relevance. This conviction had been expressed by Arthur Dent when he had declared, "For in this age wherein we liue, this Prophesie can neuer be inough [sic] opened and beaten upon, that all good Protestants may bee armed with it against future times." [28] Richard Bernard had also argued, "It as much belōgeth vnto vs now liuing, as it did vnto

---

[24]   John Cotton, *The Powring out of the Seven Vials* (1642), p. 10., cf. Ziff, *The Career of John Cotton*, pp. 171–173.

[25]   Hicks, *Revelation Revealed*, To the Judicious Christian Reader, sig. b1v.

[26]   *Loc. cit.*

[27]   *Ibid.*, Pref., sig. C1v.

[28]   Dent, *op. cit.*, sig. aair.

others in time past." [29] It was this belief that The Revelation
together with the book of Daniel spoke with meaning and authority to the present generation, which imparted to their interpretations an impetus and a vitality which was noticeably lacking
in the study of other prophetic books of the Bible. No compar-
able interest, for example, existed in the writings of Jeremiah, or
Ezekiel, or Zechariah, since it was not felt that they spoke with
specific reference to the present. With the apocalyptic prophets,
however, it is significant that men such as Richard Sibbes and
Jeremiah Burroughes, [30] who were not regarded as prophetic interpreters in the strict sense, spoke in terms which indicated an
acceptance of this attitude to Daniel and The Revelation. Pareus
had stated the point as succinctly as anyone when he had written
of The Revelation, "this Booke is not onely worthy to be con-
tinually read in the Church and meditated on: but also to containe very profitable and necessary Doctrines, especially for this
last age". [31]   Even Thomas Hall, who wrote so vituperatively
against the "Epidemical error" [32] of millenarianism, and particularly against the "Learned nonsense" and "gross nonsequitors" [33]
of Nathaniel Homes, saw fit to defend the relevance of The Revelation:

> The Book of the Revelations is an excellent prophecie of the downfal
> of the Churches enemies, and of the great things which in the latter
> dayes God will do for his people, even to the end of the world; and
> therefore the Lord would have us attentively to consider, and humbly
> and accurately to weigh what is written there ... [34]

Millenarian or otherwise, there were few indeed who were disposed to disagree with an opinion as moderate and acceptable as
that.

---

[29]   Richard Bernard, *A Key of Knowledge for the Opening of the Secret Mysteries
of St. Iohns Mysticall Reuelation* (1617), p. 4.
[30]   Cf. the statement that "in all conditions of the Church, the Church might have
recourse unto this Booke (The Revelation) to see what the issue of all would be",
Sibbes, *The Brides Longing,* p. 2, with "the very Book of the Revelations is written on
purpose for to incourage the Saints, to be willing to suffer all the time of Anti-Christ's
reign", Burroughes, *Jerusalem's Glory,* p. 86.
[31]   David Pareus, *A Commentary Upon the Divine Revelation* (Amsterdam, 1644,
tr. Elias Arnold) p. 15. The importance of this work, in addition to showing the
relationship that still existed between English and Continental eschatological thought,
is that it further establishes a continuity of opinion between the earlier and later years
of the century.
[32]   Thomas Hall, *Chiliasto-mastix redivivus,* To the Reader.
[33]   *Ibid.,* p. 13.
[34]   Thomas Hall, *Commentary,* p. 5.

"I beleeue God; I beleeue his Word; I beleeue all that is spoken
in the Scriptures: and I doe endeuour to perswade others
also," [35] Dent had declared, with reference to the Apocalypse.
While most fully concurred with him they were not insensitive to
the fact that difficulties awaited all who attempted to interpret
prophecy. The 'deeps' which Edmund Hall had mentioned were
clearly more abundant than the 'shallows' and, if the analogy
may be extended, they concealed many dangers for the unwary.
The need for care in expounding prophecy was illustrated in
what had been foretold about the first coming of Christ. Mede
had recognised that the Old Testament prophets had often
spoken of the first and second advents of Christ as one event, and
cautioned:

> For the old Prophets (for the most part) speak of the coming of Christ
> indefinitely and in general, without that distinction of First and Sec-
> ond coming, which the Gospel out of Daniel hath more clearly taught
> us. And so consequently they spake of the things to be at Christ's
> coming indefinitely and altogether, which we, who are now more fully
> informed by the revelation of the Gospel of a two-fold coming, must
> apply each of them to its proper time ... [36]

Another Presbyterian, Nathaniel Stephens, referring to the visions of Daniel, also realised that what the prophet had written
did not necessarily convey a sense of the perspective of time:

> These things are shewed to Daniel (who saw afar off) as joyned to-
> gether; and yet in experience they do not meet in the same juncture
> of time. As for example, A man that traveleth in Wales, or some
> such-like hilly Country, while he is yet at a long distance, he may see
> the tops of two great Mountains as though they were near together:
> yet when he cometh to look upon them with a more distinct view, the
> one may be ten or twelve Miles beyond the other in the distance of
> place. [37]

It was this realisation of hermeneutical difficulties and possible
misinterpretations that led some of the leading expositors to appeal for restraint and to sound a note of warning against extreme
conclusions. Mede himself wrote concerning the millennium,
"But here (if any where) the known shipwrecks of those who
have been too venturous should make us most wary and careful,
that we admit nothing into our imaginations which may cross or

---

[35] Dent, *op. cit.*, pp. 242, 243.
[36] Joseph Mede, 'A Paraphrase and Exposition of the Prophecie of St. Peter', in
Works, p. 611.
[37] Nathaniel Stephens, *A Plain and Easy Calculation of the Name, Mark, and
Number of the Name of the Beast* (1656), p. 114.

impeach any Catholick Tenet of the Christian Faith." [38] William Hicks later added a rebuke to those who had neglected, or ignored, the wisdom of such advice:

> ... as if the Actions and Revolutions of every petty City, and Commonweal, yea, the ends, Designs, and Periods of every Person that Divine Providence exalts in Power and Authority somewhat beyond the common boundaries of the ordinary Lords and Rulers of the Nations, were Comprised, Predicted, Foretold, and Prophesied of in this Book of Revelations; and so by this means makes strange and wilde Applications of the Visions and Mysteries of this Book ... [39]

Even Edmund Calamy could agree with his old adversary Joseph Hall on this point. In the preface to Stephens' *Number of the Beast* Calamy wrote of many who "by adventuring into this Sea, have made Shipwrack", and who had "built upon such weak Foundations ... that they have deceived both themselves and others". [40] This was entirely in harmony with Hall's opinion, expressed in *The Revelation Unrevealed*, where it had been stated that the book of Revelation, being a difficult part of the Bible to understand, had given rise to many strange interpretations. [41] These views, it may be noted, prevented neither Calamy from endorsing Stephens' work nor Hall from publishing *The Revelation Unrevealed*. The difficulties of interpretation did not outweigh the necessity of coming to grips with the message of prophecy.

One factor which appears to have carried some weight with many who attempted to interpret apocalyptic prophecy was the principle of progressive revelation. Not only was it believed that there were certain facets of truth which God had revealed, and would reveal, at specific key moments in history and which, indeed, He had even reserved for such times, but also that, through a diligent study of Scripture, His servants on earth could proceed from already established beliefs to the knowledge of truths hidden from earlier generations. There is no evidence to suggest that this concept was regarded as licence to depart from the fundamentals of the faith. "Present Truth" [42] was the apt term used by Nathaniel Homes in an attempt to explain the idea to his readers:

---

[38]   Joseph Mede, 'Remaines on some Passages in the Apocalypse', in *Works*, p. 603.
[39]   Hicks, *op. cit.*, To the Reader, sig. b*lr*.
[40]   Edmund Calamy, To the Reader, in Stephens, *Number of the Beast*.
[41]   Joseph Hall, *op. cit.*, pp. 1–5.
[42]   Cf. II Pet. i, 12, where the Apostle expresses a desire that his hearers may be "established in the present truth".

... there is in most Generations successively, a present Truth ... Now some Believers though they know generally all other saving Truths, yet heed not, observe not the present Truth, to contend for it in their Profession, and accordingly to put it into their Prayers and Supplications ... . What is that you call the present Truth, in any Age, or Generation of men?

We Answer, It is that Truth which the corrupt Stream of the present Times would fain drown, either by Doctrine, or Disputes, or counter Imposition, or Persecution, to the great dishonour of the God of Truth, and Prejudice to Christ ... . Thus in the time of the Arian Persecution soon after Constantines time, the present Truth was to assert the Deity of Christ. In Luthers time, at the beginning of our Henry the 8th., the Satisfaction of Christ apprehended by Faith, as the full ground of Justification was the present Truth to be asserted. And now Christs pure Worship, and Christs Glorious Kingdom (which inseparably concur) are the Truths now to be asserted. [43]

Nathaniel Stephens, again with specific reference to The Revelation, pointed out:

I may say, without prejudice to those that went before, That Bullinger in his time, Brightman in his time, Grasserus in his time, Mede in his time; each of these have made their several and respective Additions to the clearing of the Prophecie. If we endeavour to carry on the Work where they left it, at least with the same Industry and Fidelity, we may (by the blessing of God) be the instruments of bringing those Mysteries to light that were not discerned in former Ages. And for my part, I do firmly believe, That God will not cease to raise up such, in the times following, as shall clear the things that have layen dark in the Prophecies, and do yet remain hid to us. [44]

William Hicks did not think it at all strange if those who lived in his time, "coming nearer unto the accomplishment of the events and the end of all, should see a little further in the Truth of these Mysterious Prophecies, then they that went before". [45] Fortified by the immediate relevance of the doctrine of progressive revelation, earnest and devout scholars could approach Daniel and The Revelation, aware of their difficulties but not daunted by them, and in the assurance that their labours would not be in vain.

---

[43] Nathaniel Homes, *The Resurrection-Revealed Raised Above Doubts & Difficulties, in Ten Exercitations* (1661), pp. 278—279.

[44] Stephens, *op. cit.*, p. 13. On Grasserus, see J. Le Long, *Bibliotheca Sacra*, II, p. 750.

[45] Hicks, *loc. cit.* Woodhouse's comment on the "experimental spirit" of the times is apropos: "The Bible embodies a revelation complete and unalterable: but there is still room for progressive comprehension, progressive interpretation; and it is here that free discussion can (as Milton maintains in the *Areopagitica*) minister to the discovery of the truth and to agreement in the truth," Woodhouse, *Puritanism and Liberty*, Introduction, p. 45.

The circulation of such ideas was reason enough to anticipate prophetic interpretations from a host of scholars and divines well versed in the theological disciplines of the day. It was also an open invitation to others, the "mechanick" preachers with little or no formal qualifications, to unburden a variety of interpretations on a seemingly insatiable public. While this study is concerned primarily with the views of those in the former category, it will not be out of place to remark that, in the context of the prevailing religious mood of the age, which increasingly placed the emphasis upon the individual's response to the Spirit's illumination of the Word, [46] it was predictable that men and women from all walks of life should become enthused with the hopes engendered by reading Daniel and The Revelation, and proclaim views which now appear unbelievably naive. Elizabeth Avery's belief that the feet and toes of Daniel's image represented the State and Church of England, [47] Mary Cary's view that the Little Horn of the fourth beast symbolised Charles I, [48] and John More's opinion that the second beast of Revelation xiii depicted Oliver Cromwell, [49] were all strained interpretations, typical of extreme Fifth Monarchy expositors, which might have been avoided had the advice of Richard Bernard been heeded.

His *Key of Knowledge for the Opening of the Secret Mysteries of St. Iohns Mysticall Reuelation* had been concerned almost exclusively with suggesting principles and rules for a serious study of prophecy, and abounded with detailed and fascinating counsel for all would-be interpreters of the Apocalypse. [50] Bernard had carefully enunciated the idea that prophecy can only be understood completely in the light of history. Prophecies relating to the future are difficult to understand and become clear only when they have been fulfilled. Of the early Fathers he wrote, "so

---

[46] Cf. "The normal, central emphasis throughout Puritanism is upon the closest conjunction of Spirit and Word," Nuttall, *Holy Spirit,* p. 23. See further the entire chapter, 'The Spirit and the Word'.

[47] Elizabeth Avery, *Scripture-Prophecies Opened* (1647), p. 3. On Elizabeth Avery see B. F. Carr, 'The Thought of Robert Parker (1564?—1614) and his Influence on Puritanism Before 1650', Ph.D. Thesis, University of London, 1965, pp. 130, 131.

[48] Mary Cary, *The Little Horn's Doom & Downfall* (1651), p. 6. On Mary Cary (later, Mary Rande) see B. S. Capp, *The Fifth Monarchy Men,* Appendix I, s. v. Cary.

[49] John More, *A Trumpet sounded, or The Great Mystery of the Two Little Horns Unfolded* (1654), p. 8. On John More, London Baptist, see W. T. Whitley, *A Baptist Bibliography* (1916), I, pp. 224, 234.

[50] A careful examination of this work will repay all who desire to obtain an insight into the attitudes which underlay seventeenth-century apocalyptic interpretation. Napier's *Plaine Discouery* also contained thirty-six propositions relative to the correct interpretation of the Apocalypse.

much the more were they the further from beholding the things fulfilled and done; and therefore lesse able to shew the true meaning, then wee which haue the fulfilling hereof." [51] The great advantage which the present generation held over the Fathers, and even over the Apostles themselves, was time. Within the perspective of history prophecy could be understood but, by the same token, all prophecy which still pertained to the future must be approached with caution. As Joseph Hall had suggested, prophecy was not to be held as a licence for making wild guesses about the future. [52] It was this precept which, to their own discredit and largely, though mistakenly, to the calumny of more sober scholarship, the extremists chose to ignore.

There were other basic principles of interpretation which it is also necessary to understand in order to reach a fair and objective assessment of the entire prophetic movement. Some were less vital than others, but all were recognised, and clearly guided the majority of serious expositors in their attempts to explain the prophecies of Daniel and The Revelation. Joseph Mede expressed an important idea which was self-evident to all scholars of the seventeenth century when he said, "I conceive Daniel to be Apocalypsis contracta, and the Apocalyps Daniel explicate, in that ... both treat about the same subject." [53] This premise of the complementary nature of the two books was certainly fundamental to all interpreters of the time. Robert Maton drew attention to another point which others, both before and after him, accepted without question. "It is a currant [sic] axiom in our Schooles ... that wee must not forsake the literall and proper sense of the Scripture, unless an evident necessity doth require it." [54] The significance of this exception, of course, was that the greater part of both Daniel and The Revelation were written in highly figurative language.

The recognition of this particular priciple, with its implied necessity for a correct definition of the symbolic imagery used in the prophetic writings, was unquestionably one of the key factors in arriving at a satisfactory exegesis of the Scriptural passages in question. Bernard had realised this, and had made it one of his

---

[51]   Bernard, *Key of Knowledge*, p. 93.
[52]   Joseph Hall, *op. cit.*, pp. 13, 14.
[53]   Joseph Mede, 'Epistles', in *Works*, p. 787; cf. Napier, *Plaine Discouery*, pp. 16—22.
[54]   Robert Maton, *Israels Redemption* (1642), pp. 47, 48. On Maton, see *Athenae Oxonienses*, II (1692), p. 123.

major principles prerequisite to the interpretation of The Revelation:

> ... the words are figuratiue, the whole prophecie full of Metaphors, and almost altogether Allegoricall; so we must take heede that we looke further then into the letter and naked relation of things, as they are set downe, otherwise the booke should be full of absurdities, impossibilities, falsities, and flat contradictions vnto other truthes of Scripture: all which are farre from the words of Gods holy spirit, which are euer holy and true. For who can beleeue a Lambe to haue seuen eyes, a mountaine burning to be cast into the sea, and this thereby in a third part to become blood, a starre to fall from heauen, Locusts to bee of so monstrous a shape, as is set downe in chap. 9. and horses with Lions heads, fire, smoke, and brimstone comming out of their mouthes, and a hundred such things? Therefore wee must not sticke in the letter, but search out an historicall sense, which is the truth intended, and so take the words typically, and not literally. [55]

The logic of this reasoning was beyond question and made the matter of coming to grips with prophetic symbolism one of cogent necessity. No one could hope to offer an acceptable interpretation who was not conversant with the significance of beasts, or horns, or angels. While it is evident that virtually every expositor in the seventeenth century differed from every other on many points of interpretation and application, it is also clear that a remarkable unanimity of opinion prevailed regarding what were thought of as the basic symbols of prophetic imagery. Without making an artificial distinction between these varied and numerous representations, it may be said that there were five which were fundamental to even the most elementary interpretations.

In the first place, in symbolic prophecy a day represented a year of literal time. The lead given by John Napier here was followed almost exclusively for years to come, and was never wholly to be discarded again:

> So then, a propheticall day is a yeare, the week seuen yeres, the moneth thirtie yeares. (because the Hebrew and Grecian moneth hath thirtie daies) and consequentlie the propheticall yeare is 360. yeares. [56]

---

[55] Bernard, *op. cit.*, pp. 130, 131.

[56] Napier, *op. cit.*, p. 2. Napier himself was a link in a chain which stretched right back to the earliest Reformation interpretations which had been introduced into England by George Joye and further promulgated by Thomas Rogers; see *supra* pp. 18 ff. Texts usually quoted in support of the day-year principle were Numb. xiv, 34 and Ezek. iv, 5, 6, e.g. John Cotton, *An Exposition Upon The thirteenth Chapter of the Revelation* (1655), p. 85.

Napier's explanation of the thirty-day month as a basis for reckoning time is important for an understanding of the calculations of the prophetic time-periods which were so germane to the concept of the end of the age. Secondly, prophetic beasts symbolised earthly kingdoms, [57] or "Civill and Spirituall" rulers. [58] The extension of this symbol to include more than secular powers had implications of far-reaching influence. An important corollary to this second symbol, was that the heads and horns which belonged to the beasts likewise depicted "kinds of Governments", [59] again both secular and ecclesiastical. [60] In the third place, the seas or waters, out of which nearly all prophetic beasts were seen to arise, [61] symbolised peoples or nations. [62] Thus an expositor seeking to understand or explain the sense of a beast emerging from the sea, [63] could know that it represented an earthly power or government which had come into being from among the peoples of the world. A fourth symbol, although appearing in the texts less frequently than most of the others, was a woman, which was held to signify the church. [64] Hence the woman clothed with the sun in Revelation xii symbolised the true church, while the scarlet-clad woman of the seventeenth chapter depicted the apostate church. Fifthly, angels when seen in vision, were to be understood as typifying preachers of truth, "Gods Messengers" on earth, [65] "Preachers of the Gospell in the times of Antichrist". [66] It may be superfluous to add that all these meanings were derived in accordance with the elemental axiom that "the Scriptures are interpreters of the Scriptures, and the meaning of the spirit is to be found out by his owne words," [67] and texts could be produced to prove the correctness of each of

---

[57] E.g. Dent, *op. cit.*, p. 170 and Homes, Ἀποκαλυψις Ἀναστασεως, *The Resurrection Revealed* (1653), p. 70.

[58] Thomas Brightman, *A Revelation of the Reuelation* (Amsterdam, 1615) p. 430.

[59] James Durham, *Commentarie*, p. 547.

[60] E.g. Dent, *op. cit.*, p. 182; Stephens, *op. cit.*, pp. 99, 110—113.

[61] A notable exception was the second beast of Revel. xiii, which came "up out of the earth".

[62] E.g. Bernard, *op. cit.*, p. 158; Cotton, *op. cit.*, p. 8.

[63] Cf. Dan. vii, 1—7.

[64] E.g. Napier, *op. cit.*, p. 33; Joseph Mede, *The Key of the Revelation* (1643), pt. 2, p. 33.

[65] E.g. Cotton, *Seven Vials*, p. 21.

[66] Pareus, *op. cit.*, p. 337.

[67] Bernard, *op. cit.*, p. 141. Bernard also pointed out that symbols do not change their meaning, *ibid.*, p. 150, and that different symbols were sometimes used for one subject, *ibid.*, p. 151. The latter point was particularly helpful when considering the innumerable other symbols employed in prophetic writings.

the foregoing explanations. To borrow the thought which Richard Bernard had incorporated into the title of his book, these were the keys which could unlock the "secret mysteries" of both Daniel and The Revelation.

The master-key to apocalyptic interpretation, however, was not to be found among creatures, natural or supernatural. Important as all the preceding principles unquestionably were to a satisfactory understanding of the prophecies, the crucial issue was the question of time. To have any real significance, all other principles, rules, or suggestions for accurate exegesis were to be understood within the framework of thought which related all the apocalyptic prophecies to a continuous process of history. This period of time had had its beginning in the days when the prophecies were first given, and would end only when everything foretold had been brought to a final consummation. "From the beginning of the Captivity of Israel, until the Mystery of God should be finished", [68] Mede wrote of the scope of Daniel's visions. This explains the emphasis given by Richard Bernard to the necessity of an adequate knowledge of history as a background to The Revelation:

> The matter then of this prophecie is historicall, as it cometh to be fulfilled. It is therefore not a spirituall or allegoricall, but an historicall sense, which in this booke wee must attend vnto, from the beginning of the fourth chapter, to the end of the prophecie. For to Iohn was reuealed what things should come to passe here vpon the earth, before the worlds end, as far as concerned the Church; and the same he here setteth forth to vs, as to him it was reuealed. If we then doe loose the historicall sense, we loose the proper sense of this booke, what other spirituall vse soeuer we make of it. By this then we see what necessity there is to reade histories, into which wee must looke and search diligently ... according to the course of this prophetical narratiō. [69]

Professor Haller has drawn attention to the significance of historical studies in the development of Puritan thought, [70] and the importance of history and a historical discipline in the growth of the interpretative study of prophecy can hardly be over-emphasised. It was a knowledge of two millennia of history [71] that made the men of the seventeenth century certain that what

---

[68]   Joseph Mede, 'The Apostasy of the Latter Times', in *Works*, p. 654.
[69]   Bernard, *op. cit.*, p. 123.
[70]   See Haller, *Rise of Puritanism*, pp. 100, 301–303.
[71]   All seventeenth-century expositors accepted without question the traditional date for the authorship of Daniel.

Daniel and John had written with reference to the future was, in fact, by their day largely concerned with the past. While some events were then in the process of accomplishment, and while others remained as yet wholly unfulfilled, the overwhelming consensus of opinion held that the greater proportion of both Daniel and The Revelation had already reached a complete and verifiable fulfilment. The past was the master-key to both the present and the future.

Stephen Marshall's observation that "the whole Army of Protestant Interpreters" agreed "in the generall scope and meaning" [72] of The Revelation was nowhere more apposite than when applied to this historicist view. Both the early and later writers in the century were virtually unanimous in assenting to this fundamental position, which was as pertinent to Daniel's prophecies as to those of John. Of sixty-eight separate works on these two books examined during the course of this study, no less than sixty-four subscribed by statement, argument, or implication to this historicist viewpoint. Thomas Brightman, in commenting on Rev. i, 1, [73] explained "the matters should be begunne by & by, & should flowe from thence whith a perpetuall course without interruption, although the finall consummation should be afterward for many ages," [74] and David Pareus stated that the time involved was "from the giving of the Revelation, even unto the end of the world." [75] These sentiments were matched by the later testimonies of Thomas Goodwin, who said that The Revelation was a "general Prophecy from John's Time to the Worlds end"; [76] Samuel Hartlib, the economist, who described it as the "State of the Christian Church in the New Testament, and also the things which shall com to pass in the Roman Empire, or in the fourth Monarchie, under which the Church of God doth subsist"; [77] and William Guild, whose expression similarly gave

---

[72]   Stephen Marshall, *The Song of Moses ... and the Song of the Lambe* (1643), p. 3.

[73]   "The Revelation of Jesus Christ, which God gave unto him, to shew unto his servants things which must shortly come to pass ...' Rev. i. 1.

[74]   Brightman, *op. cit.*, pp. 3, 4.

[75]   Pareus, *op. cit.*, The Author's Preface, p. 16.

[76]   Thomas Goodwin, 'An Exposition Upon the Revelation' (1639), in *Works*, II (1683), p. 1. On the date of authorship, see *infra*, p. 87, n. 172.

[77]   Samuel Hartlib (tr.), 'Apocalypsis Reserata: or, The Revelation of St. Iohn Opened', in *Clavis Apocalyptica: or A Prophetic Key* (1651), p. 40. This work was a translation from an anonymous German author who, in the view of John Durie, who wrote the preface to Hartlib's translation, had based his exposition on Mede's *Clavis Apocalyptica, ibid.*, Pref. p. 11. Durie's suggestion is not sound, however, since the

no room for misunderstanding, "this Book of the Revelation is for the most part, being a Prophecy, as c. 1. 1. of things to come, and which were to fall out and befal the Church of Christ from Johns dayes to Christs second coming." [78] That the historicist construction should be applied to Daniel in conjunction with The Revelation was argued by both Joseph Mede and William Hicks:

> ... what was revealed to Daniel concerning the Fourth Kingdom but summatim ... was shewed to S. John particulatim, with the distinction and order of the several Fates and Circumstances which were to betide and accompany the same ... therefore Daniel's Prophecie is not terminated with the First, but reacheth to the Second coming of Christ ... [79]

> ... the Revelation is no longer a mystery, but a Book of History of memorable Acts and passages. Wherein is foretold the several changes that shall befall to the secular State or Roman Empire, and to the Church of Christ under the Dominion of that Empire, until it shall, as that stone prophesied of in Dan. 2. Smite the Image on his feet and become it self a great Mountaine and set up upon the top of all Mountains. [80]

It was, then, within the context of the historicist rationale, which viewed the prophecies of Daniel and The Revelation as a panorama of successively unfolding events spanning twenty centuries or more of the church's history, that all other principles of interpretation were to be applied and related. Any other approach to the interpretation of apocalyptic prophecy was effectively excluded.

The preterist interpretation, which propounded that the major prophecies had reached fulfilment in the first century or two of the Christian era, and the futurist view, which sought to postpone their accomplishment until the very last end of Christian history, were alternative constructions on the scope of the apo-

---

work he introduced stated on its title-page that "the Propheticall Numbers com to an end with the year of our Lord 1655", while Mede was notably more cautious in date-fixing, specifying only that the end would come "between the years 1625 and 1715", 'Remaines on some Passages in the Apocalypse', in *Works,* p. 600. Nathaniel Homes refers to an "anonymous German Doctor" who calculated that the millennium would commence in 1655, Homes, *Resurrection,* pp. 560—562. Professor Trevor-Roper attributes the work to Abraham von Frankenburg, Trevor-Roper, *Religion, the Reformation and Social Change,* p. 292. Hartlib's interest in prophecy may be seen as further evidence of the seriousness with which the age regarded eschatological thought.

[78] William Guild, *The Sealed Book Opened: or, A cleer Explication of the Prophecies of the Revelation* (1656), Pref. Guild, Scottish divine and chaplain to Charles I, favoured Episcopacy and took the covenant only with reservations, *DNB,* s.v.

[79] Mede, 'Epistles', in *Works,* p. 787.

[80] Hicks, *op. cit.,* Pref., sig. Clv.

calyptic prophecies which had no significant appeal whatever to the Protestant commentators of the seventeenth century. If either of these contrary propositions intruded at all into their thinking and writing, it was only in order that they could be summarily refuted or that the discreditable source of their origin could be brought to the attention of all who sought after truth.

The preterist hermeneutic, according to James Durham, had arisen through the influence of a Spanish Jesuit, Luis de Alcasar, [81] who had put forward the argument that the book of Revelation had reference only to the pre-Constantine age and related solely to the experiences of the church under the Roman Empire. [82] Henry Alford's statement that "the Praeterist view found no favour, and was hardly so much as thought of in the times of primitive Christianity", [83] is equally true of seventeenth-century Christianity. In English thought, the schoolmaster Thomas Hayne contended that Daniel's prophecies had been entirely fulfilled in the history of Israel up to the time of Christ, [84] as also did Joseph Hall, who noticeably declined to make any similar pronouncement concerning The Revelation. Henry Hammond, who in 1647 had become chaplain to Charles I, appears to have been the first English writer seriously to have adopted Alcasar's interpretation. [85] Although the work in which his views appeared went through several editions after its first appearance in 1653, there is no evidence of any wider involvement with preterism in pre-Restoration thought. [86] The failure of preterist reasoning to

---

[81] Luis de Alcasar, *Reu. Patris Ludouici ab Alcassar ... Vestigatio Arcani Sensus in Apocalypsi* (1614). Alcasar's preterism is discussed by L. E. Froom, *Prophetic Faith,* II, pp. 506–8; cf. Joseph Tanner, *Daniel and the Revelation* (1898), pp. 16, 17.

[82] James Durham, *op. cit.,* p. 667.

[83] Henry Alford, *The New Testament for English Readers* (1866), II, pt. II, pp. 348, 349.

[84] Thomas Hayne, *Christs Kingdome on Earth* (1645), pp. 5–12; and Joseph Hall, *op. cit.,* pp. 20–21. Hayne also corresponded with Joseph Mede on the interpretation of Daniel; see Mede, 'Epistles', in *Works,* pp. 735–757.

[85] Henry Hammond, *A Paraphrase, and Annotations Upon all the Books of the New Testament* (1653). On the Continent, the Dutchman Hugo Grotius, or de Groot, defended the preterist view. His *Annotata in Epistolas Canonicas & in Apocalypsim* (1650) placed the fulfilment of the Apocalypse in the past. Froom describes him as "the first Protestant recruit to Preterism", Froom, *op. cit.,* p. 506. There was little respect for Grotius's views in England for some years. John Worthington, comparing his work to that of Joseph Mede, tartly commented "The Novel way of interpreting wherein the learned Hugo Grotius is the Choragus and leads the dance, (a Dance which has made those of the Court of Rome no little sport). For me here to make a judgement upon these two so different Methods of Interpretation, it is needless", John Worthington, in Mede, *Works,* Pref.

[86] Except, perhaps, in Hugh Broughton, *Daniel his Chaldie Visions and his Ebrew* (1596); *Daniel, with a brief explication* (1607).

make any significant impact may be explained by the familiarity with ecclesiastical history which characterised the thinking of most scholars and divines, and which naturally precluded any attempt to place all those prophecies of a future bright with hope in a past which frequently had been so hopelessly dark.

Futurism, although it received more comment, made even less impression on English Protestant thought than did preterism. [87] An early attack on the futurist system came from Thomas Brightman, who defined its basic argument and at the same time identified its source of origin. Brightman contended that futurism projected all the prophecies of The Revelation into the last three and a half literal years of human history, thereby denying the historicist contention that the book of Revelation had been in the course of progressive fulfilment since the close of the first century A.D. If futurism was true, then Brightman wanted to know what comfort the church had derived, or could derive, from the special blessing promised at the time the book had been written, and which was intended for all who would read and accept its prophetic message, which even then was on the verge of fulfilment. [88] "Were men that lived by the space of theis 1500 yeares which are nowe past ... altogether devoyd of this felicity?" [89] he enquired. Brightman named another Jesuit priest, Ribera, as the originator of futurism, [90] an opinion which was quickly endorsed by Bernard [91] and accepted without further question by all succeeding expositors. [92] Half a century later James Durham could still be found maintaining an aggressive attack on the futurist system, describing it as

---

[87]   The writings of the eccentric Edmund Hall show some evidence of a leaning to futurism, in that he places more of the prophecies of The Revelation in the future than most of his contemporaries. That he remained basically within the historicist school, however, is clear from his analysis of the book, which he divided into two parts. The history of the church under her enemies had been foretold in the first thirteen chapters, while the remainder of the book proclaimed a future reign of "the Beast", and the rise of the Church to a glorious state, Edmund Hall, *op. cit.*, pp. 44, 45.

[88]   "Blessed is he that readeth, and they that hear the words of this prophecy, and keep those things which are written therein: for the time is at hand", Rev. i, 3. On Brightman's interpretation of v. 1, see *supra* p. 71.

[89]   Brightman, *op. cit.*, p. 5.

[90]   Brightman's *Revelation* had been written initially in Latin, and bore the title *Apocalypsis Apocalypseos ... et Refutatio Rob. Bellarmini de Antichristo* (Francofurti, 1609). Dr. Froom has shown that Cardinal Bellarmine "popularised" the teachings of Ribera, see Froom, *op. cit.*, p. 493. Bellarmine's *Disputationes ... de controversiis Christianae Fidei, adversus huivs temporis haereticos* (1588) was the work referred to in Brightman's title.

[91]   Bernard, *op. cit.*, p. 104.

[92]   On Ribera and futurism, see Froom, *op. cit.*, pp. 489–493.

... that conceit or dream of the Papists expounding all so literally of an Antichrist who shall come of the Tribe of Dan, and that shall reign just three years and a half, sitting in Jerusalem ... This dream [was] invented by them to keep their Pope from being apprehended as the true Antichrist ... [93]

Durham drew attention here to an aspect of the futurist construction which figured prominently in the thinking of all Protestant theologians, Episcopalian, Presbyterian, and Independent alike. Futurism, he indicated, was an invention designed to avoid the traditional Protestant historicist application of certain prophetic symbols to the Papacy and to avert the extremely unwelcome attribution of the title "Antichrist" to the papal hierarchy.

In harmony with the strong anti-Romanist convictions of the day, many Protestant expositors saw the wisdom of emphasising this ill-concealed attempt to weaken the strength of the historicist arguments. Both David Pareus and Robert Maton [94] anticipated the view expressed by Jeremiah Burroughes, that the true meaning of The Revelation had been deliberately concealed and distorted by papal scholars:

... hence it hath been, that in the time that Anti-Christ hath Reign'd, there hath been so little known of the Book of the Revelations, because it hath been applyed only in a Metaphorical way, and all the glory hath been Interpreted of the glory of Heaven, because I say there hath been a darkness on the face of the Earth in the time of Anti-christs prevailing. And it hath been the care of Anti-christ to darken this ... [95]

James Durham, with reference to the seventeenth chapter of The Revelation and the scarlet-clad woman riding on the seven-headed, ten-horned beast, stated that even many post-Reformation papal scholars conceded that the symbolism depicted Rome. But Rome at which period in time? Some, he said, naming Ribera, Blasius Viegas and Cornelius à Lapide, construed it of the city of Rome defecting to the Anti-christ during the final three and a half years of history. Others, specifically Alcasar and Bellarmine, [96] referred it to Rome in the era before Constantine. These alternative interpretations originated in papal thought "so

---

[93]   James Durham, *op. cit.*, p. 496.
[94]   See Pareus, *op. cit.*, p. 286, and Maton, *op. cit.*, pp. 20—22.
[95]   Burroughes, *Jerusalem's Glory*, p. 87.
[96]   In addition to championing futurism, Bellarmine also endeavoured to promote preterism, apparently unconcerned that the two views were mutually exclusive; cf. Froom, *op. cit.*, p. 497.

as to save their Pope and the present Rome" from the ascription of Antichrist. [97] The fact that Roman Catholic scholars had suggested alternative explanations was enough in itself to render those explanations anathema to every good Protestant. "Our Adversaries", [98] Mede wrote of the authors of futurism. Beyond this, however, the appeal of the historicist position lay in the intrinsic strength of its arguments. Carefully reasoned and subjected to the irrefutable witness of history they made historicism the only valid basis for interpretation.

In the previous chapter it was submitted that an extensive belief in the imminent second coming of Christ existed quite apart from the influence of apocalyptic prophecy. Without detracting from the validity of this argument, it is apparent that such beliefs were considerably strengthened as the interest in prophecy developed, and particularly as historicist interpretation increasingly anticipated momentous and impending changes in the present order. It is, therefore, desirable to appreciate how the historicism of the seventeenth century arrived at its major conclusion that the end of the age was at hand.

Hugh Broughton, commenting on The Revelation in 1610, had written, "I must advise the reader to learne Daniel before he learne this book". [99] This recommendation was further stressed by Mede in reply to a letter from Thomas Hayne in 1629. Referring to the first two prophetic visions of Daniel, that of the great metal image of ch. ii and that of the four beasts of ch. vii, he argued that together they constituted "The A.B.C. of Prophecie". [100] Mede later amplified this somewhat concise definition by implying that all other prophecy was related to the content of these two visions:

> For the true Account therefore of Times in Scripture, we must have recourse to that SACRED KALENDAR and GREAT ALMANACK of PROPHECY, The Four Kingdoms, of Daniel, which are A Prophetical Chronology of Times measured by the succession of Four principal Kingdoms, from the beginning of the Captivity of Israel, until the Mystery of God should be finished. [101]

---

[97]   James Durham, *op. cit.*, p. 667.
[98]   Mede, 'The Apostasy', *Works*, p. 656.
[99]   Hugh Broughton, *A Revelation of the Holy Apocalyps* (1610), p. 26.
[100]   Mede, 'Epistles', in *Works*, p. 743. Olsen comments, "From the time of the Ante-Nicene Fathers these two chapters describe prophetically and historically the linear concept of time and the one-directed movement of history towards the kingdom of God", Olsen, *John Foxe*, p. 25.
[101]   Mede, 'The Apostasy', in *Works*, p. 654.

Whatever meaning was to be placed on the ensuing visions of Daniel or John, it could be assumed that agreement would prevail with regard to the four kingdoms. The evidence suggests that this attitude was fully justified.

The four kingdoms were first mentioned in Nebuchadnezzar's celebrated dream which had subsequently been interpreted by Daniel and defined as specifically relating to "the latter days". [102] The dream, it will be recalled, had revealed an image in four main sections composed of differing metals. The head of the image was made of gold, the upper abdomen and arms of silver, the lower abdomen of brass, and the legs of iron. The feet of the image consisted in part of iron and in part of clay. The image had been shattered and the fragments thereof dispersed by the wind, when a stone of supernatural origin had struck it upon the feet. Commencing with the Babylonian empire of Nebuchad-nezzar, represented by the golden head, [103] Daniel explained that three further empires would arise successively upon the earth, the kingdoms of silver, brass and iron. The fourth kingdom would ultimately be divided into ten nations and the resultant segments would never unite again until "the god of heaven set up a king-dom". [104] This divine kingdom had been symbolised in the dream by the stone which had struck the image upon the feet, depicting that God would intervene in human affairs during the time occupied by the divided nations of the iron kingdom. "These Times once finished, all the Kingdoms of this World should become the Kingdoms of our Lord and his CHRIST". [105] The assurance that "the interpretation thereof" was "sure" [106] did not pass unnoticed. The four kingdoms again figured promi-nently in Daniel's second vision. In this instance the types were beasts; a lion, a bear, a leopard, and a fourth beast, "dreadful, and terrible, and strong exceedingly". [107] In accordance with the accepted rule of interpretation and also in accordance with the text itself, [108] the beasts were taken as symbols of the same four kingdoms which had been represented by the four main sections of the image. Even as the legs of the image had ten toes so the

---

[102]   Dan. ii. 28.
[103]   "thou art this head of gold", Dan. ii, 38.
[104]   Dan. ii, 44.
[105]   Mede, *loc. cit.*
[106]   Dan. ii, 45.
[107]   Dan. vii, 7.
[108]   Dan. vii, 17, 23.

fourth beast had ten horns, again depicting the divisions of the
fourth empire.

The counting of time on this "SACRED CALENDAR" presented little difficulty. If the Word of God explicitly stated that
Babylonia was the first kingdom of the four, history provided the
identity of the remaining three. They were the empires of Medo-
Persia, Greece, and Rome, and succeeded Babylon, and each
other, in that order. [109] Many commentators believed that the
iron legs of the image symbolised the Western and Eastern divisions of the Roman Empire, [110] but this was not as important as
the fact that, in both visions, the fourth kingdom was eventually
divided into ten parts. "For about Four hundred yeers, the
Romane Emperors continued in their Majestie, even until the end
of Constantine the Great; and then began effectually to be broken down, and to be dissolved into ten kingdoms," [111] wrote
Thomas Parker, adding that the fall of Rome was fully accomplished by 456 A.D. Mede dated the end of the Roman empire
from the death of Valentinian, in 455 A.D. [112] In practice, few
were concerned about exact dates at this juncture, recognising
that the important fact was that the prophecy now focused
upon those further nations which had arisen from the barbarian
invasions of Rome. [113] Strictly speaking, the Roman empire had
not come to an end; it had been divided, and the divisions thereof were to continue in separate existence until the advent of the
kingdom of the stone.

Daniel's second vision had drawn attention to the emergence
of another power, placed in time between the settlement of the
divisions of Rome and the inauguration of the kingdom of God.
Probably no figure in all the Bible has given rise to so many
interpretations, and misinterpretations, as the Little Horn which
Daniel now described as arising after the previous ten kingdoms,

---

[109]   See Mede, *loc. cit.;* Homes, *Resurrection,* p. 79; Ephraim Huit, *The Whole
Prophecie of Daniel Explained* (1644), pp. 46—51; Thomas Parker, *Daniel,* pp. 1—5,
inter alia. On Huit, see *Alumni Cantabrigienses,* s.v. Huitt.

[110]   E.g. Huit, *op. cit.,* p. 56, and Homes, *op. cit.,* p. 241.

[111]   Thomas Parker, *op. cit.,* p. 21.

[112]   Mede, *op. cit.,* p. 660.

[113]   Two lists will illustrate the diversity of opinion concerning the identity of
these ten kingdoms. Napier suggested Spain, France, Lombardy, England, Scotland,
Denmark, Sweden, Hungary, Italy and Exarchate of Ravenna, Napier, *op. cit.,* p. 211.
Thomas Parker accepted the Britons, Saxons, Franks, Burgundians, Visigoths, Sueves
and Alans, Vandals, Alemans, Ostrogoths, and Greeks, Parker, *op. cit.,* p. 6. Aware,
perhaps, of even greater divergences over what was not, in any case, a major issue,
Parker added that the identity of the ten divisions had not remained constant through
history, *op. cit.,* p. 21.

arrogant in its appearance and presumptuous in its claims, and resolutely bent on a course of action totally opposed to the purposes of God. [114] While a more detailed examination of the Little Horn in the prophetic exegesis of the time must be reserved until a later stage in this study, it is necessary here to remark that by far the majority of expositors saw in this cryptic symbol a definite allusion to the long-awaited, and dreaded, Antichrist. [115] It was, in brief, either the Pope, [116] or the Turk, [117] or a combination of the two, [118] both of which had emerged as a threat to the true church at the time required for a satisfactory interpretation of the prophecy. [119] Again, the Little Horn was fundamentally an extension of the fourth empire which "was to keep the dominion and Lordship of the world" [120] until the final kingdom of prophecy, a development within the era of Rome, and not a separate phenomenon beyond it. [121] In the eyes of men in the seventeenth century, both these major prophecies of Daniel had been in the course of fulfilment for some two thousand years. During that time, in the out-working of the historical process, all the salient characteristics they bore had met unequivocal identification with the single exception of the last, climactic event. If it is remembered that the remaining prophecies of

---

[114]   Cf. Dan. vii, 20, 24, 25.

[115]   E.g. Nathaniel Homes, 'The Christian Hammerers against the Antichristian Horns' (1652), in *Works,* p. 596, and Thomas Parker, *op. cit.,* p. 15.

[116]   E.g. Napier, *op. cit.,* pp. 211, 212; Goodwin, *op. cit.,* p. 63; Maton, *op. cit.,* pp. 21, 22.

[117]   E.g. Huit, *op. cit.,* p. 187; Henry Finch, *The Worlds Great Restavration* (1621), p. 55.

[118]   Pareus, *op. cit.,* p. 166; Homes, *op. cit.,* p. 255. Luther had previously held this view, see *infra,* p. 143.

[119]   On the rise of the Turco-Papal Antichrist, see *infra,* pp. 134 ff, 141 ff.

[120]   Huit, *op. cit.,* p. 181; cf. Joseph Mede, 'Diatribae', in *Works,* p. 198, and Edmund Hall, *Manus Testium movens,* p. 13.

[121]   There were a few isolated exceptions to the foregoing interpretations, exclusively among the preterist expositors of Daniel, who differed on the identification of the fourth beast, holding that it represented a later extension of the third, or Grecian, kingdom. Broughton said, "the two kingdoms which remained of Alexanders Princes: which make the fourth Beast with ten hornes", and identified them as the joint kingdoms of Ptolemy Lagides and Seleucus Nicator, Hugh Broughton, 'Daniel his Chaldy Visions, and his Ebrew', in *The Works of the Great Albionean Divine ... Mr Hugh Broughton* (1662), p. 212. Thomas Hayne and Joseph Hall both followed this view, see Hayne, *op. cit.,* p. 5., and Joseph Hall, *op. cit.,* p. 31. The logical conclusion of this argument was that the Little Horn symbolised Antiochus Epiphanes, an interpretation which Broughton, Hayne and Hall all accepted. Joseph Mede, however, pointed out that these views had first been propounded by Porphyry, the third-century neoplatonic philosopher, in an attempt to disprove the authenticity of the book of Daniel, Mede, 'Epistles', in *Works,* p. 743. On Porphyry, see *Encyclopaedia Britannica,* 1955, 18, p. 242A.

Daniel were regarded as supplying details of further events within the compass of this same time-scale, it is not hard to perceive why Daniel proved that the end of the age was at hand.

If, as Mede had suggested, Daniel was a necessary introduction to The Revelation, it was of greater consequence that The Revelation be considered an indispensable conclusion to Daniel. While the latter contained six chapters of apocalyptic prophecy the book of Revelation had eighteen, and naturally enough attracted considerably more attention than the writings of the earlier and smaller book. The resulting stream of commentaries, treatises, sermons and tracts on The Revelation, in part or in whole, grew throughout the first half of the century until by the years between 1640 and 1660 it had reached almost flood proportions. This stream, however, did not change in character as it increased in volume. It was still constituted of the same elements and continued to flow in the same direction as in its earlier reaches. Views on The Revelation which became so popular between the time of the Long Parliament and the Restoration were largely the logical development of the historicist interpretations which had been published during the first two decades of the century. Even the most extreme views of the militant Fifth Monarchy Men were ultimately derived from the serious and scholarly studies of Napier, Brightman, Mede and others of an earlier generation. It will be remembered, too, that the writings of these earlier expositors were themselves republished when the restrictions imposed under Archbishop Laud were lifted, inevitably exerting an influence upon later interpreters, as well as upon the public who continued to devour anything on the subject that was offered to them.

John Napier's *Plaine Discouery* was the first work of any significant appeal in the seventeenth century to set forth a well-reasoned approach to The Revelation. Napier held that there were two basic prophecies in the book, the first from chapter iv to chapter xi, and the second from chapter xii to chapter xxii. [122] These prophecies were repetitive, both covering the entire Christian era from the time of Christ to the last day. The first of these comprehensive prophecies contained the important visions of the seven seals of chapters vi and vii and the seven Trumpets of chapters vii-xi which, to Napier, as to all who were to follow him, were indispensable to a correct calculation of the

---

[122]   Napier, *op. cit.*, pp. 155, 156.

age of the world and the expected consummation. Napier taught that the Seals each covered seven literal years of time, and that the seventh began to be fulfilled in 71 A.D. [123] At that time the fulfilment of the seven Trumpets had commenced, which Napier believed were parallel to the seven Vials of the second prophecy. [124] The vision of the Trumpets extended right down to the last day, for with the final sounding of the seventh Trumpet the kingdom of God would come. [125] Each of the Trumpets, or vials, was to continue for a period of 245 years, which indicated that the seventh or last age of the world had commenced in 1541. [126] By this reckoning the seventh age would expire 245 years later, in 1786, but Napier added:

> Not that I meane, that that age, or yet the world shall continew so long, because it is said, that for the Elects sake, the time shall be shortned: but I meane, that if the world were to indure, that seuenth age should continew vntill the yeare of Christ 1786. [127]

The progression of this last, shortened age had been further outlined by other prophecies in both Daniel and The Revelation, enabling Napier to conclude that it was in the divine purpose for men to be aware of the approaching end. [128]

Soon after Napier's *Plaine Discouery* had appeared, Arthur Dent published *The Rvine of Rome* which provided a slightly modified interpretation, although the conclusion remained the same. Dent maintained that there were three basic prophecies in The Revelation. [129] In addition to the two suggested by Napier, concerning the importance, scope and relationship of which Dent fully concurred, [130] he also held that the first three chapters were partially prophetic in that they described the condition of the entire Christian church of the time, as well as the actual state of the seven churches named. [131] With regard to the seven Seals and seven Trumpets, Dent put forward a view which was adopted by several later scholars, namely, that these two visions were consecutive in their fulfilment. The first six Seals had fore-

---

[123]   *Ibid.*, p. 110.
[124]   *Ibid.*, pp. 2—9; cf. Rev. xv, xvi.
[125]   Cf. Rev. x, 7 and xi, 15.
[126]   Napier, *op. cit.*, p. 178.
[127]   *Ibid.*, p. 12.
[128]   *Ibid.*, p. 16.
[129]   Dent, *op. cit.*, p. 15.
[130]   *Ibid.*, p. 150.
[131]   *Ibid.*, p. 26.

told events which were to transpire from the time of the Apostolic church until "about some 300 yeares after Christ, and somewhat more". [132]   The seventh Seal included the entire vision of the Trumpets, which "doo all belong to the opening of the seuenth seale, and are as it were the seuen parts thereof". [133]   The first four Trumpets described the gradual growth of heresy within the church making way for the coming of Antichrist, [134] and had been accomplished by about 600 A.D. [135]   The fifth and sixth Trumpets respectively foretold the rise and growth of the Papacy and the Turks, and were parallel in time and fulfilment, having commenced at the completion of the fourth Trumpet, in 600 A.D. [136]   Like Napier, Dent believed that the seven Vials complemented the Trumpets, and that the sixth Vial had particular reference to the fall of Rome, which "is not yet come, but it is greatly decayed from that it was fourescore yeares ago". [137]   All this led him to conclude:

> .. wee liue under the opening of the seuenth seale, and the blowing of the sixt trumpet, and the powring forth of the sixt viall ... . Therefore when we see all things fulfilled which do belong vnto the sixt trumpet, it remaineth that wee should euery houre expect, and looke for the blowing of the seuenth trumpet, and the end of the world. [138]

Dent had reached the same conclusion as Napier, if by a slightly different route.

Six years after *The Rvine of Rome* had first been published, Thomas Brightman's *Apocalypsis Apocalypseos* appeared to give a further turn to the development of apocalyptic thought. Brightman agreed with Dent in large measure concerning the Seals and the Trumpets, but differed in his interpretation of the Vials. The first six Seals extended to the time of Constantine [139] and the seventh included the complete range of the Trumpets, the first six of which reached from Constantine to 1558. [140]   The seventh Trumpet, although it contained a review of "things past", was primarily concerned with "modern" times and things to come

---

[132]   *Ibid.,* p. 68; see pp. 58—76.
[133]   *Ibid.,* pp. 87, 90.
[134]   *Ibid.,* p. 97.
[135]   *Ibid.,* p. 103.
[136]   *Ibid.,* pp. 100—120.
[137]   *Ibid.,* p. 216.
[138]   *Ibid.,* pp. 124, 144 (the second so numbered).
[139]   Brightman, *op. cit.,* p. 236.
[140]   *Ibid.,* pp. 203, 388.

and included the remainder of the book, again emphasising the seven Vials. [141]   Thus, in Brightman's view, the vision of the Vials was not complementary to that of the Trumpets, but rather consecutive to it and was the last of "three notable termes of time, which containe in them the principall changes that are to fall out in the world, euen untill the comming of Christ ..." [142]   Lest all this should appear confusing, Brightman explained:

> It is manifest therefore that this whole space of time from Iohn to the comming of the Lord is diuided into three Periods of time, & that each of those Periods is againe diuided into seauen members so as the first member of that Period which followeth, beginneth vnder the last member of the former, that is so, that as the seauen Trumpets haue their originall from out of the last Seale, so the Seauen Violes haue their ofspring out of the last Trumpet. [143]

The Vials, of course, were symbolic and described in vivid imagery the seven steps which would lead to the final judgement of the Papacy. The pouring out of the Vials had commenced "about the yeare 1560", [144]   and when Brightman wrote out his views, three of the judgements had already fallen, the fourth was then current, and the remaining three were shortly to come. The three which were past, Brightman saw as the furtherance of the Protestant cause by Elizabeth I and other Protestant Princes, from about 1560; the conclusive demonstration of the falsity of Roman doctrine, manifested in the rebuttal of the claims of the Council of Trent by Martin Chemnitius, in 1564; and the anti-Papal legislation of 1581. [145]

Just how near the end of the age really was in Brightman's estimation may be seen from his interpretation of the vision of the seven Churches which, in effect, contained in concise form the entire message of The Revelation, and which was amplified by all the later visions. [146]   The first vision was to be understood as applying to the church in general, from its inception to its triumphant conclusion, setting forth under seven ages the decline of the church from its first purity of doctrine and its subsequent renewal in readiness for the ultimate reward. The last age, sym-

---

[141]   *Ibid.*, p. 509 ff.
[142]   *Ibid.*, p. 202.
[143]   *Ibid.*, p. 510.
[144]   *Ibid.*, p. 511.
[145]   *Ibid.*, pp. 528—536.
[146]   *Ibid.*, pp. 6, 168.

bolised by the seventh Church, had begun in 1547, and Laodicea represented the Church of England. [147]

As noted earlier, the work of David Pareus did not appear in English until 1644. It is seen in true perspective, however, if considered in its setting in the development of prophetic interpretation, between Brightman's *Apocalypsis Apocalypseos* and Joseph Mede's *Clavis Apocalyptica*. Although firmly within the scheme of historicist thought, Pareus's *Commentary Upon the Divine Revelation* showed a number of significant departures from the concepts which had guided Napier, Dent and Brightman. Pareus proposed that there were seven distinct visions in The Revelation, six of which were prophetic in nature [148] and concerned "the future condition of the whole Church, but especially the Churches of Europe". [149] The six prophetic visions were, the Seven Seals (chapters iv-vii), the Seven Trumpets (chapters vii-xi), the Woman and the Dragon (chapters xii-xiv), the Seven Vials (chapters xv, xvi), the Judgement of the Great Whore (chapters xvii-xix), and the Thousand Years and the Triumph of the Church (chapters xx-xxii). [150] These visions were all repetitive in scope, depicting different events within the entire Christian era. Pareus thus avoided Brightman's view that the basic visions of the Revelation were consecutive. A further material proposition was to the effect that the six visions variously spanned four successive periods of time, into which the entire range of The Revelation might be divided: [151]

> For the christian Church hath four periods. One under the Rome tyrants: The second from Constantine under Christian Emperours untill the times of Phocas: the third under Antichrist swaying in his full vigour, from Pope Boniface III. unto Leo X. in whose time Antichristian power began to decline: The fourth under Antichrists declining from Luthers time to the end. Unto this last period, belong the last plagues. [152]

Four of the six visions were "universal", since they covered all four epochs. They were the visions of the Seals, the Trumpets, the Woman and the Dragon, and the Thousand Years and Triumph of the Church. The other two visions, of the Vials, and the Judgement of the Great Whore, were "particular" in that they

---

[147]   *Ibid.*, p. 126.
[148]   Pareus, *op. cit.*, Pref., p. 19.
[149]   Pareus, *Commentary*, p. 84.
[150]   *Ibid.*, p. 19.
[151]   *Ibid.*, p. 25.
[152]   *Ibid.*, p. 365.

depicted events only between the rise of Antichrist and the last Judgement. [153] Thus for Pareus the Seals ran concurrently with the Trumpets, while the Vials supplied further details for the latter times of both. "This Vision belongs to the last times, and shall be finished indeed at the end of the world".[154] The church now stood in the time of the sixth Seal and the sixth Trumpet, [155] and awaited the outpouring of the third Vial. [156] Pareus could, therefore, confidently proclaim the nearness of the last events:

> The pouring out therefore of the vialls followed after the opening of five Seales, and the sounding of foure Trumpets, the sixt Seale and fift Trumpet being almost ended, and the fourth period of the Christian church begun, which as we noted on Chap. 15.1. took its beginning from the ... Reformation of Evangelicall Doctrine in the West, and is to endure unto the end. [157]

If one man stood out above the others in moulding subsequent interpretative thought, it was undoubtedly Joseph Mede. Contemporary opinion, as well as the judgement of later scholarship, [158] recognised the significance of his *Clavis Apocalyptica*. William Twisse wrote: "Master Mede hath many notions of so rare a nature, that I do not finde he is beholding [sic] to any other for them, but onely to his own studiousnesse and dexteritie, with the blessing of God upon his labours." [159] John Worthington added, ' he proceeded upon grounds never traced by any, and infinitely more probable than any lay'd down by those who before him undertook that task." [160] Mede's great contribution to the study of The Revelation was his insistence that a correct interpretation depended on the "synchronisation" of certain prophecies, and an understanding of their relationship to each other. [161] The "Key" to The Revelation was, in fact, an explanation of the seven "synchronismes" which he regarded as essential.

---

[153] *Ibid.,* Pref., p. 25.
[154] *Ibid.,* p. 362.
[155] Pareus followed Dent here, in holding that the fifth and sixth Trumpets were fulfilled simultaneously, *ibid.,* pp. 166, 167.
[156] *Ibid.,* p. 383.
[157] *Ibid.,* p. 375.
[158] Cf. Froom, *op. cit.,* II, p. 542, and Haller, *Rise of Puritanism,* p. 269. Haller's mistaken reference to Mede as "William Mede", is difficult to explain unless he is confusing him which the Quaker, William Mead (1628–1713), which is hardly likely to be the case.
[159] William Twisse, in Mede, *Key of the Revelation,* Pref.
[160] John Worthington, in Mede, *Works,* Author's Life.
[161] Mede, *Key of the Revelation,* pt. I, p. 1.

To Mede, there were only two major prophecies in the book, that of the Seals and Trumpets which outlined the destiny of Empires, particularly the Roman Empire, and that of the "Little Book opened" which foretold the destiny of the church and the Christian religion. [162]   Again, these prophecies were parallel in scope, stretching across the whole Christian era, and the purpose of the "synchronismes" was to correlate certain symbols, times, and events within each prophecy. For example, the first synchronism stated that in the first prophecy the seventh Seal, which included all seven Trumpets, corresponded in time with the Beasts of chapter xiii in the second prophecy; [163]   the second synchronism showed that the battle between Michael and the Dragon took place in the time of the first six Seals; [164]   and the third placed the seven Vials within the time of the sixth Trumpet. [165]   With seven clear rules like this to harmonize the various parts of the Revelation, Mede believed that it was possible to interpret virtually the entire book.

The first six Seals represent six stages in the history of the Roman Empire, reaching to the time of Theodosius. [166]   The seventh Seal, or first six Trumpets, depicts the fall and punishment of the Empire, [167]   and extends from the death of Theodosius in 395 A.D. [168]   to at least the destruction of Constantinople [169]   in 1453 A.D., with the seventh Trumpet reaching right down to the final consummation of the mystery of God. The second prophecy retraces the whole era, with stress upon events concerning the church. Thus, the war between Michael and the Great Red Dragon symbolises the hostility between the church and the Roman Empire in the first three hundred years or so of Christian history, [170]   and the Vials signify the destruction of the Antichrist, all within the time of the sixth Trumpet [171]   Three Vials are past, the fourth is now being fulfilled, and three only remain in the future. Apart from that, virtually every other detail in the book of Revelation has been accomplished

---

[162]   *Ibid.*, p. 13.
[163]   *Ibid.*, p. 14.
[164]   *Ibid.*, p. 17.
[165]   *Loc. cit.*
[166]   *Ibid.*, p. 61.
[167]   *Ibid.*, p. 80.
[168]   *Ibid.*, p. 85.
[169]   *Ibid.*, p. 117.
[170]   *Ibid.*, pt. II, p. 32.
[171]   *Ibid.*, pt. I, p. 17; pt. II, p. 113.

except, of course, those things which relate to the kingdom of God, which cannot be long delayed.

With all this weight of learning behind them, it cannot be surprising that the men who came later should follow the same patterns of interpretation. With Thomas Goodwin in 1639 to William Hicks in 1659, and with the host of those who came between them, the influence of Mede and his predecessors is clearly in evidence. Goodwin, who adopted the position that there were two basic visions in The Revelation, wrote:

> ... these Seals and Trumpets, which do in order succeed one another, do contain a continued Prophecy of Events following one another in a succession of Ages downward ... from the first Seal to the seventh Trumpet, is run over all the Time that the Monarchies and Kingdoms of this World ... should continue and last. [172]

The sixth Trumpet dealt with the Turkish Empire which had had its beginning around 1300 A.D., and was "not yet fulfilled or expired", [173] and would continue until the kingdom of Christ was ushered in under the seventh. [174] The book of Revelation made it most plain "that we live now in the Extremity of Times ... we are at the Verge, and as it were, within the Whirle of that Great Mystery of Christ's Kingdom, which will, as a Gulph, swallow up all Time". [175]

Hicks, who appended to his commentary of the Revelation a word to the "Quinto-Monarchians", [176] in an appeal for moderation to the militant minority, pointed out that certain prophecies were yet to be completed before the kingdom could be established. [177] What had begun as a moderate interpretation was thus to end in the same way. Among the unfulfilled parts of the prophecy he named the final downfall of the Antichrist and the completion of the pouring out of the Vials. It was true, however, Hicks added, that Antichrist had begun to fall under the second angel of chapter xiv, when the true gospel had been first restored under the Waldenses and the early German reformers. [178] It was

---

[172]   Goodwin, *op. cit.*, p. 19. As with most of Goodwin's works, they were written some time before publication. That the *Exposition Upon the Revelation* was, in fact, written in 1639, appears from his son's preface to Vol. II of his *Works* (1682).

[173]   *Ibid.*, p. 54.

[174]   *Ibid.*, p. 59.

[175]   *Ibid.*, p. 190.

[176]   William Hicks, 'Quinto-Monarchiae' (1659), *ad. cal.* with *The Revelation Revealed*.

[177]   *Op. cit.*, p. 341.

[178]   *Ibid.*, p. 342.

true also, that, with only three of the Vials remaining to be emptied upon the declining Antichristian power, [179] the end was much nearer "then the world thinks of". [180]

Hicks, then, spoke for all students of prophecy, regardless of academic background or ecclesiastical leaning, as indeed he did for virtually all Christian believers of the age when, at the conclusion of his book he proclaimed, "Therefore ye Saints of God, lift up your heads, for the Lord is at the door, and the day of your Redemption is nigh at hand." [181] Within the framework of the fulfilling prophecies of Daniel and The Revelation, set in the context of established historical fact, no other conclusion could be entertained.

---

[179]   *Ibid.*, p. 343.
[180]   *Ibid.*, p. 342.
[181]   *Ibid.*, p. 346.

CHAPTER THREE

SIGNS OF THE TIMES AND THE TIME OF THE END

Sir William Alexander was not unique among seventeenth-century writers in demonstrating that poetry as well as apologetics could advance the doctrine of Christ's near advent.[1] Both Donne and Milton spoke of "these latter days",[2] and Donne's further allusion to the approaching day[3] was strengthened by Milton in a metrical version of Psalm LXXXV:

> Surely to such as do him fear
>   Salvation is at hand
> And glory shall ere long appear
>   To dwell within our Land.[4]

Of all the poets of the period, George Wither perhaps gave fullest expression to the idea of the imminent end. As early as 1625 Wither had declared "God's patience is nigh out of date",[5] a view which he expanded in 1644 when under Parliamentary arms in the Civil War. Desirous of an early reconciliation between King and Parliament, Wither wrote:

> Our speedy Reconcilement hasten shall
> The Churches Triumph, and Great Babels fall.
> Her date is near, if I aright have hit
> The meaning of the Number, left to be
> A trial and probation of their Wit
> Who seek the fall of Antichrist to see.

---

[1] See *supra,* p. 36.

[2] John Donne, *Iuvenilia* (1633), sig. F4v; Milton, 'Eikonoclastes', in *Works*, V, p. 307.

[3] John Donne, *A Sermon of Commemoration of the Lady Dāvers* (1627), p. 84; cf. "There is scarce any amongst vs, but does expect this coming," *ibid.,* p. 87.

[4] Milton, 'Psalm LXXXV', in *Works,* I, pt. I, p. 147; cf. the "shortly-expected King", 'Of Reformation Touching Church-Discipline in England', *Works,* III, pt. I, p. 78, and "thy Kingdome is now at hand", 'Animadversions Upon the Remonstrants Defence, against Smectymnuus', *Works,* III, pt. I, p. 148.

[5] George Wither, 'A Review of Neglected Remembrances', in *Fragmenta Prophetica* (1669), p. 31. Wither's later pre-occupation with the Antichrist (infra, p. 124) may have been inspired by the earlier poet, Sir David Lindsay, whose *Dialogue betweene Father Experience & the Courteour of the miserable estate of the World* had taken up the theme of Antichrist and the Day of Judgement at some length. The work went through many editions after its first appearance in 1554, being frequently reprinted throughout the seventeenth century. The poem declared all the essentials of the coming eschatology; see 'Dialogue of the Miserable estate of the World', in *The Workes of the Famovs and Worthy Knight, Sir David Lindesay* (Edinburgh, 1619), pp. 160—193.

...
Be patient therefore, ye that are opprest;
This generation shall not pass away
Till some behold the downfall of that Beast,
Which yet among us with his Taile doth play.
...
I see as plainly as I see the Sun,
He draweth near who on the white Horse rides;
The Long expected Battel is begun.[6]

These lines were complementary to Sir William Alexander's earlier *Dooms-day* which had described latter-day conditions and which was still in circulation in the late 1630's and early 1640's. Specific signs of the end had attracted Alexander's comment:

That threatned time which must the world appall,
Is (that all may amend) by signes fore-shown;
Warres rumor'd are, the Gospell preach'd o're all,
Some Iewes convert, the Antichrist growes knowne;
Divels rage, vice raignes, zeal cooles, faith failes, stars fall,
All sorts of plagues have the last Trumpet blowne:
And by prodigious signes may plain appeare,
That of the Sonne of man the signe drawes neare.[7]

Neither Donne nor Alexander were Puritans, if Wither and Milton were, and the combined effect of these views is again to reflect the extent to which belief in Christ's imminent return had grown.

Of greater significance in this respect, perhaps, is the number of prominent laymen who similarly testified to a conviction that Christ was, to use Milton's phrase, "standing at the dore".[8] In addition to the poets Alexander, Wither, and Milton may be added the names of John Napier the mathematician, Sir Henry Finch the lawyer, and Samuel Hartlib the economist. Thomas Hayne the London schoolmaster, who ran contrary to the accepted view of his age concerning prophetic interpretation, nonetheless wrote of "these last and worst Times of the World"[9] and of "the present age ... on whom the ends of the World are come".[10] Hayne believed that it was "very probable, that the day of judgment is neer".[11] According to James Toppe,[12]

---

[6]   Wither, 'Campo-Musae' (1644), in *Fragmenta Prophetica*, pp. 50, 53, 56.
[7]   Alexander, 'Dooms-day', p. 25, in *Recreations with the Muses*.
[8]   Milton, 'Animadversions', in *Works*, III, pt. I, p. 148.
[9]   Thomas Hayne, *The General View of the Holy Scriptures* (1640), The Epistle Dedicatory.
[10]   *Loc. cit.*
[11]   Hayne, *Christs Kingdome*, p. 88.
[12]   On James Toppe, Baptist schoolmaster from Tiverton, see W. H. Burgess, 'James

Leonard Busher anticipated an end to the present order only "6 yeeres hence". [13] In 1649 the Commonwealth lawyer William Shepheard thought the last day was "neer at hand". [14] Robert Purnell, the elder and founder-member of Broadmead Baptist Church, Bristol, constrained by the double evidence of fulfilled prophecy and current "Providences", wrote that the day was "not far off" but "near, yea very near", [15] and concluded with an exhortation "to live in a continual expectation of the coming of the Lord Jesus". [16]

There is here, as indeed there is in most of the writings devoted to the second advent doctrine, a noticeable vitality, a warmth of anticipation, almost a *joie de vivre*, which is consistent in the eschatology of the seventeenth century and which particularly belongs to it. Baxter's phrases, "Oh, fellow Christians, what a day will that be", "O blessed day, when I shall rest with God", "O hasten that great Resurrection Day", [17] Sibbes's "Come Lord Iesus", [18] Love's "Cry, as the Spouse, Come, Lord Jesus, come quickly", [19] nowhere meet more simply or more fervently than in Durant:

> I have heard of a poor man (who it seems loved and longed for Christs appearance) that when there was a great Earthquake, and when many cryed out the day of judgement was come, and one cryed out, Woe is me, where shall I run? And another cryed, Alas, Alas! What shall I doe? And a third, how shall I hide myselfe? &c. That poore man onely said, And is it so? Is the day come? Where shall I go, upon what mountain shall I stand to see my Saviour? [20]

All are perhaps surpassed by the simple eloquence of the prayer recorded in an unknown seventeenth-century hand at the end of

---

Toppe and the Tiverton Anabaptists', in *Transactions of the Baptist Historical Society*, III (1912–13), pp. 193–211. Toppe's MS., referred to below, which was a reply to a lost work by Leonard Busher attacking Toppe's millenarian views, is also discussed by Burgess.

[13] James Toppe, '*Christs Monarchic* all and personall Reigne uppon Earth over all the Kingdoms of this world', British Museum, Sloane MS. 63, fol. 46*v*.

[14] William Shepheard, *Of the Foure Last and Greatest Things* (1649), p. 18. On Shepheard see *DNB*, s.v. Sheppard.

[15] Robert Purnell, *A Little Cabinet Richly Stored with all sorts of Heavenly Varieties, and Soul-reviving Influences* (1657), p. 149. Eight years earlier, the time of the seventh trumpet was "drawing neare", *Good Tydings for Sinners, Great Ioy for Saints* (1649), p. 22.

[16] Purnell, *A Little Cabinet*, p. 463.

[17] Baxter, *Saints Rest*, pp. 47, 791, 837.

[18] Sibbes, *Philippians*, p. 228.

[19] Love, *Heavens Glory*, p. 50.

[20] Durant, *Salvation*, p. 302.

Baxter's *Saints Rest*, "Even so, come, Lord Jesus". [21] This fervent vitality is so widely diffused among all writers that it can only be judged to be an essential attitude which developed wherever belief in the second advent was genuinely and discerningly cherished. It is, moreover, this warm expectancy which demands that the main stream of seventeenth-century eschatology be regarded as one of hope, rather than of fear, as has so often been the case with extremist minorities who have tended to isolate their eschatology from the main substance of Christian doctrine. The essential eschatological expectancy in the seventeenth century is characterised by its positive Christological orientation. The anticipatory ethos is well expressed by William Durham who, in his sermon of impending judgement, declares of the imminent advent, "Here's the balme of Gilead for the fainting soule, and abundant consolation for him that is opprest; 'tis (doubtless) a great asswagement to a Christian's misery, to think that Christ is ready to come to judgment". [22] That this spirit of hope was effectively transmitted from the pulpit to the pew is clear in this illuminating passage from Purnell:

> ... we should love the appearance of Christ, and look for, and haste to the coming of the day of God. O why is his Chariot so long in coming! Oh that the day should be so great, and our desires so small! Shall the Marriner desire his Port? the Apprentice his freedom? the imprisoned his liberty? the sick his health? the Spouse the day of her marriage? a malefactor his pardon? a labourer his rest? an heir his inheritance? and shall not a Christian long for that day which removes every sorrow, supplies every want, and makes us like him? [23]

Hope in a future that is Christ's is the key to expectation so clearly spiritual and lacking in any immediate political motivation.

But to what did the doctrine of the second coming owe this warmth of anticipation? What engendered such buoyant hope? The answer must be sought, to a large extent, in the consistent stress which was laid upon the imminence of the event. The focus of hope clearly lay within the horizon, not beyond it. William Durham continued, "Lift up your heads, O ye dejected spirits, for the day of your redemption draweth nigh". [24] Baxter used a

---

[21] This inscription appears on the last page of the text of the first edition in Dr. Williams's Library.
[22] William Durham, *Maran-atha*, p. 32.
[23] Purnell, *op. cit.* p. 425.
[24] William Durham, *loc. cit.*

similar expression, "the Saints lift up their heads, for their Redemption draweth nigh", [25] while Sibbes declared, "Emanuell will appeare in our flesh ere long ..." [26] John Maynard believed that the time was "at hand", [27] and William Bridge that the world had come to its final midnight, since it was both "very late" and "very darke". [28] The doctrine owed much of its vitality to this element of proximity, without which the mere promulgation of the concept of an ultimate end at some time in an indefinite future could have been little more than a formal article of faith. That this was not the case in seventeenth-century England was due to a great multitude of witnesses, drawn from a variety of ranks and professions, who united in proclaiming that Christ was near and that the last days had come.

The connotation of this phrase "the last days" and its relationship to the times then present shows an interesting development in the eschatological thought of the period, and is further comment on the expectation of an imminent advent throughout the first half of the century. Ephraim Huit's understanding of the phrase may be regarded as illustrative of a transition from the view which prevailed among earlier writers, to that which appears to have been favoured after 1640. To Huit, the biblical usage of the term "last days" [29] normally referred to the entire period between the two advents of Christ. [30] Sometimes, however, it was used specifically to denote one or other of three divisions of that period: either the time surrounding the first coming; or the Middle Ages and the time of Antichrist; or the final era, "the uttermost limits" of the Christian age. [31] Earlier writers had been content with the explanation that a two-fold meaning was implicit in the phrase, thereby overcoming the problem posed by the New Testament's apparent insistence that the last days were already present. [32] The words referred primarily to the whole Christian dispensation and, in a secondary sense, to the final part of that period. Thomas Adams wrote:

---

[25] Baxter, *op. cit.*, p. 46.
[26] Sibbes, *Emanuell*, p. 22 (the second so numbered); but not in any mystical sense.
[27] John Maynard, *A Shadow of the Victory of Christ* (1646), p. 10. On Maynard, Presbyterian vicar of Mayfield, Sussex, see *Calamy Revised*, s.v.
[28] William Bridge, *Christs coming Opened in a Sermon Before the Honourable House of Commons in Margarets Westminster: May 17, 1648* (1648), p. 19.
[29] Cf. II Tim. iii, 1, "the last days" and Heb. i, 2, "these last days".
[30] Huit, *Daniel*, p. 40.
[31] *Ibid.*, p. 41.
[32] Cf. Heb. i, 2 with I Pet. i. 20 "these last times".

> Thus the time from Christs ascension to the worlds end, is called Dies
> extrema the last day; because it immediately (without any generall
> alteration) goes before it. The end in the Apostles time was not farre
> off; now it must be very neere: if that were ultima dies, this is, ultima
> hora: or if that were ultima hora, the last houre, this is ultimum
> horae, the last minute. [33]

It fell to Joseph Mede, however, to give the most precise definition of this earlier view. Commenting on the ἐσχάτων τῶν ἡμερῶν
of II Pet. iii, 3 he explained that the last days, or last times, were
to be understood either as the "last times in general" or as "the
last times in special". [34] The "last times in general" extended
over the period of Daniel's fourth kingdom, with special reference to the era of the Christian church, while the "last times in
special" referred to the later years of the fourth kingdom, principally the reign of Antichrist for 1260 days. [35] In his *Apostasy of
the Latter Times* Mede explained, "For if the Last Times in
general are all the Times of the Fourth Kingdom, then must our
Latter times, as a part thereof, needs be the Latter times of that
Kingdom". [36] Thus the latter times of I Tim. iv. 1 are not simply
the days which "immediately precede the Second Coming of
Christ", [37] but correspond to the "ὕστεροι καιροι allotted to the Man
of sin," [38] whose reign began at the end of the Roman Empire [39]
and was to continue 1260 years. [40]

Although Huit had seen principally only a twofold application,
he had suggested nevertheless that the Christian era could be
divided conveniently into three sections, any of which might be
designated as "the last days", and it was such a threefold explanation which came to be popular with the later expositors.
Robert Maton, whose *Israel's Redemption Redeemed* appeared in
1646 as a reply to Alexander Petrie's attack on his earlier *Israels
Redemption*, outlines this development:

> There is a great difference betwixt the last dayes, and the latter dayes.
> For the (last dayes) Heb. 1 ver. 2, and the (last times) I Pet. 1 ver. 20
> doe comprehend the whole time under the Gospel; the time I say,

---

[33]   Adams, *Commentary*, p. 1132; cf. Goodwin, "it is 1600 years ago since he
called them the last daies", 'The Second Sermon on Heb. 1. 1, 2', in *Works*, I, pt. III,
p. 133.

[34]   Mede, 'A Paraphrase and Exposition', in *Works*, p. 609.

[35]   *Loc. cit.*

[36]   Mede, 'The Apostasy' in *Works*, p. 655.

[37]   *Ibid.*, p. 653.

[38]   *Loc. cit.*

[39]   *Ibid.*, p. 658.

[40]   *Ibid.*, p. 656.

from Christs first comming to his second: but the (latter times)
I Tim. 4. ver. 1. doe signifie onely the latter part of the last times. And
as the last times, or dayes, have their latter times; so againe the (latter
times) have their (last dayes) as we may see in the 2 Tim chap. 3.
ver. 1 and in the 2 Pet. chap. 3. ver. 3. and of the end of these (last
dayes) of the (latter times) are the (latter dayes) in this Prophecie to
be understood ... [41]

Nathaniel Homes, whose output of eschatological material between the years 1650 and 1666 at least equalled that of the
prolific Mede, maintained the same view in terms which strongly
resembled those employed by his illustrious predecessor. The last
times were to be understood in three ways, either "In General"
of the whole period of the Fourth Monarchy, [42] or "In Special"
of the reign of the Little Horn for 1260 years, or "In particular"
of the times of divine judgements upon the Little Horn and the
impending destruction of the Antichrist. [43] The anonymous author
of the rare little work *A Sober Inquiry: or Christs Reign With his
Saints a Thousand Years* (1660) took the definition a step further by contending that "these ὕστεροι καιροι or last times, consist
of three great periods." [44] The first two periods comprehend the
past and the present, but the third period projects the last times
into the future by applying them to the coming millennium. [45]
This does not contradict belief in an imminent end to the present
order, since the "last times" extend fundamentally from the time
of Christ to the final "consummation of all things". [46]

All this theological hair-splitting was not in vain if it hastened
that consummation by furthering the message of the advent, and
whether in terms of Thomas Adams' "ultimum horae", or of Joseph
Mede's "latter Times", or of Robert Maton's "last dayes of the
last times", or even of Bishop Brian Duppa's "terra damnata", [47]

---

[41]   Robert Maton, *Israel's Redemption Redeemed* (1646), p. 64.
[42]   It will be remembered, as with Mede's reference above to the "fourth Kingdom", that Rome, the last of the four monarchies of Daniel, was held to extend until
the end of the world; see *supra*, p. 78.
[43]   Homes, *Ten Exercitations*, p. 28.
[44]   I. F., *A Sober Inquiry: or Christs Reign With his Saints a Thousand Years*
(1660), p. 6.
[45]   *Loc. cit.*
[46]   *Loc. cit.*
[47]   In 1651 Duppa, in a letter to Sir Justinian Isham, commented on the state of
the world, noting that it "was now drawn low, and in the dreggs, little being now left,
but the tartar of it, or (as the chimists speak) the 'terra damnata' ", Sir Gyles Isham,
Ed., *The Correspondence of Bishop Brian Duppa and Sir Justinian Isham, 1650—1660*
(Northamptonshire Record Society, 1955), p. 37; cf. Hill, *Puritanism and Revolution*,
p. 325. Both Duppa, then Bishop of Salisbury, and Winchester, and Isham, later M.P.
for Northamptonshire, were Anglican Royalists.

the conclusion was consistently the same. "This is the Worlds Old age, 'tis its last and worst time", as Thomas Hall said, "for Old age is the Winter of a mans dayes, the dregges of his life, full of weaknesse, coldness, diziness, and virtiginous ... 'Tis now Winter with the World, it growes old and cold". [48] There is an obvious similarity in this analogy to the picture painted so vividly by Thomas Adams:

> Thus are wee fallen into the depth of Winter: the Spring is past, the Summer hath had her season, Autumne hath spent her fruits, and now Winter hath shaken downe the very leaves and left us nothing but naked, bare, and barren trees. The last moneth of the great yeere of the world is come upon us; wee are deepe in December. [49]

It is this catholicity of conviction that the end of time had arrived which makes it desirable to examine some of the more salient factors which even led men such as the conservative Baxter to declare, in a sermon preached before the Lord Mayor of London, "it is not a 100. years in all liklyhood, till every soul of us shall be in heaven or hell: and its like, not half or a quarter of that time ..." [50]

The "forerunners of his coming", [51] to quote Baxter again, conveniently fall into two broad categories, loosely described by Robert Purnell as "the appearances of providences" and "the fulfilling of prophecies". [52] These two comprehensive lines of argument, more specifically designated as current events and trends in world conditions, and the peculiar relevance of the chronological prophecies, seemed to converge on the middle decades of the century and were together responsible for the prevalence of the conviction that the advent was imminent. Although there was widespread recognition of the principle that the exact time of the advent was known only to the Father, [53] yet few were in disagreement with William Strong who, in a sermon entitled 'A Set time for Iudgement', stressed the validity of the signs of the times. In the divine purpose, Strong argued, there is an

---

[48]   Thomas Hall, *Commentary* p. 9.
[49]   Adams, *op. cit.*, p. 1138.
[50]   Richard Baxter, *A Sermon of Iudgement* (1655), p. 244. Baxter describes the congregation, which included the Lord Mayor, Sir Christopher Pack, as "the greatest Auditory that I ever saw", *Reliquiae Baxterianae* (1696), pt. I, p. 112.
[51]   Baxter, *Saints Rest*, p. 46.
[52]   Purnell, *op. cit.*, p. 419.
[53]   E.g. Perkins, 'An Exposition of the Symbole, or Creed', in *Workes*, I, p. 260; Seagar, *World to Come*, p. 87; Durant, *Salvation*, p. 278. While the precise month, day and hour were unknown to man, this did not preclude the possibility of determining the year in which the advent would occur.

appointed time for judgement, [54] a time which "may and must be known," [55] the approach of which would be heralded by signs of a suitable character "if a man doth wisely behold them by a spiritual eye." [56] It was this eye of spiritual discernment which enabled Strong and his contemporaries to look at the world which surrounded them and at the Bible which directed them and to conclude that they lived at the end of time.

Among the signs which were to be seen in the world none was more obvious than the extreme sinfulness of the age and the marked deterioration of morality. Every generation with an eschatological consciousness has tended to see its own age as the most sinful and corrupt in history, and to those devout students of the Word who lived in seventeenth-century England Paul's prediction that evil men would "wax worse and worse" [57] appeared to have reached its ultimate realisation. Thomas Adams, who was never at a loss for an apt simile, saw his time as the focal point of "all the vicious customes of former ages ... as the kennels of a city run to the common Sewer". [58] While many forms of wickedness had variously predominated in preceding ages, "now, like so many land-flouds from the mountaines, they meet in one chanell, and make a torrent of united wickednesse in these lower and latter dayes". [59] John Seagar, who sought to refute the millenarian concept of a golden age prior to the last judgement, based his argument largely on the teaching he found in the New Testament that conditions would grow progressively worse as the world came nearer to its final events. Christ himself had foretold an increase in latter-day wickedness, he pointed out, an added, "Wherefore I infer from what hath been said, That this present world is evil, and is likely to be get worse". [60] "We have seen how iniquity hath abounded", [61] therefore we can conlude that the end is near. For Thomas Hall also, belief that the world had come to its "Old age", its "last and worst time" [62], stemmed from a realisation that the divine indictment of the last days was particularly meaningful in view of the contemporary situation:

---

[54]   William Strong, 'A Set Time for Iudgement', in *XXXI Select Sermons* (1656), p. 449.

[55]   *Ibid.*, p. 457.

[56]   *Loc. cit.*

[57]   II Tim. iii, 13.

[58]   Adams, *op. cit.*, p. 1138.

[59]   *Ibid.*, p. 1139.

[60]   Seagar, *op. cit.*, p. 31.

[61]   *Ibid.*, p. 43.

[62]   Thomas Hall, *op. cit.*, p. 9.

> These last dayes will be the common sink and sewer, the very recep-
> tacle of all the vile abominations and heresies of former ages. As all
> the creatures met in Noahs Ark, and all the waters meet in the sea; so
> all these prodigious enormities, and flouds of error, which have ap-
> peared in former ages, will meet in this Ocean. They will come forth
> in a Third Edition, Auctiores, non Emendatiores: enlarged, but noth-
> ing bettered. [63]

If all this was true of the world at large, it was singularly
applicable to the English nation whose gross sinfulness was de-
claimed by Edmund Calamy in a sermon before the House of
Commons in December, 1641. England's sins had brought her to
the very verge of Judgement, he declared. "We in this Nation
have had many yeers warning. I feare me, that the Taper is almost burnt out: That the Sun of our prosperity is ready to set:
And that the houre-glasse of our happinesse is almost run
out." [64] Among the evils which Calamy specifically denounced
were "the beastly drunkennesse of this nation", blasphemy such
that "there is a pride taken in offending God", adultery and
fornication "which as an Epidemicall disease hath overspread the
Nation", covetousness, deceit, extortion, profanation of the Sabbath, and contempt for the Gospel. [65] This decline in moral standards called for an honest recognition of "the sins of England,
and the destruction which wee may justly expect" by way of
retribution. [66] If Calamy had a discerning eye on divine judgements of a more immediate nature, Thomas Hall, when the upheaval of the Civil Wars was over, saw in the self-same sins of the
land evidence of an impending judgement of far greater proportions:

> The common crying Sins of other nations, are rife amongst us: here
> you may find the Drunkennesse of the Dutch, the Lust of the French,
> the Italians Ambition, the Spaniards Treachery, the Laylanders Witch-
> craft, the Covetousnesse of the Jew, the Cruelty of the Turk and the
> Monsters of Munster. [67]

With reference to the opening verses of II Tim. iii, he borrowed
Calamy's title, and declared, "I may truly call these 19. sins
Englands Looking-glasse". [68] It would be tedious to recount

---

[63]   *Ibid.*, p. 8.
[64]   Edmund Calamy, *Englands Looking-Glasse* (1642), p. 20.
[65]   *Ibid.*, pp. 30, 31.
[66]   *Ibid.*, p. 33.
[67]   Thomas Hall, *op. cit.*, pp. 8, 9.
[68]   *Ibid.*, p. 13.

Hall's exposition of the entire list, but one example will illustrate his interpretation of the passage with reference to his own age. Commenting on the phrase "disobedient to parents", [69] Hall asked "Was there ever more contempt of Naturall Parents? is not the complaint generall, that the youth of our age is exceeding Haughty, Vaine, Light, Loose, Hypocriticall, and Rebellious to Parents?" [70]

Possibly the most telling analysis of this deterioration in morality was that offered by the Episcopalian divine Robert Gell. Mede had previously drawn attention to the analogy of the Noachian age, [71] but Gell's sermon before the Lord Mayor of London remains the most lucid and forthright interpretation of the parallels between the antediluvian world and the last days. [72] Sins of the flesh had been the characteristic sins of Noah's day—"The old world was overwhelmed with voluptuousnesse and sensuality" [73]—and Gell interpreted the current immorality in the light of Christ's own warning that there would be a recurrence of pre-flood standards immediately prior to His second coming. Gell condemned his own age as the one thus designated:

> All manner of iniquity abounds, in high, in low, in rich, in poore, universall iniquity, contrary to the universall righteousness of God. But the Spirit of God names onely that kind of iniquity which was then, and I believe is now, most rife and common among all men, intemperancy, incontinency, luxury, lasciviousness, all manner of uncleanness. [74]

Not satisfied with this general comparison, Gell pressed home the analogy with unflinching frankness:

> They of the old world were chast, and honest in comparison of many in this present lascivious generation ... many of this later world they bound not their unruly appetites with the lawful use of marriage, but break all bonds of God and nature, and glory as if they had attained unto some notable degree of perfection in the flesh; all women are to them alike, they are of a new world, who neither marrie nor are given in marriage, but are as the Angells. [75]

---

[69] II Tim., iii, 5.
[70] Thomas Hall, *op. cit.*, p. 66.
[71] See Mede, 'A Paraphrase and Exposition' in *Works*, pp. 613–616.
[72] The sermon was entitled 'Noahs flood Returning', and was taken from Matt. xxiv, 37–39.
[73] Robert Gell, *Noahs flood Returning* (1655), p. 11.
[74] *Ibid.*, p. 9.
[75] *Ibid.*, p. 15.

All this was an answer, if indeed any answer had been expected, to questions which Charles Hammond had asked in 1652, "Was sin ever at a greater height then it is now at this time ...? What sins is there in ye Scriptures to be pronounc'd against, but we are guilty of? What nation under ye sun, doth more abound in iniquity thē we do ...? "[76] For all that the Saints were not to despair. "The worst times are God's usuall Preface to better times", [77] as Homes said. "Heavinesse may indure for a night, but joy comes in the morning", [78] and the morning was at hand.

Morality, of course, is a term which can be applied to the relationships of nations as well as of individuals, and although theologians in the seventeenth century may not have been concerned with this principle *per se*, yet they were conscious that Christ had foretold that hostility and animosity between nations would be a further evidence of His approaching return. [79] It is probably true that this consciousness had existed in Protestant thought since Luther's observation that "the skill of waging war hath so much encreased, that more cruel and desparate arms and weapons of war, and other warlike Instruments, can hardly be invented, then are now". [80] Certainly William Perkins had drawn attention to the significance of hostility and strife among nations, [81] and the "wars and rumours of wars" referred to in the gospels had figured in discussions of the signs of Christ's advent since his 'Fruitful Dialogue' of 1585. [82] Thus Nathaniel Homes said nothing intrinsically new when he listed fifteen separate countries which were currently "either in the practise, or posture, or preparations and expectations of war." [83]

It is significant, however, that in the late 1640's and early 1650's a spate of interpretations appeared which propounded that wars were a specific sign of the end. The reasons for this are not difficult to see. On the Continent, the Thirty Years War had just dragged to a final close in 1648, bringing to an uneasy end a

---

[76]   Charles Hammond, *Englnads* [sic] *Alarum-Bell* (1652), sig. A5r. On Hammond, Royalist Captain, see *Catalogue of the McAlpin Collection* (1927), V, s.v.
[77]   Nathaniel Homes, *Plain Dealing: or The Cause and Cure of the Present Evils of the Times* (1652), p. 73.
[78]   *Loc. cit.*
[79]   Cf. Matt. xxiv, 6, 7 and Luke xxi, 9, 10 with Rev. xi, 18.
[80]   [Luther], *The Signs of Christs coming* (1661), p. 18.
[81]   Perkins, 'A Fruitful Dialogue', in *Works*, III, p. 470.
[82]   E.g. Adams, *Commentary*, p. 1136; Ussher, *Body of Divinitie*, p. 447; Bridge, *Christs Coming*, pp. 19, 20.
[83]   Homes, *Resurrection*, p. 548.

century of conflict between the nations of Europe. At home, the beginning of Charles I's reign had been marked by war with Spain and France, while its later years had embroiled the nation in the tragedy of civil war. To a generation so religiously inclined as the seventeenth century the fact that religious issues underlay so many of these conflicts added to the importance already attached to them from an exegetical standpoint. The Civil Wars were a traumatic experience for many Englishmen, particularly for those among the saints who had regarded England as the elect nation, favoured by God, and destined by Him as an instrument, perhaps the chief instrument, for the final accomplishment of the divine purpose.[84] In 1653 John Durant referred to recent events in England as signs of Christ's coming being at hand.[85] To Durant all the signs of the advent given by Christ himself could be reduced to "two heads",[86] "the darkning of the heavenly bodies, the Sun, Moon and Stars",[87] and "the disturbance of the waters ... and commotions of the earth".[88] These signs were not to be interpreted literally but metaphorically, and of the first group Durant explicitly states:

> By the signs that shall appear in Heaven, as the darkning of the Sun, obscuring the Moon, and shaking or falling of stars, I understand the debasing, dethroning and destroying of the Kings, Princes, and powers of this world, especially, and peculiarly such as at, or near the coming of Christ shal be found to be upholders of those things which Christ will destroy.[89]

---

[84] The lofty concept that Jerusalem could be built "in England's green and pleasant land" takes firm root from the early part of the century. George Wither's 'Campo-Musae' had suggested that a settlement of the conflict between the English King and Parliament would hasten the final triumph of the church. Two years later, in 1646, Thomas Goodwin declared "this Isle in which we live ... is the richest Ship, that hath the most of the precious jewels of our Lord and Saviour Jesus Christ in it, and the greatest treasure, of any kingdome in the world", Goodwin, *The Great Interest of States & Kingdomes* (1646), p. 51. In 1651 Edmund Hall wrote of Zechariah's prophecy that Christ's feet would stand at the last day on the Mount of Olives, "I am strongly induced to believe that the Mount of Olives is England and Scotland, formerly united under one King and Religion," Edmund Hall, *Manus Testium movens*, p. 80. Some find the seeds of these ideas in the much earlier writings of, for example, John Bale and John Foxe, cf. William Haller, *The Elect Nation: The Meaning and Relevance of Foxe's Book of Martyrs* (New York, 1964), *passim*, and A. J. B. Gilsdorf, 'The Puritan Apocalypse: New England Eschatology in the Seventeenth Century', unpublished Ph.D. thesis, Yale University, 1965, ch. 1.

[85] Durant, *op. cit.*, p. 278.

[86] *Ibid.*, p. 279.

[87] *Loc. cit.*; references quoted were Luke xxi, 25 and Matt. xxv, 29.

[88] *Ibid.*, p. 280.; references quoted were Luke xxi, 25, 26 and Matt. xxiv, 6.

[89] *Ibid.*, p. 289.

Durant's interpretation of this sign was unmistakable in its reference to the events of the Civil War:

> And if the late actings among our selves, and the face of things in our
> neighbour Nations, doe not clearly speake out these things to be in
> doing, beginning, and going on: I confesse I have no skill in the
> comparing of texts and times. I am altogether mistaken in these mat-
> ters if in our English Horizon we have not seen Sunne, the Moon, and
> Stars darkened and obscured. [90]

A wider viewpoint saw this tension between the nations divided over the issues of allegiance to the Christian faith. The
wicked nations, which had ever been opposed to the peoples of
God, [91] were arraigned against the nations which protected the
church. Hence ' the last attempts of the enemies shal be the
fiercest, and ... the bitterest afflictions and the sharpest persecutions of the Church of God, are reserved for these last times". [92]
The same argument was advanced by Nathaniel Homes as one of
five major signs of the approaching advent:

> When the might of the Churches enemies appeares universally, and
> irresistibly, powerful, then is the Churches great deliverance at hand
> ... Now whether at present, the might of the Churches enemies bee
> not universal and irresistible, I leave the Reader to resolve. [93]

This mounting hostility would soon culminate in the last great
battle of all, a final confrontation between the Christian nations
and that Goliath of the church's enemies, Turkey:

> ... when the power of Christians shall be no way able to chase away,
> or overthrow the Gogish Armies of the East, God will suddenly as it
> were reach out his arme from Heaven to fight for the Church, and
> extinguish the adversaries: if not before, yet certainly at the bright-
> nesse of Christs coming to Iudgement ... [94]

Moreover, as Nathaniel Homes pointed out, "Which last Warre
some thinke is not far off, in regard of their great Mathematicians
wonderfull words to that end." [95] Thus events between the na-

---

[90]   *Ibid.*, p. 293.
[91]   William Strong, *The Vengeance of the Temple* (1648), pp. 8, 9.
[92]   *Ibid.*, p. 19.
[93]   Homes, *op. cit.*, p. 545.
[94]   Pareus, *Commentary*, p. 539. "The Gogish warre ... is the TURKISH WARRE
against Christendome" which had been in progress "above these five hundred yeeres",
and which was to continue until the second advent, *ibid.*, p. 558; cf. Strong, *Vengeance*, p. 26. According to Robert Maton, Gog and Magog were to be gathered against
the Elect at the end of the Millennium. The battle of Armageddon, which was to occur
before the second coming, would see a great army destroyed by the advent, Maton,
Israels Redemption, p. 109.
[95]   Homes, *op. cit.*, p. 548.

tions, as the moral decline within them, were to increase in intensity right up until the time of the advent.

A persual of the many lists of signs that appeared from the time of William Perkins onwards reveals a consistent emphasis on trends and conditions of a religious nature. Perkins himself had divided the signs into two unequal categories. The signs in the larger group were to precede the advent and lead up to it, while a few events were to be an integral part of the advent itself. Five out of six signs in the first group were of a religious nature. [96] James Ussher listed eight signs "whereby we may discern Christ approaching", six of which concerned events in the religious world, [97] while John Seagar saw nine religious signs from a total of eleven, all of which were already fulfilled or in the process of accomplishment. [98] All nine of the signs Robert Gell observed were of a religious character, [99] and although the last sign he designated suggests a lingering influence of mediaeval superstition, [100] the remainder were in complete harmony with previous enumerations. The obvious importance thus attached to these religious trends makes it desirable to see them in the light of the contemporary thought.

What Perkins had described as a "generall departing of most men from the faith", [101] was to Gell "the abounding of iniquity, with the decay of love", [102] and all who came in the years between these two great preachers saw the degeneration in the life of the church and its individual members as one of the more prominent signs of the times. This spiritual declension showed itself in a variety of ways, but in none more lamentable than in the condition of the ministry. Calamy's *Englands Looking-Glasse*, by which he endeavoured to show the nation her sins, was written in order to produce a reformation in the country. [103] Such

---

[96]   Perkins, *loc. cit.;* cf. his list in 'An Exposition of the ... Creed', in *Workes,* I, pp. 260—261; cf. Shepheard, *op. cit.,* p. 19.

[97]   Ussher, *op. cit.,* pp. 446—447.

[98]   Seagar, *op. cit.,* pp. 78—83. A further six signs remained to be fulfilled, but since these were all "dayly expected", the final day was "near at hand", *ibid.,* pp. 84—87.

[99]   Gell, *op. cit.,* p. 17.

[100]   "The sign of the Son of man in heaven, even Christ on the Crosse with his wounds in his hand and his feet, and the Angels round about him, hath appeared in Frankenland in Germany about two yeares since, in the view of thousands, three hours together at midday", *ibid.,* p. 17. The same sign, according to reports, appeared in the East Indies; Robert Gell, *Gell's Remaines* (1676), p. 446.

[101]   Perkins, 'An Exposition of the ... Creed', in *Workes,* I, p. 260.

[102]   Gell, *op. cit.,* p. 447.

[103]   Calamy, *op. cit.,* p. 45.

a reformation could be effected, partially at least, by the action of Parliament in ensuring a godly and able ministry throughout the land. [104] This thoroughly Puritan demand for a renewed ministry noted that even "the people complain of their Ministers, that they are dumb dogs, greedy dogs, which can never have enough, and that they are superstitious ..." [105] Robert Purnell, speaking perhaps for many in the pews whose souls were starved for nourishment, declared:

> The people are saying, that there is a vast difference between Christ and his Apostles, and you: For Christ and his Apostles did feed the people with true bread; and you make the people believe, you feed them with bread in their Fathers house, and you feed them with huske ... [106]

The inadequacy of the clergy had been one of the major issues in Puritanism and in church-state relations during the earlier decades of the seventeenth century, and it had produced unhealthy effects on the spirituality of the church as a whole. Thomas Goodwin, in an early sermon, spoke of "the infant times of our first Reformation," [107] and lamented:

> Spiritual preaching was then prized, men might go far to hear Sermons, and repeat them to their Families and be reverenced ... But the memory of those godly men and their ways is now worn out, and a Generation is come on that knew not those Josephs ... [108]

Thomas Hall, who held that all nineteen sins of the last days as described in II Tim. iii, 1-5 applied particularly to "those that shall live in the bosom of the true Church", [109] attacked the superficiality of many who professed Christianity. [110] With characteristic acerbity Hall referred to the "Master-sin of this last and loose age", and asked:

> When did Pride ever more abound in City and Country, in Body and Soule, in Heart, Head, Haire, Habit; In Gestures, Vestures, Words, Works? What Painting, Poudring, Patching, Spotting, and Blotting

---

[104]   *Ibid.*, p. 56.
[105]   *Ibid.*, p. 59.
[106]   Robert Purnell, *No Power but of God* (1652), p. 172; cf. his 'A Word to the Presbyterians', in *Good Tydings for Sinners, Great Ioy for Saints* (1649), p. 42.
[107]   Goodwin, 'A Sermon on Zeph. 1. 1, 2, 3', in *Works*, I, pt. III, p. 150. The sermon was preached at Cambridge in 1628, *ibid.*, To the Reader.
[108]   *Ibid.*, p. 150.
[109]   Thomas Hall, *op. cit.*, p. 15.
[110]   Cf. "was there ever such sleeping among professors as now there is? if ever wise and foolish virgins were asleepe, they seem to be in our dayes", Bridge, *op. cit.*, p. 20.

themselves? How are men loaded, and bedawbed with yellow, red, black, blew; they have more colours then the Rain-bow, and are more like Morrice-dancers, then Professors. [111]

If all this reflected an awareness of Christ's teaching that in the last days the prevalence of wickedness would result in a declining spirituality, there was also a thorough familiarity with other statements recorded in the same passage. [112] Christ had further warned that the last days would be marked by a growth of heresy and false teaching within the church. [113] This particular prediction had received notable re-emphasis by later New Testament writers, [114] and it is not surprising that it should attract wide comment now. From its very inception the church had been concerned with defending the purity of the faith [115] and the men of the seventeenth century, many of whom were alienated from the Episcopal system, nonetheless saw themselves as a part of the true church [116] and were as quick in their denunciation of "heresy" as any of their forefathers had been, and as many of their brethren in the Establishment still were. Thus one Presbyterian could say of the Anglican church "Errors and Heresies have prevailed" and "much increased of late in the Church of England", [117] while another could denounce the millenarian views of the Independent, Nathaniel Homes, as an "Epidemical error which spreads so strangely, and hath already brought forth the malignant fruit of Schisme in the church, and Sedition in the State ..." [118] The same Independent could look at the religious scene of the day and declare with equal conviction:

And for Protestant Nations, or Peoples, I am utterly astonished in my thoughts, and distressed for words to expresse their unparallelable Apostasies. The revolt among Professours in generall. Their blasphemous words against God, Christ, the Holy Ghost, the Holy Scriptures, and consequently against Salvation, Heaven, Hell, the Immortality of the Soule, and all Fundamentals are nefanda so wicked, that they are not to be mentioned ... [119]

---

[111] Thomas Hall, *op. cit.*, p. 49.
[112] Matt. xxiv and Luke xxi were important passages for all concerned with the doctrine of the second advent.
[113] See Matt. xxiv, 11 and 24.
[114] Cf. II Tim. iv, 3, 4 and II Pet. ii, 1.
[115] Cf. Acts xx, 28—30.
[116] See Nuttall, *Visible Saints*, pp. 61—69.
[117] Seagar, *op. cit.*, p. 82.
[118] Thomas Hall, *Chiliasto-mastix redivivus,* To the Reader.
[119] Homes, *op. cit.*, p. 547.

With every group and sect contending for "the truth", it was inevitable that the imputation of heresy should become common-place. Beyond this, however, there existed on the part of the more conservative elements a genuine concern at the extremes and excesses of some of the minority groups, particularly since the Bible had foretold that many would "depart from the faith" [120] in the last days. Christopher Love's soul was "troubled to consider what an inundation of hurtful doctrines and poyson-full errours" had been "preacht ... up and down throughout our Land," [121] and Thomas Hall regarded them all as a definite indi-cation that "the time is short," [122] since

> The Devill is broke loose, and now there appeare amongst us with open face; Arians, Arminians, Socinians, Anabaptists, Familists, Sepa-ratists, Mortalists, Perfectists, and (a compendium of all these in one) Quakers. [123]

Against this background of increasing decadence without and of waning spirituality within, the church was faced with a divine mandate the accomplishment of which would finally usher in the long-awaited day. Jesus had said that the end would come only when His followers had proclaimed the gospel in all the world, [124] and by a unanimous consent it was agreed that the task already had been largely accomplished. The eschatological context of this particular statement gave it an importance which could not be overlooked. William Perkins had argued that the text did not refer to a world-wide proclamation of the gospel at one time at the end of the world, but "distinctly and successiuely at seuerall times" [125] throughout history. Thus "if we consider the time since the Apostles days wee shall finde this to be true, that the Gospel hath been preached to all the world, and there-fore the first signe of Christ's coming is already past and accom-plished." [126] Since this view could appear somewhat foreign to

---

[120]   See I Tim. iv, 1.
[121]   Christopher Love, *Englands Distemper* (1645), p. 16.
[122]   Thomas Hall, *Commentary*, p. 7.
[123]   *Ibid.*, p. 8. Many, even in the seventeenth century, would have disagreed with Hall's strictures. The inclusion of 'Mortalists' here suggests that the doctrine of condi-tional immortality or 'soul-sleep' had made appreciable headway by 1658. Hall was a contemporary of Milton, but this may not have been as significant as the publication, for instance, of Richard Overton's *Man's Mortallitie* (Amsterdam, 1643). See further, Appendix II, on mortalism.
[124]   Matt. xxiv, 14.
[125]   Perkins, *op. cit.*, p. 260.
[126]   *Loc. cit.* This sign was first in the sense that it was the initial sign listed by Perkins.

the spirit of the age, which generally demanded interpretations of more immediate relevance, Perkins further noted that the proclamation of the gospel in all parts of the world was "every day more and more accomplished". [127] It may be observed that while both emphases found acceptance with later writers, the general tendency was to stress that the work would be finished in the present generation. [128]

Few indications in the religious world were as significant as this particular sign since "all nations" included the Jewish nation, whether in the general terms of Matt. xxiv, 14 or in the more specific terms of the many prophetic passages which seemed to foretell a great latter-day movement among the Jews to turn to the Christian faith. [129] This acceptance of the gospel by the Jews, either universally or on a more limited scale, was in all eyes an indispensable prelude to Christ's coming. Joseph Mede had noted the obscure prophecy in the book of Malachi concerning the return of Elijah, [130] and had seen in it a double application. As John the Baptist had appeared with a message to prepare the way of the Lord prior to the first advent, so another messenger would appear in the last days to prepare the way for the second coming. [131] In both instances Elijah's message was to be specifically directed to the Jews. Christopher Love was typical of many who looked for an "eminent and general conversion" [132] of the Jews, maintaining that it would be a sure sign that the day was "not farr off". [133] This prevalent belief in a universal conversion of the Jews was tempered by others who held that the gospel also had to be taken to the Gentile nations. Nathaniel Homes made an important statement in this respect when he pointed out that the Jews' conversion could only occur after a more thorough work among the Gentiles. [134] It was the acceptance of this argument

---

[127]   Perkins, 'A Fruitfull Dialogue', in *Workes,* III, p. 470.

[128]   Nathaniel Homes maintained that the gospel must be preached in every part of the inhabited world immediately prior to Christ's coming, Homes, *op. cit.,* p. 378.

[129]   Early proponents of a latter-day conversion of the Jews include Martin Bucer and Peter Martyr of Strassburg. The belief was carried into English thought by William Perkins, Sir Henry Finch, and Thomas Brightman and perpetuated by Richard Sibbes and Thomas Goodwin; see J. A. De Jong, *Millennial Expectations,* pp. 9, 27, 28. Eschatological expectation among the Jews, and the anticipated role of the Jewish nation in future events, are discussed in Chapter IV, 'The Kingdoms of the World and the Kingdom of God.'

[130]   "Behold, I will send you Elijah the prophet before the coming of the great and dreadful day of the Lord," Mal. iv, 5.

[131]   Mede, 'Diatribae', in *Works,* pp. 97—98.

[132]   Love, *Heavens Glory,* p. 61.

[133]   *Loc. cit.*

[134]   Homes, *op. cit.,* p. 391.

which provoked an interest in the spiritual welfare of the Gentile nations and a concern for those which as yet needed to receive the gospel message. In this context Homes wrote:

> This salvation of the all of Israel must be, when the fulness of the Gentiles shall be brought on. But we see not yet the manner, or the meanes in any forwardnesse; the Gospel is not yet promulgated to many and mighty Kingdomes of the Gentiles, in the East and West Indies, or under the Turke, Persian and Tartar; much lesse hath the matter, the coming in of the fulnesse of the Gentiles been fulfilled. [135]

If the preaching of the gospel to the Jews was to be one of the very last signs fulfilled, and if it depended in turn on a fuller evangelisation of the Gentile nations, then any evidence of the gospel's progress among the Gentiles would be welcome. The foregoing statement drew attention to two areas of the world where missionary activity was particularly significant, the New World in the West and the Old World in the East, and from both directions the news was encouraging. In 1649 Edward Winslow published *The Glorious Progress of the Gospel Amongst the Indians in New England*. The work consisted in the main of letters from John Eliot and Thomas Mayhew describing the advances made among the Indian tribes between 1646 and 1649, and also contained an appendix by I. D. (urie) [136] which referred to the preceding reports as "palpable and present acts of providence, (which) doe more then hint the approach of Jesus Christ." [137] To this he added that "the Generall consent of many judicious, and godly Divines, doth induce considering minds to beleeve, that the conversion of the Jewes is at hand." [138] This conclusion was reinforced by a current belief that the ten lost tribes of Israel were to be found in America, [139] hence "those sometimes poor, now precious Indians ... may be as the first fruits of the glorious harvest of Israels redemption". [140] On July 27 of the same year a

---

[135]   *Loc. cit.* That this was not intended as an argument for a delayed advent appears from his further statement that "the Glorious time we speake of, is not far off, but now approacheth, especially in the introduction thereunto, viz. The Call of the Jews", *ibid.*, p. 544.

[136]   On Thomas Mayhew, first missionary to the Indians, see *Dictionary of American Biography*, s.v.

[137]   John Durie, Appendix, p. 22, in Edward Winslow, *The Glorious Progress of the Gospel Amongst the Indians in New England* (1649).

[138]   *Loc. cit.*

[139]   *Ibid.*, The Epistle Dedicatory.

[140]   *Ibid.*, p. 23. Durie also wrote a preface to Thomas Thorowgood's *Iewes in America* (1650), a fuller exposition of the theory that "the Americans are Jewes", and of the hope that "the Americans may be Gospelliz'd". In 1634 William Twisse had

charter had been granted for the Corporation for Promoting the Gospel among the Indians in New England, and the years immediately following witnessed several publications similar to Winslow's *Glorious Progress*. Henry Whitfield issued *The Light appearing more and more towards the Perfect Day* (1651) and *Strength Out of Weaknesse* (1652). [141] This latter work was the first of its kind to be published directly under the auspices of the Corporation, [142] and was commended to its readers, among other reasons, since "Hereby the fullness of the Gentiles draws more neere to be accomplished, that the calling of the Jewes may be hastned". [143]

In 1650 Henry Jessey translated a little work by Caspar Sibelius, pastor of the Dutch church in Deventer, which he called *Of The Conversion of Five Thousand and Nine Hundred East-Indians in the Isle of Formosa*. It was essentially a report of the missionary work of Robert Junius, who previously had been a minister at Delft and who had spent fourteen years labouring among the people of Formosa. He had baptised personally nearly six thousand "of persons grown up in that Isle" [144] and had seen churches established in no less than twenty-nine towns. [145] All this was again interpreted in the light of the Scripture which stated "That the fulnese of the Gentiles might come in, and that so all Israel ... might be saved." [146] It seems as though there was plenty of evidence to support the view that the church's task of

---

written to Joseph Mede of his belief that the discovery of America had been withheld in the divine purpose "till this old world of ours is almost at an end", Mede, 'Epistles', in *Works*, p. 799.

[141] On Henry Whitfield, or Whitfeld, Independent minister at Winchester and formerly pastor at Gilford (Guildford), New England, see *DNB.*, s.v. Whitfeld.

[142] Henry Whitfield, *Strength Out of Weaknesse*, To the Christian Reader, sig. B2. For other similar works published by the Corporation, see British Museum Catalogue, LONDON, III, Corporation for Promoting the Gospel among the Indians in New England.

[143] *Ibid.*, To the Reader, sig. a. The significance of this recommendation lies in the fact that the Epistles were signed by six leading Presbyterians, including Edmund Calamy and William Gouge, and by twelve prominent Independent ministers, among them John Owen, Joseph Caryl and Philip Nye. Whitfield's *Strength Out of Weaknesse* is discussed by Peter Toon in 'A Puritan Missionary Appeal', *The Gospel Magazine*, January, 1969. Contrary to the indication given by Mr. Toon, the work is in both the British Museum and the Bodleian.

[144] Caspar Sibelius, *Of The Conversion of Five Thousand and Nine Hundred East-Indians in the Isle of Formosa* (tr. Henry Jessey, 1650), p. 7. The work also contains a survey of the gospel's progress among "the west-Indians in America". On Sibelius, see *The New Schaff-Herzog Encyclopedia of Religious Knowledge*, s.v. Sibel.

[145] *Ibid.*, p. 9.

[146] *Ibid.*, To the Christian Reader, sig. A2r.

preaching the gospel to all nations was now nearly accomplished. This, added to the other religious trends of the age and to the moral conditions and political events of the time, argued strongly that the Lord's coming was nigh.

If any trace of mediaeval superstition lingered in seventeenth-century theology, it may be seen in the contemporary attitudes to what might be termed extraordinary phenomena. If God spoke through His Word, and through conditions in the church and in society, and through events among the nations, He also spoke through strange occurrences in nature which could only be explained in terms of the supernatural. Had not Jesus foretold "great earthquakes" with "famines and pestilences and fearful sights and great signs" from heaven? [147] Did not Old Testament prophets speak of "wonders in the heavens and in the earth, blood and fire, and pillars of smoke", of a flying roll, of women with wings of a stork, and of chariots traversing the skies? [148] And was not the book of Revelation almost wholly written in terms of "great wonders" and "great, marvellous" signs in heaven, and full of references to fire and blood and war and death? [149] It is understandable, therefore, that Thomas Adams should describe the six "precedent signs" as "a Drumme, a Trumpet, a Famine, A Floud, a Comet, and a new Troope", [150] and why William Strong should write:

> ... as the Lord governs the world by the Sun ... and in nature doth many times cause Comets and blazing Stars as tokens of some dangerous and dismal accidents approaching in nature: so hath the Lord set forth by the Book of the Word, some signs also hat [sic] are as so many Comets to the world .... [151]

Such signs were nature's own testimony to the truth proclaimed in the Bible. Charles Hammond's *Englnads* [sic] *Alarum-Bell* of 1652 was followed later in the same year by his *A Warning-Peece for England*. This work was occasioned by a series of violent storms which had occurred in several parts of the country that summer, particularly a thunderstorm which had struck the church in Laughton, Cheshire, killing eleven people and knocking

---

[147]   Luke xxi, 11.
[148]   Joel ii, 30; Zech. v. 1, 9; vi, 1—8.
[149]   See Rev. xii, 1; xv, 1. The word "fire" appears 25 times in the book of Revelation (πυρ, 24; πυρινος), the word "blood" 19 times, (αἱμα); "war", "battle", "fight", 15 times (πολεμος, πολεμεω), and "death" and "dead" 33 times, (θανατος, 17; νεκρος, 13; πτωμα, 3).
[150]   Adams, *op. cit.*, p. 1136.
[151]   Strong, *Sermons*, p. 457.

the minister from his pulpit. [152]   Other freak storms were recorded in which houses, barns, and churches had been flooded or
burnt down and cattle killed. Hailstones had been reported as
large as eggs. [153]   Hammond further published *The Worlds Timely
Warning-piece* (1660) which described "the nearnesse of the Day
of the Lord" [154]   specifically noting the fulfilment of the many
prophecies in Math. xxiv, Luke xxi and II Tim. iii in the various
nations of Europe. [155]   "Christ told, there should be signs from
Heauen", he said, "I am sure this land, and other Nations too,
hath both seen and felt most strange sights from Heauen." [156]
This was again with reference to the storms of 1652, and also to
1653 when, at Poole in Dorset, "it rained blood", a direct fulfilment of Joel's prophecy. [157]

   No weightier accumulation of evidence of this kind could be
found than that presented in three intriguing little works which
came from the press anonymously and without any details of
publication immediately after the Restoration. The titles, in
order of appearance were Ἐνιαυτὸς Τεραστιος, *Mirabilis Annus: or
The Year of Prodigies and Wonders* (1661); *Mirabilis Annus
Secundus, or The Second Year of Prodigies* (1662), and *Mirabilis
Annus Secundus, or The Second Part of The Second Years Prodigies* (1662). [158]   The titlepage of *Mirabilis Annus* announced that
it was "a faithful and impartial Collection of several Signs" [159]
that had been observed in the Heavens, the Earth, and the
Waters, a description which applied to all three works, each of
which recorded strange occurrences that had taken place in various parts of the land between the early summer of 1660 and the
autumn of 1662. Altogether the three accounts recorded one

---

[152]   Charles Hammond, *A Warning-Peece for England* (1652), p. 3, (the second so
numbered).
[153]   *Ibid.*, p. 7.
[154]   Charles Hammond, *The Worlds Timely Warning-piece* (1660), second title-
page.
[155]   *Ibid.*, pp. 6, 7.
[156]   *Ibid.*, p. 8.
[157]   *Loc. cit.*
[158]   For a discussion of these three works see C. E. Whiting, *Studies in English
Puritanism From the Restoration to the Revolution, 1660–1688* (1931),
pp. 547–551. Dr. Whiting believed that the author shared Fifth Monarchist sympa-
thies, and suggested that Henry Jessey was closely associated with the works. Jessey's
The Lords loud Call to England (1660) did in fact report incidents which were also
recorded in *Mirabilis Annus*, although in some cases with differing detail.
[159]   But cf. the later admission that some of the accounts were exaggerated and
unauthenticated, *Mirabilis Annus Secundus, I*, Preface.

hundred and forty-six prodigies seen in the heavens, [160] seventy-five observed on the earth, twenty-six witnessed in the rivers and seas and, in addition, ninety-one remarkable accidents which had befallen various people as judgement upon their evil ways.

The *Mirabilis Annus* contained enough evidence calculated to convince even the most sceptical. On August 1st, 1660, the appearance of "a great Ship in the Air" had been seen over Stratford, near London, "which by degrees lessened till it came to be as small as a mans Arm, but kept its form all the while, and at last disappeared." [161] In October "a fiery Meteor in the form of a Ships streamer" was observed over London which "passed with a very swift motion from West to East." [162] Three moons appeared in the sky in Surrey "of equal bigness and brightness", [163] while at Hull, also in October, a group of soldiers on guard-duty "saw the Appearance of a great Body of Fire ... as big at one end as a great Sheet, from which went a narrow stream of fire". It lasted for about half an hour and then vanished. [164] Five travellers between Hertford and London on October 30th witnessed another alarming phenomenon. As they rode along,

> ... there came a sudden Flash of Fire, which made it so light, that they could perfectly discern, as at noonday, any thing upon the ground, their Horses also seemed to be all on fire; but within a little space this body of Fire rose up again into the Aire, with a Tayl about a Pole long ... [165]

These wonders in the heavens were accompanied by fearful sights on the earth and in the waters. A storm at Dover on August 4th,

---

[160] The preponderance of phenomena seen in the sky may be an unconscious indication of the influence of astrology. Charles Hammond's *Englnads* [*sic*] *Alarum-Bell* had been written after the eclipses of March, 1652, of which he wrote "I take it as the Lord's mercy, that he shews these signs in heavē to forewarn us on earth of his judgments to come", Hammond, *Englnads Alarum-Bell*, sig. A4 *r*. In 1649, when Robert Gell preached to the learned Society of Astrologers, he had asked, that since the first advent had been announced by a star, "would not our good God vouchsafe to honour Christs second coming ... with a star also?" Robert Gell, *Stella Nova, A New Starre Leading Wisemen unto Christ (1649)*, p. 24. Gell pointed out that in 1572 a star "of the greatest magnitude" had appeared in Cassiopeia which "pointed at the great wonder in Heaven, Rev. 12:1. Christ born the second time in these last dayes, according to the Spirit", *ibid.*, p. 25. In 1643, Henry Wilkinson referred members of the Commons to certain computations of Tycho Brahe and Johannes Kepler concerning planetary conjunctions which prefigured great events in 1642 and thereafter, Henry Wilkinson, *Babylons Ruine, Jerusalems Rising* (1643), pp. 23, 24.
[161] *Mirabilis Annus*, p. 2.
[162] *Ibid.*, p. 5.
[163] *Ibid.*, p. 6.
[164] *Ibid.*, p. 3.
[165] *Ibid.*, p. 8.

1660 brought hailstones "four inches about" [166] while in Leicestershire the people had been warned both by a whirlwind and an earthquake. [167]   A plague of frogs descended out of the air at Hull, [168] while at Bury St. Edmunds "an innumberable company of Spiders of a redish colour ... marched together, and in a strange kind of order" through the town until they arrived at the house of a member of the late Parliament. [169] Abnormal births were also recorded, such as of a woman in Scotland who was delivered of a "strange and dreadfull Monster" with "two heads, one upon the top of the other, the upper like the face of a lion". [170]   A double tide had occurred at London Bridge on November 2nd, [171] and at Derby the river Derwent had completely dried up. [172]

If this impressive array was not convincing enough, *Mirabilis Annus Secundus* provided further evidence which was even more specifically related to latter-day prophecy. At Boston, in Lincolnshire, between July 4th and 6th, 1661, "the Sun was very much obscured and darkened, so that even at noon the people could behold it without the least offence to their eyesight". [173] This remarkable phenomenon was repeated on a much wider scale the following week when, on the four days July 11th-14th, a darkening of the sun occurred which this time was witnessed by "hundreds of people" in several counties:

> ... particularly it was so on the 13th day, when it cast little or no shadow for a good part of the day, especially in the morning: which in Lincolnshire, Leicestershire and Essex, with many other places, was taken notice of by Hundreds of people to their great astonishment and amazement. [174]

The record then significantly added, "The Moon also the same night, in several places and more particularly in Essex, did appear as red as Blood." [175]

---

[166]   *Ibid.*, p. 39.
[167]   *Ibid.*, pp. 40, 49.
[168]   *Ibid.*, p. 41.
[169]   *Ibid.*, p. 42.
[170]   *Ibid.*, pp. 53, 54.
[171]   *Ibid.*, p. 58.
[172]   *Ibid.*, p. 59.
[173]   *Mirabilis Annus Secundus, or The Second Year of Prodigies* (1662), p. 2.
[174]   *Ibid.*, p. 4.
[175]   *Ibid.*, p. 5. The celestial signs of the advent, which were mentioned several times throughout the Bible, had been variously interpreted in both an allegorical and literal sense. Some, as John Durant, favoured the metaphorical exposition, holding that the Sun, Moon and Stars represented earthly powers which had been, or would be,

There can be little doubt concerning the accepted meaning of all these awesome portents, or concerning the purpose of their publication. The Preface to *Mirabilis Annus* said quite clearly:

> ... let every one rather from these things be convinced, that upon us the ends of the world are come, and that God is now making hast to consummate his whole work in the earth, and to prepare the way for his Son to take unto himself his great power and reign ... [176]

The prefatory comment in *Mirabilis Annus Secundus* stated even more explicitly that the prodigious events described therein were "certain Harbengers and immediate fore-runners" [177] of the second advent. In the conclusion to *Mirabilis Annus* the author recommended "to the Readers most diligent perusal" a sermon by Luther on Luke xxi, 25, 26 dealing with the signs of Christ's coming, with the remark that "what this Famous and Eminent Light of the Church did Declare and Teach so long agoe, is exactly calculated for this Year of Prodigies and Wonders". [178] The sermon had been published in English that very year and those who read it were reminded of what the great Reformer had said of the last days:

> We see the Sun to be darkened and the Moon, the Stars to fall, men to be distressed, the winds and waters to make a noise, and whatever else is foretold of the Lord, all of them to come to pass as it were together. Besides, we have seen not a few Comets, having the form of the Cross, imprinted from heaven, both on the bodies and garments of men, new kinds of diseases, as the French Pox, and some others. How many other Signs also, and unusual impressions, have we seen in the Heavens, in the Sun, Moon, Stars, Rain-bows and strange Apparitions, in these last four years? Let us at least acknowledge these to be Signs, and Signs of some great and notable change ... [179]

---

eclipsed prior to the advent, cf. *supra*, p. 101. In this sense Richard Mercer believed that the Sun and Moon had been darkened during the time of Antichrist's rule, the Sun being the Spirit of God, the Moon symbolising the ordinances of the Church, and the Stars representing "eminent Saints", Richard Mercer, *A further Discovery of the Mystery of the last times* (1651), p. 13. The more general view, however, was that the signs in the Sun, Moon, and Stars would be fulfilled in a literal manner, although not all were agreed as to the precise time. Christopher Love followed William Perkins in saying that these signs would occur as an integral part of the advent itself, cf. Love, *Heavens Glory*, pp. 36–37, and Perkins 'A Fruitful Dialogue', in *Workes*, III, p. 470. Alexander Petrie and John Seagar looked for a literal fulfilment in the last days, Petrie, *Chiliasto-mastix*, p. 12, Seagar, *World to Come*, p. 86. Nathaniel Homes took the safe view and suggested that fulfilment would be in both a literal and allegorical manner, immediately after the reign of Antichrist, Homes, *Ten Exercitations*, pp. 289, 290.

[176]   *Mirabilis Annus*, Pref., sig. A4v.
[177]   *Mirabilis Annus Secundus, I*, Pref., sig. A3v.
[178]   *Mirabilis Annus*, p. 88.
[179]   [Luther], *The Signs of Christ's coming*, p. 14.

After a further one hundred and forty years, could diligent and sincere students of the Word come to any other conclusion?

While the foregoing circumstances argued strongly that men were now living at the end of time, they did not precisely specify the time of the end. That could be deduced only from a meticulous examination of the prophetic time periods which were to be found in the visions of Daniel and The Revelation and whose calculation was an intrinsic element of the historicist interpretation. The 1260 year period of both prophets, the 1290 and 1335 year times of Daniel and, to a lesser extent, the 2300 year period of Daniel, [180] and the mysterious number 666 spoken of by John were all variously calculated to terminate within the foreseeable future. While some commentators did not feel it necessary to defend such computations of the world's end, a majority would clearly have agreed with the argument which appeared at the beginning of Samuel Hartlib's translation *Clavis Apocalyptica* and which was repeated almost verbatim by William Hicks in his *Revelation Revealed*. The *Clavis* affirmed that God's dealings with his people in the past had been based on specific and stated periods of time. The 120 years prior to the Flood, the Israelitish bondage of 400 years in Egypt, the 70 years of the captivity in Babylon, and the 490 years of Daniel's ninth chapter were all cited as illustrations of the point in question. [181] Since all these periods had been literally and accurately fulfilled, the inference was plain enough:

> In like manner there is a certain time set, and determined upon the Church of God in the New Testament, how long shee shall bee subject and exposed to persecution, and when shee shall bee delivered from it, as it doth appear by the Prophet Daniel, and by the Revelation of St. Iohn. [182]

In similar vein Nathaniel Homes suggested that the expiry of the 1260 and 1290 year periods would "immediately precede" the coming of Christ. [183]

Among the earlier prophetic expositors there was a noticeable

---

[180] All calculated according to the day-year principle.

[181] Samuel Hartlib (tr.), *Clavis Apocalyptica*, pp. 1–3.

[182] *Ibid.*, p. 3; cf. Hicks, *The Revelation Revealed*, Pref., sig. b4v.

[183] Homes, *Resurrection*, p. 544; cf. his later statement in the rare *Miscellanea* (1666) "Scripture ... calculates the second and visible coming of Christ, by Time, and Times, and half or part of a time, Dan. 12 and Rev. 12. And by 1260 Daies with addition of 45 years more, Dan. 12. And by 1290 Daies with addition of so many years as wherein the deadly wound of Antichrist was given, and healed ...", which indicates a continuing confidence in the credibility of time prophecy, Homes, *Miscellanea*, p. 2.

reluctance to fix the date of the last day much before the end of the seventeenth century. John Napier, whose *Plaine Discouery* attracted attention for over fifty years, had not initially expected the day of judgement for another hundred years or so. Taking the 1335 years of Daniel xii, 12, Napier commenced his calculation from the time of Julian the Apostate in 363 A.D., [184] thus arriving at a final date of 1700 A.D. Further light came from the prophecy in Revelation xiv of the Seven Angels, the fulfilment of which had commenced in 1541. [185] Each of the first three angels prefigured a "Jubilee" period of 49 years, the third thus reaching to 1688. But since the last four were to be accomplished simultaneously at the very last, Napier concluded "Wherefore, appearinglie betwixt this 1688. yeare, according to the Reuelation, and the 1700 yeare, according to Daniel, the said latter day should fall." [186]

Thomas Brightman took the 1260 year period as a basis for his calculations and his work aptly illustrates the ease with which an arbitrary interpretation could be imposed on unfulfilled prophecy. It appears that the 1260 days, or 42 months, had a double application in Brightman's chronology. In the first place the period as mentioned in Rev. xi and xii, which related to the two witnesses prophesying in sackcloth and the woman fleeing into the wilderness, referred to the time when the true church was in hiding during the long ages of Antichristian domination. [187] This time had begun with Constantine in 304 A.D., but since it was to be reckoned in Julian time, or 1242 actual years, it had ended in 1546. [188] This coincided with the Council of Trent, and also with the beginning of the Laodicean church, the seventh and last in the opening prophecy of The Revelation which depicted the progressive history of the entire church, Laodicea representing its last age, of renewal, prior to the end. Laodicea was the Church of England, and her time had begun in 1547. [189] Brightman's application of the 1260 years as it appeared in Revelation xiii, related it to the time of Papal supremacy, which had also commenced with Constantine "about the yeare 300". [190] The 1260 years

---

[184] Napier, *Plaine Discouery,* p. 20. Julian fulfilled Christ's prophecy of the "abomination of desolation", Matt. xxiv, 15.

[185] *Ibid.,* p. 15.

[186] *Ibid.,* p. 21.

[187] Brightman, *Revelation,* pp. 358, 407.

[188] *Ibid.,* pp. 370, 371.

[189] *Ibid.,* p. 126.

[190] *Ibid.,* p. 451. In actual calculation, from 304 A.D., as before.

cannot here be reckoned continuously, however, and do not end simultaneously with the end of the church's "trial" in 1546, since the time to be allowed for the beast's wounding cannot be counted as belonging to the time of his supremacy. Since the "wound" lasted for the duration of the Goth's kingdom, or approximately 140 years, an allowance for this number of years must be made when calculating the 1260 years in order to reach a true date for the time of the beast's ultimate overthrow. Thus "the last ende of Antichrist shall expire at the yeare 1686, or thereabouts". [191]

In addition to this, Brightman applied the time periods of Daniel xii to latter-day events concerning Turkey and the Jews. The "time, times and a half" of v. 7 were parallel to the 395 day-years of Rev. ix, 15, which had commenced in 1300 A.D., and would therefore terminate in 1650 when he expected the conversion of the Jews to take place. [192] This was amplified by the 1290 years of v. 11 which had begun in 360 A.D. and therefore also terminated in 1650. [193] The 1335 years of v. 12 began at the same time, 360 A.D., and would thus expire in 1695 "or about the yeer 1700". [194] The forty-five years between 1650 and 1695 would see the conversion of many Jews and a revival of their nation in Palestine, the final overthrow of the fourth Empire and the destruction of the Papacy, the decline and dissolution of the Turkish power, all of which would culminate in "the marriage of the Lamb and his wife." [195]

Brightman thus made a significant contribution to prophetic dating in emphasising that the 1290 years and the 1335 years were related and that great things could be expected soon after 1650. There was, nevertheless, an essential agreement between Napier and Brightman that the last day would not occur before the end of the century, and an objective assessment of mid-seventeenth-century eschatology must overlook neither the early date at which such calculations were propounded in English theology nor the lasting influence of these early expositors on later thought. Sir Henry Finch, whose *Worlds Great Restavration, or The Calling of The Iewes* (1621) gives evidence of an awakening

---

[191]   *Ibid.*, p. 452; again reckoned in Julian time.
[192]   Thomas Brightman, 'Exposition ... of the Prophecie of Daniel' (1614), in *The Workes of That Famous, Reverend, and Learned Divine, Mr. Tho: Brightman* (1644), p. 954.
[193]   *Ibid.*, p. 967 (the first so numbered).
[194]   Brightman, 'A Commentary on the Canticles', in *Workes*, p. 1065.
[195]   Brightman, *Workes*, p. 967.

interest in the Jewish question, followed Brightman's chronology completely, predicting that 1650 would turn out to be "the time of the first conversion of the Jews", and that 1695 would see the final overthrow of the Turks. [196]

If the time of the end was to be accurately computed by any of these prophetic periods, it was clearly essential that reliable starting dates should be established from which the calculations could proceed. Joseph Mede perceived that any date subjectively suggested would be open to suspicion and argued, with reference to the 1260 year period, that there had to be a notable event from which to commence the reckoning. [197] The period related to the time of Antichrist's rule and Mede argued that the calculation should begin from the time when he first began to appear in the world, and when the Empire first began to fall. [198] The three significant events which in Mede's thinking characterised the decline of pagan Rome and the rise of the man of sin, were the death of Julian in 365 A.D., the sack of Rome by Alaric in 410 A.D., and the death of Valentinian in 455 A.D. [199] The caution which characterises all of Mede's exegesis led him to say:

> From which of these Three Beginnings of the Apostatical Times, or whether from some moment within or between them, the Almighty will reckon that his Computation of these ὑστεροικαιροι which ended shall finish the days of the Man of Sin, I curiously enquire not, but leave unto him who is Lord of times and seasons. [200]

It was quite obvious, however, that if the 1260 years began "between the years 365 and 455, they must end between the years 1625 and 1715", [201] and although Mede himself "refused precisely to determine the year of their ending", [202] others with less discretion were to follow him. Mede's academic prowess gave credibility to the dates he had suggested, and also encouraged subsequent scholars of varying repute to advance further dates from which the times could be calculated. Consequently, when restrictions on the press, which had been particularly stringent under Laud's administration, were lifted after 1640, there soon appeared, in addition to reprints of all the works cited above, a

196   Finch, *Great Restavration*, pp. 59, 60.
197   Mede, 'Remaines on some Passages in the Apocalypse', in *Works*, p. 600.
198   *Ibid.*, pp. 654, 655.
199   *Ibid.*, pp. 659, 660.
200   *Ibid.*, p. 662.
201   *Ibid.*, p. 600.
202   *Loc. cit.*

flood of new interpretations, many of which brought the time of the end appreciably nearer.

Thomas Goodwin's 'Exposition Upon the Revelation' displayed, with one notable addition, a general identity with these earlier views. Goodwin was probably influenced by Brightman in his attempt to place a double application on the 1260 year period, [203] although in extending the same principle to the 1290 years, he clearly went beyond the earlier expositor. Goodwin felt that the 1260 years could have begun, either with the removal of the Emperor to Constantinople, for which he gave no precise date, or with the final break-up of the Western Empire which he put at 406/410 A.D. This would mean that the time had already ended between 1550 and 1560, [204] or that it would end around 1666/70. [205] Similarly, the 1290 years had commenced in 69/70 A.D. with the fall of Jerusalem, or in 363 at the death of Julian, thus terminating either with Wycliffe in 1359/60, or in 1653/56. [206] The 1335 years, whose beginning coincided with that of the 1290 years, were therefore to end in 1690/1700. [207] In all these calculations Goodwin's disinclination to be rigidly specific in dating is as apparent as his insistence on the earlier view that the last day would not occur before the close of the century. [208]

Goodwin's real contribution to the development of prophetic dating is his introduction of 1666 as a year of special significance. To Goodwin, the 1260 year period was the main era of prophetic time [209] and in spite of his suggestion that two applications of the period were possible, it is quite clear that he regarded it chiefly as relating to the time of the two Antichristian beasts

---

[203]   See Goodwin, 'Revelation', in *Works*, II, pt. I, p. 147.

[204]   Events in Germany in 1550 and in England and Scotland in 1560 were seen to indicate an end to papal supremacy. By this computation, however, a date of around 300 A.D. would be required for the transfer of the empire's capital to Constantinople. The impossibility of such an early date may denote why Goodwin does not mention one, and also why he preferred the alternative method of computation.

[205]   Goodwin, *op. cit.*, p. 148.

[206]   *Ibid.*, pp. 147, 148.

[207]   *Ibid.*, p. 184.

[208]   The idea of a last day near the end of the century was perpetuated by other writers after 1640. Alsted arrived at 1694, and Ephraim Huit suggested 1695, see Johan Heinrich Alsted, *The Beloved City* (tr. William Burton, 1643), p. 13; Huit, *Daniel*, p. 356. Even Mary Cary, the militant Fifth Monarchist author, did not anticipate that the millennium would begin before 1701; Mary Cary, *Little Horn*, p. 209. On Alsted, professor of philosophy and theology at Herborn and Weissenberg, see *Encyclopaedia Britannica*, I, p. 704.

[209]   Goodwin, *op. cit.*, p. 184.

of Rev. xiii,[210] and particularly to the ending of Antichristian rule in the church.[211] Since the mysterious number of 666 of verse 8 actually stood for 1666, "the Time or Term of his ending",[212] it was only necessary to count back 1260 years to locate the date of his beginning at 406 A.D.[213] Needless to say, Goodwin could find many events of historical importance which confirmed that the Papacy had indeed risen to power[214] "not long after the Year of Christ, 400"[215] or "about an hundred Years after the beginning of Constantine's Reign".[216] Even though many were to be attracted to 1666 as a year of great portent, it was still but one of a bewildering number of dates and calculations which became available to keen students of prophetic chronology, and Jeremiah Burroughes' expectation that the 1260 years would end "in this century that is now currant",[217] is only to be noted for its restraint.

John Cotton, who for some months in 1639-40 lectured every week to his Boston congregation upon the book of Revelation, and whose *Exposition Upon The thirteenth Chapter of the Revelation* was printed in 1655 by Livewel Chapman, cautiously suggested 395 A.D. as a more likely date from which to number the 1260 years. In that year, he maintained, the Bishop of Rome had assumed the discarded Imperial title "Pontifex Maximus",[218] and although due allowance had to be made for a gradual fulfilment of prophecy and for the uncertainty of some historical dates,[219] yet,

---

[210] *Ibid.*, p. 63.
[211] The 1260 years will end with the final outpouring of the Fifth Vial on Rome and other places of papal influence, "yet Antichrist's 42 Months are not expired, we being now but under the fifth Vial", *ibid.*, p. 145.
[212] *Ibid.*, p. 67.
[213] *Ibid.*, pp. 68, 69.
[214] Events cited were, the beginning of the Goth's kingdom in 410, the coming of the Huns in 412, the succession of Innocent In 404/6, and the excommunication of the Eastern Emperor, Arcadius, in 407. Apart from the fact that the accuracy of many of these dates was open to question, none of them unequivocally established the importance of 406, which still depended entirely on the strength of a retrocessive count from the number of the beast. Possibly for this reason, Goodwin was virtually alone in holding to 406 as a starting date for any of the prophetic periods.
[215] Goodwin, *op. cit.*, p. 115.
[216] *Ibid.*, p. 61.
[217] Jeremiah Burroughes, *An Exposition of The Prophesie of Hosea* (1643), p. 749.
[218] Cotton, *Revelation*, p. 92.
[219] *Ibid.*, p. 94.

... so far as God helps by Scripture light, about the time 1655, there will be then such a blow given to this beast, and to the head of this beast, which is Pontifex maximus, as that we should see a further gradual accomplishment and fulfilling of this prophecy here. [220]

The author whose work Samuel Hartlib translated as *Clavis Apocalyptica* in 1651, held that both the 1260 and 1290 year periods would end in 1655, [221] making that year particularly auspicious because with it would expire both the six thousandth year since Creation, [222] and a period of time identical to that which had elapsed between Creation and the Flood: [223]

> Seeing the mystical numbers, which are expressed in the Prophet Daniel, and in the Revelation of St. John; the six thousand years, since the Creation of the world, and also the period since the beginning of the world until the Flood to meet with the ending of the one thousand six hundred fiftie fifth year of our Lord, which draweth neer : It is very likelie that for certain, som great things are at the door, and that wee may look for fearful and terrible revolutions. [224]

Edmund Hall arrived at the year 1650 on the basis of another commencement date for the 1260 day-years. Although he agreed that the period related to Antichrist, yet the essence of the Antichristian power was the spirit of Independency, which "the Bishop of Rome began to put in practice about the year 390". [225] Since the Two Witnesses of Rev. xi, "a lawful Magistracy and a lawful Ministry", [226] were to rise again at the close of Antichristian tyranny, their restoration could be anticipated "in the end of this year 1650" [227] or, at the most, "within twelve moneths" [228] of that time.

Only Thomas Parker allowed for the possibility of an earlier end by tentatively suggesting that all the major time periods might terminate in 1649. Nobody had previously advocated a common conclusion to so many of the chronological prophecies, but since the 1260 years and the 1290 years were to end together, [229] and since the 490 years were to end with the 1260

---

[220]   *Ibid.*, p. 93.
[221]   Hartlib, *op. cit.*, pp. 25—26.
[222]   *Ibid.*, p. 26.
[223]   *Ibid.*, p. 34.
[224]   *Ibid.*, pp. 35—36.
[225]   Edmund Hall, *Manus Testium movens*, p. 69.
[226]   *Ibid.*, p. 11.
[227]   *Loc. cit.*
[228]   *Ibid.*, p. 12.
[229]   Thomas Parker, *Daniel*, p. 133.

years, [230] it was apparent that the periods were inter-related and that the key to all lay in Daniel's 70 weeks. Parker recognised that the meaning of this particular prophecy had "been long sought, by sundry pious and learned Divines, and for many hundred yeers." [231] He also saw that any interpretation must admit that, according to the text, the overall period fell into three sections, of 7 weeks or 49 years, of 62 weeks or 434 years, and of 1 final week of 7 years. [232] But contrary to the judgement of most, Parker contended that the 70 weeks were to be placed at the end of Christian history. [233] The difficulty, as always, lay in establishing the true date at which the time had commenced, and Parker appeared to favour 1160 A.D. when the Word had begun to go forth with the Waldenses. [234] The first 49 years thus ended in 1209, the 434 years in 1643, and therefore the

> ... last & doleful week will begin precisely in 1643, and the midst of the said week will be in 1646; from which yeer the three days and half of last affliction will run down to be fully ended in the yeer 1649. Proportionately, if the One thousand two hundred and sixty yeers of the reign of Antichrist begin from the yeer 390 ... then they will precisely expire also in the said yeer 1649, and so will end together with the Seventy weeks or Four hundred and ninety yeers. [235]

Parker also contrived to make other prophetic times synchronise with 1649. The 2,300 "evening mornings" of Dan. viii, 14 were really 575 literal years because "in Scripture use, there is a morning and evening for the day time, and a morning and evening for the night time." [236] These 575 years were to be calculated from Hildebrand in 1075, which date marked the beginning of the absolute reign of Antichrist. [237] The 390 years of Rev. ix, 15, which related to the Turkish Empire, had commenced in 1260 [238] and would therefore also end in 1649, and Parker summarised his chronology with this table:

[230]   *Ibid.*, p. 62.

[231]   *Ibid.*, p. 50.

[232]   Cf. Mede, 'Daniel's Weeks', in *Works*, pp. 700—706, and Huit, *Daniel*, p. 265.

[233]   Thomas Parker, *op. cit.*, pp. 50—54.

[234]   *Ibid.*, p. 57. The text indicated that the period was to be reckoned from the issuing of a 'commandment' to restore Jerusalem, see Dan. ix, 25. Parker held that the original for 'commandment' was better translated as 'word', and that the restoring of Jerusalem applied to the 'restauration of the Spiritual Jerusalem, the Church of Christ, from the Babylon and servitude of Antichrist', *ibid.*, pp. 53, 57.

[235]   *Ibid.*, p. 64.

[236]   *Ibid.*, p. 138.

[237]   *Loc. cit.*

[238]   The hour and the day of the prophecy were seen to have applied to 1258 and 1259 respectively, thus leaving the 'round number' of the month and the year, or 390 literal years, to be counted from 1260, *ibid.*, p. 139.

1290)		(360)		
1260)	Beginning at	(390)	do end	
490)	the year	(1160)	together in	1649. [239]
575)		(1075)	the year	
390)		(1260)		

The belief that an analogy existed between the antediluvian age and the Christian era had appeared early in English Protestant thought, [240] and it is not a matter for surprise that it should recur as the expected time drew near. One thousand six hundred and fifty six years were widely held to have elapsed between Adam and the Flood, and as late as 1660 Charles Hammond availed himself of this argument, maintaining that in a similar manner the time from Christ's first coming to the day of judgement was "near 1656" years. [241] Robert Gell, in 1655, could afford to be a little more precise, "I conceive it worth your observation", he advised the Lord Mayor of London and the Worshipful Company of Drapers, "That just so many years were from the first Adam to the flood of Noah, 1656", hence "many believe that the next year will bring with it a notable change in the world, yea; many place the end of the world in that year". [242] Alternatively others found "the same Chronographical number of years, 1657. in these words MUnDI ConfLagratIo … . Surely these Synchronismes and periods of time are not to be neglected." [243] Nathaniel Homes, who in 1641 could not decide which of three possible interpretations of the 1260 years he should follow, [244] had by 1653 reached more definite conclusions. The 1290 years had begun in 367 A.D., [245] and would thus have run their course by 1657, although rather than the world being consumed by fire at that time, it would have come to the very threshold of its millennial glory. The 1260 years, starting in

---

[239]   *Ibid.*, p. 138. Parker also advanced an alternative system of chronological reckoning which anticipated an end to the same periods in 1859. This depended on the 490 years commencing from Wycliffe, in 1370, *ibid.*, pp. 59, 141. The 390 years cannot, however, be harmonised with this method of reckoning, p. 141, and since the saints are now 'to be stirred up to watchfulnesse, because the time of the end is known', p. 129, it appears that he favours the contemporaneous reckoning. Nathaniel Homes in 1653 did not like the suggestion of a last day so far removed as 1859, Homes, *Resurrection*, p. 560.
[240]   See *supra*, pp. 19 ff.
[241]   Hammond, *The Worlds Timely Warning-Piece*, p. 5.
[242]   Gell, *Noahs Flood*, p. 17.
[243]   *Loc. cit.*
[244]   Nathaniel Homes, *The New World, or the New Reformed Church* (1641), pp. 35–37.
[245]   Homes, *Resurrection*, p. 544.

410 A.D., would thus expire in 1670 [246] and these two computations formed the basis of his assessment "touching the time, when this future Glorious state of the Church on Earth ... shall begin." [247]

1670, of course, was not at all far removed from the fascinating 1666 which had attracted Goodwin and, as Edward Haughton demonstrated, the two could easily be linked if considered in relationship to the 1260 years. Although Haughton was confident that "no man alive (without extraordinary Revelation)" [248] could postulate "to a day" the commencement of the time, he nonetheless favoured 410 A.D., as the most acceptable date. [249] The destruction of Rome, however, would probably occur three or four years before 1670, since the number six hundred, threescore and six was to be understood as pointing to the final overthrow of Antichrist in 1666. [250] In 1660 another writer reached the same conclusion by arguing that four years had somehow been lost in the reckoning of time. [251] And so, if in the event, nothing remarkable had occurred in 1649 or 1650, or in 1655 or 1656 or 1657, 1666 "draws on apace" as George Wither said, [252] and remained a focal point of prophetic chronology. Wither continued:

> Seven Numerals the Roman Empire had,
> By which of old they Computations made;
> And in them was their Destiny foreshewn,
> Tho to themselves perhaps it was unknown.
> These placed single, as they valu'd are,
> Do truly, thô mysteriously, declare,
> How long that Empire, with what sprung therefrom,
> Should last, when to the full height it was come.
> For M D.C L X, with V and I,

---

[246]   *Loc. cit.*

[247]   *Ibid.*, p. 543. Homes later appears to have adopted Brightman's idea that the calculation of the 1260 years must allow for an additional 140 years, thus indicating a terminal date in the middle of the eighteenth century, Homes, *Ten Exercitations*, pp. 177, 178.

[248]   Edward Haughton, *The Rise, Growth and Fall of Antichrist: Together with The Reign of Christ* (1652), p. 108. On Haughton, see *Alumni Oxonienses* (Oxford, 1891), s.v. Houghton.

[249]   *Ibid.*, p. 110.

[250]   *Ibid.*, p. 111.

[251]   I. F., *A Sober Inquiry*, p. 19.

[252]   George Wither, 'George Withers his Prophesie, of the Downfall of Antichrist' (1660), in *A Collection of Many Wonderful Prophesies Relating to the English Nation* (1691), p. 25.

> Do number up, in Chronogrammistry,
> Years sixteen hundred sixty six, and that
> Will be of Roman Tyrannies the Date. [253]

In the unlikely event that 1666 should also pass without issue, men could still look with hope, as Napier, Brightman, Mede and Goodwin had done, to the end of the century, to 1694, 1695, or 1700 or even later. [254] Indeed, as Wither himself pointed out, the sixteen hundred and sixty six years were to be numbered from the date of the crucifixion, [255] and hence:

> And he who knows on what day it begun,
> May know the day on which it will be done;
> Which I believe will visibly appear,
> In or about the Seventeen-hundredth Year. [256]

Within the perspective of history 1700 was still near enough to give meaning to all the prevalent conditions in the church and in the world, and if men were somewhat divided as to the precise time of the end, they were singularly united in believing, as the Apostles and the Reformers had also believed, that theirs was the last age and that it heralded the consummation of history.

---

[253] *Ibid.*, p. 27.

[254] A fascinating and intricate synthesis of many mid-century views of prophetic dating appeared anonymously in 1653 with the title *Clavis Apocalyptica Ad Incudem Revocata; Vel Clavis Recusa*, bearing the imprimatur of Joseph Caryl and Henry Jessey and the recommendations of Jeremiah Whitaker and William Strong. The chronology was based on the understanding that the time, times and dividing of times, the three days and a half, the 42 months, and the 1260 days, all referred to one period of time, which had commenced in 442 A.D. Thus the 'time', or one day, equalled 360 literal years which reached down to 802 A.D. when Charlemagne had issued new laws favouring papal interests. The 'times', or two days, continued a further 720 years or to 1522 which marked the first year of Antichrist's decline, 'Hic primus est annus senectutis Antichristi'. The remaining 'half a time', or 180 years, contained five of Revelation's seven vials, each of 36 years' duration. The fifth vial would thus commence in 1666, and the prophetic times would be brought to a harmonious conclusion in 1702. Since the final 60 years of the period were the most important, relating to the fall of the ten-horned beast, it was only logical to apply 6 years to each of the ten horns, the first applying in 1642 with the outbreak of the Civil War. After the termination of the times in 1702, the last two vials still remained to be outpoured, and since they were of 30 and 45 years' duration respectively, they would conveniently extend to 1777. Thus 1666, 'numerus bestiae', is contrasted with 1777, 'numerus ecclesiae', at which time the church's glory will commence. Despite a fair amount of subjective reasoning, this rare little work displays an honest attempt to come to grips with the problems of prophetic chronology, even at the cost of postponing the last day for another century and a quarter.

[255] Wither, *op. cit.*, p. 28.

[256] *Ibid.*, pp. 29–30.

CHAPTER FOUR

THE KINGDOMS OF THE WORLD
AND THE KINGDOM OF GOD

If the doctrine of God's sovereignty was of any practical consequence in the theology of the seventeenth century, it was when
argued to its logical conclusion. Dr. E. F. Kevan's remark that the
Puritans "could never insist too much on the fact that God was
the Sovereign of all He had made, with the right to govern all
things according to His will",[1] is equally true of many who,
strictly speaking, were outside the ranks of Puritanism.[2] God, the
ultimate ruler of heaven and earth, must ultimately rule in His
kingdom. The present reign of sin must give way to a future reign
of righteousness. The New Testament portrayed Christ, not only
as Redeemer and Priest but also as Lord and King,[3] and although, as Thomas Goodwin quaintly observed, He had had "but
little takings of the world yet",[4] the time must come in the
divine purpose when the earth again would be subject to her
rightful master. "The world was made for him, and he will have it
afore he hath done,"[5] Goodwin declared. Christ had taught the
church to pray "Thy Kingdom come", and the church in seventeenth-century England looked forward to such time when He
would assert His prerogative, assume the divine right to rule, and
realise the hopes engendered by the biblical assurance that the
Kingdoms of earth would at last "become the kingdoms of our
Lord, and of his Christ."[6]

Anticipation of this kingdom was therefore founded on a confidence in the final success of the divine purpose. It is just here
that the "Essential Kingdom"[7] of John Seagar can be equated

---

[1] E. F. Kevan, *The Grace of Law* (1964), p. 47.

[2] The term Puritanism is used here in the sense in which Dr. Kevan himself initially
applies it to the 'ecclesiastical movement' for reform of the Church of England. It may
also properly be applied to that larger group 'both within and without the Anglican
fold', whose chief concern was for purity of doctrine and holiness of life, Kevan, *op.
cit.*, pp. 17—19.

[3] Cf. I Tim. vi, 14, 15; Matt. xxv, 31—46; Rev. xix, 11—16.

[4] Goodwin, 'An Exposition ... of ... Ephesians', in *Works*, I, pt. I, p. 455.

[5] *Loc. cit.*

[6] Rev. xi, 15.

[7] Seagar, *World to Come*, p. 132.

with the "Providentiall" kingdom[8] of John Archer, the ardent
millenarian. The irreconcilable difference between their concepts
of the final kingdom-state[9] must not be allowed to hide the fact
that both sprang from an acceptance of the supreme rulership of
God, and from an implicit faith in its ultimate triumph. The
contexts of both these definitions indicate that the anticipated
kingdom was not an isolated phenomenon at the end of time,
unrelated to the previous course of Christian history. Seagar's
"Essential Kingdom", which is the basis of a three-fold designa-
tion of the divine supremacy, is that absolute authority over all
creation which Christ shares co-equally in the Trinity,[10] and
which gives rise to His own unique sovereignty in the world. The
"Personal-Divine kingdom" is the spiritual rule established by
Christ at His first coming, which extends over the entire "Militant Church"[11] until the end of the present order, when it will
become the "Personal-Humane Kingdom" in which Christ will
rule bodily, visibly and eternally in a newly created world.[12]
Archer agrees with this basic concept of one kingdom in three
phases. His "Providentiall kingdom" is the divine authority over
all the world since creation vested in Christ,[13] and similarly followed by the "spirituall" and "Monarchicall" phases of His rule.
The lordship of Jesus over His own people now is to be followed
by a literal rule over the world in a future kingdom.[14] Thus,
while Archer's "Monarchicall" kingdom differs from Seagar's
"Personal-Humane Kingdom" in respect of both time and place,
in both views the eschatological aspect of the kingdom is the

---

[8] John Archer, *The Personall Reigne of Christ vpon Earth* (1642), p. 1. The incorrect 'Henry Archer' on the title-page of some 1642 editions accounts for the persis-
tence of this mistaken attribution, e.g. W. T. Whitley, *A Baptist Bibliography*, I, pp. 12,
211. Despite correction by later scholarship as in Haller, *Rise of Puritanism*, p. 270 and
Nuttall, *Visible Saints*, p. 148, more recent studies have continued with the incorrect
'Henry', e.g. P. G. Rogers, *The Fifth Monarchy Men*, p. 11, and J. A. De Jong, *Millennial Expectations*, p. 36. The original work appeared early in 1642, which accounts for
the date 1641 given by some authorities. On Archer, sometime lecturer at All Hallows,
Lombard Street, and previously pastor of the Independent Church at Arnhem, see
Georgius Hornius, *Historia Ecclesiastica et Politica* (1665), p. 331. Archer is not to be
confused with John Aucher, rector of All Hallows from 1663; nor is there ground for
classifying him as a Fifth Monarchist, e.g. Whitley, *op. cit.*, p. 238.
[9] Cf. Archer's 'Monarchicall' and 'Visible Kingdom' for a thousand years, with
Seagar's eternal 'new Heavens and new Earth', Archer, *op. cit.*, pp. 8, 38; Seagar, *op.
cit.*, pp. 58—71.
[10] Seagar, *op. cit.*, p. 132.
[11] *Ibid.*, p. 133.
[12] *Ibid.*, p. 134.
[13] Archer, *op. cit.*, p. 1.
[14] *Ibid.*, pp. 2—3.

logical culmination of Divine purpose, a process which, since the
dawn of time and more particularly since the beginning of Christian history, has been moving inexorably towards maturity.

Such reasoning argued strongly for the inevitability of the
final, visible phase of the kingdom, a conclusion which was further strengthened by the less involved kingdom concepts of other
writers. Joseph Mede believed simply that the kingdom, which he
identified with the church, [15] possessed a "Two-fold state". [16]
The church "militant" had been established at the first coming of
Christ while the church "triumphant" would be inaugurated at
His second coming. [17] Thomas Goodwin's view stemmed from an
interpretation of Daniel's vision of the stone which, he said, referred to the establishment of Christ's kingdom on earth by the
succesful preaching of the gospel in the time of the fourth world
empire. [18] The eschatological phase of this kingdom, "the world
to come", would be achieved by a transformation of the present
order. "We are but working up still to a purer world", [19] Goodwin
asserted, and explained, "Jesus Christ will never rest till he hath
not only thrown out all the dross of this world, both in Doctrine
and worship ... he will never rest till he hath brought all the
world (that is, the generality of men) to be subject to him." [20]
Nathaniel Homes also saw the kingdom in two phases. [21] Taking
his position again from Daniel's vision, Homes argued that the
kingdom of the stone represented the first stage from the found-
ing of the church to the end of the world, [22] while the kingdom
of the mountain [23] depicted the divine kingdom as it would exist
after the final overthrow of the fourth empire. [24] There is in all
these views an essential agreement with Thomas Hayne who, in
arguing against any form of latter-day millennial reign nevertheless says, "the great and famous Kingdome of Christ, that mentioned in Dan. 2. 44 & Dan. 7.13 & Psal. 2. hath already long
since begun, now is, and ever will continue ..." [25] Even Thomas

[15] Mede, 'Diatribae', in *Works*, p. 103.
[16] *Ibid.*, p. 104.
[17] *Loc. cit.*
[18] Thomas Goodwin, 'Ephesians', in *Works*, I, pt. I, p. 454.
[19] *Loc. cit.*
[20] *Ibid.*, p. 455.
[21] Homes, *Resurrection*, p. 186.
[22] *Ibid.*, pp. 236, 237.
[23] "and the stone that smote the image became a great mountain, and filled the
whole earth", Dan. ii, 35.
[24] Homes, *loc. cit.*
[25] Hayne, *Christs Kingdom*, p. 3.

Hall, who so violently opposed the "Epidemical error" of millenarianism, looked for a kingdom over which the supremacy of
Christ would eternally be established. [26]

The significance of Mede's *Clavis Apocalyptica*, or of Archer's
Personall Reigne, or of Goodwin's or Homes' expositions on Revelation or, indeed, of any of the more scholarly interpretations of
prophecy, is that they see all history moving towards the ultimate realisation of the kingdom of God. [27] When they speak of
the kingdom in an eschatological sense they speak of the reasoned culmination of an age-long development, and they cannot
fairly be accused of attempting to impose a psychologically or
circumstantially-induced Utopian phantasy on an otherwise consistently biblical theology. [28] The divine kingdom is destined to
supersede all earthly kingdoms simply because God is God. Nowhere more than here does the Calvinistic view of the divine
purpose appear more apposite. Daniel had said of God, "he re-
moveth kings, and setteth up kings", [29] and the course of empires
on earth is always subordinated to the ultimate conquest of all
by a kingdom at once both righteous and eternal.

Consequently when the historicist hermeneutic was applied to
the prophetic revelations of Daniel and the Apocalypse it identified all those nations whose fortunes were in any way related to
those of the divine kingdom. From the ancient succession of
Babylon, Medo-Persia, Greece and Rome, could be traced the
whole gamut of this intertwined history. Daniel's visions of the
four kingdoms had indicated an eventual dichotomy of the
Roman Empire, [30] and a subsequent further division into ten
kingdoms. [31] The Eastern and Western segments of Rome were
duly followed in time by the ten kingdoms of Western Europe.
By this time the kingdom of Christ had visibly appeared on earth,
but long before it grew to maturity it would be challenged and

---

[26] Thomas Hall, *Chiliasto-mastix redivivus*, pp. 33, 34.
[27] Cf. "from the first Seal to the seventh Trumpet, is run over all the Time that the
Monarchies and Kingdoms of this World (whilst they should be in the Hands of Christ's
Enemies) should continue and last", Goodwin, 'Revelation' in *Works,* II, pt. I, p. 19.
[28] Cf. Hill, 'John Mason and the End of the World', in *Puritanism and Revolution,*
pp. 323–328, and Cohn, *The Pursuit of the Millennium,* ch. 1. Even William Haller
refers to a "religious Utopianism ... inevitably conduced in the circumstances of revolution" and "Out of the desperation of the poor and humble," Haller, *op. cit.,* p. 271.
[29] Dan. ii, 21.
[30] E.g. Finch, *Great Restavration,* p. 54; Huit, *Daniel,* p. 51ff.; Homes, *Resurrection,* p. 240.
[31] E.g. Thomas Parker, *Daniel,* p. 6; Homes, *op. cit.,* p. 71; Haughton, *Antichrist,*
p. 105. Thomas Goodwin was among those who pointed out that it was the Western
Empire that was so divided, Goodwin, *States & Kingdomes,* p. 38.

thwarted by the antichristian power of the "Little Horn". The body thus cryptically symbolised referred to the Turk in the East, [32] the Papacy in the West, [33] or to a combination of both, [34] and was widely regarded as the indisputable successor to the authority once vested in pagan Rome. [35] John's Revelation concentrated on the relationship of Rome, in both its pagan and papal phase, to the developing kingdom of Christ from New Testament times onwards. The earlier chapters showed how the initial supremacy of the Empire over Christianity was reversed by the church's conquest of paganism through the conversion of Constantine. [36] Later visions again revealed how the power vacuum created by the demise of Rome was filled, in the East by Mohammedanism and Turkey, and in the West by papal Christianity. [37]

The fortunes of the divine kingdom were now bound up with these latter powers, and only after a long, drawn-out struggle involving them and the nations subject to them would righteousness prevail upon earth. Thus the Saracens and Mohammedanism were seen as Daniel's king of the north [38] and king of the south, [39] and under John's fifth [40] and sixth Trumpets. [41] Turkey was seen variously, as well as the Little Horn, also as the king of the south, [42] and the king of the north, [43] and as Gog and Magog. [44] There were few prophecies which did not, in some way, refer to the papal Antichrist. [45] Not only did it appear once

[32]   E.g. Finch, *op. cit.*, p. 55; Huit, *op. cit.*, p. 187.
[33]   E.g. Archer, *op. cit.*, p. 43; Thomas Parker, *op. cit.*, p. 15; Stephens, *Number of the Beast*, p. 113.
[34]   Homes, *op. cit.*, p. 253; cf. Pareus, *Commentary*, pp. 285, 286.
[35]   Cf. Finch, *op. cit.*, p. 54; Huit, *op. cit.*, p. 57.
[36]   E.g. Mede, *Key of The Revelation*, pt. I, pp. 39ff.; James Durham, *Commentarie*, pp. 341 ff.
[37]   E.g. Mede, *op. cit.*, pp. 85 ff.; James Durham, *op. cit.*, pp. 423 ff.
[38]   E.g. Homes, *op. cit.*, p. 155.
[39]   E.g. Brightman, 'Daniel', in *Workes*, p. 920; Huit, *op. cit.*, p. 332.
[40]   E.g. Mede, *op. cit.*, pp. 99 ff.; Goodwin, 'Revelation', in *Works*, II, pt. I, p. 53.
[41]   E.g. Pareus, *op. cit.*, pp. 185 ff.
[42]   E.g. Homes, *loc. cit.*
[43]   E.g. Finch, *op. cit.*, p. 57; Brightman, *op. cit.*, p. 921.
[44]   E.g. Pareus, *op. cit.*, p. 537; Guild, *Sealed Book Opened*, p. 313.
[45]   Wider concepts of Antichrist in the developing political scene in England are discussed by C. Hill, *Antichrist in Seventeenth-Century England* (1971), and P. K. Christianson, 'English Protestant Apocalyptic Visions, C. 1536—1642', unpublished Ph. D. thesis, University of Minnesota, 1971. The compulsion to end the reign of Antichrist as a factor in the settlement of New England is discussed by A. J. B. Gilsdorf, 'The Puritan Apocalypse: New England Eschatology in the Seventeenth Century'.

again as the Little Horn, but also as the ten-horned beast, [46] and two-horned beast of Rev. xiii, [47] and as the harlot of Rev. xvii. [48] The whole course of Western Christianity had largely been dominated by this power and it was not thought disproportionate that considerable sections of historical prophecy should have been devoted to its development. [49] The consummation of Christ's kingdom particularly depended upon the eventual overthrow of this Western Antichrist, a process of sufficient magnitude directly to involve many of the world's peoples. The Waldenses, [50] England, [51] Germany, [52] Spain, [53] the Jews [54] and, again, Turkey, [55] were prominent among many calculated to play a part of greater or lesser import in the final establishment of the kingdom. The latter-day triumph of God's people was thus inseparably bound up with the destinies of peoples and nations already established in the earth. Consequently within the historicist rationale in the seventeenth century, some knowledge of the course of empires as outlined in the books of Daniel and The Revelation was indispensable to an adequate conception of Christ's ultimate kingdom. Of all the present powers variously figuring in prophetic exegesis those which were consistently prominent were the Papacy, the Turks, and the Jews, and it now remains to examine in greater detail their historical and eschatological significance.

The fundamental scriptural allusion to the Papacy was Daniel's Little Horn which, as we have seen, was to arise after the ten-fold partition of Western Imperial Rome and which, since it constituted the final phase of that empire, was to continue until all earthly kingdoms eventuated in the kingdom of God. In this fact lay the peculiar relevance of the Little Horn to those who lived in

---

[46]   E.g. Brightman, *Revelation*, p. 429; Goodwin, *op. cit.*, p. 63.
[47]   E.g. Mede, *op. cit.*, pt. II, p. 64; Cotton, *Revelation*, p. 225.
[48]   E.g. Pareus, *op. cit.*, p. 500 (the first so numbered); James Durham, *op. cit.*, p. 630.
[49]   Thus James Durham follows David Pareus in making the fifth Trumpet "applicable to the papall Kingdom, whereof the Pope is head", James Durham, *op. cit.*, p. 442; cf. Pareus, *op. cit.*, pp. 170—180. Goodwin is again typical of many who see chapters xiii—xix given largely the rise and "Ruin" of "the Man of Sin", Goodwin, *op. cit.*, p. 24.
[50]   E.g. Mede, *op. cit.*, pp. 60, 92, 114: Cotton, *op. cit.*, p. 99.
[51]   E.g. Mede, *op. cit.*, p. 116; Cotton, *Seven Vials*, pp. 5—7, (the second so numbered).
[52]   E.g. Mede, *op. cit.*, p. 117; Goodwin, *op. cit.*, pp. 86, 99.
[53]   E.g. Goodwin, *op. cit.*, p. 99; Robert Parker, *The Mystery of The Vialls opened* (1651), p. 13.
[54]   E.g. Finch, *op. cit.*, p. 55; Mede, *op. cit.*, p. 118, Huit, *op. cit.*, p. 45.
[55]   E.g. Brightman, *op. cit.*, p. 327; James Durham, *op. cit.*, p. 616; Homes, *op. cit.*, p. 270.

the last days. "Two things are joyned together", argued James Durham, "the standing and spreading of Christs Kingdom and the decreasing of Antichrists: and these two proceed together; what bringeth Antichrist down, advanceth Christs Kingdom; and what advanceth His Kingdom, darkeneth Antichrists." [56] In equating the Little Horn with the Antichrist, and in identifying them with the Papacy, seventeenth-century expositors were following a long-established tradition. [57] Dr. Christopher Hill has emphasised the widespread identification of the Antichrist with the Papacy, both on the Continent and in English post-Reformation theology. [58] In the seventeenth century, Thomas Parker stoutly argued the historicist position when he affirmed "The fourth Beast is the Romane kingdom, and not the kingdom of the Seleucidae; and the little horn, neither Antiochus, neither Mahomet; but onely Antichrist, or the Pope of Rome." [59]

The passing of years, however, brought a new development in the comprehension of the book of Revelation, and it was soon widely held that the greater part of its prophetic message was concerned with the times and events of the fourth empire, and in particular with the rise, growth and decline of the papal Antichrist. Arthur Dent explained:

> The Church in the Apostles time had her conflicts. The ten great persecutions began euen then to be raised up. Heresies shortly after beganne to spring and sprout. Afterwards by degrees, the great Antichrist did approach towards his cursed seate. And after all this, S. Iohn foretelleth how hee should take possession of his abhominable and most execrable seate and sea of Rome: How hee should raigne and rule for a time as the Monarche of the world: How hee should preuaile against the Church, and make warre against the Saintes: How he should raigne but a short time and afterward come tumbling downe as fast as euer he rose up, and decrease as fast as euer he increased. [60]

---

[56]   James Durham, op. cit., p. 620.
[57]   Cf. "many in the ages before us, and indeed in the midst of grosse darkness have observed and constantly affirmed the Papacy to be Antichrists Kingdom, and the Pope Antichrist", Pareus, op. cit., p. 318. Among those so named by Pareus are Arnulphus, Bishop of Orleans; Eberhard, Archbishop of Salzburg; Joachim of Calabria; Francisco Petrarcha; and Michael Cesenus. The list was not original; cf. Heinrich Bullinger, A Hvndred Sermons vpō the Apocalips (1561), Pref., sigs. Biiii, Bv.
[58]   C. Hill, Antichrist in the Seventeenth Century (1971), pp. 9—33. From the political and extreme millenarian viewpoints the identification of the Antichrist was necessary as a prelude to its ultimate overthrow prior to the establishment of the Kingdom of Christ, cf. pp. 3, 104. It was, perhaps, this concern with Antichrist which died after 1660, rather than the more basically theological interest, cf. pp. 154, 164.
[59]   Thomas Parker, Daniel, p. 15; cf., e.g. Napier, Plaine Discouery p. 234, and John Trapp, 'A Commentary or Exposition upon The four Major Prophets', in Annotations Upon the Old and New Testament, III (1660), pt. II, p. 553.
[60]   Dent, The Rvine of Rome, Epistle to the Reader, sig. aa.

Dent's influential treatise, [61] which had been intended "for the comfort of Protestants and the daunting of Papists, Seminary Priests [and] Iesuites", provided an excellent foundation upon which later interpreters could build. In Dent's view the bulk of the two major visions which comprised The Revelation was related to the Antichrist. The first four trumpets of chapter viii symbolically referred to the gradual growth of heresy within the church from the time of Constantine, [62] which specifically made way for the coming of the antichristian power. [63] The fifth trumpet of chapter ix outlined the rise of papal power from "about ... six hundred yeares after Christ". [64] The star falling from heaven is the Pope, the smoke which ascends from the bottomless pit is the spiritual darkness, ignorance and superstition which covered the earth during Antichrist's rule, and the locusts which appear with the smoke are the "Pope's Cleargie, as Abbots, Monkes, Friers, Priests, Shauelings & such like vermine". [65] The final vision of the book which begins at chapter xii and runs through to the end [66] clarifies matters previously presented, with particular emphasis on the fates and fortunes of the Roman Empire and the Papacy. [67] Thus the two beasts of chapter xiii specifically represent those two great powers, [68] with the two horns of the second beast signifying the civil and ecclesiastical authority of the Roman hierarchy. [69] Chapters xiv-xx deal at length with the decline of the fourth world empire through the final overthrow of papal authority in the earth. [70] So Dent can advise "let men be studious and diligent in this booke, and they shall bee out of al doubt, that Rome is the great whoore of Babylon; that the Pope is Antichrist, and the Papacy the beast". [71] He concludes, "the vtter ouerthrow of Rome, falleth out to bee, but a little before the comming of Christ to iudgement ..." [72]

Already by this time there had been several notable works on the Apocalypse and together with the great many which were to

---

[61]   Cf. *supra*, p. 59.
[62]   Dent, *op. cit.*, p. 98.
[63]   *Ibid.*, p. 97.
[64]   *Ibid.*, p. 100.
[65]   *Ibid.*, p. 105.
[66]   *Ibid.*, p. 150.
[67]   *Ibid.*, p. 151.
[68]   *Ibid.*, p. 168.
[69]   *Ibid.*, p. 182.
[70]   *Ibid.*, p. 195.
[71]   *Ibid.*, p. 243.
[72]   *Ibid.*, p. 261.

follow, they constituted a body of literature whose influence on
the age must not be underestimated. The total number of works
on The Revelation, in part or in whole, which are dated between
1600 and 1660 makes it impossible to represent more than a
select few. [73] Fortunately, with respect to the identity of the
papal Antichrist and its place in the interpretative schemes, there
were few exceptions to the run of general opinion. Edward
Haughton is representative when he says, "The Popes of Rome
are the revealed man of sin, the (now) well known Antichrist, of
whom Daniel, Paul, and the Apostle John, have spoken such vile
and fearfull things: I say in all they have said of the great Antichrist, they have pointed the finger at the Popes of Rome." [74]

The apocalyptic delineation of this antichristian power centred
around the two beasts of The Revelation chapter xiii and the scar-
letclad whore of chapter xvii. Thomas Brightman sees both beasts as
symbolic of papal Rome and is followed here by the majority of
later writers, including Pareus, Goodwin, Cotton and Durham. [75]
The ten-horned beast with seven heads is the Papacy in a civil
role, and the two-horned beast is its ecclesiastical power. [76] Both
aspects of papal authority take their beginning from "about" 306
A.D. [77] The deadly wound inflicted on the seventh head of the
first beast applies to the Gothic invasions which heavily under-
mined the authority of the Popes, [78] and lasted in all for
140 years. [79] The healing of the wound began around 550 A.D.
and was completed by the time of Phocas in 606 A.D. [80] Thereafter the world "wondered after the beast" until its designated
time of supremacy came to an end, which would be in 1686 "or
thereabouts". [81] Mede follows Dent in applying only the second
beast directly to the Papacy. [82] This is the "religious arm" of the
Empire, "the Bishop of Rome, with his clergie". [83] Nathaniel

---

[73] Hill notes the "seminal works on Revelation and Daniel" by Brightman and
Mede, among English writers, Hill, op. cit., p. 37. Napier and Dent might also have
been included, to name two of many others, cf. supra p. 59.

[74] Haughton, op. cit., p. 3.

[75] Brightman, op. cit., p. 429; cf. Pareus, op. cit., pp. 284, 306; Goodwin, op. cit.,
p. 63; Cotton, Revelation, pp. 7, 225; James Durham, op. cit., pp. 544, 545.

[76] Brightman, op. cit., p. 430.

[77] Ibid., p. 431; but cf. "304 A.D." (p. 370), which date is necessary to his chronology, see supra, p. 116.

[78] Ibid., p. 442.

[79] Ibid., p. 452.

[80] Ibid., p. 444.

[81] Ibid., p. 452.

[82] Mede, op. cit., pp. 64—76.

[83] Ibid., p. 64.

Stephens favoured the same view since the ten-horned beast of Revelation was parallel to the ten-horned beast of Daniel which was palpably pagan Rome. [84] If, however, the precise identity of the first beast was a moot point it mattered little in perspective, and James Durham said everything when he declared "the Pope is the very Antichrist, and the papacy the very antichristian Kingdom here described." [85]

Arthur Dent had already referred to the seventeenth chapter of The Revelation as "the key of this prophesie", [86] while Mede described it as "the chiefe part of the Revelation" [87] and "the chiefest vision of all the rest." [88] The lurid picture of the scarlet whore, bedecked in splendid finery and carried in pomp upon the back of the ten-horned and seven-headed beast, by whose beguiling cup the kings of the earth had been inebriated, was certainly among the most arresting symbolic characterisations anywhere in the apocalyptic imagery of the Bible. Edward Haughton's *Rise, Growth, and Fall of Antichrist*, the purpose of which was "to discover Antichrist to you in his own colours", was based on a profound conviction that the papal hierarchy was here totally described. The logic from which he drew these conclusions issued from the premise that the beast which carried the woman could be identified with the fourth beast of Daniel. The seven heads on the beast represented seven successive kings, or forms of government. Of these, five, namely Kings, Consuls, Tribunes, Decemvirs, and Dictators, had already passed in John's time. The sixth head, then present, signified Emperors and the seventh head depicted the rule of Popes which was yet to come. [89] Mede had

---

[84]   Stephens, *op. cit.*, p. 99.

[85]   James Durham, *op. cit.*, p. 573. A factor of some importance in identifying the beasts of Revelation xiii was the mystic number 666. One widely-accepted interpretation was based on the numerical calculation of the early post-apostolic "Lateinos", e.g., Pareus, *op. cit.*, p. 317. Thomas Goodwin simply applied it to 'the Time or Term' of the beast's ending, i.e. 1666, Goodwin, *op. cit.*, p. 67. Hezekiah Holland saw it in the phrase "vicarius generalis Dei in terris", Hezekiah Holland, *An Exposition or ... Epitome on the most choice Commentaries upon the Revelation* (1650), p. 106. Haughton lists several prophetic characteristics of the Antichrist, and wisely cautions that the number of the beast can apply only to one "to whom all these particulars do agree", *op. cit.*, p. 26. Not surprisingly, he sees the significance of both "Lateinos", and "Generalis dei Vicarus [sic] in terris", but rather spoils his case by "In our English (The Pope by superioritie is the divels Leiftenant) the numeral letters hereof make up six hundred and sixty six", *ibid.*, p. 25.

[86]   Dent, *op. cit.*, Epistle to the Reader, sig. aa3*v*.

[87]   Mede, *op. cit.*, p. 107.

[88]   *Ibid.*, p. 108.

[89]   Haughton, *op. cit.*, pp. 5—6. Napier had previously applied the same reasoning to the seven heads of the beast, Napier, *op. cit.*, p. 37.

pointed out that the ten horns belonged to the seventh head and
hence referred to ten kingdoms whose allegiance would belong to
the papacy in the final era of the Roman kingdom. [90] No one put
the argument concerning the harlot Babylon as clearly as did
William Guild:

> The summe then of the mystery of this woman is this, 1. This wom-
> an as a woman, is a Church. 2. As a harlot, is a false and idolatrous
> Church. 3. As inebriating the Kings and inhabitants of the earth with
> the wine of her fornications, is a pretended Catholick Church. 4. As
> a Mother of harlots is a mother Church. And, 5. As Mystical Baby-
> lon, which Ribera and other Romanists expound to be Rome, is the
> Roman Church, all which being put together makes up here by com-
> mon consent the description of the Antichristian Church, which is
> therefore the Roman-mother-pretended Catholick Church. [91]

William Strong was in no sense in isolation when, in 1649, he
preached on 'Babylons ruine, the Saints Triumph'. [92]

The strength of such intricate dialectics, which are so alien to
contemporary interpretative thought, was reinforced by weightier and more palpable arguments. If the Papacy was in truth the
prophesied Antichrist it would exhibit the characteristics of the
Antichrist. "Him therefore we cannot but confidently judge to
be Antichrist, for as much as in him all the markes of Antichrist
do evidently concurre and agree together", [93] reasoned Pareus.
Joseph Mede's *Apostasy of the Latter Times* argued that the
essence of the Antichrist was idolatry. This persuasive work [94]
was an exposition of the latter-day departure from the faith foretold by Paul in I Timothy iv, l. Mede interpreted this predicted
defection in immediate relationship to the last verse of the preceding chapter. [95] Thus "the faith" is "the mystery of godliness"
which is the doctrine of the incarnation with its attendant Christological postulates, and the departure from that faith is simply a
deviation from these fundamental concepts, and notably from
the "assumption of this God and Man to the Throne of
Glory". [96] It is a revolt against the true worship of God through

---

[90]   Mede, *op. cit.*, pp. 110, 111.
[91]   Guild, *op. cit.*, pp. 251, 252.
[92]   See his *Sermons*, pp. 63—90.
[93]   Pareus, *op. cit.*, p. 318.
[94]   The measure of its influence may be judged from the fact that it was twice
reprinted in the nineteenth century, in 1836 and 1845.
[95]   "And without controversy, great is the mystery of godliness: God was manifest
in the flesh, justified in the Spirit, seen of angels, preached unto the Gentiles, believed
on in the world, received up into glory," I Tim. iii, 16. See Mede, 'The Apostasy', in
Works, p. 623.
[96]   Mede, *op. cit.*, p. 623.

Christ, the transference of allegiance to another. [97] This is singularly relevant since the Apostasy is occasioned by the doctrine of devils or demons, which gives it the character of a revival of "the Gentiles idolatrous Theology of Daemons". [98] The demons, so-called, were the "Deified Souls of men after death," [99] and in the prevailing philosophy of pre-Christian and early Christian times were the "middle powers" between God and men, with the right of mediation. [100] The cult of image-worship can be traced directly to the ancient manner of worship ascribed to these demonic powers, [101] hence "The worshipping therefore of Images and Columns is by its original and institution a piece of the Doctrine of Daemons." [102] The Apostasy of the last days is therefore a revival of pagan worship-forms which deny the worship alone due to Christ. Of the rites and liturgies of Rome, Mede is thus prompted to ask:

> Is it not a denial of Christ's Prerogative, to ascribe unto any other, for any respect of glory or nearness to God after death or otherwise, that whereof he alone is infeoffed by his unimitable Death, triumphant Resurrection and glorious Ascension? ... This Doctrine of Daemons comprehends in most express manner the whole Idolatry of the Mystery of iniquity, the Deifying and invocating of Saints and Angels, the bowing down to Images, the worshipping of Crosses as new-Idol columns, the adoring and templing of Reliques, the worshipping of any other Visible thing upon suppoꞩal of any Divinity therein. [103]

Manifestly, idolatry is "the very soul" [104] of the antichristian apostasy, Antichrist is a "Counter-Christ", [105] and the Papacy "wholly overshadowed with the thick darknesse of Idolatrous Antichristianism." [106]

Mede comes very close here to the view of Edward Haughton, whose Antichrist is essentially one in opposition to Christ. "The great Antichrist is one that is pretendedly for Christ, but is really against Christ." [107] The implication of this definition is beyond question:

---

[97]   *Ibid.*, p. 625.
[98]   *Ibid.*, p. 626.
[99]   *Ibid.*, p. 629.
[100]   *Ibid.*, p. 627.
[101]   *Ibid.*, p. 632.
[102]   *Ibid.*, p. 633.
[103]   *Ibid.*, pp. 640—41.
[104]   *Ibid.*, p. 643.
[105]   *Ibid.*, p. 647.
[106]   Mede, 'Diatribae', in *Works*, p. 137.
[107]   Haughton, *op. cit.*, p. 13.

> The Pope pretends to be more for Christ then any man in the World, Christs Vicar, Christs Vicegerent, the visible head of Christs Church, Saint Peters successor, to feed the flock of Christ ... I tell you he pretends to be more for Christ then any man alive: but let me tell you withall that there is no man alive so much against Christ as he is; and therefore most properly called (Antichrist) ... [108]

The gist of these allegations is that the doctrines pertaining to the redemptive work of Christ have been perverted by papal dogma. Haughton specifies the satisfaction of Christ's death, the mediatory work of Christ, His intercession, and the authority of Christ's Word, and "I profess I can hardly name one Doctrine of Jesus Christ, but the Popes of Rome have thwarted it, either directly or indirectly, and quite subverted it." [109] James Ussher is a shade nearer to the root idea of Antichrist [110] when he writes, "He is one who under the colour of being for Christ, and under title of his Vicegerent, exalteth himselfe above and against Christ, opposing himselfe against all his offices and ordinances both in Church and Commonwealth." [111] An echo, this, of the opinion already expressed by Pareus that "Antichrist under the name of Christ should oppose Christ, and labour to destroy the faith of Christ out of the harts of man". [112]

The pre-eminent demonstration of antichristianism, however, was the uncomplicated historical fact that the Papacy had corrupted the once pure teachings of the apostolic church. Romish doctrines were, to quote William Strong, "a mixture of Gods Ordinances, and carnal and heathenish superstitions". [113] This delusive syncretism which was to eventuate in the whole elabo-

---

[108]   *Ibid.*, pp. 12, 13; but cf. the Baptist Henry Denne's argument: "some think the Pope of Rome is Antichrist, some the Bishops, some the Turke, &c. But give me leave to tell you what I conceive, that to tye the name of Antichrist to a particular man, or to any particular succession of men, is to confine him unto too narrow a bound: I will not deny but that the Pope is a principall member of Antichrist, of the man of sin, the head if you please. But I do beleeve the Pope and Antichrist to differ, as the part, and the whole, as the head, and the body: And I conceive the great Antichrist to be that mysticall body of iniquity which opposeth Jesus Christ, Antichrist is as much as to say against Christ: whosoever doth seek to destroy that which the Lord Jesus hath built up, or to build up that which the Lord hath pluck'd down, the same is against Christ, and insomuch a member of the great Antichrist," Henry Denne, *The Man of Sin Discovered* (1645), pp. 15—16. Denne applied this definition to 'the Pulpits of England', a view for which he had been imprisoned.

[109]   Haughton, *op. cit.*, p. 16.

[110]   In the literal sense of the Greek ἀντι "instead of", "as a substitute for", rather than the more modern connotation "against".

[111]   Ussher, *Body of Divinitie*, p. 438.

[112]   Pareus, *op. cit.*, p. 173.

[113]   Strong, 'One Heart and one Way', in *Sermons*, p. 473.

rate structure of Rome had begun early in Christian history. If all did not trace its origin right back to the apostolic age itself, as did Haughton, [114] most were fully agreed that with the succession of Constantine to the imperial throne the stage was set for radical and lamentable changes to occur within the framework of Christian thought. [115] The ensuing degeneracy, which had been occasioned by "Constantines excessive bounty to the Church", [116] was seen both in the church's life, "for then Pastors began to be proud, luxurious, idle and fertile in vices," [117] and in her doctrine:

> ... for now infinite ceremonies and humane traditions are established: as the worshipping of the dead, images, the observation of holy dayes, orders, rites and solemnities of pagans forged by the devill himself (the names onelie altered) were forciblie imposed upon the Church, to the utter abolishing of the doctrine of free grace, and the merits of Christ. [118]

This contamination of Christian thought through the infiltration of paganism now gave rise to the actual development of the papal Antichrist, a gradual process [119] which reached maturity with the decree of Phocas in 606 A.D. [120] Of that time James Durham wrote:

> Immediately after this, the light of the Word wonderfully decayed, traditions were obtruded, all publick worship was to be performed in Latine, the Scriptures were keeped up from laick people ... Letanies, Lyturgies and Masses were brought in stead of the Word and preaching ... plurality of Mediators and worshipping of Saints and Angels were brought in ... Heathenish superstitions and ceremonies were brought again into the Church ... [121]

---

[114]   Haughton, *op. cit.*, p. 7.
[115]   E.g. Pareus, *op. cit.*, p. 117, Holland, *op. cit.*, p. 42.
[116]   Holland, *loc. cit.*
[117]   *Loc. cit.*
[118]   Pareus, *op. cit.*, pp. 117—118.
[119]   "by degrees ... the Apostolical sinceritie of faith & order did wear out: and the corruptions, superstitions and heathenish abominations & idols were brought in ... for Antichrists apostacy was not at the highest all of a sudden, but encreased by slow paces," *ibid.*, p. 277.
[120]   According to Pareus, Phocas' decree made Boniface III the "first Antichrist", *ibid.*, p. 119. Hezekiah Holland maintained that "the Pope as his Vicar took up his power in Anno 606. in Boniface third", Holland, *op. cit.*, p. 166. Those who favoured this date for the time of Antichrist's rising had difficulty in placing the 1260 prophetic years, particularly if Revelation's woman (the church) was to continue "in the wilderness" for the full extent of that time prior to the kingdom of God. Pareus overcame the problem by maintaining that the "flight" of the woman lasted from Constantine to Phocas, and that her "exile" began with Phocas and Boniface III, Pareus, *Commentary*, p. 275. In any event the 1260 day-years are "hard to be understood" and are probably not to be taken literally, *ibid.*, pp. 220, 224.
[121]   James Durham, *op. cit.*, pp. 443, 444.

The implications of these and kindred arguments exposing the true nature of the Antichrist were as clearly understood in the middle of the seventeenth century as they had been a century earlier, and both Durham's and Edward Haughton's denunciations of Antichrist are to be noted for their emphatic concern with theological issues: [122]

> ... the Pope being Antichrist, you may easily know what all Popish Ordinances are, their Doctrines, Auricular confessions, Pennances, Holy water, Crucifixes, Beads, Extream Unctions, Altars, Bloodless Sacrifices, Merits, Satisfactions, Images, the Worship of Saints and Angels with Invocation of them; Indulgences, Pilgrimages, Burying in a Franciscans-hood, Purgatory, Canonization; all this with all other appurtenances of their Religion are all Antichristianism; the Holy Ghosts expression of them is, They are the blood of a dead man. Rev. 16. 3. No better then the polluting, Choaking, Killing blood of a dead man: therefore take heed and beware of their Religion; hate it with a right perfect hatred, even all those forms of worship, Formalities, Ceremonies, anything, every thing that is a kinn to it, as you would hate, when you are athirst, drinking blood. [123]

Here was language that all could understand, substance to the less tangible denotations of prophecy, and reason enough for men to hope that the final, antichristian phase of the fourth empire would soon give way to a better and eternal kingdom.

If all this followed the earlier tradition of Robert Abbot's *Antichristi Demonstratio*, and of Andrew Willet's *Synopsis Papismi* and *Tetrastylon Papisticvm,* it also lay in the more immediate context of seventeenth-century eschatological expectation. [124] These were the very times of the fourth empire's impending demise, Antichrist's awaited downfall and judgement, and the anticipated end of Roman supremacy and when Mede, Haughton, Stephens, Guild and others wrote at length of the papal Antichrist they did so principally from the viewpoint of a generation excited at the prospect of a new age already beginning to dawn.

---

[122]   As a balance to recent interpretations which emphasise the political implications of the Antichrist concept in seventeenth-century England, e.g. C. Hill, *Antichrist in Seventeenth-Century England,* and P. K. Christianson, 'English Protestant Apocalyptic Visions'.

[123]   Edward Haughton, *op. cit.,* pp. 57, 58.

[124]   Later reprints of Abbot's *Antichristi Demonstratio, Contra Fabvlas Pontificias, & ineptam Roberti Bellarmini de Antichristo disputationem* (1603), and of Willet's *Synopsis Papismi* (1592) and *Tetrastylon Papisticvm* (1593) were in simultaneous circulation with Dent's *Rvine of Rome.* A link between earlier and later works on the papal antichrist is William Ames' *Bellarminvs Enervatvs* (1628).

The proximity of this Western Antichrist constituted an ever-present threat to Englishmen who were as unwilling as they were unable to forget a thousand years of history. The Spanish Armada, the Gunpowder plot, the Romanizing tendencies of Archbishop Laud and Charles I, and the hazardous course of Continental Protestantism had more recently served to heighten these fore-bodings and explain why, to more modern eyes, the seventeenth century appears to have had an almost inordinate preoccupation with the Papacy. [125] For all that, it could not be overlooked that the fourth empire had fallen into two, coextensive divisions. In the terms of prophecy the two legs were to continue until both were shattered by the stone. [126] Hence, while the latter-day successors of Western Rome might be of a more immediate geographical and political significance, the Eastern segment of the empire was, from an exegetical and historical viewpoint, of equal consequence. [127] Any reasoned attempt to relate history to eschatology must account for Turkey as well as the Papacy, for in the eyes of many the coming of Christ's kingdom was contingent upon the dissolution of both.

The view of Turkey as an Eastern Antichrist, although in no sense as universal as the branding of its Western counterpart, derived from reasons no less plausible. If it could be demonstrated, as Finch and Huit believed, that Daniel's Little Horn referred exclusively to the Turkish power, [128] or even as Homes contended, that it included both Pope and Turk, [129] further evidence would be superfluous. Pareus found that he could reach the same conclusion without reference to the Little Horn. Those characteristics which designated the Papacy were observable also in Turkey, and if one was an antichrist the other could be nothing else. Not only did the two share a contemporaneity of ori-

---

[125]   Cf. Haller's remark that Englishmen "hated Spain, despised France, dreaded the Pope and embraced Protestantism with the greater fervor the more these historic enemies seemed to menace England," Haller, *op. cit.*, p. 51.

[126]   Huit, *op. cit.*, p. 51; Thomas Parker, *op. cit.*, p. 4.

[127]   Pareus also believed that Turkey would remain a constant military threat to the very end, see his *Commentary*, p. 538.

[128]   Finch, *op. cit.*, p. 55; Huit, *op. cit.*, p. 187.

[129]   Nathaniel Homes, 'The Christian Hammerers against the Antichristian Horns', in *Works*, p. 596. A year later Homes wrote of the Turco-Papal little horn, "Both making up one Antichristian Body, to keep the world from imbracing [sic] Christ and his pure Gospell ... The Turke keeping off the Jewes, and the Pope the Christians ... from imbracing Christ. And both their names making exactly six hundred sixty-six," *Resurrection*, p. 253.

gin [130] and a parallel development and destiny, [131] but also a notably similar constitution. The essence of the Turkish power was Mohammedanism, "a new kind of doctrine, patched together of Judaisme, Christianisme, and Gentilisme" [132] which savoured strongly of the "deceivablenesse of unrighteousnesse" [133] of the Western Antichrist. Arthur Dent had even gone further. "The Mahometish religion", he had argued, "in very deed did spring from the darknesse of Rome, as from his proper roote and original cause". [134] If the application of the Little Horn did not always hold, there was clearly ground enough for concluding that Turkey was an antichrist.

The genesis of such persuasions can be traced to Luther whose writings betray a persistent concern over the Turkish question. Since the fall of Constantinople in 1453 the menace of the Turk had presented a growing threat to the whole of Europe. Within the succeeding fifty or so years, Turkey had extended her supremacy to the Danube. After a brief respite at the beginning of the sixteenth century when she was concerned with affairs nearer home, Suleiman the Magnificent once again directed Turkish eyes to the Christian kingdoms of Europe. In 1520 Belgrade fell to Suleiman's armies. Two years later the Turks had captured Rhodes, and in 1526 the King of Hungary and his troops were decisively beaten at the battle of Mohacs, a defeat which, according to Robert Schultz, "sent a wave of terror over Europe". A new sense of urgency was given to the Mohammedan menace in 1529 with the Turkish advance on Vienna. [135]

Luther viewed these events with the apprehension of his age.[136] In 1529 he preached his 'Army Sermon against the Turk', and in the same year wrote 'On War Against the Turk', both of which betrayed anxiety over the Turkish threat and its possible effects on the progress of the gospel. The Turk is "the servant of the devil" and "lays waste the Christian faith and our dear Lord Jesus Christ". [137] While this could apply with equal force to any

---

[130]   Pareus, *op. cit.*, p. 150.
[131]   *Ibid.*, pp. 166–188.
[132]   *Ibid.*, p. 186.
[133]   *Ibid.*, p. 173.
[134]   Dent, *op. cit.*, p. 113.
[135]   See Robert C. Schultz, Introduction, Luther, 'On War Against the Turk', *Works*, 46, p. 157.
[136]   The siege of Vienna "instilled in Luther and his central European contemporaries a proverbial dread of the Turk", see Luther, *Works*, 35, p. 300, n. 152.
[137]   Luther, 'Vom Kriege wider die Türken', in *Werke*, 30, pt. 2, p. 120, quoted from *Works*, 46, pp. 174, 175.

avowed enemy of Christian Europe, Turkey was visibly in a different category. Luther sees in the Turk the self-same characteristics of the Antichrist which denominate the Papacy:

> Mohammed highly exalts and praises himself and boasts that he has talked with God and the angels ... Therefore the Turks think that their Mohammed is much higher and greater than Christ, for the office of Christ has come to an end and Mohammed's office is still in force. [138]

Again:

> Mohammed is a destroyer of our Lord Christ and his kingdom, and if anyone denies the articles concerning Christ, that he is God's Son, that he died for us and still lives and reigns at the right hand of God, what has he left of Christ? Father, Son, Holy Ghost, baptism, the sacrament, gospel, faith, and all Christian doctrine and life are gone, and instead of Christ only Mohammed with his doctrine of works and specially of the sword is left. [139]

It is beyond doubt "that the Romane Empire is almost gone, Christ's coming is at the door, and the Turk is the empire's token of the end", [140] and Luther can pray "may our dear Lord Jesus Christ help, and come down from heaven with the Last Judgement, and strike down both Turk and Pope ..." [141] Luther's Antichrist, then, is not solely the Pope, [142] but rather "the incarnation of all that is hostile to Christ and his kingdom", [143] and more specifically the dualistic synthesis of Turkey and the Papacy:

> The head of Antichrist ... is, together with the Pope, and the Turk. For a living beast must have a bodie and soul; the spirit or soul of Antichrist, is the Pope, but his flesh or bodie, is the Turk. This devasteth [sic], destroieth, and persecuteth God's Church corporally, the Pope spiritually ... [144]

Accordingly Pareus, a century later, writes of a "spirituall affliction of the Christian world by ... the Western Antichrist", and of a "corporal" oppression "under the Mahumetane Antichrist in the East". [145]

---

[138] *Ibid.*, p. 122, *Works,* 46, pp. 176–177.

[139] *Loc. cit.*

[140] *Ibid.*, p. 144, *Works,* 46, p. 200.

[141] *Ibid.*, p. 148, *Works,* 46, p. 205.

[142] Cf. "The pretensions of the papacy suggested to Luther—as to Wycliff before him—that the Pope was Antichrist ...", see *Works,* 45, p. 60, n. 8.

[143] *Works,* 44, p. 133, n. 30.

[144] Luther, *Werke,* Tischreden I, p. 135, quoted from *Dris. Martini Lutheri Colloquia Mensalia: or Dr. Martin Luther's Divine Discourses at his Table* (tr. Henry Bell, 1652), p. 298.

[145] Pareus, *op. cit.*, p. 185.

There were on the other hand those, as Edward Haughton, who felt that Turkey could not logically be particularised as an antichrist, [146] but neither this nor the passing of a hundred years and the decline of the Ottoman empire [147] lessened the anticipation of divine judgement on the Turk. Indeed, for reasons not difficult to see, the lines were now more clearly drawn and expectancy of the impending Turkish eclipse heightened. As an integral part of the fourth empire Turkey was described by Revelation's sixth trumpet, [148] a prophecy which seemed to prove that the Turkish kingdom was to continue contemporaneously with the Papacy until the sounding of the seventh trumpet ushered in the kingdom of God. [149] If the Lord Mayor of London and his Aldermen had listened attentively to William Strong's sermon in 1648, they returned home convinced that the final end of the Roman Empire was directly contingent upon the latter-day activities of Turkey. [150]

The essential element, again, was that of time. If the duration of Western Rome had been specified in prophecy, was it not reasonable to expect some indication of the times of the Eastern Empire? The answer to this question could be found in the Trumpet prophecy, [151] and although some had declined to enumerate this particular chronology [152] many saw less reason for restraint. Turkey, which had evolved through a gradual fusion of Mohammedanism, the Saracens, the Tartars, and the Ottoman dynasty, [153] had reached its peak of power "by one consent of

---

[146]   Edward Haughton argued that Turkey did not meet all the necessary requirements concerning the prophesied antichrist, Haughton, *op. cit.*, p. 8.

[147]   See *Encyclopaedia Britannica*, 22, p. 596.

[148]   E.g. Dent, *op. cit.*, pp. 112–120; Mede, *Key of The Revelation*, pt. I, pp. 108–120; James Durham, *op. cit.*, pp. 447 ff.

[149]   E.g. Dent, *op. cit.*, p. 120; Pareus, *op. cit.*, p. 166; Goodwin, *op. cit.*, p. 59.

[150]   Strong, *Vengeance*, p. 26.

[151]   "And the sixth angel sounded, and I heard a voice ... saying to the sixth angel which had the trumpet, Loose the four angels which are bound in the great river Euphrates. And the four angels were loosed, which were prepared for an hour, and a day, and a month, and a year ..." Rev. ix, 13–15.

[152]   E.g. Dent, *op. cit.*, p. 119, and Pareus, *op. cit.*, p. 188.

[153]   Napier and Mede were among leading expositors who applied the fifth trumpet to Mohammedanism and the Saracens, rather than to the Papacy, and the sixth trumpet to the Turkish Ottoman Empire, Napier, *op. cit.*, pp. 3–5; Mede, *op. cit.*, pp. 19, 109. Brightman applied it to both the Papacy and to Mohammed, *Revelation*, p. 290. They were thus obliged to consider the further period of five months, or 150 years, of Rev. ix, 5. Mede favoured the time from 830 A.D. to 980 A.D. as most accurately fulfilling the prophecy, while Brightman offered no less than five possible alternatives, extending overall from 630 A.D. to 1223 A.D.; Mede, *op. cit.*, p. 104; Brightman, *op. cit.*, pp. 301–304.

all the Historians" in 1300 A.D. [154] It was, therefore, from the rise of Othman in 1300 that the chronology relating to the Turkish kingdom should be calculated.

The end to which this evidence pointed was inescapable. "The Number of the Turk (which is an Hour, a Day, a Month, and a Year) is not yet fulfilled or expired, being by computation 396 Years from his first breaking out". [155] The time of the sixth trumpet would accordingly close in 1696, the empire of the Turk collapse, the seventh trumpet would finally sound, and *finis* would be writ large across the last page of human history. Even so it was to be noted that 1696 was, in effect, "the last terme", "the vttermost period of the Turkish name". [156] Brightman explained: "the strength of the Turkes shall not stande intire, & vnshaken during this Terme, but shall totter, & waxe towards the ruine thereof about forty yeares before that their vtter destruction shall come." [157] This approximation of forty years was, in actual fact, forty-five years and could be deduced from the last chapters of Daniel which further foreshadowed the final throes of the Turkish Empire. The "time, times, and a half" of chapter xii related to the "king of the north" of chapter xi, an additional obscure allusion to Turkey. [158] Since a "time" in this usage signified a hundred years, [159] the whole period here was of 350 years and was also to be calculated from the rise of Othman. By this reckoning, the dissolution of the Turkish Empire could transpire in 1650, a date which is only complementary to that of 1696 since "the former number did end at the first reeling and declining power of the Turks, this second, at the defacing and utter abolishing of the same". [160] Had Luther lived a century

---

[154] "... all the Turkish families, did subject themselves to that of the Cuttomans [sic] alone ...", Brightman, *op. cit.*, p. 326. As Goodwin later explained, the four angels in the river Euphrates referred to the four major sultanates of the Turks, seated at Iconium, Aleppo, Damascus, and Baghdad. These four "about the Year of Christ 1300, over-run all Natolia [sic] or Asia the less; and joining all into one Kingdom, under Ottoman ... did not cease till they had won Constantinople it self," Goodwin, *op. cit.*, p. 54; cf. Hezekiah Holland's four angels, "Armenians, Arabians, Saracens, Tartarians (from which last came the Turk, though now all four are comprehended under the name of Turkie")", Holland, *op. cit.*, p. 64.

[155] Goodwin, *op. cit.*, p. 54.

[156] Brightman, *op. cit.*, p. 327; Finch, *op. cit.*, p. 56.

[157] Brightman, *loc. cit.*

[158] Huit, *op. cit.*, p. 333; Strong, *loc. cit.*

[159] Brightman, 'Daniel', in *Workes,* p. 954. Brightman here specifies a forty-five year period for the overthrow of Turkey.

[160] Brightman, *op. cit.*, p. 967.

later, he might well have endorsed all this for when "the blasphemous kingdome of the Turkes is at an end", [161] then will appear
the righteous kingdom of God.

Amidst this absorption with the kingdoms of Antichrist the
basic biblical dichotomy of men and nations was not to be overlooked. "The World you know consisteth of Jews and Gentiles" [162], Goodwin had said, and while Pope and Turk alike were
thoroughly Gentile, within the realm of both existed another race
of people which properly belonged to neither. This distinction
between Jew and Gentile was given a characteristic significance in
the seventeenth century by the many scriptural passages which
seemed to suggest that in the last days the Jews would return to
Palestine and there be restored to a kingdom which, by divine
appointment, had been particularly reserved for them.

As with many other aspects of latter-day thought, interest in
the future of the Jews reached its high point in the middle decades of the century. While it is true that "many of the sects with
Fifth Monarchist tendencies interested themselves greatly in
things Jewish", [163] it is at the same time to be noted that this
concern was not limited to minority groups of dubious orthodoxy as, indeed, it was not limited to the 1650's. As early as
1621 Sir Henry Finch had assured a protracted engrossment in
the Jewish question with *The Worlds Great Restavration, or The
Calling of the Iewes*, a work which enjoyed the commendation of
the famous, and moderate, William Gouge. In the epistle dedicatory Finch promised his Jewish readers that it was God's intended purpose "to bring thee home againe, & to marry thee to
himselfe by faith for euermore ... . To be the ioy of the earth, the
most noble Church that euer eye did see". [164] Sentiments like
this did indeed become the concern of John Robins the Ranter,
Thomas Tany the fanatical pantheist, of Robert Norwood, [165]
Thomas Collier, [166] Joshua Garment, [167] and other eccentrics.
They also became the confident conviction of Joseph Mede,

---

161   Finch, *op. cit.*, p. 59.
162   Goodwin, 'Ephesians', in *Works*, I, pt. I, p. 455.
163   Hill, *Puritanism and Revolution*, p. 141.
164   Finch, *op. cit.*, ep. ded., sig. A2.
165   See Hill, *op. cit.*, pp. 141—142. On Robert Norwood, see *DNB*, s.v. Thomas
Tany.
166   Thomas Collier, *A Brief Answer to some of the Objections and Demurs made
against the coming in and inhabiting of the Jews in this Commonwealth*, (1656).
167   Joshua Garment, *The Hebrews deliverance at hand* (1651). On Garment, see
DNB, s.v. John Robins.

James Ussher, John Cotton, William Strong and Thomas Adams. [168]

That such a divergent body of opinion should be concerned with the destiny of Israel partly explains the interest which centred on the wave of Jewish Messianic expectations in the 1650's. [169] Menasseh Ben Israel's celebrated תקוח ישראל, *Hoc Est, Spes Israelis* (1650) [170] drew the attention of many English theologians to the growing expectancy among Hebrew scholars that the coming of the Messiah was at hand. The hope in which Jewish people lived, declared Menasseh Ben Israel, was "the comming of the Messiah", [171] which he personally expected "about the end of this age." [172] He refuted an impressive list of Rabbis who had sought to establish the precise time of Israel's redemption, [173] but agreed that although "we cannot exactly shew the time of our redemption, yet we judge it to be neer." [174] This conclusion was founded on reasons well understood by Christians who lived in anticipation of the Messiah's second advent. Prevalent conditions fulfil those scriptural prophecies which refer to latter-day events, [175] and "the shortnesse of time" [176] indicates that "the time of redemption is at hand." [177]

The second edition of *The Hope of Israel* was bound with Moses Wall's *Considerations Upon the Point of the Conversion of*

---

[168]   Cf. Mede's evident concern for the Jews, particularly noticeable in the introduction to his *Clavis Apocalyptica* and in the *Diatribae (passim),* and Strong's sermon 'The Doctrine of the Jews Vocation', in *XXXI Select Sermons.*

[169]   Dr. Lucien Wolf suggested that the influence of Puritan eschatology was even a prominent factor in the rise of the pseudo-Messiah, Sabbathi Zevi; Lucien Wolf, *Menasseh Ben Israel's Mission to Oliver Cromwell* (1901), Introd., p. xv. The claims of Sabbathi Zevi are recorded in 'The Counterfeit Messiah; or False Christ of the Jews, at Smyrna in the Year 1666', in Nathaniel Crouch, *Memorable Remarks Upon the Ancient and Modern State of the Jewish Nation* (1786), pp. 125—163.

[170]   The English translation, *The Hope of Israel,* also appeared in 1650.

[171]   Menasseh Ben Israel, *The Hope of Israel* (1650), To the Reader. On Menasseh Ben Israel, see *The Jewish Encyclopaedia,* 8, pp. 282—284, and *DNB,* as Manasseh Ben Israel.

[172]   Menasseh Ben Israel, *op. cit.,* p. 69.

[173]   Those named are Rabbi Seadiah, Moses Egyptius, Moses Gerundensis, Selomeh Jarchi, Abraham bar Ribi Hijah, Abraham Zaculo, Mordehai Reato, Isaac Abarbanel, *ibid.,* p. 68.

[174]   *Ibid.,* p. 69.

[175]   *Ibid.,* pp. 70—71.

[176]   *Ibid.,* p. 80.

[177]   *Ibid.,* p. 82. Menasseh associated the resurrection of the dead with the coming of the Messiah, and even spoke of a second advent: "Quod resurrectio mortuorum conjuncta erit diebus Messiae ... solum in controversia relinquitur, utrum is primus, & unus, an secundus Messiae adventus futurus sit", Menasseh Ben Israel, *De Resurrectione Mortuorum* (Amstelodami, 1636), pp. 251, 254 (the first so numbered).

the Jews (1651), which concurred with Menasseh Ben Israel's view. "The age in which we live, hath been eyed by many Generations past, for the time wherin the Iewes shall be received to mercy", the author pointed out, adding "many of their owne Writers, and also of Christian Authors have pitched upon it". [178] In 1639 Thomas Goodwin had said of the period 1650-1656,

> And the Jews themselves have their Eyes upon this very Time; For it was a Secret communicated to old Mr. Forbes, by a Learned Jew, (as Mr. Forbes himself related it, not long before his Death) that the learnedest Rabby they had had in the World, of late Years, did pitch upon 1650, or thereabouts, as the utmost Time wherein they should expect their Messiah to reveal himself unto their Nation ... [179]

Goodwin had read Sir Henry Blount's *Voyage into the Levant* (1636) from which he had gleaned confirmation of a growing anticipation among the Jews, particularly in the general area of the Eastern Mediterranean. [180] In 1650 John Durie noted "the Jews, almost everie where, are also made sensible of the approaching change of their condition." [181] Further propitious news came from the East in 1655 [182] when Samuel Brett published *A Narrative of the Proceedings of a Great Councel of Jews*. The gathering he described had occurred five years previously when 300 Rabbis had met in the plain of Ageda in Hungary [183] to examine scriptural evidence concerning the Christ-Messiah "whether he be already come, or whether we are yet to expect his coming". [184] The consensus of opinion was that the Messiah had not yet appeared to His people, and the urgency of the times led the assembled Rabbis to convene another meeting in only three years. [185]

1655 saw the publication of two more significant works by Menasseh Ben Israel. His *Piedra Gloriosa o de la Estatua de Nebuchadnesar* was the culmination of a long line of Jewish exposition of the apocalyptic visions of Daniel [186] which had shown a re-

---

[178]   Moses Wall, *Considerations Upon the Point of the Conversion of the Jews* (1651), *ad. cal.* with *The Hope of Israel* (1651) p. 53. On Moses Wall, see D. Masson, *Life of John Milton*, V, p. 601.

[179]   Goodwin, 'Revelation', in *Works*, II, pt. I, p. 183.

[180]   [Goodwin], *A Sermon of the Fifth Monarchy* (1654), p. 24.

[181]   John Durie, in Hartlib (tr.), *Clavis Apocalyptica*, Pref., p. 6.

[182]   On the significance of 1655, see *supra*, p. 121.

[183]   Samuel Brett, *A Narrative of the Proceedings of a Great Councel of Jews* (1655), p. 4.

[184]   *Ibid.*, p. 7.

[185]   *Ibid.*, pp. 7, 11.

[186]   On Jewish apocalyptic interpretation see L. E. Froom, *Prophetic Faith*, II, pp. 184—240.

markably consistent similarity with that of Christian scholarship, and gave a more detailed foundation for the eschatological views set forth in his *Hope of Israel*. These beliefs constituted the basis of his petition to the Lord Protector later that year concerning the re-admission of the Jews to England. [187] "The opinion of many Christians and mine doe concurre herein", he wrote to Cromwell, "that we both believe that the restoring time of our Nation into their Native Countrey, is very near at hand". [188] The sequel to this appeal, which appeared in print as the addresses of Menasseh Ben Israel *To His Highnesse the Lord Protector*, was that Cromwell ordered a select committee to investigate the advisability of re-establishing legal entry for Jews to England. The commission, composed largely of lawyers, merchants and theologians, met in December 1655 and, although to Menasseh Ben Israel's intense disappointment it reached no final conclusion, it is of some interest to note that the plea for re-admission was supported by Thomas Goodwin and Philip Nye, on the grounds that its acceptance would expedite the conversion of the Jews. [189]

It was this latter question of the conversion of Israel and their ultimate restoration to a literal kingdom which was of prime concern to many English theologians in the seventeenth century. [190] The kingdom of Christ could not appear until the kingdom of Israel had been restored, and the kingdom of Israel could not be restored until the Jews, or at least a majority of them, had been led to acknowledge the Messiahship of Christ and the efficacy of His gospel. [191] From the time that Thomas Brightman and Henry Finch had focused attention on Israel's future, those

---

[187]   The Jews had been legally excluded from England by an edict of Edward I in 1290, although a fluctuating and inconsequential Marrano community had existed in London since 1492, Cecil Roth, *A History of the Marranos* (Philadelphia, 1932), pp. 252—259.

[188]   Menasseh Ben Israel 'A Declaration to the Commonwealth of England', sig. A4r, in *To His Highnesse the Lord Protector* (1655).

[189]   See 'The Proceedings about the Jews in England in the Year 1655', in Nathaniel Crouch, *Memorable Remarks*, p. 176.

[190]   See Nuttall, *Visible Saints*, pp. 143—146.

[191]   Nathaniel Homes was pleased to receive a letter in 1658 quoting Rabbi Nathan Sephira's report of a tendency among Jews in Jerusalem to receive Christ, Nathaniel Homes, 'A Brief Cronology Concerning the Jews, From the Year of CHRIST 1650, to 1666' (1665), in Nathaniel Crouch, *Memorable Remarks*, p. 120. Homes had previously referred to a widespread Messianic expectation centred on the year 1650, and had reported "Insomuch that one ancient learned Rabbin on his Deathbed exhorted the Jewes, that if the Messiah did not come about that time, they should imbrace the Christian Messiah, as the true Messiah," *Resurrection*, p. 96.

in England who knew anything at all about prophecy had looked anxiously for some evidence of the anticipated conversion of the Jews. As early as 1609 Brightman had written, perhaps with more optimism than realism, "... these men beinge dispersed every where amonge all Nations, shal be at last converted to the true faith, and shall mourne with an earnest sorrowe, both for theire forefathers horrible wickedness, as also for theire owne so longe obstinacy." [192]

In his *Exposition ... of the Prophecie of Daniel* [193] Brightman had asked, with reference to the resurrection foretold in Daniel xii, 2, "What is this resurrection then?", and had answered his own question, "the full restoring of the Jewish nation, and their vocation to the faith in Christ." [194]   Finch had even propounded that the kingdom of Daniel ii, v. 44, the final kingdom in the historic succession and the initial "fifth monarchy", was "the kingdome of the Iewes", [195] a view which was later expanded by Ephraim Huit, who saw all of Daniel's prophecies as the story of the Jewish people among the persecuting kingdoms of the world, assured at last of a kingdom on earth, "converted in the end of the Romaine Empire, and returning to Iudea", and planting themselves "a Christian Church, exercising dominion over their former oppressours". [196]   The eighteenth point in William Strong's sermon was that "With the calling of the Jews, the Kingdome of the God of heaven shall be set up", [197] and John Cotton pointed out that for many years the church's most respected expositors had, by "light received from the holy Ghost", interpreted Revelation xxi and xxii as applying to a Jewish Kingdom "here on earth". [198] The chief "use" that Strong drew from the doctrine of the Jews' vocation was pressed home to an undoubtedly sympathetic congregation: "Such a conversion we should help forward by faith and prayer, and so much the rather, because the time approaches, the promises are even come unto the birth, and they do draw on apace". [199] And if the faithful should question how the matter could be expedited, other than by faith and prayer, Strong would answer, "then suffer them to live

---

[192]   Brightman, *Revelation*, p. 14.
[193]   In actual fact, only an interpretation of ch. xi, 26 to the end of ch. xii.
[194]   Brightman, 'Daniel' in *Workes*, p. 941.
[195]   Finch, *op. cit.*, p. 55.
[196]   Huit, *op. cit.*, pp. 58, 59.
[197]   Strong, 'The Doctrine of the Iews Vocation', in *Sermons*, p. 287.
[198]   John Cotton, *Of the Holinesse of Church-Members* (1650), p. 94.
[199]   Strong, *op. cit.*, p. 290.

among us, that they may have the Gospel preached to them, that's the way to their conversion, to bring them into our land." [200]

It was this very suggestion, voiced so freely in the mid-1650's, that gave cogency to Menasseh Ben Israel's plea to Cromwell. Both Jewish and Christian theologians agreed that there was to be a gathering of the Jews from their dispersion, but since such a gathering could not transpire until the dispersion was itself complete it could be reasoned, with a degree of logic, that the Jews must first be admitted to England. "Therefore this remains onely in my judgement, before the Messia come and restore our Nation," argued the astute Rabbi, "that first we must have our seat here likewise." [201]   The position was well stated by the pseudonymous Philo-Judaeus who proposed Jewish entry on the grounds that it was a necessary prelude to the second advent:

> If any one that would truly further the coming of our Lord to judgment, and does desire that those evil dayes spoken of and predicted by him might be shortened; let him first study how to further their conversion, because the other cannot be accomplished untill all the elect and chosen Hebrews be made vessels ready prepared to abide for ever in those heavenly mansions above. [202]

Certainly any Jew coming to England in the time of the Commonwealth and Protectorate would be exposed to an array of influences calculated to effect his speedy conversion. [203]

The issue, however, was wider than any nationalistic tones might make it appear. The desire for Jewish entry to England was heavily undergirded by the broader theological argument concerning the general conversion of the Jews. William Strong realised that the Jewish question could not be confined to England, nor even to the countries of Europe where the scattered of Israel might be found. "The stage & place of their conversion shal not be in the Western parts of the world, where few of the are, but in the East and North." [204]   On the basis of prophecy Joseph Mede

---

[200]   *Ibid.*, p. 291.

[201]   Menasseh Ben Israel, *loc. cit.*

[202]   J. J. Philo-Judaeus, *The Resurrection of Dead Bones, or The Conversion of the Jewes* (1655), p. 122.

[203]   Cf. "inasmuch as the conversion of the Jews was an indispensable preliminary to the Millennium, their admission to England, where they might meet the godliest people in the world, was urgently necessary", Lucien Wolf, *op. cit.*, p. xxii. Sir Edward Spencer, M.P., believed that the English were "the likelyest Nation under Heaven to doe it", Edward Spencer, *An Epistle to the learned Menasseh Ben Israel* (1650), p. 2.

[204]   Strong, *op. cit.*, p. 286 (the second so numbered).

had early looked for a universal transformation of Israel. [205]
Nathaniel Homes, who maintained that at the second advent
Christ would only appear "in the clouds, personally, to convince,
and convert" Jews everywhere, [206] and who saw Jewish Messianic expectation as a basis for Judaeo-Christian dialogue, urged
the mutual study of prophecy as a means to hasten the ultimate
conversion of Israel:

> ... thereby we may search out the grounds upon which the Iewes build
> their expectation of the coming of the Messiah, and in what manner
> they expect his coming, that so we may joyne issue with them in
> knowledge, hope, and prayer, or otherwise, within our spheare, to
> help them forward ... We all, both Jewes and Gentiles, that have been
> candid enquirers into the Scriptures, have from the beginning looked
> for his further coming ... [207]

Thomas Adams related the comings of Christ to the redemptive
purpose of God for both Jews and Gentiles:

> His Legall comming, was principally to the Jewes, not excluding the
> Gentiles: his Evangelicall comming, was principally to the Gentiles,
> not debarring the Iewes: his Iudiciall comming, shall be to the Iewes
> and Gentiles, exempting none, but to judge all the world. In his first
> comming, he was a Commander; in his second, a Saviour; in his last, a
> Iudge. His first, was to give the Law; his next, to give the Gospel; his
> third, shall be to require an account of both. [208]

Viewed in this light the Gentile had no superior claim to the
gospel, no ultimate advantage over the Jew, and the last of
Adams' six "precedent signes" of the imminent advent was "a
new Troope", the converted host of Israel. [209]

Many who awaited these events were confident that this work
of grace would culminate in the return of the Jews to the land of
their fathers. The Jew who could propose to an English public of
1650 that the ten tribes were to return to Jerusalem at the
end[210] was assured of a sympathetic hearing. The soil into which
such seeds were cast was fertile indeed, and the climate favourable. For half a century or more Englishmen had been condi-
tioned to look for a literal restoration of Israel. Brightman's "restoring of the Jewish nation" was more than a call "to the faith

---

[205]   Mede, *op. cit.*, pt. II, pp. 118—120.
[206]   Homes, *op. cit.*, p. 97.
[207]   *Ibid.*, p. 126.
[208]   Adams, *Commentary*, p. 1166.
[209]   *Ibid.*, p. 1136.
[210]   Menasseh Ben Israel, *The Hope of Israel*, p. 64.

of Christ".[211] It was a national revival in Palestine,[212] and the
sixth of Revelation's seven vials, which in 1609 were already
shortly expected, foretold the drying up of the river Euphrates
that the Jews might be received in glory.[213] In 1642 Robert
Maton's *Israels Redemption* proclaimed the imminent emancipa-
tion of Israel, "a most righteous and flourishing estate of the
Jewes in their owne land",[214] and two years later Ephraim Huit
saw them "reestablished into their former Kingdome with greate
glory", a fifth apocalyptic kingdom ruling over all the world.[215]
Menasseh Ben Israel was clearly in respectable company when he
wrote that "the restoring time of our Nation into their Native
Countrey, is very near at hand."[216]

By 1647 a "certaine and credible" source of information indicated that the restoration of Israel had already begun. In various
places in Illyria, Bithynia and Cappadocia, it appeared that
groups of Jews were simultaneously "assembling themselves together into one body ... with a resolution to regaine the holy land
once more out of the hand of the Ottoman",[217] and if the
continuing authority of the Pope argued against such an immediate eventuality, it was to be remembered that the final overthrow of Antichrist was "neere, even at the doore".[218] Ten
years later those who still looked patiently to the East were
encouraged by another anonymous pamphlet, *An Information,
Concerning The Present State of the Jewish Nation in Europe
and Judea* (1658). The author began by stating that the latter-
day distress of nations was preparatory to the Jews' return, since
it would drive them from those very nations among whom they
had hitherto dwelt, and would awaken within them an earnest
desire for the realisation of the Messianic promise.[219] He then
proceeded to recount recent occurrences which were to be interpreted as evidence of divine favour turning again upon the Jews.

---

[211] Brightman, *loc. cit.*
[212] *Ibid.*, p. 930; cf. *Workes*, p. 544.
[213] Brightman, *Revelation*, p. 551.
[214] Maton, *Israels Redemption*, p. 6.
[215] Huit, *op. cit.*, p. 63.
[216] Menasseh Ben Israel, 'A Declaration', in *To His Highnesse the Lord Protector*,
sig. A4r.
[217] *Doomes-Day: or the great Day of the Lords Iudgement proved by Scripture*
(1647), p. 2.
[218] *Ibid.*, p. 5. The anonymous author of this tract, who held that "the second
coming of Christ is each day and houre to be expected", labelled millenarianism as a
"monstrous opinion to be abhorred", *ibid.*, p. 6.
[219] [John Durie], *An Information Concerning The Present State of the Jewish
Nation in Europe and Judea* (1658), pp. 3, 7.

The serious drought of 1639 had been broken in Judea when, on the third day of a solemn fast, prayer had been offered at the sepulchre of Zachary. In a manner distinctly reminiscent of Elijah's experience at Carmel, Jehovah had answered the supplications of the entreating Jews, "the clouds gathered, and with thunder they poured such a flood of rain, that all the Cisterns were filled and did run over". [220] A miraculous intervention had secured alleviation from the famine of 1655. [221] Additional evidence could be drawn from the increased productivity of Canaan. Whereas previously the land had been noticeably more barren than neighbouring countries, within the last five or six years it had become "exceeding fruitfull, yielding ten times the encrease of that which formerly it did yield." [222] Plainly enough, although 1655 had passed without a new nation in Palestine, the promises were only delayed and, as Nathaniel Homes suggested, 1666 might as acceptably prove to be the year of Jubilee. [223]

The seventh angel, then, had long since begun to sound, the remaining vials were about to be poured forth, and the final blast of the seventh trumpet would soon be heard heralding the finished mystery. [224] Everything pointed to an early transition of earthly kingdoms to the righteous kingdom of God. The Jews, together with the Papacy and the Turks, were cast in a leading role for the final act of this age-long drama and if the precise movements of the penultimate scene were yet to be observed, it was nevertheless possible to distinguish in profile the shape of things to come.

The final settlement of the converted Jews in Palestine, with the subsequent influx of Gentile peoples to the gospel, [225] would mark the beginning of divine rule upon earth. "With the calling of the Jews, the Kingdome of the God of heaven shall be set up", [226] declared William Strong. It could not occur, however, while the power of Antichrist continued unchecked and the destruction of Turkey and the Papacy were both of prior necessity.

---

[220] *Ibid.*, p. 8.
[221] *Ibid.*, p. 9.
[222] *Ibid.*, p. 10.
[223] See Homes, 'A Brief Cronology', in *Memorable Remarks*, p. 123.
[224] See Rev. x, 7.
[225] Following the vials of wrath on the Antichrist, John Cotton looked for "the fulnesse of the Gentiles to come in, and with the Jewes, multitudes of Pagans", John Cotton, *The Bloudy Tenent, Washed, and made white in the bloud of the Lambe* (1647), p. 148. "The generality of the Nations shall come flocking in as Doves to the windows", Haughton, *op. cit.*, p. 166.
[226] Strong, *op. cit.*, p. 287.

The former was to be accomplished by the impending Turco-Judean war, a conflict which would break out upon the return of the Jews [227] and which some even saw as the final Armageddon. [228] Later generations would sing "Gog and Magog to the fray", but with measurably less conviction than had they sat under the preaching of a Goodwin, a Homes, or a Strong.[229] Meanwhile the Papacy, which had been in decline since the time of Elizabeth I, [230] or earlier, [231] must likewise be brought down, if only after a brief revival of influence in the latter days. [232] In Goodwin's view this later papal revival was to follow a second reformation, in England, which would arise from the Jews' conversion. [233] Thereafter the speedy overthrow of papal power by the nations of Europe [234] could be expected and with the kingdoms of Antichrist thus defeated the way would be open at last for the kingdom of God.

Most of this had been prefigured in the seven vials of Revelation xvi and any who sought to know the times of these momentous events were directed again to the prophetic chronology of Daniel. Goodwin, who may be considered representative in the reckoning of times, regarded the two periods of chapter xii as pillars marking out the time allotted for the execution of the last

---

[227]   Cf. Finch, op. cit., p. 77, and Huit, op. cit., pp. 336–342. Robert Maton believed that Christ would come when a great army was gathered against the Jews, Maton, Israel's Redemption Redeemed, p. 36.

[228]   E.g. Finch, loc. cit.

[229]   This remains valid, even though by the middle of the century some expositors tended to place the struggle with Gog and Magog at the end of the millennium, e.g. Guild, op. cit., p. 313, and Maton, Israels Redemption, p. 114. Gog and Magog still symbolised the Turk and Mohammedanism, and a considerable body of opinion continued to hold the earlier view that Gog and Magog related to the Turk and the Papacy and the final impending conflict between the forces of righteousness and iniquity prior to the second advent, e.g. Dent, op. cit., p. 276, and Pareus, op. cit., pp. 536–38.

[230]   E.g. Brightman, op. cit., pp. 510–11.

[231]   E.g. Goodwin, 'Revelation', in Works, II, pp. 94, 84.

[232]   Nathaniel Homes, A Sermon Preached afore Thomas Andrews, Lord Maior (1650), p. 22.

[233]   Goodwin, op. cit., p. 145. The "second reformists" are the radical protestants in England who carry the work of reformation further than the disciples of Luther or Calvin, and are the "two witnesses" of Rev. xi, godly ministers and magistrates in church and state in the last days, ibid., pp. 151, 135. The final emergence of papal power is directed against the two witnesses, and is materially strengthened by "carnal Protestants", whom Goodwin fears will proceed "even to an open acknowledgement and professing the Pope's Power, (though perhaps not as infallible Head of the Church, yet as Universal Patriarch of the West) and so endeavouring to effect an Union and Reconciliation with him", ibid., p. 151.

[234]   By "the reformed Churches, in the ten Kingdoms", Strong, Vengeance, p. 28. Earlier, Dent had suggested that of the ten kingdoms of Europe referred to in Rev. xvii, 12, seven had already turned against the Papacy through the embracing of the Protestant faith, Dent, op. cit., pp. 256, 257.

events. [235]   The end of the 1290 years "shews when the first turning of the Course of Things, for the Accomplishment of all, should begin." [236]   The conclusion of the 1335 years designated "the Time of the full and final End, and compleat accomplishment of all" [237] and Goodwin, who anticipated the Jews' conversion in the mid 1650's explained:

> And so that space of Time between these two Periods (which is 45 Years or thereabouts) ... is allotted as the Time wherein those Things prophesied of by him to fall out in the last Ages of the World, should, each in their order, be accomplish'd. And so, from the first period, should begin the great turn towards the accomplishment of them, and the immediate Preparations thereunto. And in the Interim of that intermediate space of Time between 1650, or 56, and 1700, shall follow the orderly performance of those Things which are to end and consummate all, before the glorious Kingdom of Christ. As first, the Ruin of Rome, and so, the end of Antichrist's Reign; and then the destruction of the Turkish Empire; after which, shall begin that great Resurrection, even at that last Period of 1335, falling out about 1700, which is the consummation of all. [238]

By any account, all that remained to be fulfilled would have occurred, at the very latest, by 1700 and in all probability much earlier than that. The kingdoms of the world had come to the hour of their death-struggle and men watched the affairs of nations with an interest unknown in previous ages. Thomas Goodwin preached on *The Great Interest of States & Kingdomes*, and John Owen on *The Advantage of the Kingdome of Christ in the Shaking of the Kingdoms of the World*, and it is an apt reflection on the age that even Bishop Hall of Norwich could anticipate "before that great Day", [239] "the calling of the Gentiles, the conversion of the Jewes ... and (the) enlargement of his Christian Church, the subjugation, and overthrow of the publique enemies thereof." [240]

---

[235]   Goodwin, *op. cit.*, p. 184.
[236]   *Loc. cit.*
[237]   *Loc. cit.*
[238]   *Ibid.*, pp. 184, 185.
[239]   Joseph Hall, *The Revelation Unrevealed*, p. 10.
[240]   *Ibid.*, p. 17.

CHAPTER FIVE

LAST EVENTS AND THE MILLENNIAL RULE OF JESUS

The social historian will not be charged with caprice for pointing out that hopes of a coming Utopia were strengthened in the
seventeenth century by the prevalent political, social and economic conditions. In a similar way, the historian of dogma cannot be considered arbitrary for feeling obliged to observe that
preachers and divines saw that good theology required an end to
the present sinful state and the institution of a better order. That
the world was to have an end was as clear to the Anglican George
Hakewill "as that there is a Sun in the firmament".[1] Moreover, in
an age that stressed morality it was not out of place to think that
a moral obligation devolved upon the Godhead to eradicate sin
and establish the righteous rule. Such doctrinal logic served to
unite theologians who might differ on other matters and, as was
suggested in the foregoing chapter,[2] produced the broadly consistent declaration that the kingdom of God was assured and that
it was at hand.

When men thought of this kingdom they inevitably thought of
the coming of Christ. Indeed, the two basic reasons to which all
the purposes of the advent[3] could be reduced were judgement
and government,[4] and if the latter received a greater emphasis this
was because it concerned the eternal destiny of the church. Men
could aver with equal conviction that the promises of a new
heaven and a new earth[5] were to be realised, either temporally in
a glorious state of the church that would prevail in the latter days
prior to the final consummation of all, or eternally in a literal
new creation when the earth would be restored to its primitive
glory. John Cotton's *Churches Resurrection* (1642) shared a dis-

---

[1] George Hakewill, *An Apologie of the Power and Providence of God in the Government of the World* (1627), p. 441.
[2] See *supra*, pp. 126 ff.
[3] The reasons given by Richard Sibbes for desiring the advent were parallel to the
five purposes of Christ's coming as listed by John Seagar, viz., To judge and establish
the kingdom, to reward every man according to his works, to take vengeance on
sinners, to convince the ungodly of their wickedness, and to be glorified in His saints;
cf. Sibbes 'Churches Eccho', pp. 108 ff, in *Beames of Divine Light,* and Seagar, *World
to Come,* pp. 96—97.
[4] Cf. *supra,* pp. 37 ff.
[5] E.g. Isa. 1xv, 17—25, II Pet. iii, 13, Rev. xxi and xxii.

tinct synonymity with Nathaniel Homes' *New World; or the New Reformed Church*, and the premise of Jeremiah Burroughes' *Jerusalem's Glory Breaking forth into the World* was that there would come "a time that God in this Earth, shall make his Church to be the glory of the earth".[6] Hezekiah Holland, on the other hand, followed David Pareus in looking for a re-created earth in which righteousness and truth would prevail eternally at the second coming.[7] William Strong asserted:

> In the last dayes shall the great and glorious deliverances of the Churches be, when all the persecuting Monarchies shall be destroyed, and the mountayne of the Lords house be exalted on the top of the mountaynes that all nations may flow to it ...[8]

In this can be seen the essence of John Seagar's "world to come", a literal new earth to follow immediately at the advent in which Christ would reign with His saints.[9] In either case the final emphasis was upon the divine rule. The ultimate purpose of God, as Arthur Dent had perceived, was a world "redintigrated [sic] and restored to that pristinate estate, wherein it was before the fall",[10] a prospect on which both views of the new earth could agree. Nowhere did Milton write more as a child of his age than when he immortalised the saga of sin and redemption as a paradise lost and a paradise regained.

All this was not to minimise the necessity of judgement. It was manifest, both from a reading of the Bible and from an observation of human behaviour, that a day of reckoning must occur before men could receive their just rewards, and those who looked for a temporal reign of the saints were as sure of judgement to come as those who expected an imminent new creation. Nathaniel Homes thought that the visitations of divine wrath recorded in Scripture, such as the destruction of Sodom and Gomorrah and the fall of Jerusalem, were "a pledge to his people, that in time he will judge the rest of their enemies, at that day of Doom".[11] Goodwin could use the doctrine of coming judgement as an incentive to holy living[12] with as much ease as William

---

[6] Burroughes, *Jerusalem's Glory*, p. 4.
[7] Cf. Holland, *Exposition*, p. 172, and Pareus, *Commentary*, p. 550.
[8] Strong, *Vengeance*, p. 19.
[9] Seagar, *World to Come*, pp. 58, 93.
[10] Dent, *Rvine of Rome*, p. 285.
[11] Homes, 'Moderation of Spirit for quietation of Mind in trying times', in *Works*, p. 112.
[12] Goodwin, 'Of Gospel Holiness Implanted in the Heart', in *Works*, V, pt. II, p. 39.

Durham, whose Assize sermon at Warwick in 1651 was taken from James v, ix, "behold, the judge standeth before the door". The force of Durham's appeal to conscience—"only unrivet the secret Cabine of thy brest, and thou shalt find this doctrine legible" [13]—was intensified by Robert Bolton's searching portrayal of the exact account which would be required of

> ... every thought of thine heart, every word of thy mouth, every glance of thine eye, every moment of thy time, every omission of any holy duty, or good deed, every action thou hast undertaken, with all the circumstances thereof, every office thou hast borne, and the discharge of it in every point and particular, every company thou hast come into, and all thy behaviour there, every Sermon thou hast heard, every Sabbath thou has spent, every motion of the Spirit which hath been made unto thy soule ... [14]

Jesus had taught that at the end of the world the sheep were to be separated from the goats, [15] and if men could argue on other texts they had no cavil at that.

The question, then, was not 'Would there be a final judgement?' but rather, 'When would it occur?' In what sequence would Christ effect the duties of King and Judge? It would have been simple enough to provide an answer to this question, had it not been for the implications of Revelation chapter xx. Even then, for many the answer was never in doubt. Christopher Love explained that Christ's appearing meant "that glorious manifestation of Jesus Christ upon earth at that time when he shall come at the last day to judge both quick and dead". [16] But the theologian committed to the historicist interpretation of prophecy was obliged to make room in his scheme of things for the millennium, and it was clear that no attempt to set forth a rational correlation of judgement and government could exclude this difficult chapter. As the serious study of prophecy became more respectable the problem of the millennium became increasingly significant, and a new awareness arose of the difficulties associated with the thousand years of Satan's bondage and the saints' reign. With the development of millenarianism came the tendency to subordinate the issue of judgement to that of government and the second advent doctrine as a whole. The chief concerns came to be those

---

[13]   William Durham, *Maran-atha*, p. 10. Thomas Hooker, in *The Soules Preparation for Christ* (1632), had already established the force of this argument, pp. 19, 20.

[14]   Bolton, *Last Things*, pp. 89, 90.

[15]   Matt. xxv, 31—34.

[16]   Love, *Heavens Glory*, pp. 36 ff; cf. William Durham, *Maran-atha*, *passim*, and Brooks, *Glorious Day*, p. 7.

of relating the second coming to the millennium and the end of the world, of ascertaining the nature of the millennial period, and of explaining all in terms which did not contradict the general revelation of the Bible. Virtually every shade of millenarian view which developed in seventeenth-century England was exercised primarily over these issues, and the overall picture is less of the subjective imposition of fanciful theories by an extravagant minority, than of erudite and honest men genuinely wrestling with an obscure and difficult passage of Scripture. [17]

The acknowledged difficulties posed by the thousand years of prophecy were not overlooked by the opponents of millenarianism. [18] A full and objective critique of the divarications of the millenarians was given by Bishop Hall in 1650. [19] After an analysis of the current views requiring twenty pages, Hall asks, with some justification: "Now, Lord, where are we? what Reader doth not find himselfe lost in this wildernesse of opinions? Or what living man can, in such diversities of probable judgements, say, this, not the other, is the sense of the holy ghost?" [20] It is difficult to read Hall today and not be impressed by the genuine sense of bewilderment created by the millennial problem. [21] Given the perspective of history, however, it is possible to bring some order out of confusion and to see that the millenarian views of the seventeenth century fell largely into one of three categories, [22] broadly analogous to the later classifications of amillen-

---

[17]   Millenarianism was not necessarily radical *per se*. The failure to recognise who were radicals and who were not must be countered if the seventeenth-century eschatological scene is to be fully understood. Cf. F. S. Plotkin, 'Sighs from Sion', *passim*. Alsted, Mede, and Cotton do not belong together with Rogers, Aspinwall and Canne.

[18]   Pareus wrote "And the more I thinke upon it, the lesse I finde how to unty the knot that hath troubled so many," Pareus, Commentary, p. 506. The learned Mede confessed that the thousand years of the seventh trumpet was "the most abstruse of all the propheticall Scripture", Mede, *Key of The Revelation*, pt. II, p. 121.

[19]   Cf. Robert Baillie, *A Dissuasive from the Errours of the Time* (1645), p. 234.

[20]   Joseph Hall, *The Revelation Unrevealed*, pp. 63, 64.

[21]   Perhaps this may account for the continuing tendency to use the terms 'millenarian' and 'millenarianism' rather loosely, as in Tai Liu, *Discord in Zion*, Ch. I, *passim*, e.g. pp. 10, 26. All eschatological hope was not millenarian in the sense that it anticipated a literal thousand-year reign of Christ and the saints on earth.

[22]   But not the 'moderate', 'conservative', and 'left' classification as suggested by R. G. Clouse, 'The Influence of John Henry Alsted on English Millenarian Thought in the Seventeenth Century', unpublished Ph.D. thesis, State University of Iowa, 1963. There were conservative and extreme elements in both the premillenarian and postmillenarian camps. De Jong's classification of 'mild', 'complex', and 'extreme' millennialists is hardly more satisfactory. The 'complex' wing is distinguished from the 'mild' element by De Jong on account of an engrossment with dates, a literal interpretation of the first resurrection, and a literal thousand year millennium, John Cotton, however, whom De Jong cites as typical of the 'mild' group, calculated prophetic dates and

nialism, premillennialism, and postmillennialism. Strictly speaking, only the latter two positions can be described as millenarian since the amillennialist held that the thousand year period belonged to the past and had no further place in the scheme of future events. The premillennialist stressed a future millennium which was to be inaugurated by the second coming of Christ. The postmillennialist also anticipated a coming millennium but emphasised, generally, that a literal advent would not take place until its end. Although the variations upon minor interpretative detail within each classification were almost infinite, the deviations from the three main streams were surprisingly few. [23] Before proceeding to a closer examination of the millenarian impulse, it will be helpful to consider each of these basic approaches to the interpretation of the millennium and the coming of Christ.

The view which placed the thousand years in the past was a continuation of Reformation thought, and beyond that could be traced back to the eschatological teaching of Augustine who had equated the millennium with the entire era between Christ's two comings. [24] The seventeenth century began with a re-iteration of the Augustinian concept, although in a form modified by the passage of sixteen hundred years. [25] The millennium was now almost exclusively seen as a literal period of time, [26] the chief characteristics of which were the binding of Satan and the reign of the church. Among the early champions of this modified Augustinian eschatology were Dent, Broughton, Forbes and Pareus, any of whom might be regarded as more thoroughly representative than Napier or Brightman. [27] It is not to be over-

---

anticipated a literal millennium. Passages in John Owen's Parliamentary sermons of 1649 and 1651, could have been construed as encouragement for the more 'extreme' elements aspiring to establish the kingdom; cf. Tai Liu, *Discord in Zion*, pp. 65 ff. On balance it seems more appropriate to retain the later millenarian classifications.

[23] The main deviants were James Durham, who believed that the thousand years were then current, having commenced in 1560, "being in part past, but in their vigour to come", although not necessarily to be reckoned literally, James Durham, *Commentarie*, pp. 722—727, and Napier and Brightman, who both taught a double millennium on the basis that verse 6 of Revelation xx referred to a different period of time than that mentioned in verses 2—5, Napier, *Plaine Discouery*, pp. 232—243; Brightman, *Revelation*, pp. 851, 852.

[24] A summary of Augustine's eschatology will be found in L. E. Froom, *Prophetic Faith*, I, pp. 473 ff.

[25] Augustine had not anticipated that the last judgement would be delayed much beyond 1,000 A.D., Augustine, *The City of God*, (tr. M. Dods, New York, 1948), Bk. XX, ch. 7.

[26] A notable exception was James I who described the number 1000 "ane number certane for ane uncertane", *Ane Frvitfvll Meditatioun*, sig. Aiiiv.

[27] Although Napier and Brightman are described above as deviants from the main

looked, in appraising the millenarian ethos, that modified Augus-
tinianism continued to attract a considerable following, even
through the years when a more extreme millenarianism and Fifth
Monarchy teachings were in vogue. In 1656 William Guild argued
for a fulfilled millennium, [28] and a year later Thomas Hall maintained that "all the Orthodox do unanimously agree and conclude, that those thousand years are already past and gone ..." [29]

In the neo-Augustinian view the emphasis was laid on the binding of Satan, and history provided a number of satisfactory alternatives from which the time of this bondage could be reckoned.
The two most popular datings were from the beginning of the
Christian era, and from the reign of Constantine. Following the
earlier date, Satan was bound by the first preaching of the gospel
of Christ, and loosed again around the year 1,000 A.D. as the
"two great and monstrous heresies of Popery and Mahometrie"
arose in the world. [30] The later view, which brought the end of
the millennium forward by three hundred years or so, was aptly
defended by William Guild:

> ... by Constantine's conversion, heathenish and open persecution of the
> Gospel ceased, and the Christian religion by Laws was everywhere
> established, for from that time the dragon had no loose chaine ... and
> this was about the three hundredth year of Christ, which leads us also
> to the point of his losing, which falls out about the one thousand
> three hundredth year of God, in the time of Boniface the eighth, that
> monster of men ... [31]

---

stream of millennial thought, both contend strongly for the modified Augustinian view
in the interpretation of their first millennium. Brightman's views are a significant
milestone in the overall development of seventeenth-century eschatology, a watershed
from which two great streams flow in opposite directions. Christopher Love, in defending the modified Augustinian view, in 1653, refers to Brightman "that Orthodox
divine", Love, *Heavens Glory*, p. 74, and the millenarians Nathaniel Homes and John
Cotton both refer to Brightman in advocating a coming millennial state, Homes, *Resurrection*, p. 553, Cotton, *Church-Members*, p. 94. Brightman's emphasis on an age of
glory for the church during the second millennium, with Christ reigning supreme
through the saints, precludes his being considered representative of the "revised Augustinian" eschatology of the seventeenth century, as suggested by P. Toon in 'Puritan
Eschatology: 1600 to 1648', *The Manifold Grace of God*, (1968), pp. 51—54. Toon's
revised assessment of Brightman's position as "radically different" from that of Augustine is more accurate, P. Toon (Ed.), *Puritan Eschatology*, p. 31. To say that Brightman
is a deviant is not to underestimate one of the great names in the eschatological
thought of the age.

[28] Guild, *Sealed Book Opened*, pp. 304—308 (p. 304 bound at p. 290).
[29] Thomas Hall, *Chiliasto-mastix redivivus*, p. 66.
[30] Dent, *op. cit.*, p. 276. Dent specified 998 A.D. as the year in which the devil
was "fully loosed".
[31] Guild, *op. cit.*, pp. 306, 307.

Some saw 1073 as a more significant date for the loosing of Satan, since through the accession of Gregory VII to the see of Rome the Papacy had been fully established and the devil again freed to deceive the world through the notable rise of "superstition and errour" which now followed. [32] Yet other dates were known to Bishop Hall in 1650 and to James Durham in 1658, [33] which strengthens the conclusion that the modified Augustinian eschatology remained an acceptable alternative to any form of millenarianism.

With the millennium firmly placed in the past the church could look forward to an uncomplicated future, the coming of Christ, an immediate day of judgement, and the subsequent reward of the righteous. The Presbyterian Thomas Hall can thus argue "the appearing of Christ in glory, and his coming to judgment are joyned together, as being one and the self same thing at the same time," [34] the Puritan Hezekiah Holland can hope for a new earth to follow the fires of judgement, [35] and the Anglican Joseph Hall can add a note of immediacy to all:

> ... the world is near to it's last period; and ... our Lord Jesus is at hand, for his finall judgement. For if in the time of the blessed Apostles, it was justly computed to be the last houre, needs must it now be drawing towards the last minute. [36]

Clearly it is not essential to accept the doctrine of a coming millennium in order to believe in the imminent advent of the Lord.

The obvious objection to any past dating of the millennium was that no period as long as a thousand years could be found in history during which the devil had been effectively bound, and in which the church had enjoyed an era of undisturbed peace and spiritual advancement. Nathaniel Homes agreed with Bishop Prideaux of Worcester that the time of Satan's binding concurred with that of the saints' reign, but disagreed with the bishop's argument that that time was now past. "The Saints have not yet reigned; no, not in the pict thousand yeers of the Doctors; but errours, persecutions, wars &c. pressing downe the Churches, as ye have heard, have that time abounded." [37] If the thousand

---

[32]   Pareus, *op. cit.*, pp. 504—508, Hayne, *Christs Kingdome*, pp. 86, 87.
[33]   See Joseph Hall, *op. cit.*, pp. 43—49, and James Durham, *op. cit.*, p. 723.
[34]   Thomas Hall, *op. cit.*, p. 55.
[35]   Holland, *op. cit.*, p. 172.
[36]   Joseph Hall, *op. cit.*, pp. 226, 227.
[37]   Homes, *op. cit.*, p. 456.

years were to follow the reign of Antichrist, [38] and if Antichrist
was to rule for 1260 years, [39] and if the supremacy of Antichrist
was to be marked by error, blasphemy, idolatry and persecution, [40] it stood to reason that the millennium could only be
placed in the future. Such arguments spoke with force both to
the academic mind schooled in the disciplines of logic and theology, and to the more humble believer versed only in the teachings of Scripture. With the consent of both, a new explanation
was applied to the last chapters of Revelation, and for the first
time the church in England began to entertain a premillennial
hope.

The issue that divided the premillennialist from the postmillennialist was the time of the literal coming of Christ. That which
distinguished between various premillennialists was the nature of
Christ's millennial reign. A clear majority of millenarians in the
seventeenth century were premillennialist, looking for the personal, glorious, and imminent coming of Christ and His subsequent rule. These premillennialists themselves were divided, dis-
proportionately, between a conservative wing who believed in a
spiritual reign of Christ through His Saints, and a more radical
element who expected that He would reign in person on earth for
the duration of the thousand years. Apart from this important
difference, the two wings of premillennialism were broadly
agreed on the major events associated with the thousand year
period: a personal advent, two literal resurrections preceding and
following the millennium, a postmillennial judgement, and the
ultimate resignation of authority to the Father for ever. [41] Within
this broad framework of agreement there were always exceptions, and it is probably better to avoid too stringent a classification of the advocates of premillenarianism.

The conservative wing, which was the first to develop, owed its
origin to a generation of theologians who knew little of the tur-
bulence of civil war. Mede and Alsted who both wrote first in

---

[38]   It had early been observed that a chronological interpretation of the Revelation
required the millennium to come after the times of Antichrist. Hence "the downfall of
Antichrist, and the binding of Satan for a thousand years, do without any intermission
meet together", Alsted, *The Beloved City,* p. 57; cf. Mede, 'Remaines on Some Passages in the Apocalypse', in *Works,* p. 603. The 'Remaines' were written some time
before his *Clavis* and *Commentary* were first printed, *loc. cit.*

[39]   See *supra,* pp. 116, 117.

[40]   Haughton, *Antichrist,* pp. 126—136.

[41]   Christ was to reign in His kingdom during the millennium. Beyond that stretched eternity, which was to be the kingdom of God; see Mede, *Key of The Revelation,*
pt. II, p. 123.

1627, and Goodwin whose leaning to millenarianism had begun
in the 1620's while he was still at Cambridge, [42] all believed that
Christ would return in person, establish the kingdom upon earth
and vest its government in the hands of the saints, and then
return to heaven until the millennium was over. The conviction
was increasingly shared by later writers. The title of John
Archer's famous pamphlet in 1642 gave rise to an unwarranted
assumption that the author was a radical of the deepest dye. [43] In
actual fact Archer did not anticipate that Christ would remain on
earth for the millennium, and his whole exposition was hardly
more extreme than that of Mede. [44] "I do not thinke that Christ
shall ... continue raigning upon earth a thousand years, I do not
see how the Saints can spare him out of heaven so long", [45]
argued one famous preacher before the Long Parliament in 1648.
Nonetheless, the kingdom was to be Christ's and glorious, "in
this world", "his Regnum potentiae ..." and he would "rule from
sea to sea." [46] The language could understandably be mistaken to
signify a literal reign. The idea of a literal second advent and a
spiritual reign of the church continued to gain strength and some
of its most ardent exponents are to be found among writers of
Commonwealth and Protectorate times. Mede could have wished
for no more faithful a disciple than Nathaniel Homes who, between 1652 and 1666, defended the moderate millenarian position with a zeal and clarity which were matched only by his
learning. [47]

Perhaps it is wiser here to allow those who have thus far been
called conservative premillenarians to speak for themselves. In so
doing they will remind us of the numerous possibilities for difference within the overall scheme, and also provide a first-hand
account of the premillennial hope. The full title of Thomas Good-

---

[42] In the preface to Vol. I of Goodwin's *Works*, signed by Thankfull Owen and
James Barron, and published in 1681, it was pointed out that he had "preached these
lectures about Forty years ago". Goodwin himself confessed to a fascination with
millenarianism which went back "these Twenty years", *Works*, I, pt. I, p. 456.

[43] Archer, *The Personall reigne of Christ vpon Earth*. According to Robert Baillie,
Archer was "bold to set up the whole Fabricke of Chiliasme", Baillie, *Dissuasive*,
p. 224.

[44] Archer, *op. cit.*, pp. 21, 22.

[45] Bridge, *Christs Coming*, p. 6; cf. Mede, 'Remaines', in *Works*, p. 603.

[46] Bridge, *op. cit.*, pp. 3, 7.

[47] Homes's millenarian views were set forth chiefly in *Plain Dealing, or The Cause
and Cure of the Present Evils of the Times* (1652), *A Commentary ... on the whole
Book of Canticles* (1650), *The Resurrection Revealed* (1653), *The Resurrection-
Revealed Raised Above Doubts & Difficulties in Ten Exercitations* (1661), and *Miscellanea* (1666).

win's *World to Come*, published in 1655 but "preached ... many yeares since", was given as:

> Prooving That between the state of this World as now it is, and the state of things after the day of Judgement, when God shall be all in all: There is a world to come which is of purpose, and in a more especiall manner appointed for Jesus Christ to be King, and wherein he shall more eminently Reign. [48]

Mede had differed from this only in stressing that the day of judgement was to be equated with the entire millennial period:

> ... the Seventh Trumpet and the Thousand years contained therein is that Magnus dies Domini, and Magnus Dies Judicii, or Dies magni Judicii, the Great Day of the Lord, The Great Day of Judgement, The Day of the Great Judgement ... Not a Day of a few hours, as we commonly suppose, but continuatum multorum annorum intervallum, a continued space of many Years, wherein Christ shall destroy all his Enemies, and at length Death it self; beginning with Antichrist, by his revelation from heaven in flaming fire, and ending with the Universal Resurrection: during which space of time shall be the Kingdom of the Saints in the New Jerusalem. [49]

A new Jerusalem would appeal to the Jews, and Nathaniel Homes understood the drift of the times [50] when pointing out that the Kingdom belonged to an Israelite as much as to a Gentile:

> All the world of Jewes and Gentiles must be glad and rejoyce at the reigning of Christ ... Christ comes in the clouds, and every eye shall see him, Christ as the great Angel descending from heaven, binding Satan, and causing his Saints to reigne on earth; New Jerusalem, a New Heaven, and a New Earth being brought downe from Heaven, wherein ... dwelleth righteousnesse. [51]

The other wing of premillenarianism differed from the views expressed above principally in that it held to a literal presence of Christ in His kingdom, an emphasis which found its advocates among a less distinguished school of preachers. The proponents of the new view could not boast a Mede, a Goodwin, or a Homes

---

[48]   Thomas Goodwin, *The World to Come* (1655), Title-page. That this edition was probably 'pirated', and a poor version of the authorised text at that, will not be held to detract from its worth as a statement of Goodwin's position; cf. his *Works*, I, pt. I, pp. 441—456.

[49]   Mede, 'Remaines', in *Works*, p. 603. The view was dismissed by Robert Baillie as a "very strange fancie", occasioned by Mede's desire to avoid conflicting with the Creed which taught that Christ remained in Heaven until His second advent at the final judgement, Baillie, *op. cit.*, pp. 225—226. The difficulty was real, and others were inclined to follow Mede on this point, e.g. Homes, *op. cit.*, p. 473; Hicks, *Revelation Revealed*, p. 10.

[50]   Cf. *supra*, pp. 147 ff.

[51]   Homes, *op. cit.*, p. 161.

among their ranks. At best, they could look to the Kentish Independent, John Durant, and after that to the obscure William Hicks and George Hammon, or to the anonymous author of *A Sober Inquiry; or Christs Reign With his Saints a Thousand Years*. The idea seems to have received serious consideration first in the early days of the civil war. Another little-known clergyman, Robert Maton, had been exercised over the Jewish question, and had written a treatise to prove that at the second coming of Christ the Kingdom would be established through a return of the Jews to their homeland. [52] Maton had further suggested that the twelve tribes were to be united under one king, that all other nations were to be subject to the Jews, and that during the thousand years the saints were to reign principally in Judea. [53] Maton had included in his argument John i, 51, which spoke of a time in the future when the angels would be seen passing between heaven and earth in ministry to the Son of Man, and explained:

> ... that this may be fulfilled, it is requisite, that he be on earth, whither these messengers may descend unto him, and from whence againe they may ascend. Which argues too, his continuance here, for a greater space of time, then the judgement of the dead requires. [54]

Israels Redemption, in which these ideas were expressed, appeared in 1642, and drew a refutation from Alexander Petrie in 1644, [55] to which Maton replied in 1646 with *Israel's Redemption Redeemed*. In his second work he defended the earlier book, showing once more the fact of Christ's personal presence, "We reade not of his departure from the earth againe, untill the earth it selfe shall passe away at the last resurrection." [56] *Israel's Redemption Redeemed* was re-issued in 1652 as *Christ's Personall Reign on Earth One Thousand Yeares with His Saints*, and again in 1655, significantly perhaps, as *A Treatise of the Fifth Monarchy*.

Maton, who had died in 1653, might well have objected to this last publication, since nothing in it warranted his being branded as a Fifth Monarchist. It is true that he had logically applied the fifth kingdom of Daniel to the last of a line of kingdoms upon the earth, [57] but in doing this he had not differed from other premil-

---

[52] Maton, *Israels Redemption*, pp. 4—6.
[53] *Ibid.*, pp. 17, 50, 114.
[54] *Ibid.*, p. 58.
[55] Alexander Petrie, *Chiliasto-mastix*.
[56] Maton, *Israel's Redemption Redeemed*, p. 150.
[57] Maton, *Israels Redemption*, p. 52.

lennialists whose convictions were raised on the same foundation. Belief in a divine kingdom parallel to the final kingdom in Daniel's succession was not enough, *ipso facto*, to assign any man to the Fifth Monarchy movement, and revolution was no part of the general millenarian creed.

If those who preached a literal reign of Christ were radicals, they were not, by the same token, extremists. The kingdom they proclaimed in common with their more conservative brethren was not to be given to license, even as it was not to be established by violence. The accusation of reducing the millennium to a thousand years of Epicurean delights, although without foundation, was often laid at the millenarian's door. "Some are very gross and say, There shall be no sin in those dayes", charged Christopher Love with some justice. [58] "Some are so gross as to hold, there shall be sensuall pleasures in this time; though all go not thus far, yet all agree there shall be a personall reign for so many years", [59] he continued, less justifiably. A minority agreed on a personal reign but few, if any, held out for an era of unbridled hedonism. Indeed, the very thought of an earthy millennium was abhorrent to Nathaniel Homes, [60] and John Durant stoutly maintained that "no sinful carnalities shall abound". [61] Those who read Mede were warned "to beware of gross and carnal conceits ... misbeseeming the Spiritual purity of Saints." [62]

Having dwelt at some length on the arguments of the premillennialist groups, it will only be necessary to add concerning the postmillennialists that they did not expect a literal return of Christ until the end of the thousand years. The millennium itself was wholly akin to that envisaged by the conservative premillenarians, and also warrants little additional comment. It is to be noted, however, that although the postmillennial emphasis developed through the 1640's and 1650's, the seeds from which it sprang had been sown by Thomas Brightman early in the cen-

---

[58] Love, *op. cit.*, p. 68. The charge was preferred again by Thomas Hall against Nathaniel Homes, "the learned Dr." "with an excellent faculty in mangling Scripture", see Thomas Hall, *op. cit.*, pp. 5, 21. Homes' defence was that with the second coming of Christ human probation would close and men would no longer be able to accept salvation, so that "as all that time there shall be no degenerating of any beleevers, so no more regenerating of any unbeleevers", Homes, *op. cit.*, p. 510. It could be argued, therefore, that the millennium would be "sinless, sorrowless, Deathless, Temptationless, Timeless", *ibid.*, p. 507.

[59] Love, *loc. cit.*

[60] Homes, *op. cit.*, p. 373.

[61] Durant, *Salvation*, p. 195.

[62] Mede, *loc. cit.*

tury. During the final millennium, [63] Christ was to reign "by ministery of his Seruants" and thus "aduance his Church vnto the highest honour that can be." [64] Revelation xix described Christ riding forth on a white horse to commence His rule, and Brightman explained:

> It is not to be thought, that Christ will come forth in any visible forme; These things that are nowe in acting are farre of from the last coming of Christ ... but he shall openly putt forth and exercise so great power in the administration of his kingdome, as this resemblance describeth him to haue ... that glorious comming of the Lord, at which & where with S. Paul hath foretold, that this man of sinne shal be abolished, 2 Thessal. 2. 8. Is not his last comming to iudgement, but that whereby he shall cal & take the Iewes into the comunio of the holy Church; at which time indeed, his kingdome shal flourish most gloriously, & shal infinitely surpasse all brightnes of the former times ... [65]

The concept of a spiritualised advent is clearly enough enunciated, but was not to take root firmly for another thirty years.

John Cotton's Boston lectures on the book of Revelation reached England variously between two and fifteen years after they had been delivered, and it is not without significance that the first to be published in London was *The Churches Resurrection*, an exposition of Rev. xx, 5 and 6, in which he developed Brightman's views. [66] The first resurrection was interpreted spiritually as a reformation of the church, a resurrection of individuals dead in sin and of churches dead in apostasy. [67] The thousand years begin with the destruction of Antichrist, [68] which is not to be effected by the glorious appearance of Christ in the clouds, but by a revelation of Christ in His church:

> The Lord will then send such powerful Ministers into the Church that by the power of the keyes they shall take hold on Satan, that is to say, convince him and his Instruments of all Popish and Paganish Religion, and bind him by the chain, that is to say the strong chain of God's Ordinances, Word, and Sacraments, and Censures. [69]

---

[63] On Brightman's concept of a double millennium, see *supra*, p. 161.

[64] Brightman, *op. cit.*, p. 852.

[65] *Ibid.*, pp. 820, 835, 836.

[66] Other writings showing evidence of a postmillennial leaning include those of Edmund Hall, Edward Haughton and Nathaniel Stephens.

[67] John Cotton, *The Churches Resurrection or The Opening of the Fift and Sixt Verses of the 20th Chap. of the Revelation* (1642), pp. 7—9.

[68] *Ibid.*, p. 5.

[69] *Loc. cit.*

Cotton's *Powring ovt of the Seven Vials* further clarified the issue, for under the sixth and seventh vials the utter downfall of Antichrist is to be expected. Thus when Christ declares at the time of the end, "Behold, I come as a thief", [70] He speaks of a spiritual coming through the circumstances of the time, [71] and the islands and mountains which are removed at His presence are those places particularly given to Antichristian practices. [72] With the opening of the seventh vial, the true nature of the kingdom is set forth for all men to see:

> ... then shall you clearly know that the true Church is not a Catho-like visible, nor a Cathedrall, nor a Diocesan, nor a Provinciall Church. Then shall you see the Stars of heaven, you shall know who are the true officers of the Church, not Paratours, and Proctours, Deacons, and Archdeacons, Bishops and Archbishops over many Churches, they are not the lights which the Lord hath set therein: And you shall then see who were the true members of the Church, Not the Canonized Saints, not such as Saint George, who was an ancient Heretick, but you shall see them to be such as are spoken of, Phil. 2. 15, blamelesse and harmlesse, The Sons of God, without rebuke, shining as lights in the world; then shall you see the Scripture more clearly, true doctrine, and worship, and government as it is held forth in the Gospell of Christ, and when you shall see these things, then, It is done. [73]

For the minority who desired it, here was an alternative explanation to the doctrine of a literal second advent. [74]

The distinction between those who taught a literal advent and a spiritual reign, a literal advent and a literal reign, and a spiritual

---

[70] Rev. xvi, 15.
[71] John Cotton, 'The Third Sermon upon the Sixth Vial', pp. 2, 3, in *Seven Vials*.
[72] Cotton, 'The Seventh and Last Vial Opened', pp. 8, 9, in *Seven Vials*.
[73] *Ibid.*, p. 11.
[74] Postmillennialism in the seventeenth century was neither as well-developed nor as popular as it later came to be under Daniel Whitby at the beginning of the eighteenth century. Nonetheless, the marked similarity between the two periods must open to question the conclusion that Whitby was the "originator of the postmillennial theory", Froom, *Prophetic Faith*, II, p. 651; cf. H. H. Rowden, *The Origins of the Brethren* (1967), p. 13. Cotton wrote of the destruction of Antichrist referred to by Paul, "And though it be translated, (in 2 Thess. 2. 8.) The Lord shall destroy him with the brightnesse of his coming: yet the word is ἐν τηε πιφανεια [sic] της παρουσιας αὐτου and παρουσια doth as well, and more firstly signify Presence, then comming ... The Lord will destroy Antichrist with the brightnesse of his Presence in his sacred and Civill Ordinances, sundry ages before the brightnesse of his comming to Judgement", Cotton, *Bloudy Tenent*, p. 51. Edmund Hall similarly argued that παρουσια may also be used of a spiritual presence. Hence the coming of Christ in II Thess. ii, 1 and 8, at which Antichrist is destroyed, is a coming through His appointed servants "Magistracie and Ministery", Edmund Hall, *Scriptural Discourse*, pp. 129—135. In both Cotton and Hall, the first resurrection is spiritualised, the advent is spiritualised, the millennial reign is a spiritual rule, and all the essentials of postmillennialism are clearly defined. Cf. Toon, *Puritan Eschatology*, p. 31, and Brightman, 'Revelation' in *Works*, p. 824 for the seeds of postmillennialism a century before Whitby.

advent and a spiritual reign was always there for those who cared
to pursue it. There were few with sufficient detachment in the
mid-seventeenth century who did. In the ferment of the time the
differences were marginal, and a millenarian was a millenarian
regardless of how he explained the advent. In retrospect, the fact
that there was sufficient inquiry to produce three major divisions
of millenarianism is some justification of Joseph Caryl's observation that the doctrine had "gained ground in the hearts and
judgements of very many, both grave and godly men". [75]

The millenarian impulse was at its strongest between 1640 and
1660 but, like a tree whose branches spread in every direction, it
had sprung from roots reaching deep into soil which had already
nurtured a similar stock. Grave and godly men did not suddenly
stumble across a coming millennium with the approach of a civil
war. Bishop Prideaux in 1636 knew of "many ... moderne
writers" diligent for the millennium, [76] which was somewhat at
variance with Bishop Hall's contention in 1650 that, since Augustine, millenarianism had "lyen dead for this twelve hundred and
forty yeares". [77] It was advantageous, to be sure, for certain
factions to remark that "some of the Anabaptists did draw it out
of its grave", [78] but rather less than objective to add "for a long
time after its resurrection, it was by all Protestants con-
temned' . [79] The doctrine of a coming millennium was known to
both Dent in 1603 and to Napier in 1593. [80] In support of the
millenarian view the German theologian Alsted had turned to
several post-reformation expositors, including Alphonsus Conradus, Matthieu Cottière and Johannes Piscator. [81] Nathaniel
Homes was familiar with a catechism dating from the time of
Edward VI which asserted a"future glorious new Jerusalemitish
state on earth". [82] The phrase "Protestant millenaries", [83] while
coined in self-defence, was not without substance.[84]

---

[75]   Joseph Caryl, in Homes, *Resurrection,* Imprimatur.
[76]   John Prideaux, 'The Christian Expectation', p. 21, in *Twenty Sermons* (Oxford,
1636—41).
[77]   Joseph Hall, *op. cit.,* p. 71.
[78]   Baillie, *op. cit.,* p. 224.
[79]   *Loc. cit.*
[80]   Dent, *op. cit.,* p. 274; Napier, *op. cit.,* p. 63.
[81]   Alsted, *op. cit.,* pp. 58—60; e.g. Alphonsus Conradus, *In Apocalypsim D. Ioannis Apostoli Commentarius* (Basiliae, 1574); Matthieu Cottière, *Apocalypseos, Domini
Nostri Iesus Christi expositio* (Salmurii, 1615); Johannes Piscator, *Johan. Piscatoris
Commentarii in omnes libros Novi Testamenti* (Herbornae Nassoviorum, 1621).
[82]   Nathaniel Homes, 'A Commentary ... on Canticles', in *Works,* p. 461.
[83]   Homes, *Resurrection,* p. 479.
[84]   An early edition of Brightman's *Revelation of the Reuelation* was published by

The first hint of a developing millenarianism, as suggested earlier, came from John Napier and Thomas Brightman, both of whom interpreted Revelation xx to teach a double millennium. To Napier, the thousand years during which the saints were to live and reign with Christ symbolised the eternal Sabbath of rest which in due course would be the portion of the righteous. [85] Napier thus avoided the "heresie" of millenarianism to which he was opposed. [86] Brightman appeared less anxious to escape such implication. His second millennium commenced at the close of the first, in 1300 A.D., and was therefore in the main still to come. [87] In *A Commentary on the Canticles*, Brightman considerably expanded the millenarian idea to include the reign of the church on earth:

> So that where we expect the end of the world, there we finde the beginning of a new Church; which is not like to be for a day or a week or a short time. The Angel expresly affirmeth to be far and wide spread, Rev. 20. 5, 6. And giveth it a thousand yeers after the first Resurrection of the elder sister. [88] Now seeing the Church of the Iewes shall begin to flourish about 400. yeers after that Resurrection, 600. yeers at least shall be left wherein she shall raign here upon the earth. [89]

While the seeds of a coming millenarian emphasis are plainly evident here, those who were to read carefully the later editions of *A Plaine Discouery* and *A Revelation of the Reuelation* would have to conclude that neither Napier nor Brightman were thoroughgoing millenarians.

Meanwhile, in the quiet seclusion of Cambridge, one of the most learned biblical scholars of the age was wrestling with the problem of the millennium. [90] In 1627 Joseph Mede published his *Clavis Apocalyptica*, to the second edition of which, in 1632, he added *In Sancti Joannis Apocalypsin Commentarius*. The *Key* and *Commentary* together gave a sufficiently full exposition of

---

Jean de l'Ecluse, a deacon of the Brownist congregation in Amsterdam; see T. G. Crippen, 'The Brownists in Amsterdam', in *Transactions of the Congregational Historical Society*, II, p. 168.

[85]   Napier, *op. cit.*, p. 240.

[86]   *Loc. cit.*

[87]   Brightman, *Revelation*, p. 851.

[88]   The elder sister referred to true Christianity, which had been resurrected at the end of the first 1000 years, i.e., around 1300 A.D., and immediately thereafter; *ibid.*, p. 848.

[89]   Brightman, 'A Commentary on the Canticles', in *Workes*, p. 1077.

[90]   "Strangers of other Universities, who had never seen him, gave him this high Elogy, That for assailing of Scripture-difficulties he was to be reckoned amongst the best in the world", John Worthington, in Mede, *Works*, The Author's Life, p. XIII.

Revelation xx and the coming millennium to warrant the ascription to Mede of the epithet 'father of English millenarianism'. Mede was acquainted with Brightman's work, as indeed he was with other expositions, [91] but this is no reason to question the contemporary evaluation of his work. "He proceeded upon grounds never traced by any, and infinitely more probable than any lay'd down by those who before him undertook that task", [92] his biographer concluded in 1672. Dr. William Twisse, the prolocutor of the Westminster Assembly, wrote in a preface to the 1643 edition of the *Key* and *Commentary*, "M. Mede hath many notions of so rare a nature that I do not find he is beholding [sic] to any other for them, but onely to his own studiousness and dexterity, with the blessing of God upon his labours", [93] and it was Arthur Jackson's opinion that Mede's view of the thousand years was singularly distinct from the popular interpretation. [94] Without detracting from the influence of Continental antecedents, the conclusion that Mede's form of millenarianism was "a Continentally-derived departure in English eschatology" must be reconsidered. [95] It appears to be beyond doubt that Mede's contribution to English millenarianism was wholly original. [96]

---

[91] See Mede, *Key of The Revelation*, pt. II, p. 13, and *Works*, p. 603.
[92] John Worthington, *op. cit.*, p. VII.
[93] William Twisse, in Mede, *Key of The Revelation*, Pref.
[94] Arthur Jackson, in Mede, *loc. cit.*
[95] De Jong, *Millennial Expectations*, p. 16.
[96] It has been suggested that J. H. Alsted was responsible for the revival of millenarianism in England, and that his views were transmitted to the English scene by Mede, see R. G. Clouse, 'The Influence of ... Alsted', Chap. V, 'English Followers of Alsted's Millenarianism'. (See also Clouse, 'The Rebirth of Millenarianism' in Toon (Ed.), *Puritan Eschatology*, p. 60. Toon, in following Clouse, is also mistaken here; cf. De Jong, *Millennial Expectations*, pp. 9—11.) The thesis appears to stem from an isolated inference in Robert Baillie's *Dissuasive* that Mede had followed Alsted's teaching, Clouse, 'Influence of Alsted', p. 201; cf. Baillie, op. cit., p. 224. In support of this contention Dr. Clouse argues that the 1627 edition of the *Clavis Apocalyptica* makes no definite mention of a future 1000 years, while the 1632 edition clearly states the millenarian position. Since Alsted's *Diatribe de mille annis apocalypticis*, in which his millenarianism had first been fully expressed, had also appeared in 1627, Mede was thus allowed five years in which to expand the *Clavis Apocalyptica*, Clouse, *op. cit.*, p. 209. Mede's own outline, however, is clearly discernible under Synchronismus IIII in the 1627 edition of the *Clavis*. The seven vials of last wrath bring about the destruction of the beast, and occur in the time of the sixth trumpet. The seventh and last trumpet follows and is synonymous with the whole time of the thousand years or kingdom of Christ. "Ita Mille Anni ligati Satanae, ut Gentes amplius non seduceret, neque sub primis sex Sigillis, neque sub primis sex Tubis locum habere possunt: Ergo reliquendi sunt Tubae Septimae ... Quod igitur Regnum illud Christi augustum cum septima Tuba ineat, seu ab excidio Bestiae, jam est, ut ostendamus", Mede, *Clavis Apocalyptica* (1627), pp. 18, 20. In actual fact, the 1627 edition is only slightly modified in the

Mede, whose works betray a consistent devotion to the discovery of truth and its advancement, [97] approached The Revelation with a reverence in keeping with the times. It was only a
concern for objective exegesis that led him to reject the accepted
pattern and place the millennium in the future, a conclusion
which, as he later confessed to a friend, he had "tried all ways
imaginable" to avoid. [98] In framing the famous Synchronisms,
which to him were an indispensable key to unlocking the mysteries of the Apocalypse and which made up the *Clavis*, Mede had
no desire to depart from the neo-Augustinian view of a millennium beginning at the time of Constantine. [99] His critical study
of the text, however, obliged him to renounce this view and
conclude instead that the millennium could occur only at the end
of world history, and that it was inseparably bound up with the
destruction of the beast, the marriage of the Lamb, and the
realisation of a New Jerusalem. Whatever charges might be
brought against later millenarians, Mede's motive for advancing
the idea of a future millennium was purely an unshakeable regard
for the authority of the prophetic word.

While Scripture spoke equally to all men, it spoke with a special authority to those who lived in the last days. The firm biblical foundation given to the millenarian hope by Mede was imple-
mented by the twin concepts of progressive revelation and present truth. In another thirty years or so men would feel free to
imply that even Brightman and Mede were in some respects out-
of-date and that, with the blessing of God, a new generation
could expect to bring to light truths "not discerned in former
Ages". [100] It was possible, even desirable, to believe that God

---

1632 edition, from which the English translations of 1643 and 1650 were taken, and
which form the basis of Mede's entire millenarian scheme. In his *Remaines on some
Passages in the Apocalypse,* premillennialism is further stated, and it is relevant to note
again that, although the *Remaines* were published posthumously, they had been written before even the *Clavis* and *Commentary.* "They were an additional supplement to
the first Draught of his Synchronisms privately communicated to some friends, and
were not written after, but before his Clavis and 'Commentationes Apocalypticae',
which were his last labours upon that mysterious book", Mede, *Works,* Gen. Pref.
Taken together with the contemporary testimonies to Mede's originality, and with the
conspicuous absence of any acknowledgement of indebtedness to Alsted by Mede
himself, it is difficult to see how Mede's millenarianism derived from anything but a
critical and independent exegesis of Scripture. Gilsdorf's conclusion is therefore more
sound, "it seems likely that he came to his conception of the millennium ... from his
study of the text itself", 'The Puritan Apocalypse', p. 66.

[97] John Worthington, *op. cit.,* p. XXVIII.
[98] *Ibid.,* p. X.
[99] *Loc. cit.*
[100] Stephens, *Number of the Beast,* p. 13.

would raise up men to "clear the things that have layen dark in the Prophecies".[101] It could be said of the book of Revelation that men should expect to "see a little further in the Truth ... then they that went before"[102] and, since certain truths of the Christian message were particularly appropriate to specific times in history, the truth now to be stressed was that concerning Christ's coming kingdom.[103] From Mede onwards the basic factor in the millenarian upsurge was the age-long reliability of the biblical revelation, to which was given, by these arguments, an immediate relevancy. Closely identified with the authority of the Bible was the doctrinal platform of the early church. The tendency to idealise the apostolic age has always been marked among those concerned with the quest for ultimate truth, and the millenarians of the seventeenth century were quick to recognize the advantage of an appeal to antiquity. It has more recently been acknowledged that spokesmen of the ante-Nicene era were predisposed to favour an imminent, pre-millennial advent and a future millennium,[104] but it is note-worthy that the views of the Fathers were already well known in the seventeenth century.

The premillennial belief of the post-apostolic Fathers was set forth by Mede on the basis of Justin Martyr's *Dialogue With Trypho*. The coming of Christ and ensuing millennium were "so plainly perceived by the Christians of the next Age after the Apostles that Iustine Martyr witnesseth, that not onely himselfe, but if there were, at that time, any entirely Orthodoxe Christians, they did with full consent believe it."[105] The orthodox were to include, beyond the rank and file, "the choycest of the learned", Irenaeus, Tertullian, Cyprian, Methodius and Lactantius.[106] "It was the constant opinion of the Church", wrote William Burton in the preface to his translation of Alsted's *Diatribe*, "that there should be a resurrection before the generall rising at the last day, and an happy condition of the faithfull upon earth for CIↃ yeeres".[107] To this positive argument of

---

[101] *Loc. cit.*
[102] Hicks, *op. cit.*, Ep. to the Reader, sig. blr.
[103] Homes, *Ten Exercitations*, p. 278.
[104] See Philip Schaff, *History of the Christian Church* (New York, 1882–1910), II, p. 122.
[105] Mede, *Key of The Revelation*, pt. II, pp. 121, 122.
[106] Homes, *op. cit.*, pp. 7–15. Homes included Origen, whom he might well have omitted, but excluded Hippolytus and Papias both of whom might well have been included, cf. Joseph Hall, *op. cit.*, pp. 67–70, and R. G. Clouse, 'Influence of Alsted', pp. 16, 17.
[107] William Burton, in Alsted, *The Beloved City*, Pref. p. iv.

acceptance by the post-apostolic church, a negative rider could be added, namely that millenarianism was nowhere reckoned unorthodox among the early apologists when they wrote specifically against heresy. [108] Mede could thus affirm without fear of contradiction, "This dogma of the 1000 years Regnum was the General opinion of all Orthodox Christians in the Age immediately following the Apostles". [109] Consequently the early Fathers were frequently cited by the seventeenth-century millenarians, [110] not primarily because they felt the need to rebut a charge of novelty, [111] but more because they felt a need to draw closer to the fountain of truth.

The millenarians were aware that a corrupt version of the premillennial doctrine had occurred fairly early in Christian history, and Mede suggested that due to this distortion later generations of believers were reluctant to accept the purer version. [112] The heterodoxy of the Montanists [113] and the deviant stresses given to the millenarian doctrine by Cerinthus were sufficient to surround millenarianism with suspicion until, by the end of the fourth century, it was discredited enough for Augustine to renounce it in favour of a spiritualised interpretation. [114] It is essentially correct, therefore, that from the end of the second century chiliasm, which had always been confronted with a charge of Judaism, was forced to labour under the added stigma of fanaticism and sensualism. [115] That stigma was to gather a more relevant justification in the excesses of John Mathijs and John Beuckels and their followers at Münster, and the opponents of the revived millenarianism in England were not slow to recognise the value of such implications. Some even, it seems, were not beyond overlooking the distinction between the corrupted chiliastic teaching and the earlier and purer premillennialism of

---

[108] Homes, *op. cit.*, p. 7. In addition to Irenaeus and Tertullian, Homes mentions Epiphanius and Augustine. The strength which Epiphanius, Bishop of Salamis (d. 403 A.D.) brought to the argument, may be judged from the fact that he was "an authority on Christian deviations of all kinds, past and present", Henry Chadwick, *The Early Church* (1967), p. 184. Augustine, again, does not really belong here.

[109] Mede, *Works*, p. 602.

[110] E.g. Burton, *op. cit.*, p. IV; Burroughs, *op. cit.*, p. 72; Durant, *op. cit.*, p. 196.

[111] R. G. Clouse, op. cit., p. 27: cf. "you may see that this doctrine is no new licht reveled in this last age (as yow have heard some teach)", Alexander Petrie, *Chiliastomastix*, Pref., sig. *4.

[112] Mede, *Key of The Revelation*, pt. II, p. 122.

[113] A brief statement of Montanist eschatology is given by Henry Chadwick, *op. cit.*, p. 52.

[114] See Augustine, *op. cit.*, pp. 356–368.

[115] See R. G. Clouse, *op. cit.*, p. 22.

Irenaeus, Tertullian, and Hippolytus, with the result, no doubt intended, that the millenarian hope was often indiscriminately denounced as a "Cerinthian fable", [116] "an old error new vamped ... an old harlot new painted". [117] In an age when the history of the church was an important study, it was simple enough to defend the early post-apostolic doctrine against such charges, and Homes was quite right in saying "that Millenarianism ... is no Heresie, may appear to the objector who is an Honourer of Antiquity." [118] To those who came within this category the calumny was inconsequential, [119] and the millenarian cause was strengthened, rather than weakened, by the appeal to the early Fathers.

The combined authority of Scripture and the Fathers in the developing millenarian thought was strengthened by a further influence common to both. It was readily accepted in the seventeenth century, and not in any way regarded as an embarrassment, that the Christian message was rooted in Judaism. The Old Testament was as authoritative a source of truth as the New. Of six sermons preached by John Dod for the essentially New Testament Ordinance of the Lord's Supper, five were taken from Old Testament texts. [120] The book of Revelation itself was perceived to allude frequently to Hebrew scripture and practice. The early Fathers inevitably shared the sense of affinity with traditional Judaism felt in general by the first Christians, and their expectation of an imminent advent was understandably coloured by a knowledge of Hebrew thought. [121] It was as true of eschatology as of every other aspect of truth that new revelation "must be consistent with that spoken in the past by the prophets." [122] This intrinsic element of Judaic thought was understood in the seventeenth century, and Mede was well able to appeal to a school of rabbinical teaching which maintained the necessity for a "Renovation of the World". [123]

[116]   Petrie, *loc. cit.*

[117]   Thomas Hall, *op. cit.*, p. 98.

[118]   Homes, *op. cit.*, p. 7.

[119]   Bishop Hall did better by recognising the existence of a strong millenarian movement in the early church, and by endeavouring to counteract it on the grounds that it was not a matter of faith, "neither imports salvation, either way", Joseph Hall, *op. cit.*, p. 66.

[120]   John Dod and R. Cleaver, *Ten Sermons tending chiefly to the fitting of men for the worthy receiuing of the LORDS Supper*, (1614).

[121]   See James Hastings (Ed.), *Encyclopaedia of Religion and Ethics* (New York, 1928), 5, p. 388.

[122]   Chadwick, *op. cit.*, p. 9.

[123]   Mede, 'A Paraphrase and Exposition of the Prophecie of St. Peter', in *Works*, p. 610.

The basic theory which came down from pre-Christian Judaism through the Talmud and the Fathers to the millenarians of the seventeenth century, was that the world was to last in all for 6000 years. [124]   The analogy was taken from the six days of creation and from a text in Psalms which implied that a thousand years in the sight of God were as a day. [125]   The argument had been known in the middle of the sixteenth century and had attracted the attention of Luther and Osiander on the Continent, and of Latimer and Joye in England. [126]   With the early Reformers there was no juxtaposition of the seventh day of creation's week with a final period of one thousand years. The Sabbath was rather seen to represent that everlasting rest to which the saints would be called. This view remained unchanged at the end of the century, when John Napier wrote, "it is thought by the most learned, that the six daies of labor, weekly obserued, doth meane & beare the symbole of 6000. yeares, that mankinde shall indure the trauels and cares of this world". [127]   Napier, however, specifically mentioned a seventh thousand year period, although he still applied it to an "aeternal Sabboth & rest" in heaven, and not upon the earth. [128]

Among English millenarians, the idea found its fullest development and expression in Nathaniel Homes, who maintained that the seventh thousand period of years was regarded in Jewish literature as a literal period of time, a sabbath of years, in "the last thousand yeares of the world". [129]   A particular school of rabbinical thought provided Homes with further support. Referring to Rabbis Ketina, David Kimchi, and Schelomo, he found in the Jewish sabbatical year additional significance for the cryptic and recurring seventh. "Their words in summe are these; 'As every seventh yeare is a yeare of release, so the seventh thousand of yeares of the world is the time of the release of the world'." [130]   Homes was impressed by the scriptural tone of the rabbinical arguments and turned himself to the fourth chapter of the epistle to the Hebrews where he found that a period of rest, a σαββατισμος, still remained for God's people to enjoy. "A Sab-

---

[124]   There is evidence of pagan influence in the development of this idea, see Froom, *op. cit.*, I, p. 304.
[125]   Psal. xc, 4.
[126]   See *supra*, p. 19.
[127]   Napier, *op. cit.*, p. 18.
[128]   *Ibid.*, p. 19.
[129]   Homes, *Resurrection*, p. 174.
[130]   *Ibid.*, p. 175.

batisme signifies a rest upon a seventh, most likely ... in the seventh and last Age of the world, and its remaining signifieth, it is yet to be fulfilled ..." [131] Homes interpreted this future rest, not only in the immediate context of Hebrews iv, but in the wider setting of the many 'sabbatismes' granted to Israel throughout her history, all of which were governed by the mystical seven:

> You have had the seventh dayes rest ever since the Creation, as God on the first seventh having finished his Workes, rested; and you have had your sevenths of restes in Canaan; First, your seventh yeare; then secondly, your Jubilean seven seventh: Thirdly, your seventieth Jubilean of seven sevens, and yet there is another Sabbatisme, or Septenary rest still remaining. [132]

What else could this one outstanding 'Sabbatisme' be, but the thousand years corresponding to the seventh day of the week and the seventh year of release?

Lest this question should be answered as Napier had answered it, the eternal rest of the saints in heaven, Homes pointed out that σαββατισμος denoted a determined period of time, a seventh day or a seventh year. [133] To apply it to eternity was to rob the word of its inherent meaning and to divest the seventh day of a significance granted to it by the wisdom of antiquity. Therefore:

> ... as the former great Ages of the world were distinct on earth by some eminent notes, as they shall easily find that consult Chronologers; so shall this be as distinct likewise. The rest of the Sabbath began with God's rest after the finishing of his workes; the rest in Canaan began with the conduct and wonders done under Joshua, and etc., so this Sabbatisme of the last thousand years is begun, and bounded with notable landmarkes; it begins with the binding of Satan, the fall of the beast, and with the first Resurrection; and terminated with the loosing of Satan, the rising of Gog and Magog in armes, and the second resurrection, so that great things are acted between the end of the Sabbatisme and ultimate glory. [134]

In 1651 Samuel Hartlib translated a work which computed that the world's six thousand years would expire in 1655, [135] and John Durie, who wrote the preface, commented on the wide-

---

[131] *Ibid.*, p. 174. William Gouge had compared the world's history to a week. The first six days were, respectively, from Adam to Noah, Noah to Abraham, Abraham to David, David to the Captivity, the Captivity to the Ascension, and the Ascension to the Second Coming. Then would follow "an eternall Σαββατισμος, keeping a Sabbath, a rest after the day of judgement", William Gouge, *The Progresse of Divine Providence* (1645), p. 13.

[132] Homes, *loc. cit.*

[133] *Ibid.*, p. 176.

[134] *Loc. cit.*; cf. Strong, *Vengeance*, p. 1.

[135] Samuel Hartlib (tr.) *Clavis Apocalyptica*, p. 26.

spread eschatological hopes in Germany, Poland, France, the Low Countries, and among the Jews. [136] Not every calculation culminated in 1655 but, for all that, the millenarian belief was substantially reinforced by the idea that earth's last long day was drawing to its close. "The sunne of worldly pompe is declining towards Sun-set, the shadowes grow long, it begins to be duske upon all Secular splendour". [137] Time's last night was at hand and, beyond it, a new day on which the Son of Righteousness would rise and reign.

When a distinguished theologian argued "The full accomplishment of the salvation of the Believers, shall not bee vntill Christ's second comming," [138] it revealed an element of personal involvement with the doctrines of the last events. "Though their soules bee blessed before, yet the full blessednesse of soule and bodie, is deferred till then." [139] Much clearly depended on the second coming and the subsequent kingdom. In the Puritan ethos the quest for salvation was the pre-eminent issue of life, a drama that was played out, as Professor Haller remarks, in the theatre of each human breast. [140] "Election-vocation-justification-sanctification-glorification was more than an abstract formula. It became the pattern of the most profound experience of men through many generations." [141] If the final act in this drama was glorification, if "full blessednesse of soule and bodie" came only at the second coming, then men could be expected to take a keen interest in all that would transpire at that day. The kingdom and the glory were not merely necessities imposed by the logic of Calvinistic determinism, however attractive that theology might be. The kingdom was a place where individual piety would obtain its just reward, and the glory the saints would there enjoy an experience every whit as personal as justification had been or as sanctification was now proving to be. "Thy kingdom come" was infinitely more than a repetitious phrase to be uttered dutifully in church whenever occasion demanded. It was at the same time the essence of personal aspiration and the end of divine purpose.

A substantial proportion of those holding the second advent doctrine were not circumscribed by millenarianism in any

---

[136]   John Durie, in *Clavis Apocalyptica*, Pref., p. 6.

[137]   Homes, *op. cit.*, p. 498.

[138]   David Dickson, *A Short Explanation Of the Epistle of Paul to the Hebrewes* (Aberdene, 1635), p. 193. Dickson was professor of divinity at Glasgow, 1640–50, and at Edinburgh, 1650–60.

[139]   *Loc. cit.*

[140]   See Haller, *Rise of Puritanism* p. 91.

[141]   *Ibid.*, p. 93.

form,[142] and simply believed that Christ would come and rule. "Hee shall come as a King, full of maiesty and glory, guarded and attended vpon with many thousands of heauenly Souldiours",[143] wrote Samuel Smith, and men cherished his words for almost a century. "At his second appearing he shall appear in Majesty as a King",[144] and the effulgence of the event would "constrain all the world to acknowledg his Soveraignty."[145] Between the advent and the eternal kingdom, however, the millenarians interposed the thousand-year rule of Christ. The larger proportion, as we have seen, favoured a spiritual kingdom, a few only expecting Christ to reign in person. It could therefore be said of the coming rule of Christ, that while a majority expected Him to come and inaugurate a Kingdom *for* the saints, the millenarians held that He would either reign *through* the saints or *with* them. All were agreed that the work was of God and that He would order it in His own good time. John Archer specifically stated "we cannot hasten its time",[146] a view that was endorsed by John Durant, similarly an advocate of the more restrained millenarianism.[147] Beyond these more moderate opinions, however, there developed an extremer creed which ultimately proclaimed that the kingdom was to be established *by* the saints. With the Fifth Monarchy Men, Robert Browne's axiom of 'Reformation without tarrying' and his spirit of divine impatience with the second-best reached the extreme limit of their development.

The political opinions and involvements of the radical Fifth Monarchists have received sufficient study elsewhere to justify the exclusion of further detailed examination here.[148] It is

---

[142]   The exact proportion is difficult to assess. B. S. Capp's estimate of 70% is too high, Capp, *The Fifth Monarchy Men*, p. 38. Based on an analysis of writers publishing three or more theological works between 1640 and 1653, this assessment overlooks the fact that many prominent writers published less than three works during this period, e.g. Alexander Petrie, William Sclater, Joseph Hall. Moreover, Capp's list of "authors showing millenarian ideas" is suspect, since it includes several who openly disclaimed millenarianism, e.g. Christopher Love, Thomas Brooks, John Trapp, William Gouge, Edmund Calamy, Capp, *op. cit.*, pp. 46—48. Less than 50% of the writers whose works were examined in the preparation of this study, with one or more published works between 1640—1660, were millenarian.

[143]   Smith, *Great Assize*, p. 31.

[144]   Love, *op. cit.*, p. 38.

[145]   Baxter, *Saints Rest*, p. 47.

[146]   Archer, *Personall Reigne*, p. 53.

[147]   Durant, *op. cit.*, p. 274.

[148]   Recent studies include P. G. Rogers, *The Fifth Monarchy Men* (1966) and the more scholarly work by B. S. Capp, *The Fifth Monarchy Men: A Study in Seventeenth Century Millenarianism* (1972). Tai Liu's *Discord in Zion* is a helpful study of the political involvements and aspirations of the Fifth Monarchists.

known that soldiers in the Parliamentary army, politicians in the Barebones parliament, and pamphleteers of various loyalties espoused Fifth Monarchy hopes between 1640 and 1660, and that some openly advocated rebellion against the state and twice endeavoured, in 1657 and 1661, to put their ideas into practice. The names of preachers including John Rogers, Christopher Feake, Vavasor Powell, John Simpson and John Canne, and of army officers such as Major-General Harrison, Major-General Goffe, Colonel Rainborough, Colonel Rich, Colonel Okey and others are familiar enough to those acquainted with the development of the Fifth Monarchy faction. Indeed, it can be argued that owing to the concentration of interest on the activities of the Fifth Monarchy Men in general, the wider and saner eschatology of the time has received rather less than its due share of attention. It is true that for a few years in the middle of the seventeenth century there were radical Fifth Monarchists, a Parliament containing a fair sprinkling of Fifth Monarchy Men and more of their sympathisers, and Fifth Monarchist risings against established government, all of which have had their fascination for historians. [149] It is equally true, and perhaps more important, that these men and their farfetched schemes were not representative of general eschatological doctrine. Notoriety has tended to exaggerate their theological significance. The more sober brotherhood of the saints, as well as the government which was already as godly as any practical Englishman might hope, were embarrassed by the strange notions which they advocated. [150] It will not be out of place, therefore, to see the Fifth Monarchy movement in its proper theological context and to note its relationship to the contemporary eschatological thought.

It is necessary to determine initially who were Fifth Monarchy Men and who were not. In this respect it is to be stressed that the mere use of the term "fifth monarchy" is not in itself sufficient to denominate any writer or preacher as a Fifth Monarchist. Robert Barclay recognised this nearly a century ago and his distinction still merits emphasis. "The idea of the near approach of a 'Fifth Monarchy' was most widely spread, and this must not be

---

[149] See C. H. Firth, *The Last Years of the Protectorate 1656—1658* (1909), I, pp. 201—219.

[150] "There were hundreds who repeatedly and emphatically disavowed them, finding their interest in religion and not in politics", W. T. Whitley, 'Militant Baptists 1660—1672', in *Transactions of the Baptist Historical Society*, I, p. 155. The conclusion is equally true of the years preceding 1660.

identified with the opinions of the few crazy enthusiasts called
'Fifth Monarchy Men'."[151] Masson's comment is also apropos:

> The Fifth Monarchy notion was by no means an upstart oddity of
> thought among the English Puritans of the seventeenth century. It was
> a tradition of the most scholarly thought of medieval theologians as to
> the duration and final collapse of the existing Cosmos; and it may be
> traced in the older imaginative literature of various European na-
> tions. [152]

Such an unlikely combination as Ben Jonson, John Donne,
Nathaniel Stephens, Menasseh Ben Israel and William Strong all
employ the term as a matter of course, [153] but not by the
widest stretch of the imagination could any one of them be
thought of as a Fifth Monarchy Man. The same caution is therefore necessary when reading Thomas Goodwin, Nathaniel Homes,
John Archer or William Hicks, among others. They too preached
a final fifth kingdom, but it would betray a lack of rapport with
the seventeenth century scene to confuse them with the radical
diehards. Perhaps the phrase 'Fifth Monarchy Men' would be
better used exclusively of the extremists whose creed was revolution and whose weapons came to be material rather than spiritual. [154]

It is also necessary to see the Fifth Monarchy movement in the
context of millenarianism, for all the elements found in the developing millenarian impulse can also be traced in the Fifth Monarchy literature. The study of Daniel's prophecies and the delineation of the four major kingdoms of history in Babylon, Medo-
Persia, Greece, and Rome, the ten-fold partition of Rome, the
rise and fall of the Little Horn, the impending destruction of
Antichrist, and the final kingdom of God, all this the Fifth Monarchists shared in common with the standard eschatological
teaching of the age. [155] The intricacies of the Revelation, and the

---

[151]   Barclay, *The Inner Life,* p. 182.
[152]   Masson, *Life of John Milton,* V, p. 17.
[153]   Jonson, *The Alchemist,* Act 4, Sc. 5; Donne, 'Elegie' in *Iuvenilia,* p. 296;
Nathaniel Stephens, *op. cit.,* Pref.; Menasseh Ben Israel, *The Hope of Israel,* p. 68;
Strong, 'The Doctrine of the Iews Vocation', in *Sermons,* p. 287.
[154]   De Jong notes this distinction in the works of Thomas Goodwin, De Jong, *op.
cit.,* p. 41.
[155]   William Aspinwall's *An Explication and Application of the Seventh Chapter of
Daniel* (1654) illustrates the basis of Fifth Monarchy theology, although in equating
the Little Horn with Charles I, Aspinwall goes much further than the average millenarian
was prepared to go. The importance of the Little Horn in the Fifth Monarchy scheme
was argued by John Tillinghast, "this Prophecy of Daniels little Horn is so materiall,
that an error here turns the streams of all Daniels Prophecies out of their proper
channel", John Tillinghast, *Knowledge of the Times* (1654), p. 61. This was no licence,

peculiarly special place of England as an elect nation in the divine scheme of last events were an important part of the historico-prophetic foundation on which they built,[156] as recent studies have correctly emphasised. With the millenarian emphasis they shared a belief in the coming millennium, Christ's kingdom on earth before the last judgement, in which the principles of divine rule would prevail and the saints be elevated to the highest honour.[157] They understood prophetic chronology, and none calculated more meticulously than they the significance of days and years.[158] They computed the number of the beast,[159] counted on the realisation of the seventh millennial day,[160] and knew that the saints were destined to play a significant role in the last events.[161] Yet all this put together still fell short of the real essence of Fifth Monarchism. Neither a fifth monarchy, nor a final millennium, nor belief in the destiny of the church were of themselves ideas strong enough to turn a revolution or breed militancy. A catalyst was needed to fuse all, and it was to be found in a doctrine which had already furthered the general growth of millenarianism.

There was little doubt at the time that millenarianism bred the Fifth Monarchy movement. Nathaniel Stephens, who stood firmly for a "Fifth Monarchy and the Reign of Christ upon the Earth", withdrew from the extreme millenarian construction because it was associated with "many Heterogeneal Falsities, and Unsavoury Errors".[162] In Thomas Hall's view millenarianism brought forth "the malignant fruit of Schisme in the Church, and Sedition in the State", since the Fifth Monarchy Men advocated the abolition of both Magistracy and Ministry "as that Beast ... which hindreth the coming of their King Jesus."[163] "I see now whence our fifth Monarch men have their New-light", he con-

---

however, for wild interpretations, and if Tillinghast was at odds with Aspinwall over the exact identity of the Little Horn, he was still further away from John More's strained view that it depicted Cromwell, see John More, *A Trumpet sounded*, p. 5. On all known Fifth Monarchists, see Capp, *The Fifth Monarchy Men*, Appendix.

[156]   E.g. Mary Cary, *Little Horn*, ep. ded., sigs. A3, 4.

[157]   E.g. Tillinghast, *op. cit.*, p. 307, and *Generation Work: The Second Part, ... an Exposition of the Seven Vials* (1654), p. 164.

[158]   E.g. Tillinghast, *Knowledge of the Times, passim*.

[159]   John More did little to improve the image of Fifth Monarchy writers by deriving six hundred and sixty-six from "Rex Oliver Lord Protector", More, *op. cit.*, p. 8.

[160]   John Canne, *A Voice From the Temple* (1653), p. 29.

[161]   Tillinghast, *Generation Work. or A Brief and Seasonable Word*, pt. I, *passim*.

[162]   Stephens, *op. cit.*, To the Conscientious Reader, sig. aiv.

[163]   Thomas Hall, *op. cit.*, To the Reader.

tinued, "from this Tenet of the Millenaries, which opens a gap to Anarchy and confusion ..." [164] To *The Revelation Revealed* the ardent and radical millenarian William Hicks added "A Glass for the Quinto-Monarchians", a plea to the militants for moderation and a defence of the "Magistrates just Power and Jurisdiction shining in its full luster and glory as an Ordinance of God and not to be touched with unhallowed hands." [165] The distinction between millenarians and Fifth Monarchists begins to become apparent, and a more recent view may be noted here:

> The Fifth Monarchy men were millenarians who were not content to wait quietly for the millennial reign to begin in God's own good time. They believed that prophecy could only be fulfilled with the active help of the believers and they were prepared to spread their views by the sword. [166]

The full title of the pirated *A Sermon of the Fifth Monarchy* proclaimed that the present fourth monarchy was to be destroyed "by the Sword of the Saints". John Evelyn wrote in his diary on returning from church in 1657, "our Viccar 18 Joh. 36 declaiming at the folly of a sort of Enthusiasts and desparat Zealots cald the Fift Monarch-Men, pretending to set up the Kingdome of Christ with the Sword." [167] It was the sword that set the Fifth Monarchists apart. [168] Militancy was their hallmark. While millenarianism gave rise to Fifth Monarchism it was not synonymous with it. To the creed of violence no respectable millenarian could be a party.

Where, then, was the element in millenarianism which fostered thoughts of militancy and anarchy? While the Fifth Monarchy movement was developing, Nathaniel Stephens, William Hicks, Nathaniel Homes and other leading millenarian spokesmen were propounding the doctrine of progressive revelation and linking it with present truth. It was the application of these principles to the belief that the saints were to be involved in the affairs of the last days that gave a distinctive nuance to the theology of the Fifth Monarchy Men. "The crown must be laid at the feet of Jesus, for the government would be upon his shoulders." [169] But

---

[164]   *Ibid.*, p. 51.
[165]   William Hicks, 'Quinto-Monarchiae', Title-page, *ad. cal.* with *The Revelation Revealed.*
[166]   A. J. Woodfield, 'The Life and Works of Joseph Stennett 1663—1713', unpublished M. A. thesis, London University, 1958, p. 207.
[167]   John Evelyn, *The Diary of John Evelyn* (ed. E. S. De Beer, 1955), III, p. 196.
[168]   Cf. Capp. *Fifth Monarchy Men*, pp. 131 ff.
[169]   Nuttall, *Welsh Saints*, p. 46.

the crown and the government must first be wrested from those who now enjoyed them, and who better to accomplish the work than the elects heirs of the coming kingdom?

The idea that God's people were to show an active concern for the advancement of truth was as old, and as acceptable, as the gospel itself. In the seventeenth century it drew particular support from the ranks of millenarianism. Thomas Goodwin argued the case from the viewpoint of an incomplete Reformation. Doctrinal truth had been largely recovered by the Reformers, but matters of order and discipline were still outstanding and were now to be settled. [170] Under the guidance of Parliament, the two witnesses or olive trees, Magistrates and Ministers, were to lead out in this work. [171] Goodwin, however, was careful to point out that men were not to be exalted. "The building of Gods Church is his owne businesse ... It is not of the ordinary make that other societies of men ... are, but by the Spirit ... it is not made with hands, (with humane wisdome or power, as they are) ..." [172] In the work of the last days, though, the saints are God's instruments. "God doth give these his Saints a Commission to set up and pull down," [173] he declared, but hastened to add, "by their prayers and intercessions". [174] Similar thoughts were expressed by William Strong. Preaching on the impending destruction of Antichrist, Strong declared that it was to be accomplished by "the reformed Churches", [175] and continued:

> ... it is out of Zion that the fire comes that consumes the enemies ... They that are with the Lamb, called and chosen and faithfull, they shall burne Rome with fire ... The Lord Jesus having made the Saints together with himselfe Heyres of the world, hee hath also given them a great hand in the Government of the world ... [176]

---

[170]   Thomas Goodwin, *Zerubbabels Encouragement to Finish the Temple* (1642), p. 17.

[171]   *Ibid.*, p. 55.

[172]   *Ibid.*, pp. 48, 49.

[173]   Goodwin, *States & Kingdomes*, p. 42.

[174]   *Ibid.*, p. 43. Even the earlier *A Glimpse of Sions Glory* (1641) is far from preaching incitement to rebellion. It was the author's purpose "to show ... how upon the destruction of Babylon Christ shall reigne gloriously, and how we are to further it ... It is the work of the day to cry downe Babylon, that it may fall more and more, and it is the worke of the day to give God no rest, till he sets up Ierusalem as the praise of the whole World ... This is the work of the day, for us to lift up our voice to Heaven ..." *A Glimpse of Sions Glory*, pp. 2, 7. On the authorship of this work see Nuttall, *The Holy Spirit*, p. 110, to which may be added, "Possibly by Thomas Goodwin, whose name appears on the title-page in some copies", *Dictionary of Anonymous and Pseudonymous English Literature*, IX, p. 119.

[175]   Strong, *Vengeance*, p. 28.

[176]   *Ibid.*, p. 33.

This would have sounded well in the ears of any Fifth Monarchy congregation, and Strong was careful to explain:

> ... though your power bee small and your party few and weake, that by power you have little hope to prevayle, yet by the meanes you have, prayers and prayses, and by them God hath ordayned that he shall still the enemy and the avenger: the fire with which they must bee killed, must proceed out of your mouths. [177]

There could be little harm in prayer and praise, and it was justifiable, even necessary, to maintain that Archer, Homes, Mede, and Alsted were not subversive writers. [178]

The Fifth Monarchy Men, however, saw that these arguments had stopped short of their logical end. If it was right to preach, it was right to practise. If the saints could pray in the spirit for the downfall of Antichrist and the uprising of Christ's kingdom, could they not also in the flesh help the matter forward? An early Fifth Monarchy writer, Mary Cary, [179] argued that the fate of Charles I was an act of God working through the saints, [180] and defended "the lawfulness of fighting against the enemies of Christ with the material sword." [181]   Reprehensible though the doctrine was to most religious people of the time, it could not be cast aside as merely the new light of deceived visionaries. Ironically enough, the seeds of this extreme teaching had been sown by James I. In upholding the legitimacy of armed resistance against the invading armies of Antichrist, he wrote:

> It is all our duties in this Ile at yis tyme [182] to do twa thingis. Ane, to consider our estait; Another to conforme our actiounis according thairunto. Our estait is, we ar thrie foldie beseagit; First, spirituallie be ye heresies of ye Antichrist. Secundlie, corporallie and generallie, as memberis of that Kirk ye quhiik in haill they persecute. Thridlie, corporallie & particularlie be yis present armie. Our actiounis then conformed to our estait are thes: First to call for help at God-dis handis: Nixt to assure us of ye same, seeing we have ane sufficient warrend, his contant promeis expressed in his word. Thirdlie sence with guid conscience we may, being in ye Tentis of ye Saintis and belovit Citie, stand in our defence: Incourage ane another to use lawfull resistance, and concur ane with another as warriouris in ane camp and citizenis of ane belovit citie, for mantenance of ye guid caus God hes cled us with, and defence of our liberties, native countrie and lyfes. [183]

---

[177]   *Ibid.*, p. 47.
[178]   Hicks, *op. cit.*, ep. ded., sig. Aaa4.
[179]   There is little, if any, Fifth Monarchy literature before 1650.
[180]   Cary, *op. cit.*, pp. 35, 36.
[181]   *Ibid.*, p. 122.
[182]   First written in 1588.
[183]   James I, *frvitfvll Meditatioun*, sig. Bivr.

If this applied when the nation was threatened from without, it also applied when Antichrist sat at Westminster and the Little Horn signified Cromwell or the Protectorate. In their own eyes, at least, the Fifth Monarchy Men stood on solid ground.

Not all Fifth Monarchy writers, particularly in the early days, were as inflammatory or as bold as Mary Cary. [184] Indeed the more restrained and spiritual reasoning of John Tillinghast can be reckoned to have had a deeper influence on Fifth Monarchy theology. [185] It was Tillinghast who coined the phrase "Generation-work" and made it relevant to the purposes of the militants. If "Generation-truth" was the doctrine of a fifth monarchy, [186] "Generation-worke" was the duty suggested by present truth and "the light of the age." [187] Noah's work had been to build an ark and warn the people; Abraham's vocation was to leave his home and go in search of a better country; Solomon's task was in the building of the temple, and John the Baptist had been called as a forerunner of the Christ. [188] For the present "the master-piece of worke in this generation is the Advancement of the Kingdome of Jesus Christ", [189] and its seriousness was difficult to exaggerate:

> ... the obligation whereby I stand bound unto the worke of my generation, is a greater obligation then that whereby I stand bound to any other duty, and my fault or error herein is a greater error then any other of my errors ... it is the duty of a Christian man, employed in generation-worke, when other workes and this do stand in competition, to choose neglect in any duty, rather then in that, wherein the worke of his generation lies ... [190]

The saints were to be ready at all times to accept "new light", [191] and in 1653 Tillinghast's exhortations fell on willing ears.

---

[184]   The second part of the *Little Horn,* entitled *A new and more exact mappe or Description of New Ierusalems Glory,* bore the explanation "That great Question, whether it be lawfull for the Saints to make use of the materiall Sword in the ruining of the enemies of Christ, and whether it be the mind of Christ to have it so, is at large debated and resolved in the Affirmative from clear Scriptures".

[185]   On Tillinghast's moderation and influence, see Nuttall, *Visible Saints,* pp. 152, 153.

[186]   Tillinghast, *Knowledge of the Times,* To the Faithful Witnesses of Christ, sig. A 3v.

[187]   Tillinghast, *Generation Work,* pt. I, p. 6; cf. Aspinwall's *Work of the Age* (1655).

[188]   *Ibid.,* pp. 13—16.

[189]   *Ibid.,* p. 67.

[190]   *Ibid.,* pp. 26, 27.

[191]   *Ibid.,* p. 86.

The second part of *Generation Work* was an exposition of the seven last vials, which had commenced with the first decline of Antichrist and the rise of the true church with Luther. [192] Tillinghast followed the customary interpretation of seeing human agents portrayed by the angels which proceeded from the heavenly temple, "such as have renounced the false Idolatrous worship of Antichrist", [193] and his exposition of coming events was all that might have been expected. Three vials were past already, the fourth and fifth were to be fulfilled between 1654 and 1656, [194] and the sixth, under which the Turks were to be overthrown and the Jews return to their homeland, would follow immediately. [195] In the pouring out of these latter vials the saints were to establish the righteous rule throughout Europe, and by 1656 were to have overrun Germany, invaded Italy, and destroyed Rome. [196] As the Jews began their return from Italy, and the Turks were rising to oppose them, the saints would be "waiting upon God to see what further worke" he had for them. [197] The sixth vial is now put into their hands, and upon its accomplishment all is ready for the personal appearing of Jesus and the millennium. [198] Tillinghast did not omit to make it clear that the work of the age required spiritual saints, men with "a strong breathing after the Lord." [199]

Posterity has rightly judged that not all who approved of Tillinghast's theology were men of that calibre. John Canne, it is true, in 1653 was anxious to dissociate himself and his cause from any taint of extravagance, and set about to prove "the absurdity, ignorance and malice" of all who sought to disgrace "the glorious work of God now begun amonst us, by raking into the businesse of Munster." [200] The Little Horn was an evil system rather than a person, an Antichristian State which was to end in 1660, [201] although the 1260 years had terminated in 1648 when God had begun to establish His kingdom. [202] Cromwell and his colleagues were "seasonable and good instruments" in the hand of the Lord, [203] and Canne confidently expected them to "effectually finish" the work in England, Scotland, and Ireland well before the date he had suggested. [204] Six thousand years from

[192] *Ibid.*, pt. II, p. 13.
[193] *Ibid.*, p. 5.
[194] *Ibid.*, p. 51.
[195] *Ibid.*, pp. 57, 58.
[196] *Ibid.*, p. 69.
[197] *Ibid.*, p. 70.
[198] *Ibid.*, p. 117.
[199] *Ibid.*, p. 85.
[200] Canne, *op. cit.*, pp. 5, 6.
[201] *Ibid.*, pp. 19, 20.
[202] *Ibid.*, p. 13.
[203] *Ibid.*, p. 16.
[204] *Ibid.*, p. 21.

creation would end "about 1655", when the present righteous rule would widen to enjoy "supream Power ... four or five yeares without interruption, untill they have broken in pieces the fourth Monarch." [205] In another three years, however, Canne's patience had run out and he turned on the government at Whitehall, denouncing its pride and craft, [206] and decrying it as the "last Apostacie" and the "Little Horn." [207] A further study of the prophetic word had brought new light, and Canne now declared that the time of this Little Horn's rule was almost over and that God would soon reveal to the saints their part in the Horn's mortification. [208] This coming revelation would verify that the Horn was to be "given up to the Saints of the Most High", [209] the agents of divine punishment, and in the event there would be "fighting, and instruments of war used." [210]

Much of William Aspinwall's advice to the saints stemmed from a similar desire that "with holy zeale" they should "fall close to the worke of this present generation." [211] Aspinwall followed Mary Cary in defending the trial and execution of Charles I as a good and necessary act, justifiable by the authority delegated by Christ to His saints. "God gave them a just occasion to take up Armes for their own defence, and afterwards to proceed to Judgement of the King for Blood-guiltiness and Enmity against Christ." [212] Antagonism to the cause of Christ could not be viewed lightly, and the inference was ominous for the future. In *The Work of the Age*, written two years later, Aspinwall described the work of the saints, now much closer at hand, in language that even then would have been difficult to understand in a purely spiritual sense. "Christ's heralds do so smite and thrash these Image Governments consisting of Heterogeneal parts, to wit, iron and clay ... that they bruise them to dust." [213] Such an unlikely work for saints would not be difficult for "the Lambs Military Officers, with whom he betrusteth the Militia ..." [214]

---

[205]   *Ibid.*, pp. 29, 30.
[206]   Canne, *The Time of the End* (1657), pp. 217, 218.
[207]   *Ibid.*, pp. 44f, 130.
[208]   *Ibid.*, p. 168.
[209]   *Ibid.*, p. 189.
[210]   *Ibid.*, p. 200.
[211]   Aspinwall, *An Explication and Application of the Seventh Chapter of Daniel*, p. 36.
[212]   *Ibid.*, p. 32.
[213]   Aspinwall, *The Work of the Age* (1655), p. 14.
[214]   Aspinwall, *A Brief Description of the Fifth Monarchy* (1653), p. 4.

John Roger's scurrilous *Sagrir, or Doomes-day drawing nigh*, which showed less concern for the scriptural foundation of Fifth Monarchism than an almost inordinate anxiety with politics and affairs of state, nonetheless sprang from an outlook similar to that which motivated Tillinghast, Canne and Aspinwall. Addressing the members of the present Parliament about their "generation-work" in view of the coming Fifth Monarchy, Rogers advised "your worke is about the Lawes and Tithes, to strip the Whore both of her outward Scarlet-array, and to rend the flesh off of her bones by thorwing [sic] down the standing of Lawyers, and Priests." [215] To soldiers of the New Model Army he added, "let me tell thee, thou wilt not lye quiet long; for God hath a worke to doe yet by thee, or upon thee: and such men must not be idle in this age." [216] Rogers' interpretation of the Fifth Monarchy could be calculated to appeal to those of a less spiritual sort whose aspirations of eternal bliss rose no higher than a future derived from a modification and betterment of the present. Redemption was to be freedom from "Ecclesiastick Bondage, Decrees, Councels, Orders, and Ordinances, of Pope, Priest, Prelate or the like ... From Civil bondage and slavery, or those bloody, base, unjust, accursed, tyrannicall Laws." [217] The Fifth Monarchy had already begun in 1648, [218] by 1660 the work would have reached Rome, and by 1666 would "be visible in all the earth." [219] Since, however, it had commenced and was to continue first among the saints in England, Rogers cautioned, "if so be the fifth Monarchy is so nigh us, it concernes them to set upon their Generation-worke then in these dayes, which is to model and conforme the Civil affaires for Christs coming ..." [220]

It will thus be evident that theology formed no small part of the Fifth Monarchist platform. Historians have tended to see various reasons for the rise of the Fifth Monarchy men, [221] but in an exceedingly religious age the force of spiritual ideas and the motivation of religious belief cannot lightly be discounted. The hopes of men have generally been stirred more deeply by a

---

[215] John Rogers, סגריר, *Sagrir. or Doomes-day drawing nigh* (1654), To the Reader, sig. A4r.

[216] *Ibid.*, sig. b 2r.

[217] *Ibid.*, pp. 130, 131.

[218] *Ibid.*, p. 129.

[219] *Ibid.*, p. 128, 129.

[220] *Ibid.*, p. 136.

[221] E.g. "The economic crisis of the sixteenth and early seventeenth centuries bred Fifth Monarchism, a form of revolutionary anarchism", Hill, *Puritanism and Revolution*, p. 56.

prophet with a vision, or a preacher with a message, or a seer who can cry with conviction 'Thus saith the Lord', than by any earthly promises of mere human devising. With the Fifth Monarchy Men, the vision and the message were suited to the present need, and the seers brought a word direct from God. "I have had much light and encouragement in this present Undertaking", [222] wrote John Canne in 1657. "Gods Word to me is, to declare against their Injustice and Tyranny", [223] said John Rogers. He had not intended to write so much, but "the Lord will have it so." [224] "My experience tels mee how to prophesie by the Spirit of the Lord, when the Spirit brings me into a fruitive discovery of the latter days ... I am able to foretell, and testifie to the approach of Christ, and his promises." [225] Here the root of the Fifth Monarchist deviation is laid bare. The doctrine of progressive revelation becomes the doctrine of personal inspiration, and the prophet can tell his people to take the sword and cut off the ear of the evil servant.

Few would question that these men or their followers were sincere and none would doubt that they were zealous, but sincerity and zeal alone are often the marrow of bigotry, and the judgement of history has been that the Fifth Monarchy Men were deluded fanatics. Later generations have tended to ignore, if not to scorn, the eschatology of the seventeenth century, and for this the excessive and bellicose enthusiasm of the Fifth Monarchists must largely be held responsible. In context, however, the movement was a fringe element, the extreme limit of an eschatology which had been growing in scope and in popular appeal for a century or more. Between 1640 and 1660 it was still possible to believe in the Fifth Monarchy without being fanatical, it was acceptable to be a millenarian without believing in a Fifth Monarchy, and it was normal to expect the imminent second advent without being a millenarian at all. Men of every persuasion and shade of opinion could pray with equal conviction "Thy Kingdom come", and the devout Thomas Brooks spoke for a wider eschatology than that of either millenarians or Fifth Monarchy Men when he affirmed "the year of Jubile is at hand." [226]

---

[222]   Canne, *op. cit.,* p. 32.
[223]   Rogers, *op. cit.,* p. 13. The allusion was to lawyers.
[224]   *Ibid.,* p. 19.
[225]   John Rogers, 'Channuccah, A Tabernacle for the Sun', in *Dod or Chathan: The Beloved: or The Bridegroom going forth for his Bride* (1653), p. 27.
[226]   Brooks, *Heaven on Earth,* p. 596.

CHAPTER SIX

THE END OF FAITH AND THE GODLY LIFE

Any representative bibliography or book-list reveals two characteristic and related elements of faith in Puritan England. Titles like William Gouge's *The Saints Sacrifice*, Robert Bolton's *The Saints svre and Perpetvall Gvide*, John Preston's *The Saints Daily Exercise*, *The New Covenant, or The Saints Portion*, and *The Saints Qvalification*, John Downame's *The Christian Warfare*, and Richard Sibbes' *The Saints Cordials* and *The Sovles Conflict with itselfe* are a handful of the great many works by eminent divines which illustrate the essentially personal nature of religious belief in the seventeenth century. "You are a Seale upon Christs heart, you are engraven on the palms of his hand; Your names are written upon his Breasts."[1] To make the saints aware of this direct relationship with Christ, and to bring each one of them into the fulness of its eternal benefits was the burden of the spiritual preacher. Popular works like Lewis Bayly's *The Practise of Pietie*, John Downame's *A Gvide to Godlynesse*, Robert Bolton's *Some Generall Directions For a Comfortable Walking with God*, and Richard Sibbes' *The Spiritvall-Mans Aime*, and works less frequently published such as Walter Cradock's *Gospel-Holinesse* or John Ball's *The Power of Godliness* exemplify the other aspect of Puritan faith, the pursuit of a holy life. "You are the Epistle of Christ; You are the anointed of Christ; You have the spirit of discerning; You have the mind of Christ ... such souls will keep their garments pure and white, and will follow the Lamb wheresoever he goes,"[2] continued Thomas Brooks. Religion can scarcely be personal without devotion, and the end of faith was the godly life.

The two themes were discerningly brought together in Thomas Taylor's *The Progresse of Saints to Full Holinesse* (1630), which expounded the doctrine of sanctification and left no doubt in the minds of readers regarding its needfulness:

> No Christian must content himselfe with the beginnings of holinesse, but must proceede to full sanctification ... the whole life of a Christian must be a continuall progresse in sanctification ... . It must begin in

---

[1] Brooks, *Heaven on Earth*, Ep. to the Saints, sig. a7r.
[2] *Ibid.*, sigs. a7r, a8v.

the spirit and minde, and then change the heart and will, and so come forth into the body and actions, that the whole man consisting of these parts, may be blameless.[3]

The whole treatise was rooted in the closing verses of I. Thess. v, and in the context of verse 23 [4] Taylor maintained that a particular necessity for piety arose from the doctrine of Christ's second coming. Although Taylor fully accepted the doctrine of a literal and glorious advent at the last day, he advised caution in the study of prophecy, particularly of the book of Revelation,[5] and it is the more significant that he so pointedly draws attention to the relationship of the godly life and belief in Christ's coming:

> ... a Christian should never set the second comming of Christ out of sight; as being a strong meanes to keepe him in a generall preparation or readinesse ... every one that would be found unblameable then, must be so now ... onely an unblameable holinesse will bestead us at that day, and therefore we must preserve ourselves unblameable till that comming of Christ, all things else leave us at that day: Riches, honours, pleasures then forsake us ... Onely a good conscience and study of holinesse, and practise of holy duties goe along with us to meete Christ in his second comming ...[6]

George Hakewill thought that a profession of the Creed, which spelt out the fact of a coming day of judgement, should be seen to lead to a sanctified life.[7] Thus, at a relatively early date, eschatological hope was held to have a direct bearing on the present life of the believer.[8]

Across the theological spectrum there came to be a wide acknowledgement of this relationship. The process of election, through justification, sanctification and ultimately on to glorification, through which men passed to salvation was understood in less theological language to mean that the present life was granted in order to prepare for that which was to come. Men expected to dwell at last in the presence of a holy God. It was unthinkable that they could do so without being holy themselves. God had said to His people of old "Ye shall be holy; for I the Lord your God am holy", and the author of the Epistle to the Hebrews had

---

[3] Thomas Taylor, *The Progresse of Saints to Full Holinesse* (1630), p. 201.

[4] "And the very God of peace sanctify you wholly; and I pray God your whole spirit and soul and body, be preserved blameless unto the coming of our Lord Jesus Christ".

[5] See his *The Principles of Christian Practice* (1635), p. 250.

[6] Taylor, *Progresse of Saints*, pp. 301, 303, 310.

[7] Hakewill, *Apologie*, p. 471.

[8] Early, that is, for those who see the main eschatological surge after 1640. Hakewill wrote in 1627, and Taylor in 1630.

reminded the elect of a new Israel that without such holiness no man would see the Lord.[9] This was but the outworking of the basic postulates of Calvinistic theology that all religion and religious experience began with a knowledge of God and a knowledge of man. If at first that knowledge was essentially theoretical, it became in the end essentially experiential.

None came to this conclusion more readily than George Fox and the early Quakers, and if they reached it by a somewhat different theology they reached it nonetheless. "The creature is a perfect creature out of transgression: He that is borne of God doth not commit sin".[10] "The life of the Saints is Christ, not sinfull at all".[11] "The lusts and affections must be mortified", even to the exclusion of "ribbons and cuffs, and scarfs, and ... double Boot-hose tops."[12] Fox is neither being facetious nor Pharisaical here. Holiness is real, it is practical, and it must, as Thomas Taylor had said, extend to the whole man. Indeed, Fox's chief disagreement with the orthodoxy of his day was that it failed just at this point. Preachers "did ... Roare up for Sinne in their pullpitts", and professors could, without compunction, "plead for Unholynesse".[13] Professor Hugh Barbour has drawn attention to the fact that spiritual idealism and a high ethical standard were inherent in the Puritan setting of Quaker development, and has noted also the presence of an eschatological expectation in early Quaker thought.[14] Before proceeding to look more closely at the ideal of a godly life in the broader eschatological context, it may be helpful to examine first this element in Quakerism and to note its relationship to the Quaker concept of holiness.

The literature of early Quakerism shows a conspicuous affinity with the general eschatology of the age. Its language and symbolism is, to a large extent, the language and symbolism of a wider theology. In 1653, Fox wrote:

> Now the Stone cut out of the mountain without hands, begins to strike at the Feet of the Image, that the head of Gold begins to fall,

---

[9] Lev. xix, 2; Heb. xii, 14.
[10] George Fox, *The Great Mistery of the Great Whore Unfolded* (1659), p. 280; cf. I John iii, 9.
[11] *Ibid.,* p. 281.
[12] *Ibid.,* pp. 228, 231.
[13] Fox, *Journal* (Ed. Norman Penney, Cambridge, 1911), I, pp. 2, 3.
[14] Hugh Barbour, *The Quakers in Puritan England* (1964), ch. 1, 'A Holy Nation: The Puritan Setting of Quakerism'. T. L. Underwood comments on this eschatology, which takes "a significant place within the spectrum of Puritan views of the millennium and related eschatological events", in Toon, *Puritan Eschatology,* pp. 91 ff.

> and the breast of Silver, and thighes of Brasse, and Feet part Iron, and part Clay; and his dominion is a Dominion for ever, over all ... and before him the Hills shall move, and the mountains shall melt, and the rocks shall cleave ... great Earthquakes shall be, the terrible day of the Lord drawes neer ... [15]

Fox speaks also of the false Prophet, the Beast and the judgement of the great Whore, of the day of the Lord and judgement to come, [16] and in the following year wrote *The Vials of the Wrath of God Poured Forth upon the Man of Sin.* Francis Howgill writes of Antichrist, Gog and Magog, and of "the Angel ... flying through the midst of heaven", [17] and in 'A Warning to all the World', declares:

> Woe woe unto all the Inhabitants, for the Lord God of power is coming in Power and great glory with ten thousand of his Saints to judge the Earth ... a day is at hand wherein you shall see him whom you have peirced [sic], yea, behold the Judge of all the World stands at the doore, even of the quick and the dead, and he comes in the Clouds with power & great glory, and every eye shall see him, and every heart shall melt ... [18]

The climate of the age, as the previous chapters of this study have suggested, was essentially eschatological and Quakerism, which grew out of that climate, [19] did not withdraw from its implications. To the credit of the early Quakers it will be granted that at least they understood the age in which they lived.

The relationship may be judged to have been deeper than that, however. The language of this early Quaker literature often approaches that of the radical millenarians, even the provocative rhetoric of the Fifth Monarchy Men. Fox writes:

> Now is the Lord comming to sit as Judge, and reigne as King ... Now shall Zion arise and thresh to beat the hills, and thresh the mountains; now is the Sword drawn, which glitters, and is furbished, the Sword of the Almighty, to hew down Baals Priests, corrupt Judges, corrupt Justices, corrupt Lawyers, fruitless Trees which cumber the ground. [20]

Edward Burrough said that God was going to come down from heaven "to burn up and destroy, and to consume to ashes" all who had worshipped the beast, and that the enemies of truth

---

[15]   George Fox, *To all that would know the Way to the Kingdome* (1653), p. 5.

[16]   *Ibid.,* pp. 5, 10, 13.

[17]   Francis Howgill, *An Answer to a Paper called, A Petition of one Thomas Ellyson* (1654), pp. 7, 10 (the first so numbered).

[18]   Francis Howgill, 'A warning to all the World' (1655), in Christopher Fell, *A few words to the people of England* (1655), pp. 10, 12.

[19]   Nuttall, *Holy Spirit,* p. 150.

[20]   Fox, *op. cit.,* p. 5.

were about to be "swept away with the besom of destruction". [21] Francis Howgill was even plainer:

> The Lord is proclaiming himself to be King ... and all who rule as
> Kings and Conquerors shall bow ... the Trumpet is blown, the Stan-
> dard is lifted up, there is open War proclaimed between Michael our
> Prince and all the Inhabitants of the Earth. Arm you selves, O ye
> Mountains and gather your selves on heaps O ye Isles, the glittering
> Sword of the Lord is drawn ... . Glory unto him for evermore; its hard
> for you to kick against the pricks, for we witness the two edged
> Sword of the Lord shall bathe itself in the blood of his Enemies, and
> shal be made fat with slaughter. [22]

While Fox and his men were thus proclaiming the Lamb's War
across the counties of England, others with bolder motives were
advocating the use of the sword. [23] It is hardly surprising that by
1658 the Quakers were described as a complete compendium of
all the devil's heresies. [24] In pointing to this affinity with extremist eschatology it is not suggested that the early Quakers shared
the same spirit. The power of the Friends was a different power
from that of mere "Mechanick professors" and the kingdoms of
men would not be reduced through human strivings alone. Nevertheless it is very clear that the two principles which turned pacif-
ist millenarians into violent Fifth Monarchists were both present
and strong in early Quaker thought.

The first, Professor Barbour describes in the chapter he calls
'The Terror and Power of the Light'. It was that conviction, so
intrinsically a part of all Quaker belief and action, that the individual should sense the immediate and continual direction of the
Spirit in his life. The work of Dr. Barbour and the earlier work of
Dr. Nuttall [25] combine to show that this sense of immediate
inspiration is the essence of Quakerism. This conclusion can never
be in doubt once the pages of Quaker literature between 1650
and 1660 are opened and read with due discernment. In his
Journal Fox repeatedly refers to specific instances of such guidance. "I was moved to go into Derbyshire ... . And I went to
Chesterfield where one Britland was Priest ... . (and) I was mooved
to speake to him & ye people." [26] Only months after this Fox

---

[21]   Edward Burrough, *The Walls of Ierico Razed down to the Ground* [1654],
pp. 1, 14.
[22]   Francis Howgill, *A Woe Against the Magistrates, Priests, and People of Kendall*
(1654), pp. 5, 6.
[23]   See *supra*, Ch. V on the Fifth Monarchy Men.
[24]   Thomas Hall, *Commentary*, p. 8.
[25]   See his *Holy Spirit*, ch. X, 'The Spirit in Every Man'. Cf. Underwood, *op. cit.*,
pp. 94—96.
[26]   Fox, *Journal*, I, p. 1.

was led, for reasons which even he did not then understand, to walk barefoot through the streets of Lichfield and cry "Woe unto ye bloody citty of Lichfeilde". Afterwards "ye fire off ye Lorde was soe In my feete & all over mee yt I did not matter to putt my shooes one any more & was att a stande whether I shoulde or noe till I felt freedome from ye Lorde soe to doe." [27] Francis Howgill records the very hour and place at which he was moved to write to Cromwell, and begins his testimony "Therefore hear the word of the Lord: thus saith the Lord ..." [28] James Nayler heard a voice calling him to leave home and preach, [29] and Fox himself went out into a hostile world and willingly endured vilification because the Lord had sent him. There is in all these instances of direct guidance an immediacy which defies the analysis of pure reason.

There were also revelations and day-to-day experiences which similarly could only be explained in terms of the Spirit's operation. Fox tells how, shortly after he had been "moved to sounde ye day of ye Lorde" from the top of Pendle Hill, he saw a vision of "a great people in white raiment by a rivers syde comeinge to ye Lorde." [30] The *Journal* mentions other visions. At the same time that Margaret Fell foresaw "a man in a white hatt ... come & confounde ye priests," another believer saw that a man in leather breeches would also "come and confounde ye priests". [31] When Fox came and preached, and the priest was duly convinced, it was an unsurprising endorsement of the Spirit's revelation. After attempting to speak in the church at Ulverston, Fox was attacked by an angry crowd, and beaten unmercifully. "They fell upon mee", he says, "& knockt mee doune & kikt mee & trampeld upon mee". [32] He was then dragged from the church to a nearby common, where, to use his own words again, "they then fell upon mee as aforesaid with there stakes & clubbs & beate mee on my heade & armes & shoulders till they had mased mee ... . And my body & armes was yellow blacke & blew with ye blowes & bruises ..." [33] Fox then recounts how, in the presence of his

---

[27] *Ibid.*, p. 15.
[28] Francis Howgill, in John Camm and Francis Howgill, *This Was the word of the Lord which Iohn Camm and Francis Howgill Was moved to declare and write to Oliver Cromwell, Who is named Lord-Protector* (1654), sig. A4.
[29] James Nayler, *A Collection of Sundry Books, Epistles and Papers* (1716), p. 12.
[30] Fox, *op. cit.*, p. 40.
[31] *Ibid.*, p. 52.
[32] *Ibid.*, p. 57.
[33] *Ibid.*, pp. 58, 59.

persecutors, his whole body seemed to be infused with the restoring power of God:

> ... I lay a little still & ye power of ye Lord sprange through mee & ye
> eternall refreshinges refresht mee yt I stoode uppe againe in ye eter-
> nall power of God & stretched out my armes amongst ym all & said
> againe with a loude voice strike againe heere is my armes my head &
> my cheekes: & there was a mason a rude fellow a professor (caled) hee
> gave mee a blowe with all his might Just a toppe of my hande as it was
> stretched out with his walkinge rule staffe; & my hande & arme was
> soe nummed & bruised yt I coulde not draw itt in unto mee againe:
> soe as ye people cryed out hee hath spoiled his hande for ever have-
> inge any use of it more (& I looket att it in ye love of God & I was in
> ye love of God to ym all yt had persecuted mee).
>
> And after a while ye Lords power sprange through mee again &
> through my hande & arme yt in a minute I recovered my hande &
> arme & strength ... [34]

Enough has been quoted to convey a sense of the early Quaker
conviction of the Spirit's presence. The first fifty pages alone of
Fox's *Journal* provide sufficient evidence for Professor Barbour's
conclusion that "serenity and trust and the sense of daily direction from the Spirit finally became the most characteristic part
of the Quaker way of life." [35] In theory, however, if not in fact,
Quakerism could not claim a monopoly of such immediate direction. When a Quaker saw a vision, or heard a voice, or felt a
compulsion to go to Derby or Lichfield or Bristol, or sensed the
urgency of sending a message to Cromwell, or the King of Spain,
the stimulus of his action was fundamentally the same as that of
the Fifth Monarchy Man who prophesied "by the Spirit of the
Lord", who was "able to foretell and testifie to the approach of
Christ", and who also could bring a word from God to the Lord
Protector. [36]

The other link in early Quaker thought with radical eschatology was the conviction that the saints were to have a part in the
establishment of the divine kingdom upon earth. In language that
again is barely distinguishable from that used by millenarians and
Fifth Monarchy Men, Fox speaks of the coming of Christ. "With
him are the Saints singing victory over the Beast, and the false
Prophets, great Whore, mother of Harlots, Babylon, Antichrists.
Babylon is fallen, the Lamb and the Saints shall have the vic-

---

[34] *Ibid.*, p. 58.
[35] Barbour, *op. cit.*, p. 94. Professor Barbour also notes the difficulty which confronted many early Quakers, that of distinguishing whether or not the Spirit was really
at work. "This was a deep and frequent problem in early Quakerism," *op. cit.*, p. 63.
[36] As did John Rogers in 1654.

tory." [37] It is always the Lamb *and* the Saints, both now and in the future. Christ is in the Saints, and they with Him, and the conquest of the powers of darkness is theirs as much as His. Without the city are the dogs and whoremongers, the liars and deceivers, but the elect of God "shall reign with the Lamb in the new Jerusalem for ever and ever." [38] "Your City is new Jerusalem ... your little Seed shall become a great Nation, and the whole earth shall be replenished there with ... your Beginning is the little Stone cut out without a hand, and it shall fill the Earth, and become a great mountain ..." [39] This was to be the ultimate outcome, but it depended on the present participation of the saints. The Generation-work of Fifth Monarchy Men was, for the Quakers, the Lamb's War. "The Lamb ... hath called us to make War ... against ... all the powers of darkness." [40] The war was as real as the task to which the militants believed they had been called, and demanded the same degree of commitment from the Lamb's followers. Howgill sounds the call to battle thus:

> Lift up your voyces, blow the Ttumpet [sic], sound an Alarum out of the holy mountain; proclaime the acceptable year, and the day of vengeance of our God. Gird on your sword upon your loins, put on the tried Armour ... Ride on, ride on, my beloved brethren and fellow souldiers ... thresh on with the new threshing instruments which hath teeth: beat the mountaines to dust ... make the Heathen tremble, and the uncircumcised fall by the sword: the Lord of hosts is with us, and goes before us. [41]

In the past, the Beast and the False Prophet have warred against the Saints and overcome them; now "the Lamb and the Saints must have the victory". [42] Hitherto Antichrists have reigned in the earth; "now the Lamb and the Saints shall rule". [43] The domination of mystical Babylon is over, and "the Lamb and the Saints is trampling him to pieces ... getting the victory". [44] The Quakers saw themselves arraigned against an evil world at the time when God was "enlarging his Kingdom". The elect were in the forefront of the battle, the sword of the Lord in their hands,

---

[37] Fox, *Great Mistery*, p. 172.

[38] Edward Burrough and Francis Howgill, *Answers to Severall Queries* (1654), p. 13.

[39] Edward Burrough, *A Trumpet Of the Lord sounded out of Sion* (1656), pp. 34, 35.

[40] Burrough, in Fox, *op. cit.*, Ep. to the Reader, sig. b2r.

[41] Francis Howgill, *This is onely to goe amongst Friends* [1655], p. 7.

[42] Fox, *op. cit.*, p. 75.

[43] *Ibid.*, p. 83.

[44] *Ibid.*, p. 122.

and their reward would be "the Inheritance of the Saints in Light."

What has thus far been observed of the writings of Fox and other early Friends has indicated that a strong eschatological element persisted in the Quaker theology of the 1650's. The terminology in which it found expression and the roots from which it sprang both suggest an affinity with the more radical eschatology of the day, and it is initially somewhat surprising to find that a mutual antipathy existed between the Quakers and other extreme camps. [45] Quite clearly the Quakers were not fighting on the same front as the Fifth Monarchy Men, and it might justifiably be questioned whether they were fighting in the same war. One cannot imagine John Rogers being "in ye love of God" to a mob who had just beaten him to unconsciousness, [46] or Thomas Venner advising an armed soldier to "putt uppe his sworde". [47] The eschatological factor in early Quakerism was more than the fusion of the two concepts of individual inspiration and collective and physical participation in the kingdom struggle. This might have been sufficient to produce a narrow sectarian revolution with strong political overtones. It was not sufficient to initiate the kingdom according to Quaker understanding. The Lamb's War was to be fought on the basis of an eschatological stress distinctive to Quakerism, and the war would be won and the final victory obtained only as that distinctive emphasis was communicated by the Friends to all men everywhere.

The expression of this eschatology emerged in the Quaker view of the kingdom. Quakers were as dissatisfied as any thoughtful men of the age with the state of the world in which they lived, and the vision of an ultimate divine order was fundamental in their outlook. "He will ... establish his own truth, his own truth in righteousnesse, his owne Kingdome". [48] So Fox in 1652, but in 1660 the ungodly and the unclean, the carnal and the disobedient still constituted the majority and still ordered the affairs of men, [49] and the first decade of Quaker activity is marked by faith in a kingdom which is largely still to come. [50]

---

[45] See Fox, *Journal*, I, p. 246, and Burrough, *A Trumpet, passim*, where it is declared that the Lord's controversy is, amongst others, with Anabaptists, Ranters, Seekers, and all who await "the Coming of Christ to Reigne in Person upon Earth", *A Trumpet*, p. 25. Cf. Underwood, *op. cit.*, pp. 99, 100.
[46] Cf. Fox, *op. cit.*, p. 58.
[47] *Ibid.*, p. 59.
[48] Fox, *The Kingdom*, p. 5.
[49] Edward Burrough, *A General Epistle to all the Saints* (1660), pp. 12,13.
[50] Cf. Barbour, *op. cit.*, p. 185.

The future tense appears repeatedly in the earlier writings of Fox. "Then shall the Lord alone be exalted ... the Lord will send a fire to devour them ... the Everlasting Gospel shall be preached again to them which dwell upon the earth ..." [51] "An Earthquake is coming upon you that hath not been since the foundation of the world ... but the Lamb and the Saints shall get the victory." [52]   In 1656 Edward Burrough was asking "How long Lord? how long? ... . Is it not the fulness of thy time which thou hast promised?", [53] and with many a devoted heart he prayed "Come, Lord Jesus, come quickly." [54] Babylon had not fallen by 1660 and the judgements of the Lord were still to be seen, although he would "speedily do great things in the world" and the righteous would soon "see the marvelous works of his hand." [55] Only when the work now swelling through England had spread through the whole world would truth prevail and the Lord be king. To a degree worthy of note the strength of early Quakerism lay in the challenge of an unfinished task and the hope of a future consummation.

To say that and no more, however, would be to convey a wholly superficial impression of Quaker eschatology. In the last analysis, the Friends were not so much concerned with the future as with the present. Their first interest lay less in a temporal kingdom in time than in a spiritual kingdom within the soul. Others might see the rule of God as promised for tomorrow — they saw it as present today. Those things which to other Christians signified that the day of the Lord was at hand were of little import to Quakers for whom the kingdom had already been established. "And as for all the confusions, and distractions, and rumors of Wars, what are they to us? What have we to do with them? and wherein are we concerned in these things? is not our Kingdome of another World?"[56] The questions were rhetorical, and Burrough answered them himself. "Our Kingdome is inward, and our weapons are spiritual, and our victory an [sic] peace, is not of this world ... " [57] This was in 1660. In 1654 he had already written that God had begun to set up his kingdom in the

---

[51]   Fox, *op. cit.*, pp. 9, 13, and *The Lambs Officer is gone forth with the Lambs Message* (1659), p. 13.

[52]   Fox, *Great Mistery*, pp. 44; cf. pp. 146, 172.

[53]   Burrough, *A Trumpet*, p 41.

[54]   *Loc. cit.*

[55]   Burrough, *A General Epistle*, p. 16.

[56]   *Ibid.*, p. 15.

[57]   *Loc. cit.*

earth, [58] and the doctrine received repeated emphasis from Fox and others:

> We witness the happy day of the Lord is come ... . The Lord Jesus Christ is come to reign, and his Everlasting Kingdom and Scepter is set up, and the Bar of Judgment ... now is the day of your tryal come, the Lambs Throne is set up ... now is the judgement of God come, and the man Christ Jesus, whom he ordained to judge the world in Righteousness ... [59]

The final events portrayed in the book of Revelation are already in course of fulfilment. The reapers are going forth to reap the harvest of the world. The winepress of divine wrath is about to be trodden. [60] Ordinary Christians likened the times to winter. "The Summer hath had her season ... The last moneth of the great yeere of the world is come upon us; wee are deepe in December," Thomas Adams had said. [61] In the climate of Quaker thought the seasons were more advanced. "The winter is past, and the summer is come, and the Turtle Dove, and the singing of the Birds is heard in our Land." [62] A wider eschatology declared that the world had come to its midnight and awaited the glorious dawn. [63] Quakerism could proclaim already "... the morning is broak, the Sun is rising, the day-Star is risen ..." [64] Throughout the 1650's the heart of the Quaker message was that the kingdom of God had already come.

The gist of this affirmation of an already-present kingdom is found in two succinct phrases from Fox, "the appearance of Jesus Christ in your souls", and "the Kingdom of heaven within". [65] The wide gulf which separated the eschatology of Quakerism from the general eschatology of the day was the insistence that the coming of Christ was not a final and general revelation from heaven but a present and personal revelation in the lives of men, and that His kingdom was not established once at the end of time but continuously as individuals yielded to the influence

---

[58]   Burrough, *Walls of Ierico*, p. 1.
[59]   George Fox, 'To all who love the Lord Jesus Christ', in George Fox and James Nayler, *Several Papers* (1654), p. 12; *The Lambs Officer*, pp. 1, 21.
[60]   George Fox, 'To the King of Spain' (1660), in *Gospel-Truth Demonstrated, in a Collection of Doctrinal Books* (1706), p. 198.
[61]   Thomas Adams, *Commentary*, p. 1138.
[62]   Edward Burrough, 'To the Camp of the Lord in England', in Howgill, *This is onely to goe amongst Friends*, p. 18.
[63]   Cf. William Bridge, *Christs Coming*, of which the running head reads 'Christ's Coming is at Our Midnight'.
[64]   Fox, *Great Mistery*, p. 233.
[65]   Fox, *Several Papers*, p. 7, and *A Word From the Lord to all the World* (1654), p. 6.

of the Spirit. The Quaker "war" was to convert people from sin
and death by bringing them into the new life of the Spirit, from
which they would derive true blessedness both "in this world,
and in the world to come." "Through all these things", said
Edward Burrough, "the Lord will set up his Kingdome." [66] The
Quaker was committed to preaching the gospel of a kingdom at
once invisible and inward, and when Burrough wrote his *General
Epistle to all the Saints* it was to the "whole Flock of God; who
are called and gathered into the Spiritual Kingdom of Righteousness and Peace." [67] The eschatology of Quakerism was clearly a
realised eschatology, perhaps the most significant such interpretation in early post-Reformation theology. [68]

The extent to which this consummated hope ran through
Quaker thought can be seen in the interpretation of biblical passages referring to last-day events in terms of individual and personal experience. The evidence available is vast and three illustrations must suffice. The usual view of Revelation xix and the
marriage of the Lamb was that it referred to the coming of
Christ at the end of time to claim His Bride, the church: "The
marriage shall be in the end of the world: for then the Bridegroom shall returne, and the Bride shal be prepared in her perfect
beautie for the embracing of her bridegroom." [69] The Quaker,
however, saw the union as a present experience: "The marriage of
the Lamb is come unto many ..." [70] Every believer in Christ had
not entered this relationship, only those "in whom his innocent
and heavenly nature is begotton and brought forth; for this is of
his flesh and of his bone; and here is his wife that hath made her
self ready, and is prepared for the Bridegroom." [71] All who
through the effectual mediation of the Spirit had thus partaken
of the divine nature, "quickened into Life, and adorned with
Beauty," were "married to the Lamb, to live with him for ever-
more." [72] That for which so many in the churches were longingly
waiting the Quakers had already experienced.

Fox preached the same message from the parables of the pearl
and the grain of mustard-seed. The pearl lies hidden in the field,

---

[66] Burrough, *A General Epistle*, p. 16.
[67] *Ibid.*, Title page.
[68] "... in eschatological questions (the Quaker) emphasis fell upon the present,
inward, spiritual experience in contrast with outward, physical events expected in the
future", Underwood, *op. cit.*, p. 96.
[69] Pareus, *Commentary*, p. 480; cf. Brooks, *Glorious day*, p. 4.
[70] Burrough, *op. cit.*, p.,7.
[71] *Loc. cit.*
[72] *Ibid.*, p. 8.

but the field is the world and since the world is in the hearts of all men, it is necessary to dig deep within in order to find the pearl. [73] Christ is the Light which enlightens every man coming into the world, and those who come to the Light are enabled to discover that which erstwhile has been dark and hidden. Thus "the Pearl that hath been hid in the Earth is found, and the Morning star is risen, and the day is dawned, and the true light shines ..." [74] Similarly the kingdom is like "a grain of mustard-seed, which is within ... like unto leaven ..." [75] The seed, again, is in all men and the leaven will produce a "new lump", and those who yield to its influence will come to see "the Kingdom of the world, to become the Kingdom of the Son of God ... the Kingdom of heaven ..." [76] Both parables teach the basic truth that the kingdom exists in embryo within, and Fox can proclaim with conviction the good news of a kingdom already begun:

> ... so the Pearl is within you that is found in the Nation of England, and all people upon the earth come in to your selves, find the Pearl in you ... and the Kingdom there within you, though it be like a grain of mustard-seed, its like unto leaven, it will leaven you up into a new lump ... . The Pearl in you come to know, the seed in you come to know, which seed is Christ ... which now is risen in thousands, who are come to be Heirs of the promise, & Heirs of God, and Heirs of the world that has no end. [77]

No single instance portrays the fulfilled eschatology of early Quakerism so vividly as that in which Francis Howgill describes his own conversion. In *The Inheritance of Jacob Discovered* he tells of a search for peace of mind which begins at the tender age of twelve and which leads him to forsake the world for a rigorous discipline of outward religious observance in the most depressing form of the Puritan tradition. He reads the Bible, prays regularly, meditates, fasts, listens to sermons, talks with men of faith but, like Luther, is still weighed down beneath an overpowering sense of guilt which no amount of sermons or sacraments will relieve. Turning from the fear and condemnation of this "Evangelical obedience" he pursues the search in the fellowship of Independents, and later among Anabaptists, but "after all this, no Peace nor no Guide I found." At last he hears a Quaker preacher declare that the light of Christ within is the way to eternal truth.

---

[73] George Fox, *The Pearle Found in England* (1658), sig. A2r.
[74] *Ibid.*, pp. 2, 3.
[75] *Ibid.*, p. 4.
[76] *Ibid.*, p. 5.
[77] *Ibid.*, pp. 4, 5.

The scales fall from his eyes and he discovers the presence of Jesus, Rest, Peace and Glory. [78] It is the traumatic effect which this revelation has upon his tortured soul that deserves notice:

> ... the Ark of the Testament was opened, and there was thunder, and lightning and great haile, and then the trumpet of the Lord was sounded, and then nothing but war, and rumour of war, and the dreadful power of the Lord fell upon me, plague, and pestilence, and famine, and earthquake, and fear, and terror ... and all that ever I had done was judged and condemned ... and the Seals were opened, and seven thunders uttered their voyces; ... the pillars of Heaven was shaken, and the earth reeled as a cottage; one woe poured out after another. And I sought death in that day, and could not find it, and it fled from me ... for the indignation of the Lord was upon the Beast and the false prophet; and Babylon came into remembrance in that day ... and as I bore the indignation of the Lord, something rejoyced, the Serpents head began to be bruised, and the Witnesses which were slain, were raised ... and a great famine there was; and the Sun was darkned, and the Moon turned into blood, and the Stars did fall, and all the grasse of the earth withered, and every green tree, and all the springs were dryed up ... and the Heavens passed away with a noyse, and the Elements melted, and the earth was scorched with the flame which proceeded from the Throne of God, and the Judgement Seat of Christ was seen ... and my heart was broken ... I saw the Crosse of Christ, and stood in it ... and the new man was made ... and eternall life was brought in through death and judgement ... [79]

The entire range of seventeenth-century eschatological expectation appears here as a direct and personal fulfilment. The last days have past, Christ has come, judgement and wrath have been poured forth, a new creation is here, and all within the experience of one man. [80] In an insignificant way a work had begun in England. In Quaker eyes, it would end gloriously as the kingdom was thus realised in men everywhere.

The effect of such doctrine in the lives of men and women was immediate. When the kingdom of God was realised within, as in the case of Howgill and thousands more, [81] it demanded a submission to the new, divine authority and a transformation in the

---

[78] Francis Howgill, *The Inheritance of Jacob Discovered: After his return out of Aegypt* (1656), pp. 5—11.

[79] *Ibid.*, pp. 11—13.

[80] In this context the significance of James Nayler's pseudo-Messianic entry into Bristol in 1656, riding on an ass and preceded by a group of women strewing flowers and garments in his path, can perhaps only be seen completely from an eschatological standpoint. If Scriptures with an eschatological import had been explicitly realised within the experiences of Burrough, Fox, and Howgill, then why not also in Nayler, a claimant to the leadership of the early Quakers?

[81] Professor Barbour suggests that the number of convinced Friends had reached 20,000 by 1657, Barbour, *op. cit.*, p. 182.

life. If the Quakers spoke much of the Spirit, it was because this work was essentially that of the Spirit, "ye Spiritt of God in mee", [82] as Fox would say. But they spoke equally of God and of Christ, and phrases such as "God in you", "the life of God in thee", "Christ made manifest within" [83] are frequent in the early literature. The momentous truth was that a new life had dispossessed the old and that that new life was the very life of God himself. The Quaker saw it clearly enough:

> ... he that hath received the holy Ghost ... knowes the Creator, and the dwelling of him in the heart ... for the Elect are one with the Creator, in his nature, enjoying his glory ... . Christ and the Father is one, and the same Spirit that dwels in the Son dwels in the Father which is one, I and my Father is one, the same dwels in the Saints, not distinct nor divided ... and he that is joyned to Christ is one spirit, and not distinct nor separate ... [84]

Francis Howgill, on the strength of his own experience, adds "so its no more the creature, but Christ who is all in his Saints." [85]

The realisation of the rule of Christ within the individual brought unavoidable consequences. If God possessed the believer as completely as Quakers seemed to believe He did, a holy life was inevitable. Old bottles could not take new wine. The deduction was thoroughly logical, and although Quakers generally were not moved as much by logic as by impulse, the force of this particular argument did not pass unnoticed. "Is not the new creature in Christ?" asked Fox. Then

> He that is in Christ is a new creature, and is not distinct from him ... . And Christ is justification, sanctification, and wisdome, and righteousnesse; and if he be not within ye, ye are Reprobates: And where Christ is, he is not without righteousnesse. Therefore they are not without righteousness, and wisdome, Justification, and Sanctification, if Christ be within, that is within; for where he is, that is not wanting: And the Apostle said they were made free from sin: And let not sin have dominion over your mortall bodies; minde, mortall bodies which sin was not to have dominion over: And old things passe away, and all things become new. Sin is an old thing, from the old deceiver: So while any sin is standing, all things is not made new, and sin hath its dominion.[86]

Two points are argued here that are basic to the Quaker concept of the holy life. In the first place, Quakers tended to avoid

---

[82] Fox, *Journal*, I, p. 20.
[83] George Fox, *An Epistle to all People on the Earth* (1657), pp. 3, 20; Burrough, *op. cit.*, p. 47.
[84] Burrough and Howgill, *Several Queries*, pp. 12, 18.
[85] Howgill, *Inheritance of Jacob*, p. 14.
[86] Fox, *Great Mistery*, p. 117.

the normal theological distinction between justification and sanctification. If Christ dwelt within, both justification and sanctification were simultaneously accomplished, and sin was taken
away in fact as well in theory.[87] Secondly, sin was evidence of the
old life and therefore evidence that Christ did not yet rule within. This was but a step from the ultimate idea of perfectionism
and the Quaker message was that all who were "in the light ...
come into perfect holiness."[88] Indeed, justification is not merely
the imputation of righteousness, but "a believer that is justified,
he is a new Creature ... and comes to enter into his rest where sin
is not."[89] Those who preach the bare doctrines of justification
and sanctification are no better than Jews, witches, or reprobates,
"but where Christ is within, there is Justification, Sanctification,
and Redemption."[90] The end of the Protestant doctrines of justification and sanctification, in the Quaker view, is that sin remains in the believer, a position which cannot be reconciled with
the apostolic faith,[91] for sin "continuues [sic] not in the godly;
for the godly are like God, out of sin ..." Conversely, sin can be
seen "in the ungodly, that is not like God."[92]

The Quaker ideal of holiness was absolute, and the man who
acceded to the Quaker call had to be prepared for total separa-
tion from the world. Sin was to be put off, God was to be
glorified, and the holy life was to be seen in body as well as in spirit. "The Saints are the Temples of God, and God dwels in them,
and walks in them, and they come to witnesse the flesh of Christ,
and they glorifie him in their souls and bodies ..."[93] Since "the
Saints bodies are the Temples of God,"[94] the Quaker aversion to
outward adornment is more understandable. Display and ostenta-
tion are incompatible with the fundamental objective of Christian living which is to glorify God. Soberness and modesty bring
glory to Him, but "silver lace, and your Jewels, and your spots of
your faces, and your feathers, and your wearing of Gold"[95] are
evidence of pride and vanity, and glorify the creature more than
the Creator.[96] If Quakers took the campaign for simplicity to an

---

[87]   *Ibid.*, p. 157.
[88]   *Loc. cit.*
[89]   *Loc. cit.*
[90]   *Ibid.*, p. 158.
[91]   *Ibid.*, p. 101. Hence Underwood comments on the Quaker antipathy to the
doctrines of imputed righteousness and justification by faith, *op. cit.*, p. 95.
[92]   *Ibid.*, p. 160.
[93]   *Ibid.*, p. 135.
[94]   *Ibid.*, p. 174.
[95]   George Fox, *To the High and Lofty Ones* [1655], p. 3.
[96]   *Ibid.*, p. 4.

extreme they did so because display was ungodly, and no saint in whom the kingdom had been realised could lend his body to ungodliness. "The new Jerusalem is come down from Heaven, and no unclean can enter." [97]

Quakers who thus witnessed latter-day events taking place within themselves were thereby powerfully motivated to the godly life. The standard by which that life was measured was high, but if Christ had once lived a sinless life in the flesh it was altogether possible that He should do so again in His Saints. "He is come, whose flesh is the life of the Saints, and his body is known which is prepared to take away sin ..." [98] The Quaker testimony of a kingdom which had already come was not primarily in preaching but in living. It was just at this point that Quakers challenged the eschatological doctrine of the day. The Lord had a controversy with those who claimed to believe in the coming of Christ and who said that they waited for His reign on earth. "Your hope of his coming hath no whit purified you", charged Edward Burrough, "and to you, what purpose is it for to desire the day of his coming?" [99] The theology of a share in the divine glory had not, in Quaker eyes, been reduced to the experience of submission to the divine nature:

> Your high nature stands, and Satan is not bound, nor one of the days of the thousand years of his limit is not yet come; your minds are outward in your own thoughts, which are vain, and you know not of what Spirit you are; The sufferings of Christ must you know, before you can see him Reigne, and thorow his War must you strive, before you can obtain his victory, and him must you own, in his convincing you of sin, before you can witness his Reigne in glory upon Earth over sin. [100]

Fox himself, in *The Vials of The Wrath of God,* cries "Repent, for the day of the Lord is coming ... the righteous God is coming to give every one of you according to your works ..." [101] Yet the works he sees on every hand are evil, the works of "Earthly-minded Men". Pride, ambition, malice, selfishness, conceit, deceit, pleasure-seeking, drunkenness, lust, gluttony, oppression — the list is formidable and long. "The glittering sword is drawn to hew down your fruitless trees which cumber the ground, ye lust-

---

[97] Burrough, 'Camp of the Lord', in Howgill, *This is onely to goe amongst Friends,* p. 18.

[98] Francis Howgill, *A Lamentation for the Scattered Tribes* (1650), p. 14.

[99] Burrough, *A Trumpet,* p. 25.

[100] *Ibid.,* pp. 25, 26.

[101] George Fox, *The Vials of The Wrath of God* (1654), pp. 4, 3.

ful fleshly ones ... ye heady high-minded ones ... ye scorners, ye lyers, ye dissemblers ... ye do not see your selves to be these trees which cumber the ground ..." [102] But to whom is Fox speaking? In part, undoubtedly, to the unbeliever, the worldling who has not yet come to know the light within, but initially, and principally to "professors, Priests and people" who know "their Deeds are evil", who have seen "the light" but hate it and walk contrary to it, whose consciences are their condemnation. [103] All who "act such things, must never inherit the kingdom of God." [104] Quakers did not doubt that others, by their lives, were excluded from the kingdom. The enthusiasm of such conviction was intense, even in an enthusiastic age, and time has shown that in their judgement the Quakers were a little harsh. They alone did not pursue godliness, as the following pages will indicate, nor were they unique among the saints in recognizing that belief in the divine kingdom should effect holiness. Given the charity and toleration of later generations, Quakers would surely have welcomed the strivings and sincerity of others who agreed that the end of faith was a godly life.

Divergent as it was from the more popular eschatological schemes, Quaker eschatology touched them at a point where they also met each other. The seventeenth century believed that it had recovered the letter of New Testament eschatology. The multiformity of interpretations argues against this assumption, yet does not nullify the fact that it did recapture its spirit. That spirit was one of hope, "the fundamental attitude determinative of the Christian life", and the orientation of that life "towards the coming of Jesus Christ and thus towards the future generally". [105] Apostolic faith was certainly fortified by such positive attitudes and the men of the seventeenth century, in opting for a biblical eschatology, inevitably imbibed of its spirit. "True Hope keeps up the heart from sinking, and desponding or apostatizing", reasons Nathaniel Homes. "As the Cork bears up the Net, that it may catch the Prey", he continues, "so doth Hope bear up the Soul, till it catch Salvation." [106] In this sense salvation is not fully wrought until the last events have run their course, and if

---

[102]   *Ibid.,* p. 4.
[103]   *Ibid.,* p. 1.
[104]   *Ibid.,* p. 4.
[105]   H. Quistorp, *Calvin's Doctrine of the Last Things* (1955), p. 15. The point of Dr. Quistorp's argument is that Calvin's entire theology is permeated with eschatological hope.
[106]   Homes, *Ten Exercitations,* p. 268.

men are saved by faith, they are also saved by hope. [107] "Why
should a godly man be discouraged, whatever his condition be?",
asked one. The world has come to its midnight, its coldest and
darkest hour, but at this very point Christ says, "this is my time,
it is now darke, and night, and midnight with my servant, now
will I go and comfort and deliver him." [108] "Is is not a blessing
to know that Antichrists raign is but 42 moneths a certain definite time, which is now drawing to its period?", [109] asks another.
For centuries the church has been trodden down by her enemies,
her doctrines subverted by error, and her people oppressed by
persecution. The knowledge of prophecy and coming events is of
inestimable value in the life of the Christian who lives in the age
of fulfilment:

> Is it not a blessing to know that the time of the woman in the
> Wilderness, and the witnesses mourning in sackcloth, the treading
> down the true Church of Christ and the Professours thereof is but for
> 1260. dayes, which term is also neer expiring. Is it not a great blessing
> after all the troubles and afflictions of the Church and Saints here on
> earth to be assured, that Christ their head with Myriads of his Angels
> and Saints departed, will appear to the finall destroying of all their
> enemies? ... [110]

Mortality is soon to be changed into immortality, and the saints
will then understand the deepest mysteries of God in Christ. That
which is perfect must replace that which is imperfect, that men
may no longer look darkly through a glass but face to face.
Sorrow, sin, and death are to be swallowed up in victory, that the
victors may walk in the light of the new Jerusalem. [111] The
language of hope might appear ethereal to those who did not
understand. To those who did, its substance was real enough. The
nearness of the last day is as the balm of Gilead to the faint-
hearted, [112] and the good news of a kingdom at hand is "a Doctrine that nourisheth Faith, Hope, Patience, and Comfort". [113]
The expectancy is joyful without being ecstatic, positive and at
the same time restrained.

These declarations of hope are neither confined to the more
enthusiastic groups nor tied to the prolix style of theology. Richard Sibbes gives it a homely expression when he pursues the

---

[107] See Rom. viii, 24.
[108] Bridge, *Christs Coming,* p. 13.
[109] Hicks, *Revelation Revealed,* Pref., sig. c3r.
[110] *Loc. cit.*
[111] *Loc. cit.*
[112] William Durham, *Maran-atha,* p. 32.
[113] Homes, *op. cit.,* p. 221.

biblical analogy of the church as the bride of Christ. In the usual
course of a human relationship, in "civill Marriage" as Sibbes
calls it, [114] there is first an exchange of promises between the
parties. This solemn betrothal, which is wrought in love, sets
apart each for other in a manner as binding as any contract. The
very nature of this relationship engenders hope and the engage-
ment period is bright with anticipation. In spiritual terms Christ,
the heavenly bridegroom, came once to earth to make the contract with His bride and therefore must "come againe to marry
us, and to take us where he is." [115] "It shall be our Marriage day,
now we are but betrothed to Christ", [116] said John Cotton.
Sibbes can thus call a sermon *The Brides Longing for her Bridegroomes second comming*, and can picture the bride-to-be as
yearning for her husband and for her "Marriage day". [117] To
quote another respected preacher, "A loving wife cannot but
looke for, and long for the returne of her husband from a farre
countrie." [118] Indeed, the bride's loving entreaties may even hasten the bridegroom's appearing and the day of consummation. [119]

Although in a different vein, Richard Baxter transmits this
eschatological hope with equal verve. His *Saints Everlasting Rest*
undoubtedly owed much of its popular appeal to a consistently
optimistic vocabulary. The last day is a "blessed day", a "joyful
day", a "wonderful" event, a doctrine of "cordial consideration"
to the saints, [120] who can therefore "rejoice", look for it with
"gladness", and allow its leavening influence to be seen with
"believing Joyes and Praise". [121] Baxter had served as an army
Chaplain during the Civil War, and his memories were still fresh
when he wrote the *Saints Rest*:

> I have thought on it many a time, as a small Emblem of that day,
> when I have seen a prevailing Army drawing towards the Towns and
> Castles of the Enemy: Oh with what glad hearts do all the poor
> prisoners within hear the news, and behold our approach? How do
> they run up to their prison windows, and thence behold us with
> Joy? How glad are they at the roaring report of that Cannon, which is

---

114   Sibbes, *The Brides Longing*, p. 15.
115   Sibbes, 'Churches Eccho', p. 107, in *Beames of Divine Light*.
116   Cotton, *A Practical Commentary, or an Exposition with Observations, Reasons, and Vses upon The First Epistle Generall of John* (1656), p. 227.
117   Sibbes, *The Brides Longing*, p. 15.
118   Taylor, *Principles of Christian Practice*, p. 255.
119   Homes, 'Canticles', in *Works*, p. 462.
120   Baxter, *Saints Rest*, pp. 791, 776 (numbered 176), 48.
121   *Ibid.*, pp. 48, 804.

> the Enemies terror? How do they clap each other on the back, and cry Deliverance, Deliverance! [122]

The illustration was too pertinent for a good preacher to miss, and Baxter pressed the lesson well home. "O what thought should Glad our hearts more, then the thought of that day ... . Fellow Christians, what a day will that be, when we who have been kept prisoners by sin, by sinners, by the grave, shall be fetcht out by the Lord himself?" [123]

This last sentence provides the key to a hope which is rooted in a climactic event in time. It is "by the grave" as well as by sin that men have been fettered and prevented from enjoying that fulness of fellowship with the divine for which they were created. Only as the grave is conquered and its captive released can the believer enter eternal life in its widest sense. The limitations of mortality must be overcome, and when Baxter speaks of an ever-lasting rest for the saints he is talking of more than the liberation of the soul at death. It is true that the saints' rest begins at death, when the soul is freed from the body to enter the presence of God. [124] But in Baxter's view this is only a partial rest. The full glory and blessing of that rest is not achieved until after the resurrection when soul and body are united once more, and Baxter looks to the day when his "perfect soul and body together" will come into the presence of God. [125] This essential reunification will take place at "that most blessed joyful day" which "comes apace", that is at the last coming of Christ and, although the Lord may seem "to delay his coming, yet a little while and he will be here." [126] In such assurance Baxter can trustingly commit his whole being to the grave:

> O hasten that great Resurrection Day! when thy command shall go forth, and none shall disobey; when the Sea and Earth shall yield up their Hostages, and all that slept in the Graves shall awake, and the dead in Christ shall first arise; when the seed that thou sowedst corruptible shall come forth incorruptible; and Graves that received but rottenness, and retained but dust, shall return thee glorious Stars and Suns; therefore dare I lay down my carcass in the dust, entrusting it, not to a Grave, but to Thee: and therefore my flesh shall rest in Hope, till thou raise it to the possession of the Everlasting REST. Return, O Lord, how long? O let thy kingdom come! [127]

---

[122] *Ibid.*, p. 49.
[123] *Ibid.*, pp. 50, 47.
[124] *Ibid.*, p. 836.
[125] *Ibid.*, p. 791.
[126] *Loc. cit.*
[127] *Ibid.*, pp. 837, 838.

The body has shared in the sufferings and obedience of time, it must therefore share the blessedness of eternity. Through the redemptive act on the cross "Christ bought the whole man, so shall the whole partake of the everlasting benefits of the purchase." [128] In short, the fulness of eternal life can only be realised through the resurrection of the body. [129]

This is precisely Christopher Love's message when he argues that the "maine end of Christs coming againe" is the resurrection of the body. [130] Again, it is what John Durant means when he says "salvation is onely yours: at the last day". [131] Love agrees with Baxter, "though Christ brings soules to heaven before his coming, yet hee doth not compleatly glorifie any of his servants till his coming againe," [132] thus the "totall and compleat" blessedness of believers waits until the second advent. [133] The Creed as well as Scripture could be cited in support of this position, and Durant pointed out "you are already redeemed in your soules, but your bodies are not yet redeemed ... in that day you shall have not only soule-salvation, but body-salvation". [134] The whole doctrine of the resurrection was thus very much a question of personal salvation, and the nature of the resurrection body came to be a reason for individual hope, as the following passage from Durant perceptively shows:

> The bodies of you that are alive are subject to sicknesses, pains, weaknesses, death: And the bodies of the Saints departed, are subjected to corruption ... Well, but yet in that day, your bodies shall bee redeemed ... all your bodies shall then bee saved from sicknesses, weaknesse, yea, and death ... Now we groan under stones, and gouts, and feavors, and agues, and other distempers and paines; yea, and all the day long we are liable to death. But chear up ... in that day it shall not be so ... When Christ shall appear the second time, it shall be for salvation unto our bodies. [135]

The hope offered here to the dead was also offered to the living. A real body, at once tangible yet spiritual and incorruptible, might be difficult to imagine. Nevertheless Christ had appeared in such a form after the Resurrection, and Paul had promised that the living saints would be changed at the last trump. Archbishop

---

128 *Ibid.*, p. 29; cf. Sibbes, *A Fountain Sealed* (1637), pp. 191–195.
129 See Appendix II, 'The Resurrection of the Body'.
130 Love, *Penitent Pardoned*, p. 197.
131 Durant, *Salvation*, ep. ded., sig. A4v.
132 Love, *op. cit.*, p. 139.
133 *Ibid.*, pp. 187, 188.
134 Durant, *op. cit.*, pp. 224, 225.
135 *Ibid.*, p. 225.

Ussher had much in mind when he wrote that Christ would "change the living, so that it shall be with them as if they had been a long time dead and were now raised to life againe." [136]

There was nothing naïve about a resurrection of the body. Christ had raised the dead and this, together with His own victory over the grave, was sufficient surety of a general resurrection at the last day. The same power that had brought Christ from the tomb would "in a moment both raise the dead with their own bodies and every part thereof though never so dispersed." [137] Time and space were no obstacle to a Creator and resurrection was, in fact, re-creation. He who had first fashioned man from the dust of the ground and pronounced him perfect, would yet bring forth a multitude of men from the grave in bodies not subject to "diseases and distempers, infirmities and deformities, maimednesse and monstrous shapes." [138] Baxter, Ussher, Bolton, Love and Durant all suggest that Christian hope in the seventeenth century lay less in the survival of the soul after death, universal as that doctrine undoubtedly was, than in the new creation of the whole being. When a professor of divinity spoke of "the full accomplishment of the salvation of the Believers", he spoke in terms of Christ's coming and the resurrection of the body. [139] Men learned from their Bibles of a hope set before them, of a hope laid up in heaven, of a hope of the resurrection of the dead. They were told that believers were begotten unto a lively hope, that they were heirs of the hope of eternal life, that they were to look for the blessed hope, the glorious appearing of Christ. [140] It all told of a future consummation in time, and in professing that hope the saints were not ashamed.

It was precisely this hope that spurred on the believer in his pursuit of godliness. The evidence of fitness for the companionship of a holy God and holy angels was a holy life. The bride did not spend the time of her betrothal dreaming of bliss to come, but in the exacting task of preparation for a new life. "If a man hope for this comming of Christ, he will purifie himselfe for it, even as hee is pure. He will not appear in his foule cloathes, but ... will fit himselfe as the Bride for the comming of the Bridegroome." [141] An unfeigned belief in Christ's second coming, in

---

[136]   Ussher, *Body of Divinitie*, p. 447.
[137]   *Loc. cit.*
[138]   Bolton, *Last Things*, p. 129; cf. Ussher, *op. cit.*, p. 448.
[139]   Dickson, *Short Explanation of ... Hebrewes*, p. 193.
[140]   Cf. Sibbes, *Philippians*, pp. 225, 226.
[141]   Sibbes, *Brides Longing*, pp. 73, 74.

the view of Alexander Nisbet, "is a special mean to make Christians thrive in grace and holinesse." [142] Conversely, if the doctrine cannot be seen to work efficaciously in the life, "it is but a false conceit and lying fancy." [143] True Christians, therefore, "always live in expectation of the Lord Iesus in the Clouds" with oil in their lamps and "prepared for his comming." [144]

> If we say this truly, Come Lord Iesus, undoubtedly it will have an influence into our lives, it will stirre up all graces in the soule; as Faith, to lay hold upon it; hope, to expect it; love, to embrace it; patience, to endure anything for it; heavenly-mindednesse, to fit and prepare for it ... [145]

All this was manifestly in the tradition of New Testament exhortation and was therefore the more welcome, since those early believers were the epitome of godly hope. Thomas Goodwin recognised that it was essential to apostolic faith to live constantly in the expectation of the coming of Christ. They "had that Day in their Eye", they "walk'd in view of it", consequently they were "set forth as a Pattern" to later generations. [146] The whole gamut of eschatological doctrine, the interpretation of apocalyptic symbolism, the times of chronological prophecy, an understanding of the age, the future of the Papacy, Turk, and Jew, the millennium and the kingdom, all, in the last analysis, was to be measured by one criterion. "The only use of knowiug [sic] them", declared Goodwin, is "to prepare for them". [147] "Latet hic Dies, ut observetur omnis Dies; The Day and Year of the Accomplishment of the great Matters are hid from us, so that each Day and Year we may be found ready, when-ever they shall come". [148] This could be construed in the same sense as Joseph Hall's comment that a Christian is always ready for the coming of the Lord, [149] and Goodwin could not refrain from adding "as in this Age wherein we live, they are likely to do." [150] The eschatological stress of scripture constrains Durant's word "it is your worke and wisdome, to cleanse yourselves from all filth, and to

---

[142]   Alexander Nisbet, *A Brief Exposition of the first and second Epistles General of St. Peter* (1658), p. 330. On Nisbet, see *Fasti Ecclesiae Scoticanae* III (Edinburgh, 1920), p. 99, s.v. Nesbitt.
[143]   Sibbes, *loc. cit.*
[144]   Ussher, *op. cit.*, p. 451.
[145]   Sibbes, *op. cit.*, p. 79; cf. Cotton, *A Practical Commentary*, p. 229.
[146]   Goodwin, 'Gospel Holiness' in *Works*, V, pt. II, p. 25.
[147]   Goodwin, 'Revelation', in *Works*, II, pt. I, p. 190.
[148]   *Loc. cit.*
[149]   Joseph Hall, *op. cit.*, p. 233.
[150]   Goodwin, *loc. cit.*

perfect holinesse in a filiall feare of God." [151]

Thus, while the believer looked forward to a definitive point in time for the realisation of his hopes, he was also conscious that the future emerged from the present. The full eschatological hope did not rest solely in an isolated event at the end, but rather in the culmination of an agelong process. For the world this process had been in operation throughout history, for the individual it had begun with the outworking of divine grace at conversion. There was no future for the man who in the present lived only for the present. The true hope of the last things led both church and saint towards a future event only along the path of present, and total, commitment. Christopher Love preached ten sermons on the coming of Christ and the future glory of heaven from Col. iii, v. 4, all of them posited on three propositions, that Christ is the life of the believer now, that Christ will appear in glory at the end, and that when He does appear the saints will appear in glory with Him. [152] To Love, there are three appearings of Christ taught in Scripture, His appearing in the flesh when He lived a holy life, His appearing in the lives of believers through the gospel, and His appearing in glory at the last day. [153] The saints will appear with Him in glory then, only as His holy life is manifest in them now. Sibbes understands the relationship, again, from the viewpoint of the Bride's marriage to her heavenly spouse. Before the marriage can be finally effected there is to be a threefold union of Christ with His Church, a union of nature, of grace, and of glory. The union of nature came through the incarnation when Christ took upon Himself man's nature. The union of grace comes through the gospel when man partakes of the divine nature. The union of glory will be at the end when the church, duly prepared and perfected, will be in heaven in the presence of Christ. [154] The marriage cannot be regarded as consummated until the union of glory, but that union is not possible without either those of nature or grace. The future, then, does not stand in distinction from the present. It is part of it, a culmination in time of a process in history and in life.

The reality of this hope in personal experience finds expression in many ways, all of them compelling to the believer whose chief end in life is the pursuit of holiness. Sibbes sees it as an

---

[151]   Durant, *op. cit.*, ep. ded., sig. A5r.
[152]   Love, *Heavens Glory*, p. 4.
[153]   *Ibid.*, pp. 4, 5.
[154]   Sibbes, 'Chvrches Eccho', p. 102, in *Beames of Divine Light*.

antidote to sin. "The Soule is never in such a tune, as when the thoughts of those glorious Times have raysed the Affections to the highest pitch ... so long as it is so affected, it cannot sinne ... . So long then, as wee keepe our hearts ... in a love of the appearing of Christ, they are impregnable ..." [155] To Goodwin, it is a barrier against the machinations of Satan. "The Devil, the shorter his time is, the more he rages and ... seeing these are the last daies ... the more should we endeavour to do God service." [156] Taylor regards it as a timely preservative against the cares of this life. "The buriall of the father, the tending of the farme, the marriage of a wife, the care of the family, the bidding of friends farewell; many will be the occasions of looking backe, and plucking backe the hands from this spirituall plough." But what better way to resist such temptations than to remember that the coming of the Lord draweth nigh? [157] To Brooks, it is a challenge to prepare the whole man for eternity. "Those that have hopes to reign with Christ in glory, that have set their hearts upon that pure and blissful State ... they will purifie both their insides, and their outsides, both body and soul." [158] It is an incentive to duty and obedience. [159] It is the spring of brotherly love. [160] It is a stimulus to work and pray for others. [161] It is the root of happiness and contentment in the present. [162] There is, in short, no aspect of Christian life and doctrine that is not quickened and ennobled by the influence of a positive eschatological expectancy. The theology of hope is a catalyst which breaks down the tension between present and future by bringing the future into the present in a form that is accessible to every aspiring believer. In the language of the time, it is summarised by Thomas Brooks in his conclusion to *Heaven on Earth*:

> Holiness is the very marrow and quintessence of all Religion: Holiness is God stamped and printed upon the Soul; it is Christ formed in the Heart; it is our Light, our Life, our Beauty, our Glory, our Joy, our Crown, our Heaven, our All. The holy Soul is happy in Life, and blessed in Death, and shall be transcendently glorious in the Morning of the Resurrection, when Christ shall say, Lo, here am I, and my holy Ones, who are my Joy; Lo, here am I, and my holy Ones, who are my

[155]   Sibbes, *The Brides Longing*, pp. 105—106.
[156]   Goodwin, *Works*, I, pt. III, p. 133.
[157]   Taylor, *Titvs*, p. 93.
[158]   Brooks, *op. cit.*, p. 540.
[159]   Love, *Heavens Glory*, p. 47 ff.
[160]   Homes, *Resurrection*, p. 542.
[161]   Sibbes, *Philippians*, p. 230.
[162]   Taylor, *op. cit.*, pp. 492, 493.

Crown; and therefore, upon the Heads of these holy Ones, will I set an Immortal Crown. Even so Amen, Lord Jesus. [163]

Most preachers who held out this high standard to their people were aware that Paul's despairing cry would be re-echoed within many breasts, "for to will is present with me; but how to perform that which is good I find not." [164] The pursuit of holiness was not made easier by the associations of hope, and the faithful shepherd understood that his flock needed much guidance if they were to escape the corruptions of the world. If Baxter is to be followed, there were three notable preparatives to the second coming: the Word, the Sacraments, and the Spirit. [165] The efficacy of Word and Spirit as means of grace was not likely to be questioned in Puritan England, and if the bread and wine were not always understood in a sacramental sense their importance in the life of faith was generally undisputed. To receive the Sacraments, or "the Ordinances", or "the Lord's Supper" was, in the eyes of most saints, one of those God-given "seasons and opportunitites of grace" granted "to make use of for .. salvation." [166] The soteriological significance of the elements was beyond dispute, even with those who denied them any sacramental power. No-one doubted that the bread and wine pointed back to the sacrifice of the cross, but in the seventeenth century an eschatological meaning was widely acknowledged which hitherto had not received much notice. Baxter, Homes, and Pareus all stress that in celebrating the Lord's Supper, believers witness to the Lord's death "till He come". [167] Morgan Llwyd, in 'Our Lord is Coming Once Againe', writes: "By breaking bread we show thy death and mind thy wondrous love Untill thou come to us againe in glory from above", [168] and in 'Canticls. Some Select Verses of the Song of Songs, or the Churches Hymne After Breaking Bread', he adds:

My love among the lillyes feed
    Untill the breake of day
Then light in stead of darknesse comes
    and shaddowes flee away. [169]

---

[163] Brooks, *op. cit.*, pp. 606, 607.
[164] Rom. vii, 18.
[165] Baxter, *op. cit.*, p. 46.
[166] Love, *op. cit.*, p. 52.
[167] Baxter, *loc. cit.*, Homes, 'Canticles', in *Works*, p. 426; Pareus, *Commentary*, p. 15.
[168] Morgan Llwyd, *Gweithiau Morgan Llwyd*, I (1899), ed. T. E. Ellis, p. 9. Llwyd and his expectant spirit are discussed by G. F. Nuttall in *The Welsh Saints, passim*, but particularly ch. III.
[169] *Ibid.*, p. 10.

There is clearly an eschatological meaning here, and Baxter will go even further and suggest that it may be the supreme message of the Lord's Table:

> What consolation also have we oft received in the Supper of the Lord? What a priviledge is it to be admitted to sit at his Table? to have his Covenant sealed to me by the outward Ordinance, and his special Love sealed by his Spirit to my heart? Why, but all the life and comfort of these, is their declaring and assuring me of the comforts hereafter; their use is, but darkly to signifie and seal those higher mercies: when I shall indeed drink with him the fruit of the vine renewed, it will then be a pleasant feast indeed. [170]

Participation at the Lord's Table may be a means of grace. To Baxter it is also quite clearly the hope of glory.

The reasons for this emphasis, in addition to the declarations of scripture, [171] are numerous. Some see the eschatological significance of the sacraments primarily as doctrinal and theological, while others regard it more in a spiritual sense. Pareus comes to the point through a defence of the literal and personal second advent against the Roman doctrine of the mass. From Rev. i, 7 it may be seen that at the last day Christ descends bodily and visibly from heaven in the clouds. It is the testimony of scripture that He does not come to earth again *until* the last day, and it is not therefore possible that He can be corporally present on earth in space or time prior to His second appearing, much less in the ubiquitous sense of the mass. All of which "is a strong reason to prove that his body is not in the mean time invisibly hid in, under, or about their host, altar, or chalice." [172] Further, "for men to believe as necessarie to salvation that Christ ... is present, in or under the sacrament of the Altar, or that his humane nature is in all places, and filleth all things, is a most false doctrine." [173] It is as a witness against such theology that "when we celebrate the Lords supper, we are commanded to shew forth his death till hee come." [174] The mass denies the work of Christ at its two cardinal points in time and the sacraments can only be of total relevance when they are seen to symbolise the entire work of Christ as begun at the cross and finished at the second coming. John Archer therefore stresses a kingdom significance in the Lord's Supper, since its celebration will cease when Christ comes to

---

[170]   Baxter, *op. cit.,* p. 771.
[171]   See Matt. xxvi, 29 and I Cor. xi, 26.
[172]   Pareus, *op. cit.,* p. 15.
[173]   *Ibid.,* p. 52.
[174]   *Ibid.,* p. 15.

establish His divine rule. Archer is evidently familiar with the more evangelical form of the service where the worshippers meet the minister in fellowship around the table, for it is in the table that he sees the real meaning of the act. "The gesture of a Table is necessary at the receiving of the Sacrament, or else a maine use and comfort of the Sacrament is lost, which is the signification of our Raigning with Christ in his Kingdom ..." [175] Archer adds that the kingdom signified will be "in this World", and if many could not accept that, few would disagree that the Lord's Supper was "a consolation for the future." [176] It is a strange paradox of history that those who believed most ardently in the Lord's coming should come to meet least frequently at His table.

For the more spiritual view we may turn again to Brooks, and to John Dod. When saints are at the Lord's Table they are at the "Gate of Heaven". [177] They can "see Christ at the right hand of the Father". [178] To illustrate the longing of the soul that had seen this vision Brooks refers to Plutarch, "once the Gauls had tasted of the sweet Wine, that was made of the Grapes of Italy, nothing would satisfie them but Italy, Italy." [179] This is hope again, and to Brooks it is never stronger than at the Lord's Table. He who had caught a glimpse of God in the Sacrament can never be satisfied with anything less than a complete revelation. "It is not a lap and away, a sip and away, that will suffice such a soul: No, This soul will never be quiet, till it sees God face to face." [180] But hope cannot come to such fruition in this life, hence the Lord's Supper stands between the believer and the future, pointing forward to the full accomplishment of the gospel promise:

> ... as the espoused Maid longs for the marriage day, the Apprentice for his freedom, the Captive for his ransom, the condemned man for his pardon, the Traveller for his Inn, and the Mariner for his Haven; so doth a soul that hath met with God in his Ordinances, long to meet with God in Heaven. [181]

With John Dod we return from hope to holiness. His sixth sermon for the Lord's Supper was from the parable of the marriage feast. To the man without a wedding garment the King says

---

[175] Archer, *Personall Reigne*, p. 17.
[176] *Loc. cit.*
[177] Brooks, *op. cit.*, p. 119.
[178] *Loc. cit.*
[179] *Ibid.*, p. 127.
[180] *Loc. cit.*
[181] *Ibid.*, pp. 126, 127.

"How darest thou come to the Royall table ... having no repentance for sinne; no freedome from the guilt, or from the power of sinne ...?" [182] It is "the foule and loathesome garments of the old man" which so "displease the eyes of the Lord." [183] Only after "due preparation, and with all feare, and care, and good conscience" is it proper to "draw neere unto his Table" and come "before his Maiestie."[184] Therefore, he urges, "let us labour to put on this wedding-garment seeing it is so requisite and needfull for every worshipper of God to be cloathed therewith." [185] Dod's message is clear enough. Holiness is essential in the life of those who partake of the sacraments, and anything less is an affront to God. [186] But the guest without a wedding garment is cast into hell at the last day, [187] and Dod must draw from the parable its full meaning. If it is necessary to be holy in the presence of the elements which signify the body and blood of the Saviour on the cross, it is necessary to be holy in the presence of God Himself. The consequences of holiness, or unholiness, are eternal and the preparation of life demanded for the ordinances is a reminder of the preparation required of those called to the Marriage Supper of the Lamb:

> ... sith God hath chosen you to eternall glory in the heavens, and provided unto you a kingdome, that you may raigne with his owne Sonne, therefore doe you leade such a life as becomes heires of such a Kingdome, and adorne your selves with such graces as may beseeme the Spouse of Christ, and those that are the chosen people of the Lord, even such as are called unto holinesse. [188]

In the sacraments, then, could be found tangible evidence of the end of faith, and a means towards the godly life that was its goal.

In keeping these thoughts before their congregations the spiritual preachers and writers accomplished a far greater task than of merely preparing men to receive the sacraments. It might be concluded that those who were ready to meet God at His table were ready also to meet Him at the throne. The wedding garment enabled a man both "to sit at the Lords Table" [189] and "to have boldnesse in the day of Iudgement." [190] The saints on whose

---

[182]   Dod and Cleaver, *Ten Sermons*, p. 158.
[183]   *Ibid.*, p. 160.
[184]   *Ibid.*, p. 161.
[185]   *Ibid.*, p. 165.
[186]   For those who desired it, the *Ten Sermons* contained detailed instruction on how to make adequate preparation to receive the Lord's Supper.
[187]   *Op. cit.*, p. 173.
[188]   *Ibid.*, p. 166.
[189]   *Ibid.*, p. 162.
[190]   *Ibid.*, p. 172.

willing ears such exhortations fell, however, were men of clay, children of Adam, and given to the weaknesses of the flesh. "Labour more and more to be like to Christ", [191] urged William Bridge, but even the most upright men in the land to whom he had been called to preach had never faced a more impossible demand. How to perform that which was good was a real and recurring problem for believers of every station, and the advocates of the godly life would have failed at the most crucial point of all if they had not made plain the way by which frail humanity could achieve the goal of holiness. There is no lack of spiritual directives or devotional aids in the literature of the seventeenth century, nor of later evaluations of their significance, but it would be an omission if in concluding this study no mention was made of their relationship to the eschatological hope. "Be wise, now, therefore, O ye Princes, Nobles, Rulers, Judges, Gentlemen, and others and Kiss the Son, lest ye perish in the way, for Christ is upon his way unto his kingdom." [192] The words were becoming enough for the pulpit, but how were they to be understood in practice? How were men to be "Blamelesse till the day of Christ"? [193] How were they to proceed to full holiness? [194]

The terms by which the 'physicians of the soul' sought to impress the need for practical godliness in view of the imminent advent were seemingly without end. "Put on your garments ... Gird your loyns ... Light your Lamps ... Doe the worke of your places," [195] advised John Durant. "Acquaint thy self with thy Judge aforehand ... Part from sinne ... Get sinceritie and uprightnesse of heart ... Get love of the Saints ..." [196], counselled Thomas Taylor. "This Doctrine of Christ's appearing in glory to judge the world, gives direction to you to set about the practise of seven practical duties", [197] specified Christopher Love. They were: to repent, to keep a clear conscience, to be patient under trials, to improve the talents, to desire the coming of the Lord, to practise moderation, and to be watchful.[198] Watchfulness, with prayer, had been enjoined by Christ as being needful at the end-time and both now found a relevant expression in the exhor-

---

[191] Bridge, *op. cit.*, p. 16.
[192] *Ibid.*, p. 13.
[193] Taylor, *Progresse of Saints*, p. 236.
[194] *Ibid.*, p. 201.
[195] Durant, *op. cit.*, pp. 299, 300.
[196] Taylor, *Principles of Christian Practice*, pp. 280, 281.
[197] Love, *op. cit.*, p. 47.
[198] *Ibid.*, pp. 47—52.

tations of the church. Believers were to watch against the deceitfulness of their own hearts, against the subtle temptations of the Devil, and for every special opportunity of grace. [199] Failure to watch and to understand the significance of the times had been the tragic mistake of men in the days of Noah and Lot. The end had been condemnation and judgment. "Let us therefore not be secure ... . Let us rather watch and waite for Christs comming and appearance ..." [200] Labour for grace, [201] advised Thomas Hall. Keep God's commandments, [202] urged William Durham. Meet Him in the way, be devout in duty, show a holy conversation, [203] admonished others. In Dod's exposition of the parable, the wedding garment is mercy, kindness, humility, meekness, long-suffering, forgiveness. [204] Each thought was set in the context of eschatological hope, and all could be reduced to the two principles enunciated by Richard Sibbes, "Labour to bee reconciled to God ... labour to grow in the New creature." [205] It was desirable counsel at any time for the Christian who knew that the holy life was the evidence of his calling. To those who sought how to prepare for the second coming of Christ it was doubly acceptable.

All this is undoubtedly the language of the people, the language of religion rather than of theology. Theology, however, at least before 1660, is the mother of religion and the relationship must be understood. The godly life was a religious experience necessitated by a theological truth and in the end men must be brought to face the reality of truth. Religion and theology begin and end in Christ, and in turning their people to the Christ of the future the preachers and spiritual guides of the seventeenth century turned them also to the Christ of history. "Wee have heard what the wedding-garment is: now it is further to be considered, how wee come by it." [206] Dod's way is unambiguous. "The way is, to goe unto Christ Jesus for it." [207]

---

199   *Ibid.,* p. 52.
200   Hayne, *Christs Kingdome,* p. 89.
201   Thomas Hall, *Commentary,* p. 8.
202   William Durham, *Maran-atha,* p. 14.
203   Taylor, *op. cit.,* p. 256; Homes, 'Moderation of Spirit', in *Works,* p. 114; Goodwin, 'Gospel Holiness' in *Works,* V, pt. II, p. 39.
204   Dod, *op. cit.,* pp. 166, 167.
205   Sibbes, *The Brides Longing,* pp. 81, 84. "We must labour for true repentance, which doth consist in contrition, confession, faith, and reformation," William Shepheard explained, *Four Last Things,* p. 24.
206   Dod, *op. cit.,* p. 168.
207   *Loc. cit.*

Sibbes' principle of reconciliation was the theological dictum of justification. In the language of theology the holiness men pursued could be found only in the holiness of God Himself. "Iehovah is our righteousnesse, that is, he is made righteousnesse unto us." [208] Pareus explains the apparel with which the bride is clothed in readiness for the Lamb's supper thus: "this fine linnen or wedding garment is Christ himself with his righteousnesse, with which we being clothed are acceptable to God." [209] "Would you know what to doe in the day of God's Anger?", asks William Bridge. "Seek Righteousnesse ... the Righteousness of Christ", is the answer. [210] Herein lies the only safe shelter for saints in the time of divine wrath. Christ's righteousness, then, is the ground of men's holiness. "Therefore above all, let us get the assurance of the grand point of justification, of being clothed with the righteousnesse of Christ", [211] urges Sibbes. That truth it is essential to grasp more than any other:

> If wee be cloathed with the Garments of Christ's righteousnesse, wee may goe through the wrath of God: for, that alone is wrath-proofe; that will pacifie God, and pacifie the Conscience, too. It is a righteousnesse of God's owne providing ... Be sure that you understand it well; that you appeare not in your owne, but in his: and then may you thinke of that day with comfort. [212]

The way is through faith. The wedding garment is "freely given by the bridegroom" [213] and is not provided by the bride herself. Dod says the "Spouse must be cloathed and decked by himself, who is the Bridegroome." [214] Pareus points out, "The Guest in the Gospel had good works: in that he obeyed the call and sate down with others at the banquet." [215] Yet he still lacked the necessary robe. Righteousness is appropriated by faith and, as Dod further maintains, to be covered with that righteousness now makes a man as thoroughly holy here as he will be hereafter in heaven. [216]

This does not negate the rightful place of effort and works in the life of the believer who is preparing for Christ's coming. Dod

---

[208] Pareus, *op. cit.*, p. 482.
[209] *Loc. cit.*
[210] William Bridge, *The Saints Hiding-Place in the Time of God's Anger* (1646), p. 24.
[211] Sibbes, *op. cit.*, p. 82.
[212] *Ibid.*, p. 83.
[213] Pareus, *loc. cit.*
[214] Dod, *loc. cit.*
[215] Pareus, *loc. cit.*
[216] Dod, *loc. cit.*

does not contradict Pareus when he affirms that in the search for holiness the saint "must come to the places and shops where he may buy" the wedding-garment, that is to the places "where the Word is powerfully preached, and the Sacraments duely administered." [217] Between justification and glorification there is always sanctification, and Sibbes' second principle was that the justified believer must "labour to grow in the New creature." In the view of most Puritans sanctification was a middle road between legalism and antinomianism and along that road the saints were to travel towards the kingdom. Dod, again, is explicit:

> If then we would be able to stand before the Lord, when he shall come ... at the last dreadful day of judgement, ... then let us take that course which will make us able to doe so: and that is, to get holy and sound love, to testifie our loving heart by our loving behaviour; not to love in word alone, but in deed ... Christian love with the fruits of it, is the best meanes to make us with confidence and comfort to hold up our heads in the day of accounts. [218]

From the moment of justification, the saint's life is a new life in which the affections are motivated by love and the will is bent to obedience. [219] It is a life which is oriented towards Christ in the present and in the future. "The more wee have of Christ in us, the more shall wee desire his coming to us." [220] The outcome is a constant growth in grace occasioned by the indwelling of God's Spirit and culminating in a "suitablenesse" for "the glorious condition to come." [221]

It is in this context that preachers of the Word commend devotion to duty, holiness in conversation, keeping God's commandments, and likeness to Christ. Sibbes sets forth the very marrow of eschatological hope when he says:

> ... where this hope is ... it stirres up and quickens the soule to a holy conversation ... it stirres us up to be pure, even as hee is pure ... this hope will stirre us up to doe all good duties and to right performance of good duties, to doe all things sincerely ... And this hope will also incourage us, and put us forward, that in our several callings and standings, we should help on the performance of them, as much as is in our power to performe, by helping on the building of the Church, and the inlargement of Christs kingdome and the confusion of his enemies. [222]

---

[217]   *Ibid.*, p. 169.
[218]   *Ibid.*, p. 172.
[219]   Sibbes, *op. cit.*, p. 84.
[220]   *Loc. cit.*
[221]   *Ibid.*, p. 85.
[222]   Sibbes, *Philippians*, pp. 228—230.

This is not the isolationist, the heady enthusiast, the militant paranoiac, the narrow sectarian. This is the man who loves God supremely and his neighbour sincerely; mature, rational, and concerned, whose life and influence are a blessing to the church and to society. If the doctrine of Christ's imminent second coming needed a stronger recommendation than the state of the world, or the declarations of scripture, or the fulfilment of prophecy, it could find it in the daily life of the saint whose watchword had been that of the apostle Paul, "Maranatha ... the Lord is at hand." [223]

---

[223] I Cor. xvi, 22; Phil. iv, 5.

CONCLUSION

"I beleive, that the light which is now discovered in England ... will never be wholly put out, though, I suspect, that contrary principles will prevayle, for a time ...".[1] Dr. Hill sees the light of which John Davenport wrote to Lady Mary Vere as the light of human equality and international brotherhood, kindled in the mid-seventeenth century by expectations of a coming kingdom.[2] Had that thought been uppermost in Davenport's mind, or that conclusion regarding the eschatological impulse the most valid, it would be difficult to find a more discerning comment on the expectant stirrings of the time. Christ's kingdom was at hand, and this was the light of the age; its establishment was to begin in England, from whence it would proceed to conquer the world. It may be remarked, however, that at this precise point Davenport is more concerned with principles of congregationalism than collectivism, more convinced that the brotherhood of society will be subordinated to the brotherhood of the saints.[3] Nonetheless, his letter may justifiably be quoted as a pertinent reminder that by 1647 latter-day expectancy had penetrated far beyond the bounds of preachers and the proletariat. The passage as a whole reveals a strong eschatological tone,[4] for to John Davenport, as to John Cotton his New England contemporary and friend, the new light of congregationalism was an intrinsic factor in the fulfilling *eschaton*.[5] Others might have expected Christ "to settle the Kingdom" in different ways, but most would readily have endorsed Davenport's hope that Lady Vere "be preserved blameless to the coming of our Lord Jesus."[6] That by this time the

---

[1] 'John Davenport to Mary, Lady Vere', in I. M. Calder, *Letters of John Davenport, Puritan Divine* (New Haven, 1937), p. 82.

[2] Hill, *Puritanism and Revolution*, p. 152. On Davenport, pastor at New Haven, see *Dictionary of American Biography*, s.v.; on Lady Vere, see Calder, *op. cit.*, p. 18.

[3] The phrase omitted from the above quotation, as by Hill, is "concerning church order and governm(en)t."

[4] "... the most high shaketh heaven, earth, and seaes, and all hearts ... that he may, at last, settle the Kingdom of our Lord Jesus, and bowe all nations under his scepter ... worse things are yet to come, till the slaughter of the witnesses shall be finished, which, I suppose, is not yet past, when I seriously compare the description of that time, as it is in Rev. 11. with the providences of God which have passed upon his people, to this day," Davenport, in Calder, *op. cit.*, p. 82.

[5] See Cotton, *Churches Resurrection*, pp. 5, 6, and 'The Fift Viall' pp. 3 ff. in *Seven Vials*. Cotton's *Keyes of the Kingdom* (1644) appeared after his most important eschatological works.

[6] Davenport, in Calder, *loc. cit.*

advent hope was being sent back across the Atlantic is a further measure of its popularity and influence.

Most of the conclusions to be drawn from the evidence offered in this study have been suggested as the argument has developed. In recapitulation, however, it is helpful to recall that the investigation began with the moderate views of theologians who were not too far either to the right or to the left of a fairly broad middle road between conservative Anglicanism and extreme Puritanism. In the main principles of eschatological doctrine the views of the moderates were remarkably analogous. Variations inevitably appear, and these become progressively more complex the further one moves from the middle path. For this reason it is inadvisable to attempt to establish an absolute norm. There can be little doubt, nevertheless, that a large measure of conformity existed in the structures of the various eschatological schemes. Austere Anglican bishops and rabid Fifth Monarchy Men alike raised their hopes on similar foundations, and the finished fabric of each bore an observable resemblance. The overall view of the moderate Baxter, who clearly anticipated a well-defined course of future events, may be cited as representative. The world had come to its expected last age and the personal and glorious second coming of Christ was imminent. The resurrection of the dead would occur at the advent and would be accompanied by the translation of the living saints. The last judgement would then follow, the saints would inherit eternal rest in the kingdom of God, the wicked would be cast into hell.[7] For a survey of the broad principles of prevailing eschatological thought Baxter can hardly be bettered.

The importance of the eschatological emphasis to the age as a whole, as well as to those who proclaimed it, is equally certain. The man of the seventeenth century, rooted as he was in a thoroughly biblical theology, saw the end of the age from more than one angle. Presupposing the questionings of later generations more than his own, Sibbes argues, "But some may say, Christ hath saved us already, when need is there therefore of his second comming?".[8]

> I answer, it is to perfect our salvation: for redemption of our bodies, and glorious libertie are reserved to his second comming, wee looke not that he should die any more, but appear as a Lord of glorie, without humiliation for sinne, having already gotton victorie of it.[9]

---

[7] See Baxter, *Saints Rest*, pp. 44—68.
[8] Sibbes, *Philippians*, p. 231.
[9] *Loc. cit.*

Dogmatic theology thus imposed a necessity for the second advent. John Owen urges the needfulness of understanding times and events, and the heavenly wisdom for which every Christian should strive is to know the will of God for the present. That will was not inscrutable. "His way is not so in the dark, nor his footsteps in the deep, but that we may perceive what he is about". [10] and Owen's argument is that enlightened eyes may see in the affairs of the age evidence of the fulfilling *eschaton*. [11] J.F. Wilson remarks that "the eschatological framework of Revelation possessed general meaning for the puritans beyond whatever specific expectations they derived from it." [12] That that meaning was relevant to more than the conventional Puritan, vital as it unquestionably was to him and all his brethren, is beyond doubt. What else can be inferred from the fact that John Napier, Joseph Mede, and Joseph Hall, to recall a few, wrote commentaries on The Revelation, or that Pareus, the famed continental theologian who was widely read in England, as well as Nathaniel Homes and William Hicks, defended its place in the New Testament canon? "It is to be admired that an opinion once so generally received in the Church should ever have been so cryed down, and buried," [13] wrote Homes of the coming millennium. Multitudes cherished similar thoughts of a wider eschatology of which millenarianism was only one manifestation.

It is indeed the breadth of eschatological involvement that emerges as the major conclusion to this study, a breadth that is evident from more than one standpoint. Ecclesiastically, Puritanism, although it may be granted to have provided the larger proportion of the advocates of a fulfilling eschatology, could claim no monopoly of them. In addition to those Anglicans of an earlier generation who anticipated Christ's coming, Hugh Latimer, Edwin Sandys, John Bradford, George Joye and Thomas Rogers, and to those mentioned above who wrote on The Revelation, may be added the names of Patrick Forbes, George Hakewill, John Donne, James Ussher, John Prideaux, Richard Baxter, and Robert Gell, all of whom ecclesiastically were closer to Episcopacy and the Establishment than they were to Puritanism. There was substance to John Durant's claim that among Protes-

---

[10]   John Owen, ΟΥΡΑΝΩΝ ΟΥΡΑΝΙΑ, *The Shaking and Translating of Heaven and Earth* (1649), p. 28.

[11]   *Ibid.*, pp. 30—40; cf. his *The Advantage of the Kingdome of Christ* (1651), *passim.*

[12]   Wilson, *Pulpit in Parliament*, p. 151.

[13]   Homes, *Resurrection*, p. 437.

tants of every shade of opinion, "Prelatical, or Presbyterian, or
Independent, or Anabaptist", advocates could be found even of
the extremer millenarian emphasis. [14] It is not superfluous to add
that in each of these ecclesiastical groupings some of the most
prominent names of the time were associated with the eschatological surge. [15]

Socially, the doctrines of the end were evident on an even
broader plane. The voluminous works of scores of clergy from
virtually every rank in the ecclesiastical hierarchy were complemented by the writings of laymen from a wide cross-section of
public and private life. At a time when the press was the only
means of mass communication and the reading of religious books
a recognised means of grace, literature of every quality became
the vehicle for the advancement of eschatological doctrines. [16]
The theology of an archbishop, bishops, and learned doctors of
divinity, blessed with the authority of a king, statesmen, and men
of letters, provided a corpus of opinion which the average man
was unable to resist. From James I to James Ussher, from John
Napier and the Earl of Stirling to John Donne, George Wither,
and John Milton, the eschatological hope found a lucid and compelling expression. Topics investigated by Sir Henry Finch the
lawyer, Samuel Hartlib the economist, and the schoolmasters
Thomas Hayne, William Burton, and James Toppe were re-exam-
ined and re-stated not only by theologians, but by other laymen,
by Leonard Busher, for example, the early advocate of religious toleration, by Robert Purnell the Baptist elder from Bristol, and
by William Shepheard the Commonwealth lawyer.

Geographically, although London and southern counties
would figure prominently in any precise locational analysis, the
national spread of the eschatological arguments was broad in-

---

[14]   Durant, *Salvation*, p. 197.

[15]   A typical list might include: James Ussher, Archbishop of Armagh; Patrick
Forbes, Bishop of Aberdeen; Joseph Hall, Bishop of Norwich; George Hakewill, Arch-
deacon of Surrey; John Donne, Dean of St. Pauls; William Twisse, Prolocutor of the
Westminster Assembly; William Guild, Chaplain to Charles I; John Trapp, headmaster
of Stratford-upon-Avon school, and rector of Welford; Christopher Love and William
Jenkyn, Presbyterians; Jeremiah Burroughes and William Strong, Independents; Henry
Jessey and Robert Maton, Baptist divines. Richard Baxter, Thomas Goodwin, Richard
Sibbes, John Cotton, John Owen, Thomas Brooks, Nathaniel Homes, and Thomas
Taylor cannot be omitted from any roll of influential clergy who espoused an eschato-
logical hope during the first half of the seventeenth century.

[16]   For literary merit, Richard Mercer's poorly written *Some Discoveries of the
Mystery of the last times* (1649), or Elizabeth Avery's barely comprehensible *Scripture-Prophecies Opened* (1647) could not even be compared with the prose of Thomas
Adams or the verse of a Milton or a Wither. The message, however, was essentially the
same, and men generally were more concerned with content than style.

deed. Certain areas of the country, in view of their associations with early Protestantism and the Puritan movement, might be expected to have been more susceptible to the challenge of a new biblical emphasis. [17] East Anglia and the South East are accordingly found to have provided a number of the second advent preachers and prophetic expositors. Joseph Mede worked at Cambridge; John Tillinghast was rector at Trunch, in Norfolk, when he wrote his *Generation-Work*; William Bridge had been appointed town preacher at Great Yarmouth; and Joseph Hall, nominally at least, was still bishop of Norwich when he wrote *The Revelation Unrevealed*. In Kent, Hezekiah Holland's *Exposition or ... Epitome of the most choice Commentaries upon the Revelation of St. John*, and John Durant's *Salvation of the Saints* were both stronger for the local influence of their authors. Henry Symons at Maidstone and John Maynard, not far away at Mayfield in neighbouring Sussex, both proclaimed the imminent second advent. Beyond the counties immediately facing the continent men were no less involved in the eschatological surge or with the obligations of living in the last days. In the West, Richard Bernard the Anglican rector of Batcombe in Somerset, the Presbyterian John Seagar, from Broadclyst in Devon, and Robert Purnell of Bristol all contributed to the eschatological literature. Wales could boast Vavasor Powell and Morgan Llwyd, and Ireland the renowned James Ussher. Among the names that could be cited from Midland counties are Thomas Hall from Warwickshire who wrote at least two books concerned with the last events, Robert Bolton from Northamptonshire, author of *The Foure last Things*, and Samuel Smith from Shropshire whose *Great Assize, or, Day of Ivbilee* enjoyed thirty-nine editions before the turn of the century. Richard Baxter wrote the celebrated *Saints Everlasting Rest* at Rous Lench in Worcestershire. Scotland provided as impressive a selection of men as any area in the nation: John Napier, mathematician; William Alexander, poet and statesman; James Durham, David Dickson, and William Guild, university professors, all of whose writings betray a deep and sustained interest in the last days. The weight of evidence indicates that at no other time in England's history has the doctrine of the second advent been so widely proclaimed or so readily accepted.

---

[17] Cf. the distributions of Protestantism and Puritanism as indicated in the maps given in Owen Chadwick, *The Reformation* (1964), p. 139, and Barbour, *The Quakers in Puritan England*, Fig. 1, facing p. 42.

The corollary to this conclusion is that eschatological expectation belonged more to orthodoxy than it did to heterodoxy. Lamont rightly concludes that the book of Revelation has too often been identified exclusively with fanatical groups like Fifth Monarchists, [18] and Wilson suggests that millenarianism was only one possible sequel to the study of apocalyptic prophecy. [19] In many instances, as the preceding pages have indicated, the most eloquent advocates of the prevalent eschatology were men of undeviating loyalty to the accepted patterns of doctrinal orthodoxy. That there were extremists and that on occasion they were more in evidence than the sober brotherhood of spiritual preachers is not to be denied, but Thomas Hall patently overstated the case in arguing that millenarianism jeopardised the future of both church and state. [20] Some might have dated their letter from the New Jerusalem, [21] but more were intent on reaching it first and for every William Sedgwick [22] there was a Baxter, a Taylor, a Sibbes, a Love, and a Mede.

That it was not necessary to be a millenarian to believe in Christ's imminent coming was proved by Joseph Hall, Christopher Love and William Sclater, [23] and the total number of millenarians in the adventist ranks may have been considerably less than has often been assumed. At the same time, many would have agreed with Hall that millenarianism in any event was not a cardinal point of faith affecting the destiny of the believer, [24] and therefore a millenarian was not, *ipso facto*, a heretic or even necessarily an extremist. [25] Millenarianism lent itself more to the ideas of fanatics when it became associated with time-setting and many followed Hall, again, in avoiding chronological computations as a step away from moderate exegesis. [26] Jeremiah Burroughes struck an acceptable note in deciding that God had not

---

[18] Lamont, *Godly Rule*, p. 97.

[19] Wilson, *op. cit.*, p. 147.

[20] Thomas Hall, *Chiliasto-mastix redivivus*, To the Reader.

[21] Joseph Hall, *Revelation Unrevealed*, p. 15.

[22] Of 'Doomsday' Sedgwick, Hill comments that he was imprudent only in "predicting the end of the world for next week"; Hill, *op. cit.*, p. 325.

[23] See Joseph Hall, *op. cit.*, pp. 7, 10; Love, *Heavens Glory*, pp. 5, 6; William Sclater, *The Grand Assizes* (1653), p. 37.

[24] Hall, *op. cit.*, p. 66.

[25] In 1690 Baxter could look back over a century of eschatological debate and conclude "the chief Writers for the Millennium are Conformists, (and men of greatest Learning and Piety among them)", Richard Baxter, *The Glorious Kingdom of Christ* (1691), ep. ded.

[26] Hall, *op. cit.*, p. 232; cf. Henry Symons, *The Lord Jesus His Commission*, pp. 35, 36.

fully revealed the times of the last events [27] and that prophetic chronology would mature only within "this century that is now currant." [28] Few understood the desirability of a moderate second advent doctrine better than Thomas Taylor, whose learning had convinced him of the folly of attempting to set a date for the coming of Christ and the end of the world. Taylor could cite an impressive list of scholars who had variously computed that the end would come between the middle of the thirteenth century and the beginning of the twentieth century, most of whose calculations time had already proved wrong. [29] This, however, did not diminish the basic credibility of belief in Christ's coming. One extreme was as unfortunate as the other and Taylor constantly returned to the second advent in his writings. His *Commentary on Titus*, published first in 1619, provides as clear a survey of the various aspects of the doctrine as may be found, his *Progresse of Saints* relates it to the present life of the believer, and *The Principles of Christian Practice* advises on how to prepare to meet Christ in peace. Despite the rashness of some, Taylor can declare with evident conviction "yet a very little while, and he that shall come, will come, and will not tarrie." [30] Taylor was one of many who demonstrated that the church could have hope apart from "blazing chiliastic expectancy." [31]

It has been easy to dismiss mid-seventeenth century eschatology as the wishful thinking of a hare-brained minority, only relevant, if relevant at all, to the troubled decades of the Civil Wars, the Commonwealth, and the Protectorate. It is clear, however, that the roots of this eschatology went back to the relative calm of Elizabeth's reign, [32] and that its influence was felt long after the last radical Cromwellian pamphleteer had laid down his pen. If after the Restoration men ceased to believe in a millen-

---

[27]   Burroughes, *Jerusalem's Glory*, p. 79.
[28]   Burroughes, *Exposition of ... Hosea*, p. 749.
[29]   The names of the writers concerned and the respective dates they suggested for the end of the world, as given by Taylor are: Joachim Abbas, 1258; Arnold de Villanova, 1345; Michael Stiphelus, 1533; Cyprian Italus, 1583; John Regiomontanus, 1588; Adelbert Thermopedius, 1599; Nicholas of Cusa, 1700; Cardanus, 1800; Osiander, 1689; and Picus Mirandula, 1904: Taylor, *Principles of Christian Practice*, pp. 249, 250. On Joachim Abbas and Michael Stiphelus, see *The New Schaff-Herzog Encyclopedia*, s.vv. Joachim of Fiore and Stiefel; on Arnold de Villanova see *Encyclopaedia of Religion and Ethics*, s.v. On John Regiomontanus, Nicolas of Cusa, Cardanus, Osiander, see *Encyclopaedia Britannica*, s.vv.; on Picus Mirandula, see *Encyclopaedia Britannica*, s.v. Pico Della Mirandola.
[30]   Taylor, *Titus*, p. 490.
[31]   Zagorin, *History of Political Thought*, p. 57.
[32]   Cf. P. Collinson, *The Elizabethan Puritan Movement* (1967), pp. 104, 123.

nium,[33] if with the return of the monarchy, there is no longer need for a divine kingdom,[34] if the concept of Antichrist has evaporated after 1660,[35] then with them go the books of Daniel and The Revelation, significant passages from other biblical writers, the apparently consistent emphasis on an ultimate end, and hence the authority of the scriptural revelation. This, of course, is impossible at any time in the seventeenth century and although the eschatology of its later years remains largely an unexplored field, there is reason enough to conclude that the apocalyptic hopes kindled between the accessions of Elizabeth I and Charles II continued to burn in many breasts long after the reasons often alleged to have contributed to their rise had disappeared, and long after their dissemination had been supposedly curtailed by the Clarendon Code. [36]

A certain continuity was provided by Edward Bagshaw, who followed *A Discourse About Christ and Antichrist* (1661) with *Signes of the Times* (1662) and *The Doctrine of the Kingdom And Personal Reign of Christ* (1669). Samuel Whiting published *A Discourse of the Last Judgement* (1664), and in 1668 Thomas Vincent added *Christ's Certain and Sudden Appearance to Judgment*. The bulk of Hanserd Knollys' work appeared well after the Restoration. Much of it was concerned with a continuing eschatology, and included *An Exposition of the Eleventh Chapter of the Revelation* (1679), *Mystical Babylon Unvailed* (1679), *The World that Now is; and the World that is to Come; Or the First and Second Coming of Jesus Christ* (1681), and *An Exposition Of the whole Book of the Revelation* (1689). Other commentators on the Apocalypse included Richard Hayter, in 1675, William Sherwin in 1676, who quoted frequently from Mede, and Drue Cressener, 1690. Thomas Beverley's *The Catechism of the Kingdom of our Lord Jesus Christ in the Thousand Years* (1690) drew a reply from Richard Baxter entitled *The Glorious Kingdom of Christ* (1691), some evidence that the millenarian argument was not yet dead. Popular works of the earlier decades

---

[33] Lamont, *op. cit.*, p. 158.

[34] Cf. Hill, *op. cit.*, p. 152.

[35] Trevor-Roper, *Religion, the Reformation, and Social Change*, p. 293.

[36] In 1666 Samuel Pepys wrote in his diary, "Read an hour, to make an end of Potter's Discourse of the number 666, which I like all along, but his close is most excellent; and, whether it be right or wrong, is mighty ingenious ... This is the fatal day that every body hath discoursed for a long time ... What the meaning of all these sad signs is, the Lord knows; but every day things look worse and worse," Samuel Pepys, *The Diary of Samuel Pepys*, ed. Henry Wheatley (1895), VI, pp. 56, 57. The work referred to was Francis Potter's *An interpretation of the Number 666* (Oxford, 1642).

continued to be republished. Smith's *Great Assize*, Brooks' *Heaven on Earth,* and Baxter's *Saints Rest* appeared again both in the eighteenth and nineteenth centuries. The works of Goodwin, Homes, and Mede were all reprinted between 1833 and 1844. The eschatological thought of Love and Mede is known to have influenced interpretation towards the end of the eighteenth century and as late as 1850. The immediate influence of English thought on New England and the subsequent development of eschatology in the New World cannot be overlooked. John Cotton, Ephraim Huit, and Thomas Parker are to be counted among those who carried the apocalyptic tradition across the Atlantic and transplanted it in a soil that was to nurture its growth for centuries. [37] It is reasonable to regard the mid-seventeenth century eschatological stress in English theology, not as an isolated phenomenon, but as part of a long and continuing involvement.

To return to the more immediate significance of the eschatological hope in the life of both saint and church, we come again to Richard Sibbes. The fundamental unity of the believer with Christ and the consequential unity of believer with believer in the church were both seen in direct relationship to belief in Christ's coming. Sibbes had variously maintained "The contracted Spouse must needes say Amen, to the Marriage-day", "it is the disposition of a gracious heart, to desire the glorious comming of Christ Iesus", "the more wee have of Christ in us, the more shall wee desire his comming to us", [38] and the conclusion of such a consistent emphasis is to be noted:

> Let us desire and labour to have all the corners of the heart filled up with the Spirit of Christ; our understandings, with knowledge; our affections, with love and delight; and our wills, with obedience. The Scripture calls it, being filled with all the fullnesse of God. Now, the more wee enter into the Kingdome of Heaven, by growth in grace here, the fitter shall wee be for it, and the more shall wee desire it. [39]

Fellowship with Christ in glory was measurably dependent on fellowship with Christ in grace. The relationship was unalterable, but not unattainable, and belief in the second advent materially contributed to the believer's present spiritual condition.

Yet the end of unity was more than a personal relationship culminating in an individual salvation in the future. The entire

---

[37] See A. J. B. Gilsdorf, 'The Puritan Apocalypse', *passim,* for New England eschatology in the seventeenth century.

[38] Sibbes, *Brides Longing,* pp. 15, 48, 84.

[39] *Ibid.,* pp. 84—85.

church was to draw a blessing from the second advent hope, and it was at this very point that Sibbes found cause for concern. In the preface to *The Gloriovs Feast of the Gospel* he deplores the fact that this necessary relationship appears to be in decline, "Alas! Christians have lost much of their Communion with Christ and his Saints".[40] The very experience upon which the future glory of church and believer rests was being eroded and the reason was clear: "they have woefully disputed away, and dispirited the life of Religion and the power of Godlinesse into dry and sapelesse Controversies about Government of Church and State."[41] Let the message of the church take precedence over its machinery. Let believers recapture the unity with Christ and with each other through a re-emphasis of essentials. Sibbes went on to write *The Glorious Feast of the Gospel* in which the doctrine of the second advent duly appeared as an integral part of the New Testament message. Other moderates could be heard to voice similar sentiments. Both Edmund Calamy and Stephen Marshall specifically decried the divisions in church and kingdom,[42] and Marshall described the multiplicity of sects into which the church had been divided as an "epidemical disease" and "pleasing ... to Satan."[43] The divisions within the church were clearly an obstacle to the realisation of the divine purpose. While some evidently expected unity to be realised through Parliament and the establishment of a state church, others discerned matters of a deeper significance. William Strong's eschatological hope of "perfect and sweet Communion one with another" is contingent upon the communion of each individual believer with God, in Christ.[44] The cure for division, according to the moderator of the Westminster Assembly, lay in a universal acceptance and individual application of the essentials of the Christian faith, and the last word thus belongs to Jeremiah Whitaker:

> The way to cure the bleeding distempers of Christendome is for all men to endeavour to get inward perswasions answerable to their outward professions; for as these main principles are more or lesse beleeved; so is the heart and life of man better, or worse ordered. When the soul is once fully perswaded, that Christ is God, that he is the true Messiah, that there is another life besides this, that the Lord Christ is ready to come to judgement, and his reward is with him; then the soul

---

[40] Sibbes, *Gloriovs Feast*, Pref.
[41] *Ibid.*
[42] Calamy, *Englands Looking-Glasse*, p. 32; Marshall, *A Sermon ... The Unity of the Saints with Christ* (1653), p. 21.
[43] Marshall, *op. cit.*, pp. 21, 37; cf. Durant, *Salvation of the Saints*, ep. ded.
[44] William Strong, *The Trust and the Account of a Steward* (1647), p. 29.

begins to seek and beg an interest in Christ, to flee from wrath to come, to assure the hopes of Heaven, whilst we are on earth: and this hope, when once truly attained, carries the soul farre above the comforts of life, and beyond the fears of death ... [45]

There is more here than concern with ecclesiastical politics or church government, more than the unrealistic yearnings of a radical millenarian minority.[46] Hope, the future, Christ's coming, eternal life, these, in the context of a complete gospel, and in the experience of each believer, are the basis of a valid ecumenism, the assurance of an ultimate triumph.

Christ had taught His disciples to look forward in praying 'Thy kingdom come', and as long as that prayer remains central in the worship of the church there is always a valid basis for the eschatological stress. It was in this spirit that the men of the seventeenth century read the Bible, recited the Creed, and repeated that particular phrase in the Lord's Prayer with more conviction than any other generation in the English church as a whole. His coming and His kingdom were at hand, and if they were not all to see it with the physical eye they would deem it a privilege to be counted among those who died in hope, not having received the promises, but having seen them afar off. The unassailable strength of such convictions lay in the assurance that if time was to prove them wrong in detail eternity would prove them right in principle. In this the seventeenth-century spirit was essentially one with that of the New Testament, and men could pray with equal fervour, 'Even so, come, Lord Jesus'.

---

[45]   Jeremiah Whitaker, *The Christians Hope Trivmphing* (1645), ep. ded.

[46]   This is not to overlook the immediate religio-political aspirations of many mid-seventeenth century divines. These cannot be doubted in view of the recent work of William Lamont, John Wilson and Tai Liu. Perhaps it can be argued that the eschatological radicals failed to establish the kingdom on earth partially because they failed to grasp the full content of biblical eschatology and to assimilate its real spirit. Whitaker is a good example of those who may have been nearer to the truth than some would have allowed.

APPENDIX I

The Apocalyptic Significance of the Song of Solomon

In addition to the books of Daniel and The Revelation, the Song of Solomon attracted erudite scholars with interests in the last things. A number of interpretations of the book appeared between 1610 and 1650, constituting an important extension of the apocalyptic literature.[1] It is only possible to examine a selection, but these can be regarded as having particular significance in view of the wider eschatological convictions of their authors. Brightman's 'A Commentary on the Canticles', published in his *Works* (1644), Cotton's *A Brief Exposition of the whole Book of Canticles* (1642), and Homes' *A Commentary ... On the whole Book of Canticles* were all firmly set in the historicist approach to apocalyptic prophecy. The inscription on the titlepage of Cotton's book reads:

> ... describing the Estate of the Church in all the Ages thereof, both Jewish and Christian, to this day: And Modestly pointing at the gloriousnesse of the restored Estate of the Church of the Iewes, and the happy accesse of the Gentiles, in the approaching daies of Reformation, when the Wall of Partition shall bee taken away.[2]

Homes stated that the book was "a Prophetical History, or Historical Prophesie ... from Solomon's time, down to the second coming of Christ."[3] He compared it to the book of Daniel[4] and Thomas Brightman stressed its similarity to The Revelation: "They foreshew the same events in the like times."[5] To see this thought in the middle decades of the century, however, it is necessary to begin with two earlier works.

Henry Finch, whose *World's Great Restavration* of 1621 did much to awaken popular interest in the Jewish question, had previously issued, in 1615, *An Exposition of the Song of Solomon: called Canticles*. This work, which was recommended by William Gouge, has as its theme the love between Christ and the

---

[1] An extension, perhaps, of typology as an element in millenarian exegesis, as noted by Plotkin, 'Sighs from Sion', pp. 24–29.

[2] Cotton, *A Brief Exposition Of the whole Book of Canticles* (1642), Title-page.

[3] Homes, 'A Commentary ... On the whole Book of Canticles', in *Works*, (1652), Pref., sig. A2r.

[4] *Loc. cit.*

[5] Brightman, 'A Commentary on the Canticles', in *Workes*, p. 981.

church. Finch refers to the espousal between the heavenly Bridegroom and His bride and describes the sojourn of the church on earth "as it were a bidding of the banes vntill by his second comming from heauen our spirituall marriage with him shall be solemnized and made vp."[6] The cry of the spouse in chapter viii, 14, "Flee to us", echoes the church's anticipation and is "a speciall note of the childe of God to desire still the comming of Christ."[7] Henry Ainsworth's *Solomons Song of Songs* (1623), while in the main a highly spiritualised interpretation of the relationship between Christ and the believer, also gives evidence of a development in the apocalyptic view. "The mysteries of Christ and his Church" extend throughout the era of the church's existence in history. Thus chapter ii, 9 refers to the incarnation "when he dwelt in our house of clay ... and in our flesh ... to draw us after him into the Kingdome of his Father ..."[8] In chapter viii, 8 the little sister with no breasts is "a new Church arising ... as yet having no stablished ministerie"[9] (perhaps the Jews at the end?), and chapter viii, 14 is, again, the longing of the spouse for her beloved "desiring the end of his Kingdome in this world ... and the translating thereof into the highest heavens."[10] Ainsworth concludes: "Thus as this Song began with desire of Christs first comming to kisse her with the kisses of his mouth, by preaching his Gospell: so it endeth with desire of his second comming, to remoue his Church out of all misery, into the place of endlesse and incomprehensible glorie."[11] Both Finch and Ainsworth had been preceded by Joseph Hall with 'An Open and plaine Paraphrase upon the Song of Songs' (1609), in which pointed reference to the second advent could be found at chapter ii, 17, iii, 6, and vi, 12.[12]

With Brightman's 'Commentary on the Canticles' we move to a much developed apocalypticism with regard to the Song of Solomon. Although the work was not published until 1644, Brightman had died in 1607 and the 'Commentary on the Canticles' therefore antedates the work of both Finch and Ainsworth. The interpretation is markedly more advanced than that of either of the previous two, and suggests the conclusion that Brightman was

---

[6] Finch, *An Exposition of the Song of Solomon: called Canticles* (1615), pp. 1, 2.
[7] *Ibid.*, p. 129.
[8] Ainsworth, *Solomons Song of Songs* (1623), sig. E3*v*.
[9] *Ibid.*, sig. M4*r*.
[10] *Ibid.*, sig. N1*v*.
[11] *Loc. cit.*
[12] Joseph Hall, 'An Open and plaine Paraphrase, upon the Song of Songs', pp. 25, 38, 66, in *Salomons Diuine Arts* (1609).

here well ahead of his time, a fact which may account for the
delay in publication. As it is, the 'Commentary' is an important
link between the earlier published works and those of Cotton and
Homes. Brightman divides the book between the first three and a
half chapters, which outline the "Legall" history of the church
from David until Christ, and the remainder which extends over
its "Evangelicall" era "unto the second comming of Christ." [13]
From chapter six onward may be found a portrayal of major
events leading to the full restoration of truth in the last days.
Thus in chapter vi, 8 the queens, concubines, and virgins refer to
various churches of the Reformation "according to their degrees
of purity". [14] Queens represent the main churches to have sprung
from the Reformation, particularly the churches in England, Ireland, Scotland and Geneva. Concubines are other reformed
churches, lower in esteem than the foregoing, as the churches in
Germany and Denmark, and virgins "without number" are the
lowest of all those constituting the Bride of Christ, as Anabaptists, Antitrinitarians, and Arians. [15] From this point onwards
future events are depicted, including the call of the Jews "about
the yeer 1650", the destruction of Antichrist, [16] the conversion
of Eastern nations, [17] and a flourishing new church in the end-
time. [18] At this early date Brightman brings in the millennium,
interpreting the first resurrection to have been fulfilled around
1250 A.D., and therefore expecting more than 600 years in
which the church "shall raign here upon the earth". [19]

Cotton and Homes were able to build solidly on such a well-
laid foundation, and Cotton provides a useful chapter synopsis
which sets out the scope of Solomon's predictions. The first
chapter depicts the period from Solomon to Josiah. Chapter two
runs from Josiah to the Maccabees, with the next chapter carry-
ing events from Nehemiah to John the Baptist. Then comes the
period of the early church, ending with the ten persecutions of
the third century. The fifth period is the long era from Constantine to Luther, and chapter six covers events from the Reformation until the call of the Jews, the Gentiles, and the ultimate
triumph of the church. [20] Cotton revises Brightman's interpreta-

---

[13]   Brightman, *op. cit.,* p. 981.
[14]   *Ibid.,* pp. 1047, 1048.
[15]   *Ibid.,* p. 1048.
[16]   *Ibid.,* p. 1051.
[17]   *Ibid.,* p. 1072.
[18]   *Ibid.,* p. 1075.
[19]   *Ibid.,* p. 1077.
[20]   Cotton, *op. cit.,* pp. 42, 52, 83, 101, 141, 169, 205, 245.

tion of chapter vi, 8, making the queens the true "Reformed Churches" following the Congregational way, the concubines churches with a ministry "thrust upon them" and the virgins those groups without any satisfactory ministry. [21]

Homes had had the advantage of reading Ainsworth, Brightman and Cotton, [22] and his *Commentary on Canticles* appropriately combines the various eschatological emphases reflected in each during the preceding half century. He follows the apocalyptic historicism of Brightman and Cotton, adopting the latter's chapter analysis with little alteration, but returns also to the second advent stress of Ainsworth and Finch. Homes defends the historicity of the doctrine of Christ's coming, claiming for it apostolic and post-apostolic belief, and alluding to its recovery through the Reformation. [23] From the theological standpoint he upholds the necessity of the doctrine in the scheme of truth, expressing its purpose and describing its accomplishment on both righteous and wicked. [24] He concludes with a seven-fold summary of events stemming from the advent, commencing with the resurrection and culminating in the restoration of all things and the sabbath of rest for the saints. [25]

To bring the church and the faithful, through faith in Christ, to that rest was the purpose of The Song of Solomon, and Brightman, Finch, Ainsworth, and Cotton would all have agreed with Homes, "Christ will come with salvation to them that look for him ... We must pray ... that He would make haste". [26] The doctrine was in keeping with the thought of the time and with the general tone of the biblical revelation, but it may be indicative that none of these works, with the exception of Cotton's book, were ever reprinted. Other studies, such as John Robotham's *An Exposition On the whole booke of Solomons Song* (1651) or William Guild's *Loves Entercovrs Between The Lamb & his Bride* (1658), failed to perpetuate the apocalyptic interpretation of Solomon. [27] This approach to a book that contained little obvious apocalyptic imagery was perhaps too fanciful even for the mid-seventeenth century and remains as a caution against an over-enthusiastic subjectivity in prophetic interpretation.

---

[21]   *Ibid.*, pp. 185–189.   [24]   *Ibid.*, p. 462.
[22]   Homes, *loc. cit.*   [25]   *Loc. cit.*
[23]   *Ibid.*, p. 461.   [26]   *Loc. cit.*
[27]   Thomas Beverley returned to it, however, in 1687 with *An Exposition of the Divinely Prophetick Song of Songs which is Solomons.*

APPENDIX II

The Resurrection of the Body

The dualistic concept of the soul as an incorporeal, immortal entity distinct from the body, to be released at death, met little opposition from Protestant theologians during the sixteenth and seventeenth centuries. Although inherently necessary to the believer's hopes of heaven and his fears of hell, this traditional view of the nature and destiny of man did not, in early Protestant eschatological thought, seek to establish the primacy of the soul to the exclusion of the body in the final soterio-eschatological drama. Hence the resurrection of the body at the last day remained as an essential element in the salvation-process of each individual believer.

Richard Baxter representatively argues the necessity of the resurrection in this process:

> ... as the soul separated from the body, is not a perfect man, so it doth not enjoy the Glory and happiness so fully and so perfectly as it shall do after the Resurrection, when they are again conjoined.

In Baxter's eschatology, while the soul is distinct from the body and obtains a degree of bliss between death and the last day, the resurrection of the body is ultimately as necessary to eternal life as is the immortality of the soul. Christopher Love likewise speaks of a "partiall and incompleat receiving" of the believer to heaven at death, and of a "totall and compleat reception" when body and soul are reunited at the last day.[2] There are discernible echoes here of the monistic Hebrew concept of the "wholeness" of man, restored in eternity, as opposed to an eternal dichotomy of body and soul.

Thus to both Baxter and Love the resurrection of the body is one of the chief reasons for Christ's second coming. Of Baxter's "four great preparatives" to the saint's everlasting rest, the first two are given as:

1. The most Glorious Coming and Appearing of the Son of God.
2. His powerful and wonderful raising of our Bodies from the Dust, and uniting them again with the Soul.[3]

---

[1] Baxter, *Saints Rest,* p. 255.
[2] Love, *Penitent Pardoned,* p. 187.
[3] Baxter, *op. cit.,* p. 45.

Love declares, "it is one great end of Christ's coming again for to receive the bodies of all the Elect unto himselfe into Heaven".[4]

Deep-rooted though the doctrine of the soul's separate existence and innate immortality was in Reformation theology, many English Protestants were aware of alternative interpretations of the nature and destiny of man. Generally known during the sixteenth and seventeenth centuries as "mortalism" or "soul sleep", advocates of these views held that after death the soul either slept in an unconscious state, or ceased to exist as a separate entity apart from the body. Such doctrines were so radical to contemporary thought that those holding them were inevitably castigated as heretics, even though most mortalists were thoroughly "Christian", as Norman Burns suggests in his important study of English Reformation mortalism, *Christian Mortalism from Tyndale to Milton* (1972), and despite the fact that most Christian mortalists ardently looked for the resurrection of the body at the last day.

The Forty-Two Articles of Religion of 1553 gave clear indication of the early appeal of English mortalism in its various forms by condemning it, together with millenarianism, as unsound doctrine. Three of the Articles, later to be omitted from revisions of the church's official statement of faith, had eschatological significance:

XXXIX   *The resurrectiō of the dead is not yet broughte to passe.*

The resurrecciō of the dead is not as yet brought to passe: as though it only belonged to the soule, which by the grace of Christ is raised from the death of synne: but it is to be loked for at the laste day. For then (as Scripture doth most manifestly testifie) to all that be dead theyr owne bodies fleshe, and bone shal be restored: that the whole mā may (according to hys workes) have ether reward, or punishment, as he hath lived vertuously or wickedly.

XL   *The Soules of them that depart this life doe neither die wyth the bodies, nor sleepe idly.*

They which say, that the soules of suche as depart hence, dooe sleepe, beyng wythout al sence feling, or perceiving, untyl the day of iudgmente: or affirme that the soules dye with the bodies, and at the last day shal be raised up wyth the same: do utterly dissente from the right belefe, declared to us in holye Scripture.

---

[4] Love, *op. cit.*, p. 186.

XLl   *Heritikes called Millenarii.*

> They that go aboute to renewe the fable of heretickes called
> Millenarii, be repugnant to holy Scripture, and cast thẽselves
> headlong into a Jewish dotage.[5]

Burn's study of early mortalism is significant for its clarification of the three major schools of mortalist thought which developed during the first century or so of the English Reformation.
The earlier Annihilationists held that the soul died eternally with
the body and that there would be no literal resurrection of body
or soul at the end. This view appears to be condemned in the
thirty-ninth Edwardine Article. The Thnetopsychists maintained
that the soul had no existence as an entity distinct from the
body, and that it therefore "died" when the body died, to await
resurrection with the body at the last day. The Psychopannychists declared the soul to be a separate entity which did not,
however, enjoy existence in isolation from the body, and which
slept in unconsciousness after death until the resurrection. These
later views appear to be condemned in Article XL of the 1553
Articles. Both Thnetopsychists and Psychopannychists looked
for the resurrection of the body at Christ's coming and could
argue, with some logic, that the resurrection meant more to them
than it did to the majority who anticipated a partial reward at
death.[6]

Thnetopsychism drew its ablest support in the seventeenth
century from Richard Overton and John Milton, and from the
philosophical rationalist Thomas Hobbes. Froom omits from his
Conditionalist Faith of our Fathers Hobbes' treatment of the
subject in the *Leviathan* (1651), presumably since Hobbes is not
normally regarded as a theological writer.[7] Overton's strictures
against the received doctrine of the soul's immortality could reasonably be expected to have met with wide approval in the seventeenth century:

> ... it fighteth against the Attributes of God ... it vndermineth Christ,
> vndervallueth and lesseneth the Purchase of his sufferings, and deny-
> eth the Resurrection ... the most grand and blasphemous Heresies that

---

[5]   *A Short Catechisme ... (and) the Articles agreed upon by the Bishoppes & other
learned and godly men, in the last convocatiō at London, in the years of our Lord
MDLll. for to roote out the discord of opinions, and stablish the agremēt of trew
religion,* 1553, fol. lxxxv–lxxxvi.

[6]   See N. T. Burns, *Christian Mortalism from Tyndale to Milton,* (Cambridge, Mass.,
1972), pp. 16–18.

[7]   L. E. Froom, *The Conditionalist Faith of our Fathers,* II (Washington, D.C.
1965).

are in the world, the Mysterie of Iniquity, and Kingdome of Anti-christ depend upon it ... [8]

The writer who attacked a doctrine which at the same time depreciated the work of Christ and strengthened the claims of Anti-christ had at least a semblance of respectability, and Burns' conclusions that mortalism was essentially Christian, and that it attracted a greater following than hitherto may have been recognised, appear well-founded.

In mortalism, as in immortalism, the resurrection of the body appears as the focus of Christian hope, and Burns' comment here may be cited:

> Christian mortalism, then, appealed to the more radical temperaments among those who feared the return of Roman superstition or who were convinced that Holy Scripture contained yet undiscovered truths that must be searched out diligently without human prejudgments. The orthodox compromise with the Roman doctrine of immortality not only left these Christians restive, but it seemed to some of them that the compromise denied to the resurrection of the body the central importance it seemed to have for St. Paul. If the souls of the departed were already in joy or misery, how could the resurrection of the body be important to eternal life? [9]

Overton's chief "use" of mortalism substantiates the conclusion that the doctrine in the seventeenth century was essentially Christian and that it tended towards a Christological eschatology. The believer is to

> cast himselfe wholy on Jesus Christ with whome in God our lives are hid, that when he who is our life shall appeare, he might also with him appeare in glory, to whome be the honour of our immortality for ever, and for ever. [10]

---

[8] R[ichard] O[verton], *Man's Mortallitie* (Amsterdam, 1643), p. 55. A second, revised, edition appeared in 1655 as *Man Wholly Mortal.*

[9] Burns, *op. cit.,* p. 34.

[10] Overton, *op. cit.,* p. 57.

BIBLIOGRAPHY

The date given at each entry is the original date of publication, which, except where followed by a bracketed date, indicates the edition used. As in the footnotes, the place of publication, unless otherwise stated, is London.

I. PRIMARY SOURCES

(a) *Printed Works*

Abbot, Robert: *Antichristi Demonstratio, Contra Fabvlas Pontificias & ineptam Roberti Bellarmini de Antichristo disputationem*, 1603.

Adams, Thomas: *A Commentary or Exposition upon the Divine Second Epistle Generall, written by the Blessed Apostle St. Peter*, 1633.

Ainsworth, Henry: *Solomons Song of Songs. In English Metre: with annotations and References to other Scriptures, for the easier understanding of it*, 1623.

Alcasar, Luis de: *Reu. Patris Ludouici ab Alcassar ... Vestigatio arcani Sensus in Apocalypsi*, Antwerp, 1614.

Alexander, Sir William: *Recreations with the Mvses*, 1637.

Alsted, Johann Heinrich: *Diatribe de mille annis apocalypticis*, Francofurti, 1627 (quoted from the Eng. trans. by William Burton, *The Beloved City, or the Saints Reign on earth a thousand yeares, Asserted, and Illustrated, from LXV places of Holy Scripture*, 1643).

Ames, William: *Bellarminvs Enervatvs, a Gvilielmo Amesio S. S. Theologiae Doctore in Academia Franekerana*, Amstelodami, 1628.

Archer, John: *The Personall Reigne of Christ vpon Earth, In a Treatise, wherein is fully and largely laid upon and proved, That Iesus Christ, together with the saints, shall visibly possesse a Monarchicall State and Kingdom in this World*, 1642.

Arnold, Elias: see Pareus, David, *In Divinam Apocalypsin*.

Aspinwall, William: *A Brief Description of the Fifth Monarchy, or Kingdome That shortly is to come into the World ... When the Kingdome and Dominion, and the greatnesse of the Kingdome under the whole Heaven shall be given to the people, the Saints of the Most High ... And in the Conclusion there is added a Prognostick of the time when this fifth Kingdome shall begin*, 1653.

——: *An Explication and Application of the Seventh Chapter of Daniel; with a Correction of the Translation. Wherein is briefly shewed The State and Downfall of the four Monarchies; But more largely of the Roman Monarchy, and the Ten Horns or Kingdomes; And in Particular, the Beheading of Charles Stuart, who is proved to be the Little Horn, by many Characters ... And what is meant by the Carkass of the beast, which yet remains to be burned. Together with a Hint of the Slaying and Rising of the Two Witnesses*, 1653.

——: *The Work of the Age; or, the sealed Prophecies of Daniel opened and applied ... Amending sundry places in our Common Translation*, 1655.

Augustine: *De Civitate Dei* (quoted from the Eng. trans. by M. Dods, *The City of God*, New York, 1948).

Avery, Elizabeth: *Scripture-Prophecies Opened, Which are to be accomplished in these last times, which do attend the second coming of Christ*, 1647.

B., R.: see Crouch, Nathaniel: *Memorable Remarks*.

B., T.: *The Saints Inheritance After the Day of Iudgement. Being also An Answer to certaine scruples of late delivered, and others printed, especially in that Booke intituled: (The Personall Reigne of Christ upon Earth)*, 1643.

Bagshaw, Edward (1629-1671): *A Discourse About Christ and Antichrist: or, a Demonstration That Jesus is the Christ From the Truth of His Predictions, Especially, The Coming and the Seduction of Antichrist. To which is added A Treatise about the Resurrection*, 1661.

——: *The Doctrine of the Kingdom and Personal Reign of Christ Asserted and Explained in An Exposition upon Zach. 14. 5. 9*, 1669.

——: *Signes of the Times: or Prognosticks of Future Judgements, with The way how to prevent them*, 1662.

Baillie, Robert: *A Dissuasive from the Errours of the Time: wherein the Tenets of the principall Sects, especially of the Independents ... are examined by the Touchstone of the Holy Scrptures* [sic], 1645.

Bale, John: *The Image of bothe churches after the moste wonderfull and heauenly Reuelacion of Sainct John the Euangelist*, [1548?]

Baxter, Richard: *The Glorious Kingdom of Christ, Described and clearly Vindicated, Against the bold Asserters of a Future Calling and Reign of the Jews, and 1000 years before the Conflagration*, 1691.

——: *Reliquiae Baxterianae: or Mr. Richard Baxters Narrative of The most Memorable Passages of his Life and Times*, ed. Matthew Sylvester, 1696.

——: *The Saints Everlasting Rest: or, a Treatise of the Blessed State of the Saints in their enjoyment of God in Glory*, 1650.

——: *A Sermon of Iudgement*, 1655.

Bellarmine, Robert: *Disputationes Roberti Bellarmini ... de controversiis Christianae Fidei, adversus huius temporis haereticos, tribus tomis comprehensae*, 3 Vols., Ingolstadii, 1588-1593.

Bernard, Nicholas: *The Life and Death of ... Dr. James Usher, Late Arch-Bishop of Armagh, and Primate of all Ireland*, 1656.

Bernard, Richard: *A Key of Knowledge for the Opening of the Secret Mysteries of St. Iohns Mysticall Reuelation*, 1617.

Beverley, Thomas: *The Catechism of the Kingdom of our Lord Jesus Christ, in the Thousand Years*, 1690.

——: *An Exposition of the Divinely Prophetick Song of Songs which is Solomons*, 1687.

Blount, Henry: *A Voyage into the Levant*, 1636.

Bolton, Robert (1572–1631): *Mr. Boltons Last and Learned Worke of the Foure last Things, Death, Ivdgement, Hell, and Heaven*, 1632.

——: *The Saints Sure and Perpetuall Guide, or, A Treatise concerning the Word. Which, as the Israelites Cloud, conducts us from Aegypt to Canaan; whereunto wee must take heed, as unto a light that shineth in a darke place, till the Day dawne, and the Day-starre arise in our hearts*, 1634.

——: *Two Sermons Preached at Northampton at Two Severall Assizes There*, 1635.

Bradford, John: *The Hvrte of Hering Masse*, [1561?]

——: *The Writings of John Bradford, M.A.*, 2 Vols., ed. A. Townsend, Cambridge, 1848, 1853.

Brett, Samuel: *A Narrative of the Proceedings of a Great Councel of Jews assembled in the plain of Ageda in Hungaria ... to examine the Scriptures concerning Christ*, 1655.

A Brief Description Of the future History of Europe, from Anno 1650 to An. 1710, Treating principally Of those grand and famous Mutations yet expected in the World, as, The ruine of the Popish Hierarchy, the final annhilation of the Turkish

Empire, the Conversion of the Eastern and Western Jews, and their Restauration to their ancient Inheritances in the holy Land, and the FIFTH MONARCHIE of the universall Reign of the Gospel of Christ upon Earth ... out of that famous ms. of P. Grebner extant in Trinity College library in Cambridge, 1650.

Bridge, William: *Christs coming Opened in a Sermon Before the Honourable House of Commons in Margarets Westminster: May 17. 1648*, 1648.

——: *The Saints Hiding-Place in the time of Gods Anger*, 1646.

Brightman, Thomas: *The Workes of That Famous, Reverend, and Learned Divine, Mr. Tho: Brightman*, 1644.

——: *Apocalypsis Apocalypseos. Id est, Apocalypsis D. Ioannis analysi et scholiis illustrata ... Huic Synopsis praefigitur universalis: & Refutatio Rob. Bellarmini de Antichristo*, Francofurti, 1609.

——: *A Revelation of the Reuelation, that is the Revelation of St. John opened clearely, with a logicall Resolution and Exposition*, 2nd Eng. edit., 1615.

——: *A most Comfortable Exposition of the last and most difficult part of the Prophecie of Daniel*, 1614 (1644).

Brooks, Thomas: *Heaven on Earth; or, a Serious Discourse touching a wel-grounded Assurance of Mens Everlasting Happiness and Blessedness*, 1654.

——: *The Glorious day of the Saints Appearance; calling for a glorious conversation from all Beleevers*, 1648.

Broughton, Hugh: *Daniel his Chaldie Visions and his Ebrew*, 1596.

——: *Daniel, with a brief explication*, 1607.

——: *A Revelation of the Holy Apocalyps*, 1610.

——: *The Work of the Great Albionean Divine ... Mr. Hugh Broughton*, ed. John Lightfoot, 1662.

Bullinger, Heinrich: *A Hundred Sermons vpō the Apocalips of Jesu Christe, reveiled in dede by Thangell of the Lorde: but seen or receyued and written by thapostle and Euāgelist, S. John*, tr. John Daws, 1561.

Burrough, Edward: *A General Epistle to all the Saints: Being a Visitation of the Fathers Love Unto the whole Flock of God; Who are called and gathered into the Spiritual Kingdom of Righteousness and Peace*, 1660.

——: *A Trumpet Of the Lord sounded out of Sion ... a true noyse of a feerfull earthquake at hand*, 1656.

——: *The Walls of Ierico Razed down to the Ground, or An Answer to a lying Book, called the Quaking principles dashed in peices* [1654].

——: (and Howgill, Francis): *Answers to Severall Queries Put forth to the despised people called Quakers, by Philip Bennett ... also Answers To Severall other subtil Qveries Put forth by one Iohn Reeve*, [1654].

Burroughes, Jeremiah: *An Exposition of The Prophesie of Hosea ... in Divers Lectures Vpon the first three Chapters*, 1643.

——: *Jerusalem's Glory Breaking forth into the World, being a scripture-discovery of the New Testament Church in the Latter Days Immediately before the Second Coming of Christ*, 1675.

Burton, William: see Alsted, Johann Heinrich: *Diatribe de mille annis apocalypticis*.

Calamy, Edmund (1600-1666): *Englands Looking-Glasse, presented in A Sermon Preached before the Honourable House of Commons ... Dec. 22. 1641*, 1642.

Calvin, John: *Sermons of M. John Caluin on the Epistles of S. Paule to Timothie and Titus*, tr. Laurence Tomson, 1579.

——: *Sermons de Iean Calvin sur les deux Epistres Sainct Paul à Timothee, & sur l'Epistre à Tite*, Genève, 1563.

Camm, John (and Francis Howgill): *This Was the word of the Lord which Iohn Camm and Francis Howgill Was moved to declare and write to Oliver Cromwell, Who is named Lord-Protector, ... so the Kingdoms of the world may become the Kingdom of Christ*, 1654.

Canne, John: *The Time of the End: shewing, First, until the three years and a half are come ... the prophecies of the Scripture will not be understood, concerning the Duration and Period of the Fourth Monarchy and Kingdom of the Beast. Then, Secondly, When that Time shall come ... the Knowledge of the End ... will be revealed, By the Rise of a little Horn, The last Apostacy, and the Beast slaying the Witnesses*, 1657.

——: *Truth with Time: or, Certain Reasons Proving That none of the seven last Plagues, or Vials, are yet poured out: neither will the time of their pouring out begin, till after the rising of the Two Witnesses, and the fourty two months of the Beast's reign be expired*, 1656.

——: *A Voice From the Temple to the Higher Powers. Wherein is shewed, that it is the work and duty of Saints, to search the Prophesies and Visions of holy Scripture, which concern the Later Times*, 1653.

Cary, Mary: *The Little Horn's Doom & Downfall; or a Scripture-Prophesie of King James, and King Charles, and of this present parliament unfolded*, 1651.

Certain most godly, fruitful, and comfortable letters of such true Saintes and holy Martyrs of God, as in the late bloodye persecution here within this Realme, gaue their lyues for the defence of Christes holy gospel: written in the tyme of theyr affliction and cruell imprysonment, ed. Miles Coverdale, 1564.

Clavis Apocalyptica Ad Incudem Revocata, Vel Clavis Recusa; Apocalypsis quoad temporis supputationem, reclusa, 1653.

Clavis Apocalyptica: or, a Prophetical KEY: by which the great Mysteries in the Revelation of St. John, and the Prophet Daniel are opened; It being made apparent That the Prophetical Numbers com to an end with the year of our Lord, 1655, tr. Samuel Hartlib, 1651.

Cleaver, Robert: see Dod, John: *Ten Sermons*.

A Collection of many Wonderful Prophesies Relating to the English Nation, 1691.

Collier, Thomas: *A Brief Answer to some of the Objections and Demurs made against the coming in and inhabiting of the Jews in this Commonwealth*, 1656.

Conradus, Alphonsus: *In Apocalypsim D. Ioannis Apostoli Commentarius*, Basiliae, 1574.

Conti, Lothario: *The Droomme of Doomesday*, tr. George Gascoigne, 1576.

Cottière, Matthieu: *Apocalypseos, Domini Nostri Iesus Christi expositio*, Salmurii, 1614.

Cotton, John: *The Bloudy Tenent, washed, and made white in the bloud of the Lambe*, 1647.

——: *A Brief Exposition of the whole Book of Canticles, or Song of Solomon; Lively describing the Estate of the Church in all the Ages thereof, both Jewish and Christian, to this day: and Modestly pointing at the Gloriousnesse of the restored Estate of the Church of the Iewes, and the happy accesse of the Gentiles, in the approaching daies of Reformation, when the Wall of Partition shall bee taken away*, 1642.

——: *The Churches Resurrection, or The Opening of the Fift and Sixt verses of the 20th. Chap. of the Revelation*, 1642.

——: *An Exposition Upon The thirteenth Chapter of the Revelation*, 1655.

——: *The Keyes Of the Kingdom of Heaven, and Power thereof, according to the Word of God*, 1644.

——: *Of the Holinesse of Church-Members*, 1650.

——: *A Practical Commentary, or an Exposition with Observations, Reasons, and Vses upon The First Epistle Generall of John*, 1656.

——: *The Powring out of the Seven Vials: or an Exposition, of the 16 Chapter of the Revelation, with an Application of it to our Times*, 1642.

Coverdale, Miles: see *Certain most godly, fruitful and comfortable letters*.

Crouch, Nathaniel: *Memorable Remarks Upon the Ancient and Modern State of the Jewish Nation*, 1786.

Denne, Henry: *The Man of Sin Discovered: Whom the Lord shall destroy with the brightnesse of his Coming. The root and foundation of Antichrist laid open in Doctrine*, 1645.

Dent, Arthur: *The Rvine of Rome: or An Exposition vpon the whole Reuelation. Wherein is plainly shewed and proued, that the Popish Religion, together with all the power and authoritie of Rome, shall ebbe and decay still more and more throughout all the churches of Europe, and come to an vtter ouerthrow euen in this life before the end of the world*, 1603.

Dickson, David: *A Short Explanation Of the Epistle of Paul To The Hebrewes*, Aberdene, 1635.

Dod, John: (and Cleaver, Robert): *Ten Sermons tending chiefely to the fitting of men for the worthy receiuing of the LORDS Supper*, 1609 (1614).

Donne, John: *Iuvenilia: or Certaine Paradoxes, and Problemes*, 1633.

——: *A Sermon of Commemoration of the Lady Dāvers, late Wife of Sr. Iohn Dāvers*, 1627.

Doomes-Day: or The great Day of the Lords Iudgement proved by Scripture; and two other Prophecies the one pointing at the yeare 1640. the other at this present yeare 1647 to be even now neer at hand, 1647.

Durant, John: *The Salvation of the Saints By the Appearances of Christ, 1. Now in Heaven, 2. Hereafter from Heaven*, 1653.

Durham, James: *A Commentarie Upon the Book of the Revelation*, 1658.

Durham, William: *Maran-atha: The Second Advent, or, Christ's Coming to Judgement*, 1652.

[Durie, John]: *An Information concerning the present state of the Jewish Nation in Europe and Judea*, 1658.

Ενιαυτος Τεραστιος, *Mirabilis Annus: or The Year of Prodigies and Wonders*, 1661.

Evelyn, John: *The Diary of John Evelyn*, ed. E. S. De Beer, 6 Vols., Oxford, 1955.

F., I: *A Sober Inquiry; or Christs Reign With his Saints a Thousand Years; Modestly Asserted from Scripture*, 1660.

[Fell, Christopher]: *A few words to the people of England, who have had a day of visitation, not to slight time but prize it, least ye perish*, [1655].

[Finch, Henry]: *An Exposition of the Song of Solomon: called Canticles*, 1615.

[——]: *The Worlds Great Restavration, Or The Calling of the Iewes, and (with them) of all the Nations and Kingdomes of the earth, to the faith of Christ*, 1621.

Forbes, Patrick: *An Exquisite Commentarie upon the Revelation of Saint Iohn*, 1613.

Fox, George: *An Epistle to all People on the Earth; And the Ignorance of all the World, both Professors and Teachers Of the Birth that must be silent, and of the Birth that is to speak, which declares God; and the difference betwixt silence and speaking*, 1657.

——: *Gospel-Truth demonstrated, in a Collection of Doctrinal Books, Given forth by that Faithful Minister of Jesus Christ, George Fox: Containing Principles, Essential to Christianity and Salvation, held among the People called Quakers*, 1706.

——: *The Great Mistery of the Great Whore Unfolded: and Antichrists Kingdom Revealed unto Destruction*, 1659.

——: *The Journal of George Fox*, ed. N. Penney, 2 Vols., Cambridge, 1911.

——: *The Lambs Officer is gone forth with the Lambs Message, Which is the witnesse of God in all Consciences, to call them up to the Bar, the judgement of the Lamb, in this his day which is come*, 1659.

——: *The Pearle Found in England*, 1658.

——: *To all that would know the Way to the Kingdome, Whether they be in Forms, without Formes, or got above all Forms*, 1653.

[——]: *To the High and Lofty Ones*, [1655].

——: *The Vials of The Wrath of God Poured forth Upon the seat of the Man of Sin, And Upon all professors of the World*, 1654.

——: *A Word From the Lord to all the World, and all Professors in the world*, 1654.

——: (and Nayler, James): *Several Papers; some of them given forth by G. Fox, others by James Nayler*, 1654.

Foxe, John: *Actes and Monuments of these latter and perillous dayes ...*, 1563.

——: *Ecclesiasticall History, Contayning the Actes and Monumentes ...*, 1576.

——: *Eicasmi sev Meditationes in Sacram Apocalypsin*, 1587.

Garment, Joshua: *The Hebrew's deliverance at hand*, 1651.

Gascoigne, George: see Conti, Lothario: *The Droomme of Doomesday*, 1576.

Gell, Robert: *Gell's Remaines: or, Several Select Scriptures of the New Testament Opened and Explained*, 1676.

——: *Noah's flood Returning, a sermon Preached ... before the Lord Major of the Honourable Citie of London, and the ... Company of Drapers*, 1655.

——: *Stella Nova, A New Starre Leading wisemen unto Christ*, 1649.

Geveren, Sheltoo à: *Of the ende of this worlde, and second comming of Christ*, tr. Thomas Rogers, 1577.

Goodwin, Thomas: *The Works of Thomas Goodwin, D.D.*, ed. Thankfull Owen, James Barron, Thomas Goodwin, younger, 5 Vols., 1681-1704.

[——]: *A Glimpse of Sions Glory; or, the Churches Beautie specified*, 1641.

——: *The Great Interest of States & Kingdomes*, 1646.

[——]: *A Sermon of the Fifth Monarchy, Proving by Invincible Arguments That the Saints shall have a Kingdom here on Earth, which is yet to come, after the Fourth Monarchy is destroy'd by the Sword of the Saints*, 1654.

[——]: *The World to Come; or the Kingdome of Christ asserted In two Expository Lectures on Ephes. 1. 21, 22 verses*, 1655.

——: *Zerubbabels Encouragement to Finish the Temple*, 1642.

Gouge, William: *A Learned and very useful Commentary on the Whole Epistle to the Hebrewes*, 1655.

——: *The Progresse of Divine Providence*, 1645.

Grebner, Paul: see *A Brief Description*.

Groot, Hugo de: *Annotata in Epistolas Canonicas & in Apocalypsim*, Amstelodami, 1644.

Guild, William: *The Sealed Book Opened, or A cleer Explication of the Prophecies of the Revelation*, 1656.

Hakewill, George: *An Apologie of the Power and Providence of God in the Government of the World*, Oxford, 1627.

[Hall, Edmund]: *Manus Testium movens: or, A Presbyteriall Glosse Upon many of those obscure prophetick Texts In Canticles, Isay, Jeremiah, Ezekiel, Daniel, Habbakuk, Zachary, Matthew, Romans, and the Revelations: which point at The great Day of the Witnesses rising, Antichrists ruine, and the Jews conversion, neare about this time*, 1651.

H[all], E[mund]: Ἡ Ἀποστασια ὁ ἀντιχριστος: *or, a Scriptural discourse of the Apostasie and the Antichrist*, 1653.

[Hall, Joseph]: *The Revelation Unrevealed. Concerning the Thousand Yeares Reigne of the Saints with Christ upon Earth*, 1650.

——: *Salomons Diuine Arts, Of 1. Ethickes, 2. Politickes, 3. Oeconomicks ... With an open and plaine Paraphrase vpon the Song of Songs*, 1609.

Hall, Thomas: *Chiliasto-mastix redivivus, sive Homesus enervatus: A confutation of the Millenarian Opinion ... Plainly demonstrating that Christ will not Reign Visibly and Personally on earth with the Saints for a thousand yeers either before the day of Judgement, in the Day of Judgement, or after it*, 1657.

——: *A Practical and Polemical Commentary or Exposition Upon The Third and Fourth Chapters of the latter Epistle of Saint Paul to Timothy*, 1658.

Hammon, George: *Syons Redemption, and Original Sin Vindicated ... Published for the instruction and comfort of all that wait for the appearing of the Lord Jesus and Zions Redemption. Being an Answer to a Book of Mr. Hezekiah Holland*, 1658.

Hammond, Charles: *Englnads [sic] Alarum-Bell to be rung in the eares of all true Christians, to awaken them out of dead sleep ... before the evill day commeth*, 1652.

——: *A Warning-Peece for England, By that sad and fearefull Example that hath happened to Men, Women, and Children ... by Stormes, Tempests, Hail-stones, Lightning and Thunder, June 25. 1652*, [1652].

——: *The Worlds Timely Warning-piece*, 1660.

Hammond, Henry: *A Paraphrase, and Annotations Upon all the Books of the New Testament*, 1653.

Hartlib, Samuel: see *Clavis Apocalyptica: or, a Prophetical KEY.*

Haughton, Edward: *The Rise, Growth, and Fall of Antichrist: Together with The Reign of Christ*, 1652.

Hayne, Thomas: *Christs Kingdome on Earth, Opened according to the Scriptures. Herein is examined, what Mr. Th. Brightman, Dr. J. Alstede, Mr. I. Mede, Mr. H. Archer, The Glympse of Sions Glory, and such as concurre in opinion with them, hold concerning the thousand years of the Saints Reign with Christ, And of Satans binding*, 1645.

——: *The General View of the Holy Scriptures; or, The Times, Places, and Persons of the Holy Scriptures*, 1640.

Hicks, William: 'ΑΠΟΚΑΛΥΨΙΣ 'ΑΠΟΚΑΛΥΨΕΩΣ *or, the Revelation Revealed: Being a Practical Exposition on the Revelation of St. John. Whereunto is annexed a small Essay, Entituled Quinto-Monarchiae cum Quarto* ὁμολογια*, or a Friendly Complyance between Christ's Monarchy, and the Magistrates*, 1659.

Holland, Hezekiah: *An Exposition or ... Epitome of the most choice Commentaries Upon the Revelation of Saint John*, 1650.

Homes, Nathaniel: *The Works of Dr. Nathanael Homes*, 1652.

——: *A brief Cronology concerning the Jewes from ... 1650 to 1666*, 1665. (quoted from N. Crouch, *Memorable Remarks upon ... the Jewish Nation*, 1786).

——: *A Commentary Literal or Historical, and Mystical or Spiritual on the whole Book of Canticles*, 1650 (1652).

——: *Miscellanea; consisting of three treatises; I. Exercitations extricated: resolving ten questions; touching the glorious kingdom of Christ on earth, yet to come ... II. A Review of; or a fresh enquiry after Gog and Magog, where to find them. III. Some Glimpses of Israel's Call approaching*, 1666.

——: *The New World; or the New Reformed Church*, 1641.

——: *Plain Dealing; or The Cause and Cure of the Present Evils of the Times ... in a sermon ... Upon the Lord's Day after the great eclipse*, 1652.

——: ΑΠΟΚΑΛΥΨΙΣ ΑΝΑΣΤΑΣΕΩΣ : *The Resurrection Revealed: or the*

Dawning of the Day-star about to rise ... For a Thousand yeers Yet to come, before the ultimate Day of the Generall Iudgement, 1653.

——: *A Sermon Preached afore Thomas Andrews, Lord Maior*, 1650.

——: *The Resurrection-Revealed Raised Above Doubts & Difficulties in Ten Exercitations. 1. That Chiliasme, or the Opinion of the Future Glorious state of the Church on Earth ... is no Errour. 2. Of the Manner, and Measure of Burning the world ... 3. Touching Gog and Magog*, 1661.

[Hooker, Thomas]: *The Soules Preparation for Christ*, 1632.

[Howgill, Francis]: *An Answer to a Paper called, A Petition of one Thomas Ellyson, late Shepheard of Easington in the County of Durham, to his Highness the Lord Protector of England, Scotland, and Ireland, and to all Emperors, Kings and Princes through the world*, 1654.

——: *The Inheritance of Jacob Discovered. After his return out of Aegypt: and the Leading of the Lord to the Land of Promise, declared, and some information of the way thither*, 1656.

——: *A Lamentation for the Scattered Tribes, Who are exiled into Captivity, and are now mingled among the heathen, and are joyned to the Oppressor, and refuses to return*, 1656.

[——]: *This is onely to goe amongst Friends*, [1655].

[——]: *A Woe Against the Magistrates, Priests, and People of Kendall ... Pronounced from the Lord by one of his Prophets*, 1654.

——: see Burrough, Edward: *Answers to Severall Queries*.

——: see Camm, John: *This Was the word of the Lord*.

Huit, Ephraim: *The whole Prophecie of Daniel Explained, by a Paraphrase, Analysis and briefe Comment*, 1644.

The Humble Advice of the Assembly of Divines ... Concerning A Confession of Faith, 1658.

The Humble Advice of the Assembly of Divines ... Concerning A Larger Catechisme, 1658.

An Information, Concerning The Present State of the Jewish Nation Europe and Judea, 1658.

J., J. Philo-Judaeus: *The Resurrection of Dead Bones, or The Conversion of the Jewes*, 1655.

James I: *Ane frvitfvll Meditatioun contening ane plane and facill expositioun of ye 7. 8. 9. and 10 versis of the 20 chap. of the Reuelatioun*, Edinburgh, 1588.

——: *The Workes of the most High and mightie Prince, Iames ... Kinge of Great Brittaine, France & Ireland*, 1616.

Jenkyn, William: *An Exposition of the Epistle of Jude*, 1652.

J[essey], H[enry]: *The Lords Loud Call to England; Being a True Relation of some Late, Various, and Wonderful Judgments, or Handyworks of God, by Earthquake, Lightening, Whirlewind ... in several places; for what Causes let the man of wisdome judge, upon his serious persual of the Book it self*, 1660.

——: see Sibelius, Caspar: *Of the conversion of five thousand*.

Jewel, John: *An Exposition upon the two Epistles of St. Paul to the Thessalonians*, 1583.

Joye, George: *The exposiciovn of Daniel the Prophete gathered oute of Philip Melancthon, Johan Ecolampadius, Chonrade Pellicane & out of Johan Draconite*, Geneva, 1545.

——: see Osiander, Andreas: *The coniectures of the ende*.

Knollys, Hanserd: *An Exposition of the Eleventh Chapter of the Revelation. Wherein*

All those Things therein Revealed, which must shortly come to pass, are Explained, 1679.

——: *An Exposition Of the whole Book of the Revelation. Wherein The Visions and Prophecies of Christ Are opened and Expounded: Shewing The great Conquests of our Lord Jesus Christ for his Church over all His and Her Adversaries, Pagan, Arian and Papal; and the glorious State of the Church of God in the New Heavens and New Earth, in these Latter Days*, 1689.

——: *Mystical Babylon Unvailed. Wherein is Proved, I. That Rome-Papal is mystical-Babylon. II. That the Pope of Rome is the Beast. III. That the Church of Rome is the great Whore. IV. That the Roman-Priests are the false Prophet. Also a Call To all the People of God To come out of Babylon*, 1679.

——: *The World that Now is; and the World that is to Come: Or the First and Second Coming of Jesus Christ. Wherein several Prophecies not yet fulfilled are Expounded*, 1681.

Latimer, Hugh: *Certayn Godly Sermons*, 1562.

——: *The Works of Hugh Latimer, Sometime Bishop of Worcester, martyr, 1555*, ed. George Corrie, Cambridge, 1845.

Lindsay, David: *The Workes of the Famovs and worthy Knight, Sir David Lindsay of the Movnt, alias, Lyon King of Armes*, Edinburgh, 1619.

Llwyd, Morgan: *Gweithiau Morgan Llwyd o Wynedd*, I, ed. T.E. Ellis, 2 Vols., Bangor and London, 1899, 1906.

Love, Christopher: *A Christians Duty and Safety in Evill Times*, 1653.

——: *Englands Distemper, having Division and Error, as its Cause: wanting Peace and Truth for its Cure*, 1645.

——: *Heavens Glory, Hells Terror. or, Two Treatises; the one, Concerning the glory of the Saints with Jesus Christ, as a spur to Duty: the other, Of the Torments of the Damned, as a Preservative against Security*, 1653.

——: *The Penitent Pardoned ... Together with a Discourse Of Christ's Ascension into Heaven, and of his coming again from Heaven. Wherin the opinion of the Chiliasts is considered, and solidly confuted*, 1657.

Luther, Martin: *D. Martin Luthers Werke*, 58 Vols., Weimar, 1883-1948.

——: *Luther's Works*, ed. J. Pelikan and H.T. Lehmann, St. Louis, 1958—.

——: *Dris. Martini Lutheri Colloquia Mensalia: or, Dr. Martin Luther's Divine Discourses At his Table*, tr. Henry Bell, 1652.

[——]: *The Signs of Christ's coming, and Of the last Day*, 1522 (1661).

Marshall, Stephen: *The Song of Moses the Servant of God and the Song of the Lambe*, 1643.

——: *A Sermon ... wherein The Unity of the Saints With Christ, the Head, and especially with the Church, the Body; With the duties thence arising, are endeavoured to be cleared*, 1653.

Mather, Cotton: *Magnalia Christi Americana: or The Ecclesiastical History of New-England, from Its First Planting in the Year 1620. into the Year of our Lord, 1698*, 1702.

Maton, Robert: *Israels Redemption, or the propheticall history of our Saviours Kingdome on earth ... With a Discourse of Gog and Magog, or the battle of the great day of God Almightie*, 1642.

——: *Israel's Redemption Redeemed, or the Jewes generall and miraculous conversion to the faith of the Gospel; and returne into their owne land: And our Saviours personall Reign on Earth, cleerly proved out of many plaine Prophecies of the Old and New Testaments*, 1646.

Maynard, John: *A Shadow of the Victory of Christ*, 1646.

Mede, Joseph: *Clavis Apocalyptica ex innatis et insitis visionvm characteribvs ervta et demonstrata*, Cantabrigiae, 1627.

——: *The Key of the Revelation searched and demonstrated out of the Naturall and proper Charecters of the Visions*, tr. R. More, 1643.

——: *The Apostasy of the Latter Times; ... or, the Gentile's Theology of Daemons Revived in the Latter Times amongst Christians, in Worshipping of Angels, Deifying and Invocating of Saints, Adoring of Reliques, Bowing down to Images and Crosses, & C.*, 1641.

——: *Daniel's Weeks: an interpretation of part of the prophecy of Daniel*, 1643.

——: *Diatribae ... as many Discourses on divers texts of Scripture as there are Sundays in the Year*, 1642.

——: *Epistles, being Answers to divers Letters of Learned Men*, 1652.

——: *A Paraphrase and Exposition of the Prophecie of St. Peter, concerning The Day of Christs Second Coming*, 1642.

——: Παραλειπομενα: *Remaines on some Passages in the Apocalypse*. 1650.
(The above six works are quoted from *The Works of ... Joseph Mede, B.D.*, ed. J. Worthington, 1672.)

Menasseh Ben Israel: *Menasseh Ben Israel de Resurrectione Mortuorum*, Amstelodami, 1636.

——: מקוה ישראל , *Hoc Est, Spes Israelis*, Amstelodami, 1650. (quoted from the Eng. trans. *The Hope of Israel*, 1650).

——: אבו יקוה *Piedra Gloriosa o de la Estatua de Nebuchadnesar*, Amsterdam, 1655.

——: *To His Highnesse the Lord Protector of the Commonwealth of England, Scotland, and Ireland; the humble addresses of Menasseh Ben Israel ... in behalfe of the Jewish Nation*, 1655.

Mercer, Richard: *A further Discovery of the Mystery of the last times*, 1651.

——: *Some Discoveries of the Mystery of the last times, bordering upon the Comming of the Lord Jesus*, 1649.

Milton, John: *The Works of John Milton*, 18 Vols., ed. F.A. Patterson, New York, 1931-38.

Mirabilis Annus Secundus, or The Second Year of Prodigies, 1662.

Mirabilis Annus Secundus, The Second Part of the Second Year's Prodigies, 1662.

More, John: *A Trumpet sounded: or, The Great Mystery of the Two Little Horns Unfolded. Being as a Candle set up in the dark Lanthorn of Daniel*, 1654.

Napier, John: *A Plaine Discouery of the whole Reuelation of Saint John*, Edinburgh, 1593.

Nayler, James: *A Collection of Sundry Books, Epistles and Papers, written by James Nayler*, 1716.

——: see Fox, George: *Several Papers*.

Nisbet, Alexander: *A Brief Exposition of the first and second Epistles general of St. Peter*, 1658.

Osiander, Andreas: *The coniectures of the ende of the worlde*, tr. George Joye, Antwerp, 1548.

——: *Vermutung von den letzten Zeiten und dem Ende der Welt aus der heiligen Schrift gezogen*, Nürnberg, 1545.

O[verton], R[ichard]: *Mans Mortallitie or a Treatise Wherein 'tis proved, both Theologically and Phylosophically, that whole Man (as a rationall Creature) is a Compound wholy mortall, contrary to that common distinction of Soule and Body: And that the present going of the Soule into Heaven or Hell is a meer Fiction:*

And that at the Resurrection is the beginning of our immortallity, and then Actuall Condemnation, and Salvation, and not before, Amsterdam, 1643.

[——]: *Man Wholly Mortal*, 1655.

Owen, John: *The Advantage of the Kingdome of Christ in the Shaking of the Kingdoms of the World: or, Providentiall Alterations in their Subserviency to Christ's Exaltation*, Oxford, 1651.

——: *A Sermon Preached to The Parliament, Octob. 13. 1652 ... Concerning the Kingdome of Christ*, Oxford, 1652.

——: *A Continuation of the Exposition of the Epistle of Paul the Apostle to the Hebrews, Viz. on the Sixth, Seventh, Eighth, Ninth, and Tenth Chapters*, 1680.

——: ΟΥΡΑΝΩΝ ΟΥΡΑΝΙΑ *The Shaking and Translating of Heaven and Earth*, 1649.

Pareus, David: *In Divinam Apocalypsin. S. Apostoli et Evangelistae Johannis Commentarius*, Heidelbergae, 1618.

(quoted from the Eng. trans. by E. Arnold, *A Commentary Upon the Divine Revelation of the Apostle and Evangelist John*, Amsterdam, 1644).

Parker, Robert: *The Mystery of the Vialls opened: being a short Exposition upon the pouring out of the four last Vialls mentioned in the 16 Chapter of the Revelation*, 1651.

Parker, Thomas: *The Visions and Prophecies of Daniel Expounded: Wherein the Mistakes of former Interpreters are modestly discovered, and the true meaning of the Text made plain*, 1646.

Pearson, John: *An Exposition of the Creed*, 1659.

Perkins, William: *An Exposition of the Symbole, or Creed of the Apostles*, 1595.

——: *A Fruitfull Dialogue Concerning the end of the World*, 1587.

——: *A godly and learned Exposition or Commentarie vpon the first three Chapters of the Reuelation*, 1595.

(The above are quoted from *The Workes of That Famous and Worthy Minister of Christ in the Universitie of Cambridge, M.W. Perkins*, 3 Vols., Cambridge, 1626-1631.)

Pepys, Samuel: *The Diary of Samuel Pepys*, ed. H.B. Wheatley, 8 Vols., 1895.

Petrie, Alexander: *Chiliasto-mastix, or, The Prophecies in the Old and New Testament concerning the kingdome of our Saviour Iesus Christ, Vindicated from the misinterpretationes of the Millenaries, and specially of Mr. Maton in his book called "Israel's redemption"*, Roterdame, 1644.

Piscator, Johannes: *Johan Piscatoris Commentarii in Omnes libros Novi Testamenti*, Herbornae Nassoviorum, 1621.

Potter, Francis: *An interpretation of the Number 666*, Oxford, 1642.

Prideaux, John: *Twenty Sermons*, Oxford, 1641.

Purnell, Robert: *Good Tydings for Sinners, Great Ioy for Saints*, 1649.

——: *A Little Cabinet Richly Stored with all sorts of Heavenly Varieties, and Soul-reviving Influences*, 1657.

——: *No Power but of God: and yet a Power in every Creature. or, a word in season to all Men, not void of Grace, or deprived of Reason*, 1652.

Rogers, John: סגריר , *Sagrir, or Doomes-day drawing nigh, With Thunder and Lightening to Lawyers ... Making Discoverie of the present ungodly Laws and Lawyers of the Fourth Monarchy, and of the approach of the Fifth; with those godly Laws, Officers, and Ordinances that belong to the Legislative Power of the Lord Iesus*, 1653.

——: אהל *Ohel or Bethshemesh. A Tabernacle for the Sun: or Irenicum evangelicum. An idea of church-discipline, in the theorick and practick parts*, 1653.

Rogers, Thomas: see Geveren, Sheltoo à: *Of the ende of this worlde*.

Sandys, Edwin: *Sermons made by the most reuerende Father in God, Edwin, Archbishop of Yorke*, 1585.

——: *The Sermons of Edwin Sandys, D.D.*, ed. J. Ayre, Cambridge, 1841.

Sclater, William (1609-1661): *The Crowne of Righteousnes: or The glorious Reward of Fidelity In the Discharge of our Duty*, 1654.

——: *The Grand Assizes: or, the Doctrine of the Last Generall Judgement, with the Circumstances thereof*, 1653.

Seagar, John: *A Discoverie of the World to Come According to the Scriptures ... Wherein, I. The Doctrine of the World to come, is propounded, explicated, confirmed, and applyed ... 2. The Doctrine of Millenaries, touching a New Reformed Church in the latter Times ... is confuted*, 1650.

Shakelton, Francis: *A blazyng Starr or burnyng Beacon, seene the 10. of October laste (and yet continewyng) set on fire by Gods prouidence, to call all sinners to earnest and speedie repentance*, 1580.

Shepheard, William: *Of the Foure Last and Greatest Things: Death, Iudgement, Heaven and Hell. The Description of the Happinesse of Heaven, and misery of Hell ... with The way or means to passe through Death, and Judgement, into Heaven, and to avoid Hell*, 1649.

A Short Catechisme ... (and) the Articles agreed upon by the Bishoppes & other learned and godly men, in the last convocatiō at London, in the yeare of our Lord MDL^ll. for to roote out the discord of opinions, and stablish the agremēt of trew religion, 1553.

Sibbes, Richard: *Beames of Divine Light, Breaking forth from severall places of holy Scripture*, 1639.

——: *The Brides Longing for her Bridegroomes second comming*, 1638.

——: *An Exposition of the Third Chapter of the Epistle of St. Paul to the Philippians*, 1639.

——: *A Fountain Sealed: or, The duty of the sealed to the Spirit, and the worke of the Spirit in Sealing ... also Of assurance and Sealing what it is, the priviledges and degrees of it, with the signes to discerne, and meanes to preserve it*, 1637.

——: *The Gloriovs Feast of the Gospel. or, Christ's gracious Invitation and royall Entertainment of Believers*, 1650.

——: *A Miracle of Miracles or Christ in our nature ... The Wonderfull Conception, Birth, and Life of Christ, who in the fulnesse of time became man ... to make reconciliation betweene God and man*, 1638.

Sibelius, Caspar: *Of the Conversion of Five Thousand and Nine Hundred East-Indians in the Isle of Formosa, neere China*, tr. Henry Jessey, 1650.

Smith, Samuel: *The Great Assize, or, Day of Ivbilee*, 1618 (1628).

Spencer, Edward: [*An Epistle to the learned Manasseh Ben Israel in answer to his dedicated to the Parliament*, 1650] (The title-page is missing from the only known copy. The title is quoted from the British Museum Catalogue).

Stephens, Nathaniel: *A Plaine and Easie Calculation of the Name, Mark, and Number of the Name of the Beast*, 1656.

Strong, William: *XXXI Select Sermons, Preached On Special Occasions*, 1656.

——: *The Trust and the Account of a Steward*, 1647.

——: *The Vengeance of the Temple*, 1648.

Stubbs, Philip: *The Anatomie of Abuses: Containing, A Discoverie, or briefe Summarie of such Notable Vices and Imperfections, as now raigne in many Countreyes of the Worlde*, 1583.

Symons, Henry: ʾΑνδριδικαστης ʾΑρχιδικαστης *The Lord Jesus His Commission ... to* be the alone *Judge of Life and Death, in the Great and General Assize of the World*, 1657.

Taylor, Thomas: *A Commentarie upon the Epistle of Saint Paul written to Titvs*, Cambridge, 1619.

——: *The Principles of Christian Practice. Containing the Institution of a Christian man, in twelve heads of Doctrine*, 1635.

——: *The Progresse of Saints to Full Holinesse, Described In sundry Apostolicall Aphorismes, or short precepts tending to sanctification*, 1630.

Thorowgood, Thomas: *Iewes in America, or Probabilities that the Americans are of that Race. With the removall of some contrary reasonings, and earnest desires for effectual endeavours to make them Christian*, 1650.

Tillinghast, John: *Generation Work. Or a Brief and Seasonable Word offered to the view and consideration of the Saints and people of God in this Generation, relating to the work of the present age, or generation wee live in*, 1653.

——: *Knowledge of the Times; or the resolution of the Question how long it shall be unto the end of Wonders*, 1654.

Trapp, John: *Annotations Upon the Old and New Testament*, 5 Vols., 1654-1662.

——: *A Commentary or Exposition upon All the Epistles and the Revelation of John the Divine*, 1647.

Ussher, James: *A Body of Divinitie, or the Summe and Substance of Christian Religion*, 1645.

Vincent, Thomas: *Christ's Certain and Sudden Appearance to Judgment*, 1668.

Wall, Moses: *Considerations Upon the Point of the Conversion of the Jewes*, 1651.

Whitaker, Jeremiah: *The Christians Hope Trivmphing In these glorious Truths; That Christ the ground of hope, is God ... That there is another life besides this ... How the hope of Heaven should be attained ... for the comfort of every poor Christian*, 1645.

White, John: *The Troubles of Jerusalems Restauration, or The Churches Reformation*, 1646.

Whitfield, Henry: *The Light appearing more and more towards the perfect Day: or, A farther Discovery of the present state of the Indians in New England, Concerning the Progress of the Gospel amongst them*, 1651.

——: *Strength Out of Weaknesse; or a Glorious Manifestation of the further progresse of the Gospel among the Indians in New-England*, 1652.

Whiting, Samuel: *A Discourse of the Last Judgement, or, Short Notes upon Mat. xxv. from Ver. 31 to the end of the Chapter. Concerning the Judgement to Come, and our Preparation to stand before The Great Judge of Quick and Dead*, Cambridge, 1664.

Wilkinson, Henry: *Babylons Ruine, Jerusalems Rising*, 1643.

Willet, Andrew: *Synopsis Papismi, that is a generall viewe of papistry: Wherein the whole mysterie of iniquitie, and summe of Antichristian doctrine is set downe, which is maintained this day by the Synagogue of Rome*, 1592.

——: *Tetrastylon Papisticvm, That is, the fovre principal pillers of Papistrie*, 1593.

Winslow, Edward: *The Glorious Progress of the Gospel Amongst the Indians in New England*, 1649.

——: *Hypocrisie Unmasked: By a true Relation of the Proceedings of the Governour and Company of the Massachusetts against Samvel Gorton*, 1646.

Wither, George: *A Collection of many Wonderful Prophesies Relating to the English Nation*, 1691.

——: *Fragmenta Prophetica; or, the remains of George Wither Esq., being a Collection of the Predictions dispers'd throughout his works*, 1669.

(b) *Manuscripts*

British Museum, Sloane MS. 1004: A most sure and certaine prophecie of That which is past, present and to come, Rev. 15. 1. Historically comprised in the seven last plagues, probably interpreted of yt which is past from ye times of ye Waldenses, and yet to come in and before ye second comming of Christ to iudgment.

British Museum, Sloane MS. 63: Toppe, James: CHRISTS MONARCHICall and personall Reigne uppon Earth over all the Kingdoms of this world.

II: SECONDARY SOURCES

(a) *General Works of Reference*

Alumni Cantabrigienses, Pt. I, 4 Vols., ed. J. Venn and J.A. Venn, 1922-1927.
Alumni Oxonienses 1500-1714; 4 Vols., ed. J. Foster, Oxford, 1891-1892.
Athenae Oxonienses, 2 Vols., ed. A. Wood, 1691, 1692.
The Babylonian Talmud, ed. I. Epstein, 1938-1952.
A Baptist Bibliography, 2 Vols., ed. W.T. Whitley, 1916, 1922.
Bibliotheca Sacra, 2 Vols., ed. J. Le Long, Paris, 1723.
Cambridge Modern History, 13 Vols., ed. A. Ward, G.W. Prothero, S. Leathers, Cambridge, 1902-1911.
Catalogue of the McAlpin Collection of British History and Theology, 5 Vols., ed. C.R. Gillett, New York, 1927-1930.
Dictionary of American Biography, 20 Vols., ed. A. Johnson, 1928-1937.
Dictionary of Anonymous and Pseudonymous English Literature, 7 Vols., ed. J. Kennedy, W.A. Smith, A.L. Johnson, Edinburgh, 1926-1934.
Dictionary of National Biography, 63 Vols., ed. L. Stephen and S. Lee, 1885-1900.
Encyclopaedia Britannica, 24 Vols., 1955.
Encyclopaedia of Religion and Ethics, 13 Vols., ed. J. Hastings, Edinburgh, 1908-1926.
An Encyclopedia of World History, ed. W.L. Langer, Boston, 1948.
Fasti Ecclesiae Scoticanae, 9 Vols., ed. H. Scott, Edinburgh, 1915-1961.
The Jewish Encyclopedia, 12 Vols., ed. I. Singer, New York, 1925.
The New Schaff-Herzog Encyclopedia of Religious Knowledge, 13 Vols., ed. S. Jackson, New York, 1908-1914.
A Short-Title Catalogue ... 1475-1640, ed. A.W. Pollard and G.R. Redgrave, 1926.
Short-Title Catalogue ... 1641-1700, ed. D. Wing, 3 Vols., New York, 1945-1951.

(b) *Other Printed Works*

Alford, H.: *The New Testament for English Readers*, 2 Vols., 1863, 1866.
Armytage, W.H.G: *Heavens Below: Utopian Experiments in England, 1560-1960*, 1961.
Barbour, H: *The Quakers in Puritan England*, New Haven and London, 1964.
Beasley-Murray, G.R: *A Commentary on Mark Thirteen*, 1957.
Barclay, R: *The Inner Life of the Religious Societies of the Commonwealth: Considered principally with reference to the influence of church organisation on the spread of Christianity*, 1876.
Brown, L.F: *The Political Activities of the Baptists and Fifth Monarchy Men In England During the Interregnum*, Washington, D.C. 1912.

Burns, N.T: *Christian Mortalism from Tyndale to Milton*, Cambridge, Mass., 1972.
Calder, I.M. (Ed.): *Letters of John Davenport, Puritan Divine*, 1937.
Capp, B.S: *The Fifth Monarchy Men*, 1972.
Chadwick, H: *The Early Church*, 1967.
Chadwick, O: *The Reformation*, 1964.
Cohn, N: *The Pursuit of the Millennium*, 1957.
Collinson, P: *The Elizabethan Puritan Movement*, 1967.
Conklin, G.N: *Biblical Criticism and Heresy in Milton*, New York, 1944.
Cullmann, O: *Christ and Time*, 1951.
——: *Immortality of The Soul or Resurrection of the Dead?* , 1958.
Davies, D.H.M: *The Worship of the English Puritans*, 1948.
De Jong, J.A: *As the Waters Cover the Sea: Millennial Expectations in the Rise of Anglo-American Missions 1640-1810*, Kampen, 1970.
Dexter, H.M: *The Congregationalism of the Last Three Hundred Years, as seen in its Literature*, [1880].
Edwards, D.L: *Religion and Change*, 1970.
Firth, C.H: *The Last Years of the Protectorate 1656-1658*, 2 Vols., 1909.
Froom, L.E: *The Conditionalist Faith of our Fathers: The Conflict of the Ages Over the Nature and Destiny of Man*, 2 Vols., Washington, D.C., 1965-66.
——: *The Prophetic Faith of our Fathers: The Historical Development of Prophetic Interpretation*, 4 Vols., Washington, D.C., 1946-1964.
George, C.H. & K: *The Protestant Mind of the English Reformation 1570-1640*, Princeton, 1961.
Haller, W: *The Rise of Puritanism, Or, The way to the New Jerusalem as set forth in pulpit and press from Thomas Cartwright to John Milton, 1570-1643*, New York, 1938.
——: *Foxe's Book of Martyrs and the Elect Nation*, New York, 1963.
——: *Liberty and Reformation in the Puritan Revolution*, New York, 1955.
Hill, C: *Antichrist in Seventeenth Century England*, 1971.
——: *Puritanism and Revolution: Studies in Interpretation of the English Revolution of the 17th Century*, 1958.
——: *Society and Puritanism in Pre-Revolutionary England*, 1964 (1969).
Huehns, G: *Antinomianism in English History*, 1951.
Isham, G. (Ed.): *The Correspondence of Bishop Brian Duppa and Sir Justinian Isham, 1650-1660*, Lamport Hall, 1955.
Jeremias, J: *The Parables of Jesus*, tr. S.H. Hooke, 1954.
Kevan, E.F: *The Grace of Law; A Study in Puritan Theology*, 1964.
Ladd, G.E: *Jesus and the Kingdom: The Eschatology of Biblical Realism*, 1966.
——: *The Presence of the Future*, Grand Rapids, 1974.
Lamont, W.M: *Godly Rule: Politics and Religion 1603-60*, 1969.
——: *Marginal Prynne 1600-1669*, 1963.
Liu, Tai: *Discord in Zion: The Puritan Divines and the Puritan Revolution 1640-1660*, The Hague, 1973.
Lundström, G: *The Kingdom of God in the Teaching of Jesus*, 1963.
Martin, J.P: *The Last Judgment in Protestant Theology from Orthodoxy to Ritschl*, 1963.
Masson, D: *The Life of John Milton*, 7 Vols., 1859-1894.
Matthews, A.G: *Calamy Revised. Being a revision of Edmund Calamy's Account of the Ministers and others ejected and silenced, 1660-2*, Oxford, 1934.
——: *Walker Revised. Being a revision of John Walker's Sufferings of the Clergy during the Grand Rebellion, 1642-60*, Oxford, 1948.

Miller, P: *Errand Into the Wilderness*, Cambridge, Mass., 1956.
——: *Orthodoxy in Massachusetts*, Gloucester, Mass., 1965.
Moore, A.L: *The Parousia in The New Testament*, Leiden, 1966.
Myers, T. (Ed.): *Commentaries on the Book of Daniel by John Calvin*, Edinburgh, 1852.
Nuttall, G.F: *The Holy Spirit in Puritan Faith and Experience*, Oxford, 1946.
——: *Visible Saints: The Congregational Way 1640-1660*, Oxford, 1957.
——: *The Welsh Saints 1640-1660; Walter Cradock, Vavasor Powell, Morgan Llwyd*, Cardiff, 1957.
——: *The Puritan Spirit; Essays and Addresses*, 1967.
New, J.F.H: *Anglican and Puritan: The Basis of Their Opposition, 1558-1640*, 1964.
Olsen, V.N: *John Foxe and the Elizabethan Church*, Berkeley, Los Angeles and London, 1973.
Payne, E.A: *The Baptists of Berkshire Through Three Centuries*, 1951.
Perrin, N: *The Kingdom of God in the Teaching of Jesus*, 1963.
Quistorp, H: *Calvin's Doctrine of the Last Things*, 1955.
Roth, C: *A History of the Jews in England*, 1941.
——: *A History of the Marranos*, Philadelphia, 1932.
Rogers, P.G: *The Fifth Monarchy Men*, 1966.
Rowden, H.H: *The Origins of the Brethren, 1825-1850*, 1967.
Schaff, P: *History of the Christian Church*, 12 Vols., Edinburgh, 1883-93.
Shaw, W.A: *History of the English Church ... 1640-1660*, 2 Vols., 1900.
Simpson, A: *Puritanism in Old and New England*, Chicago, 1955.
Solt, L.F: *Saints in Arms: Puritanism and Democracy in Cromwell's Army*, Stanford, 1959.
Strong, A.H: *The Great Poets and Their Theology*, Philadelphia, 1899.
Strype, J: *Annals of the Reformation, and Establishment of Religion ... in the Church of England during Queen Elizabeth's ... Reign*, 4 Vols., Oxford, 1824.
Tanner, J: *Daniel and the Revelation: The Chart of Prophecy and our Place in it. A Study of the Historical and Futurist Interpretation*, 1898.
Taylor, A: *The History of the English General Baptists*, 1818.
Toon, P. (Ed.): *Puritans, The Millennium, and the Future of Israel: Puritan Eschatology 1600 to 1660*, Cambridge, 1970.
——: *Puritans and Calvinism*, Swengel, Penn., 1973.
Torrance, T.F: *When Christ Comes and Comes Again*, 1957.
Trevor-Roper, H.R: *Religion, the Reformation and Social Change, and other essays*, 1967.
Tuveson, E.L: *Millennium and Utopia: A Study in the Background of the Idea of Progress*, New York, 1949 (1964).
Wolf, L: *Menasseh Ben Israel's Mission to Oliver Cromwell*, 1901.
Whiting, C.E: *Studies in English Puritanism From the Restoration to the Revolution, 1660-1688*, 1931.
Woodhouse, A.S.P: *Puritanism and Liberty, Being the Army Debates (1647-9) from the Clarke Manuscripts with Supplementary Documents*, 1938.
Walzer, M: *The Revolution of the Saints: A Study in the Origins of Radical Politics*, 1966.
Wilson, J.F: *Pulpit in Parliament: Puritanism during the English Civil Wars 1640-1648*, Princeton, 1969.
Zagorin, P: *A History of Political Thought in the English Revolution*, 1954.
Ziff, L: *The Career of John Cotton,*, Princeton, 1962.

(c) *Articles*

Burgess, W.H: 'James Toppe and the Tiverton Anabaptists', *Transactions of the Baptist Historical Society*, III, 1912-1913.

Crippen, T.G: 'The Brownists in Amsterdam', *Transactions of the Baptist Historical Society*, I, 1908-1909.

Nuttall, G.F: 'Dissenting Churches in Kent before 1700', *The Journal of Ecclesiastical History*, XIV, 2, 1963.

Thrupp, S.L. (Ed.): 'Millennial Dreams in Action', *Comparative Studies in Society and History*, Supplement II, The Hague, 1962.

Toon, P: 'Advice to the Churches in 1654', *The Gospel Magazine*, December, 1968.

——: 'A Puritan Missionary Appeal', in *The Gospel Magazine*, January, 1969.

——: 'Puritan Eschatology: 1600 to 1648', *The Manifold Grace of God*, 1968.

Whitley, W.T: 'Militant Baptists 1660-1672', *Transactions of the Baptist Historical Society*, I, 1908-1909.

(d) *Theses*

Carr, B.F: 'The Thought of Robert Parker (1564?-1614) and his Influence on Puritanism before 1650', Ph.D. Thesis, University of London, 1965.

Christianson, P.K: 'English Protestant Apocalyptic Visions, c. 1536-1642', Ph.D. Thesis, University of Minnesota, 1971.

Clouse, R.G: 'The Influence of John Henry Alsted on English Millenarian Thought in the Seventeenth Century', Ph.D. Thesis, State University of Iowa, 1963.

Gilsdorf, A.J.B: 'The Puritan Apocalypse: New England Eschatology in the Seventeenth Century', Ph.D. Thesis, Yale University, 1965.

Plotkin, F.S: 'Sighs from Sion: A Study of Radical Puritan Eschatology in England, 1640-1660', Ph.D. Thesis, Colombia University, 1966.

Woodfield, A.J: 'The Life and Works of Joseph Stennett, 1663-1713', M.A. Thesis, University of London, 1958.

INDEX OF BIBLICAL REFERENCES

INDEX OF NAMES

Most names referred to in the text and footnotes are included. Separate references to footnotes are not given where the name appears in the text on the same page.

INDEX OF SUBJECTS